Advances in Pattern Recognition

For further volumes:
http://www.springer.com/series/4205

Venu Govindaraju · Srirangaraj Setlur
Editors

Guide to OCR for Indic Scripts

Document Recognition and Retrieval

Springer

Editors
Prof. Venu Govindaraju
Center for Unified Biometrics and Sensors
520 Lee Entrance
Amherst NY 14228
Suite 202
USA
govind@buffalo.edu
venu.govindaraju@gmail.com

Srirangaraj (Ranga) Setlur
Center for Unified Biometrics and Sensors
520 Lee Entrance
Amherst NY 14228
Suite 202
USA
setlur@buffalo.edu
setlur@gmail.com

Series Editor
Professor Sameer Singh, PhD
Research School of Informatics
Loughborough University
Loughborough, UK

ISBN 978-1-4471-2518-1 e-ISBN 978-1-84800-330-9
DOI 10.1007/978-1-84800-330-9
Springer London Dordrecht Heidelberg New York

British Library Cataloguing in Publication Data
A catalogue record for this book is available from the British Library

Printed on acid-free paper

Springer is part of Springer Science+Business Media (www.springer.com)

Foreword

The original motivations for developing optical character recognition technologies were modest to convert printed text on flat physical media to digital form, producing machine-readable digital content. By doing this, words that had been inert and bound to physical material would be brought into the digital realm and thus gain new and powerful functionalities and analytical possibilities.

First-generation digital OCR researchers in the 1970s quickly realized that by limiting their ambitions primarily to contemporary documents printed in standard font type from the modern Roman alphabet (and of these, mostly English language materials), they were constraining the possibilities for future research and technologies considerably. Domain researchers also saw that the trajectory of OCR technologies if left unchanged would exclude a large portion of the human record. Digital conversion of documents and manuscripts in other alphabets, scripts, and cursive styles was of critical importance. Embedded in non-Roman alphabet source documents, including ancient manuscripts, papyri scrolls, clay tablets, and other inscribed artifacts was not only a wealth of scholarly information but also new opportunities and challenges for advancing OCR, imaging sciences, and other computational research areas. The limiting circumstances at the time included the rudimentary capability (and high cost) of computational resources and lack of network-accessible digital content. Since then computational technology has advanced at a very rapid pace and networking infrastructure has proliferated. Over time, this exponential decrease in the cost of computation, memory, and communications bandwidth combined with the exponential increase in Internet-accessible digital content has transformed education, scholarship, and research. Large numbers of researchers, scholars, and students use and depend upon Internet-based content and computational resources.

The chapters in this book describe a critically important area of investigation – addressing conversion of Indic script into machine-readable form. Rough estimates have it that currently more than a billion people use Indic scripts. Collectively, Indic historic and cultural documents contain a vast richness of human knowledge and experience.

The state-of-the-art research described in this book demonstrates the multiple values associated with these activities. Technically, the problems associated with Indic script recognition are very difficult and will contribute to and inform related script recognition efforts. The work also has enormous consequence for enriching and enabling the study of Indic cultural heritage materials and the historic record of its people. This in turn broadens the intellectual context for domain scholars focusing on other societies, ancient and modern.

Digital character recognition has brought about another milestone in collective communication by bringing inert, fixed-in-place, text into an interactive digital realm. In doing so, the information has gained additional functionalities which expand our abilities to connect, combine, contextualize, share, and collaboratively pursue knowledge making. High-quality Internet content continues to grow in an explosive fashion. In the new global cyberenvironment, the functionalities and applications of digital information continue to transform knowledge into new understandings of human experience and the world in which we live. The possibilities for the future are limited only by available research resources and capabilities and the imagination and creativity of those who use them.

Arlington, Virginia

Stephen M. Griffin
Program Director
National Science Foundation

Preface

In the past few years, we have seen many ambitious large-scale efforts to make all written material accessible online in a digital format. University-led efforts such as the Million Book Project and industry-led efforts such as the Google Books Library Project have made this goal seem attainable, though there still remains a lot to be achieved. Government sponsored programs such as the Digital Libraries Initiative, which is currently in its second phase, jointly supported by the National Science Foundation (NSF), the Defense Advanced Research Projects Agency (DARPA), the National Library of Medicine (NLM), the Library of Congress (LoC), the National Aeronautics and Space Administration (NASA), the National Endowment for the Humanities (NEH) and others have led to the acceleration of development of technologies and applications that make it possible to create, access and manage digital library content in a quick and easy manner. The Million Book Project was in fact, a product of the Digital Libraries Initiative. Advances in scanning technologies have resulted in the creation of large libraries of digitized content under these initiatives.

The objective of the creation of digital library content is to enable the query and retrieval of relevant documents from the digital library. Technologies such as keyword spotting and optical character recognition (OCR) are crucial elements in the creation of indexed digital library content. The state of the art today is still a long way from being able to reliably recognize the text in many of documents that have been digitized to date. This is especially true in the case of documents in non-Latin scripts and in the case of most historical documents.

Most of the scripts of south and Southeast Asia are derived from the ancient *Brahmi* script (The Unicode Standard v3.0). Since a majority of these scripts are mainly prevalent in the Indian sub-continent, they are also called *Indic* scripts. The basic character set for Indic scripts can be seen in Figs. 1 and 2.

The Eighth Schedule of the Constitution of India contains a list of 22 major languages that are currently used in India. Additionally, there are hundreds of minor languages or dialects that are spoken by populations in small geographical pockets making south Asia a highly multi-lingual region. The scripts used by contemporary speakers of these languages for writing are *Devanagari* (Sanskrit, Hindi, Marathi, Nepali, Konkani, Santhali, Bodo, Dogri, Kashmiri, Maithili, Sindhi), *Bengali* (Bengali or Bangla, Assamese or Asomiya, Manipuri, Santhali), *Gurmukhi*

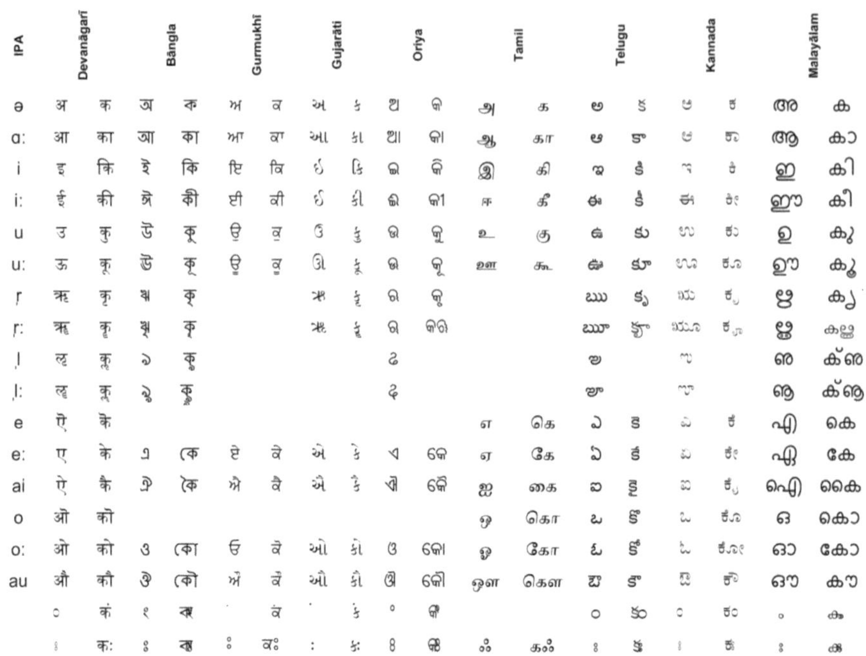

Fig. 1 Vowels and a consonant with vowel modifiers in Indic scripts

(Punjabi), *Gujarati* (Gujarati), *Oriya* (Oriya, Santhali), *Tamil* (Tamil), *Telugu* (Telugu), *Kannada* (Kannada), *Malayalam* (Malayalam). Many of these languages were also historically written in other related scripts. Urdu, spoken in many parts of India and Pakistan, is usually written in the Perso-Arabic *Nastaliq* script. Some languages such as Kashmiri, Sindhi, Dogri are also written using the Perso-Arabic script in certain regions. Given the widespread use of Urdu in India, we have loosely defined the term *Indic* scripts in the context of this book to include the Perso-Arabic script used for Urdu. Most Indic scripts follow a writing system that is written from left-to-right and has the orthographic syllable as the effective unit consisting of a consonant and vowel core optionally preceded by one or more consonants. The Perso-Arabic script used for Urdu is written from right-to-left.

An enormous body of literature spanning a range of topics that would be of interest to researchers and lay people alike exists in these languages and scripts. There is very little digital access to these contemporary and cultural heritage materials in *Indic* scripts. These scripts present some challenges for OCR which are different from the issues faced with Latin and Oriental scripts. There are also heritage materials in these scripts that are written on media such as palm leaf that pose problems in digitization as well as image pre-processing to render them potentially suitable for down-the-line indexing via keyword spotting or partial or complete OCR.

All major research groups working in the area of *Indic* OCR and information retrieval from *Indic* documents are represented in this book. The groups include

IPA	Devanagari	Bangla	Gurmukhi	Guj arati	Oriya	Tamil	Telugu	Kannada	Malayalam
k	क	ক	ਕ	ક	କ	க	క	ಕ	ക
kʰ	ख	খ	ਖ	ખ	ଖ		ఖ	ಖ	ഖ
g	ग	গ	ਗ	ગ	ଗ		గ	ಗ	ഗ
gʱ	घ	ঘ	ਘ	ઘ	ଘ		ఘ	ಘ	ഘ
ŋ	ङ	ঙ	ਙ	ઙ	ଙ	ங	ఙ	ಙ	ങ
c	च	চ	ਚ	ચ	ଚ	ச	చ	ಚ	ച
cʰ	छ	ছ	ਛ	છ	ଛ		ఛ	ಛ	ഛ
ɟ	ज	জ	ਜ	જ	ଜ	ஜ	జ	ಜ	ജ
ɟʱ	झ	ঝ	ਝ	ઝ	ଝ		ఝ	ಝ	ഝ
ɲ	ञ	ঞ	ਞ	ઞ	ଞ	ஞ	ఞ	ಞ	ഞ
ʈ	ट	ট	ਟ	ટ	ଟ	ட	ట	ಟ	ട
ʈʰ	ठ	ঠ	ਠ	ઠ	ଠ		ఠ	ಠ	ഠ
ɖ	ड	ড	ਡ	ડ	ଡ		డ	ಡ	ഡ
ɖʱ	ढ	ঢ	ਢ	ઢ	ଢ		ఢ	ಢ	ഢ
ɳ	ण	ণ	ਣ	ણ	ଣ	ண	ణ	ಣ	ണ
t̪	त	ত	ਤ	ત	ତ	த	త	ತ	ത
t̪ʰ	थ	থ	ਥ	થ	ଥ		థ	ಥ	ഥ
d̪	द	দ	ਦ	દ	ଦ		ద	ದ	ദ
d̪ʱ	ध	ধ	ਧ	ધ	ଧ		ధ	ಧ	ധ
n	न	ন	ਨ	ન	ନ	ந	న	ನ	ന
n	ऩ					ன			
p	प	প	ਪ	પ	ପ	ப	ప	ಪ	പ
pʰ	फ	ফ	ਫ	ફ	ଫ		ఫ	ಫ	ഫ
b	ब	ব	ਬ	બ	ବ		బ	ಬ	ബ
bʱ	भ	ভ	ਭ	ભ	ଭ		భ	ಭ	ഭ
m	म	ম	ਮ	મ	ମ	ம	మ	ಮ	മ
j	य	য	ਯ	ય	ଯ	ய	య	ಯ	യ
r	र	র/ৰ	ਰ	ર	ର	ர	ర	ರ	ര
r	ऱ					ற	ఱ	ಱ	റ
l	ल	ল	ਲ	લ	ଲ	ல	ల	ಲ	ല
ɭ	ळ		ਲ਼	ળ	ଳ	ள	ళ	ಳ	ള
ɻ	ऴ					ழ		ೞ	ഴ
ʋ	व	ৱ	ਵ	વ		வ	వ	ವ	വ
ɕ	श	শ	ਸ਼	શ	ଶ		శ	ಶ	ശ
ʂ	ष	ষ		ષ	ଷ	ஷ	ష	ಷ	ഷ
s	स	স	ਸ	સ	ସ	ஸ	స	ಸ	സ
h	ह	হ	ਹ	હ	ହ	ஹ	హ	ಹ	ഹ

Fig. 2 Consonants in Indic Scripts

university researchers and industry labs in India as well as in the United States. This book is divided into two parts: recognition of Indic scripts and retrieval of Indic documents. The recognition part covers topics such as data set creation for OCR development and the current state of the art in the development of OCR technologies for many of the Indic scripts. We also include a chapter on online handwriting recognition for Indic scripts that is critical for the development of applications built around digital pen input of Indic script. The second part discusses issues related to facilitating query and retrieval of Indic documents from digital libraries.

1 Part I: Recognition of Indic Scripts

Indic scripts are *abugidas* or *alpha-syllabaries*, i.e., the basic writing unit consists of a consonant–vowel core and phonetically, they largely share the same basic character set (vowels and consonants) as shown in Figs. 1 and 2. A vowel has two forms, an independent form when not part of a consonant and a dependent form. In the written form, the manner in which the dependent vowel signs or *maatraas* are attached to the base consonant exhibit a large variation among the Indic scripts. These scripts are also characterized by a large number of consonant conjunct forms where the characters tend to change shape depending on their context. This results in a large set of character glyphs and poses a challenge for OCR systems Indic numerals are shown Fig. 3.

Availability of data sets is a critical requirement for the development of OCR systems. The chapter on data sets describes the ongoing work at IIIT, Hyderabad, on the creation of a large data corpus that currently has over 600,000 document images representing many Indic scripts. This chapter comprehensively details the steps involved in the creation of a good data set including the identification of documents, procedure for scanning and creation of images, consistent procedures

Roman numerals	0 1 2 3 4 5 6 7 8 9
Devanagari	० १ २ ३ ४ ५ ६ ७ ८ ९
Bangla	০ ১ ২ ৩ ৪ ৫ ৬ ৭ ৮ ৯
Gurmukhi	੦ ੧ ੨ ੩ ੪ ੫ ੬ ੭ ੮ ੯
Gujarati	૦ ૧ ૨ ૩ ૪ ૫ ૬ ૭ ૮ ૯
Oriya	୦ ୧ ୨ ୩ ୪ ୫ ୬ ୭ ୮ ୯
Tamil	0 ௧ ௨ ௩ ௪ ௫ ௬ ௭ ௮ ௯
Telugu	౦ ౧ ౨ ౩ ౪ ౫ ౬ ౭ ౮ ౯
Kannada	೦ ೧ ೨ ೩ ೪ ೫ ೬ ೭ ೮ ೯
Malayalam	൦ ൧ ൨ ൩ ൪ ൫ ൬ ൭ ൮ ൯

Fig. 3 Numerals in Indic scripts (0 in Tamil and Malayalam are not native)

for annotation, and structured storage of the metadata to allow for efficient indexing and retrieval.

The next nine chapters describe OCR systems that cover eight different scripts: Bangla, Devanagari, Gurmukhi, Gujarati, Kannada, Malayalam, Tamil, and Urdu (Perso-Arabic). It may be noted that while these scripts share some similarities they are also quite disparate. The methods described in these chapters span the use of a multitude of features and classification techniques giving the reader a good insight into the efficacy of these methods for the various Indic scripts.

The work on Bangla and Devanagari OCR at ISI, Kolkata, uses sequential rules to segment characters followed by template matching for classification using a bank of classifiers. The chapter also describes the use of post-processing of recognition results to improve classification performance and a methodology for error evaluation.

A system for recognition of machine-printed Gurmukhi documents has been presented by the researchers at Punjabi University. Local and global structural features are used with a multi-stage classification approach using binary tree and k-nearest neighbor classifiers.

The next chapter describes work on Gujarati documents by researchers at the University of Baroda and the University of Hyderabad. The work explores multiple feature extraction techniques such as fringe maps, discrete cosine transforms and wavelets and multiple classifiers such as a nearest neighbor classifier and a neural network-based classifier. Experimental results are presented comparing various feature–classifier combinations.

The system developed at IISc Bangalore for recognition of bilingual documents (Kannada and English) addresses a frequent challenge encountered in the sub-continent, viz., documents containing multiple scripts. A script identification method based on Gabor filters and discrete cosine transforms is proposed and classification using nearest-neighbor, linear discriminant classifiers, and support vector machines are compared. Graph-based features and an SVM for based classifier have been used for the OCR.

The chapter on Malayalam documents describes work on both machine-printed documents and online handwriting at IIIT Hyderabad. A novel approach has been used to learn features automatically from large quantities of training data, i.e., to derive a statistical feature extraction suitable for the script from examples, rather than defining intuitive features from experience. An ensemble of binary SVM classifiers using decision-directed acyclic graphs is used for classification.

The work on OCR of Tamil magazine documents at IIT Madras includes layout analysis and segmentation of body text, titles, and images using a modified smeared run-length approach. The character recognition is based on a radial basis function neural network and uses Gabor filter features.

The chapter on recognition of Urdu handwriting presents an overview of existing research on Urdu documents and reports preliminary experiments at the University at Buffalo on handwritten Urdu documents using GSC features and k-NN and SVM classifiers.

The BBN Byblos Hindi OCR system uses a script-independent methodology for OCR using hidden markov models. The chapter from BBN Technologies describes their efforts in training of the system for Hindi (Devanagari) documents and presents experimental results on Hindi documents.

The chapter from University at Maryland describes a novel technique using font models for script identification and segmentation of Hindi characters in machine-printed documents. In the recognition system, three feature extraction methods are used to demonstrate the importance of appropriate features for classification.

The last chapter in this part from HP Labs, Bangalore describes challenges in the recognition of handwriting in Indic scripts in the online domain and provides an overview of the state of the art in isolated character and word recognition. It also describes the progress in the development of applications such as handwriting-based text input systems.

2 Part II: Retrieval of Indic Documents

The first chapter in this part describes ongoing work at Brown University in enhancing access to cultural heritage materials of India for researchers through The Sanskrit Library at Brown. The methodology could be extended to other digital library collections throughout the world.

The next chapter describes techniques developed at the University at Buffalo to enhance images of historical Indic manuscripts such as palm leaf manuscripts and render them at the very least readable for human eyes and potentially enable segmenting of lines of text and even keyword spotting or partial OCR for indexing and retrieval. Novel methods for image enhancement using background normalization and text line location and extraction using an adaptive local connectivity map have been presented.

The following two chapters describe two different techniques for word spotting. The first work of IIT Delhi uses a geometric feature graph to encode word image features for word spotting. The graph is encoded as a string that serves as a compressed representation of the word image skeleton. The GFG-based word image spotting is augmented with latent semantic analysis for more effective retrieval.

The other work on word spotting from the University at Buffalo describes two techniques, a script-dependent, recognition-based approach using a block adjacency graph representation and a script-independent recognition-free approach based on image moments.

The last chapter reviews the state of the art in mono-lingual and cross-lingual information retrieval in Indic languages. A framework for evaluation of Indian language information retrieval has been described.

3 Target Audience

This unique guide/reference is the very first comprehensive book on the subject of OCR for Indic scripts, providing an overview of the state-of-the-art research in this field as well as other issues related to facilitating query and retrieval of Indic documents from digital libraries. We hope that this guide will serve as an excellent reference for researchers and graduate students studying OCR technology and methodologies for Indic scripts.

Acknowledgments

We are extremely thankful to all the chapter authors who have contributed to making this book an invaluable resource to researchers in the area of OCR for Indic scripts. The 16 chapters are the combined efforts of 37 authors. Interaction with the authors through the concept, draft, and finalization stages has been truly stimulating and enjoyable. We would like to thank Stephen Griffin, Program Director at NSF for his foreword and his continued support for the development of multilingual OCR technologies. We would also like to thank Achint Thomas and Anurag Bhardwaj for helping with submissions, proofreading, and a myriad of other tasks. We are also grateful to Springer for their encouragement and persistence in driving us to complete this work in a timely manner.

Buffalo, New York

Venu Govindaraju
Srirangaraj Setlur

Contents

Part II Retrieval of Indic Documents

Contributors

Mudit Agrawal LAMP of UMIACS, University of Maryland, College Park, MD 20742, USA, mudit@umd.edu

A. Bharath Hewlett-Packard Laboratories, Bangalore, India, bharath.a@hp.com

Anurag Bhardwaj Department of Computer Science and Engineering, Center for Unified Biometrics and Sensors, University at Buffalo, Amherst, NY, USA, ab94@cubs.buffalo.edu

Srinivasa Chakravarthy Department of Biotechnology, IIT – Madras, Chennai, India, schakra@ee.iitm.ac.in

B. B. Chaudhuri Indian Statistical Institute, Kolkata, India, bbcisical@gmail.com

Santanu Chaudhury IIT Delhi, New Delhi, India, schaudhury@ee.iitd.ac.in

Michael Decerbo BBN Technologies, Cambridge, MA, USA, mdecerbo@bbn.com

Jignesh Dholakia Department of Applied Mathematics, M S University of Baroda, Vadodara, Gujarat, India, jignesh.dholakia@gmail.com

David Doermann LAMP of UMIACS, University of Maryland, College Park, MD, USA, doermann@umd.edu

Ritu Garg IIT Delhi, New Delhi, India, ritu2721a@gmail.com

Venu Govindaraju Department of Computer Science and Engineering, Center for Unified Biometrics and Sensors, University at Buffalo, Amherst, NY, USA, venu@buffalo.edu

Gaurav Harit IIT Delhi, New Delhi, India, gharit@ee.iitd.ac.in

Malcolm Hyman Department of Classics, Brown University, Providence, RI, USA

C. V. Jawahar International Institute for Information Technology, Center for Visual Information Technology, Hyderabad, India, jawahar@iiit.ac.in

K. J. Jinesh International Institute for Information Technology, Center for Visual Information Technology, Hyderabad, India

Aparna Kokku Department of Biotechnology, IIT – Madras, Chennai, India, ee01m03@ee.iitm.ac.in

Anand Kumar International Institute for Information Technology. Center for Visual Information Technology, Hyderabad, India

Gurpreet Singh Lehal Department of Computer Science, Punjabi University, Patiala, India, gslehal@gmail.com

Huanfeng Ma Drexel Hill, PA 19026, USA, huanfeng@gmail.com

Ehry MacRostie BBN Technologies, Cambridge, MA, USA, emacrost@bbn.com

Sriganesh Madhvanath Hewlett-Packard Laboratories, Bangalore, India, srig@hp.com

Prasenjit Majumder CVPR Unit, Indian Statistical Institute, Kolkata, India, prasenjit_t@isical.ac.in

Mandar Mitra CVPR Unit, Indian Statistical Institute, Kolkata, India, mandar@isical.ac.in

Omar Mukhtar Department of Computer Science and Engineering, Center for Unified Biometrics and Sensors, University at Buffalo, Amherst, NY, USA, omukhtar@buffalo.edu

Anoop Namboodiri International Institute for Information Technology, Center for Visual Information Technology, Hyderabad, India, anoop@iiit.ac.in

P. J. Narayanan International Institute for Information Technology, Center for Visual Information Technology, Hyderabad, India, pjn@iiit.ac.in

Prem Natarajan BBN Technologies, Cambridge, MA, USA, prem@bbn.com

N. V. Neeba International Institute for Information Technology, Center for Visual Information Technology, Hyderabad, India

Atul Negi Department of Computer and Information Sciences, University of Hyderabad, Hyderabad, India, atulcs@uohyd.ernet.in

Peeta Basa Pati Department of Electrical Engineering, Indian Institute of Science, Bangalore, India

A. Phaneendra International Institute for Information Technology, Center for Visual Information Technology, Hyderabad, India

S. Rama Mohan Department of Applied Mathematics, M. S. University of Baroda, Vadodara, Gujarat, India, srmmsu@gmail.com

A. G. Ramakrishnan Department of Electrical Engineering, Indian Institute of Science, Bangalore, India, ramkiag@ee.iisc.ernet.in

Peter M. Scharf Department of Classics, Brown University, Providence, RI, USA, scharf@brown.edu

Srirangaraj Setlur Department of Computer Science and Engineering, Center for Unified Biometrics and Sensors, University at Buffalo, Amherst, NY, USA, setlur@buffalo.edu

Zhixin Shi Department of Computer Science and Engineering, Center for Unified Biometrics and Sensors, University at Buffalo, Amherst, NY, USA, zshi@buffalo.edu

R. S. Umesh Department of Electrical Engineering, Indian Institute of Science, Bangalore, India

Part I
Recognition of Indic Scripts

Building Data Sets for Indian Language OCR Research

C.V. Jawahar, Anand Kumar, A. Phaneendra, and K.J. Jinesh

Abstract Lack of resources in the form of annotated data sets has been one of the hurdles in developing robust document understanding systems for Indian languages. In this chapter, we present our activities in this direction. Our corpus consists of more than 600000 document images in Indian scripts. A parallel text is aligned to the images to obtain word- and symbol-level annotated data sets. We describe the process we follow and the status of the activities.

Keywords OCR Data sets · Indic scripts · Annotation Tools

1 Introduction

The rapid growth of digital libraries (DLs) worldwide poses many new challenges for research and development in document image analysis (DIA) [1–4]. The primary challenge being the conversion of the scanned images to a textual representation with the help of OCRs. For Roman scripts, we have commercial OCRs which can produce reasonably accurate text, for a wide variety of documents. However, robust and efficient recognizers are not yet commercially available for Indian languages [5]. Data sets are prerequisites for the development, performance enhancement, and evaluation of data-driven document analysis systems [6]. Lack of resources in the form of annotated data sets has been one of the hurdles in building robust document understanding systems for Indian languages. There is a pressing need for very large collections of data if robust systems have to be built for Indian language document understanding.

Generation of large database of annotated document images involves (i) identification of the content/source; (ii) employing a well-defined and repeatable preprocessing steps for creation of multiple images suited for various DIA tasks;

C.V. Jawahar (✉)
Center for Visual Information Processing, International Institute for Information Technology, Hyderabad, India
e-mail: jawahar@iiit.ac.in

V. Govindaraju, S. Setlur (eds.), *Guide to OCR for Indic Scripts*, Advances in Pattern Recognition, DOI 10.1007/978-1-84800-330-9_1, © Springer-Verlag London Limited 2009

(iii) consistent labeling procedures for annotation; and (iv) structured storage of annotation information for effective access. Annotation involves labeling image components (often with text) along with additional details such as layout information, language or script, scanning parameters, printing parameters. For document understanding, documents need to be annotated at the structural, functional, and content level for building robust systems. Out of which, content-level annotation is critical for developing OCRs [6]. Our primary focus is on content-level annotation.

In this chapter, we discuss the challenges associated with the generation of data sets required for Indian language OCR research. Moreover, we present the process as well as the status of the annotation activities we have undertaken. A hierarchical approach to the annotation is presented, which finally results in image and text corpus along with the truth information. The data storage schema is also discussed.

Our data set mainly comprises of (i) a comprehensive image corpus with large number of document images scanned at multiple resolutions and processed with a set of well-defined algorithms; (ii) an unaligned parallel text corpora corresponding to these document images; (iii) annotation information for document images at different granularity levels. Such a data set help researchers/developers to evaluate the performance in a consistent and repeatable manner. Needless to say, such data sets are useful for training and validation of pattern classifiers. We focus on generation of corpus from printed document images for Indian language document understanding. Presently, the generated data set is available to the members of a consortium of prominent universities and institutes in India.

2 Datasets

We start by describing the basic constituents of the corpus.

2.1 Image Corpus

One of the primary component of the corpus is a set of document images collected from different sources. The diversity and popularity of the source helps to make the system designed with this corpus practically applicable in a variety of situations. Digitization of paper documents to obtain document images is quite straightforward. Unfortunately, there are no standard/public domain data sets available for Indic documents. Most of the previous research evaluated their character recognizers on a very small set of documents. To suit the diverse requirements of the present and future generations of document image analysis systems, we decided to scan the documents in multiple resolutions. We broadly classify the documents we scan into two classes: (i) documents with simple layout and (ii) documents with complex layout.

In our corpus, documents with simple layout comes primarily from printed books published after 1950. They follow mostly a Manhattan layout. Segmentation and preprocessing of such document images are relatively easy compared to those of documents in complex layout. These documents are primarily useful for the development and evaluation of character recognizers. Such documents are ideal for collecting the content-level ground truth information at character level, which is used for performance enhancement of recognizers. In addition to books, we also propose to add some content from sources like newspapers.

Design and development of next-generation document analysis systems also require data set from multitude of sources. It should comprise data sets required for segmentation and layout analysis tasks. In such data sets, the documents are of complex layout with text spread over multiple columns, possibly embedded with pictures and graphs, and printed in special and fancy fonts. Annotation of such data set is a challenging task. The "truth" itself need not be uniquely defined. Such documents in the corpus are primarily useful for tasks related to segmentation and layout analysis. These documents are often printed in multiple colors. The primary focus of our ongoing activities is to develop a corpus of documents with simple layout and annotate for the content-level information.

2.1.1 Digitization

The documents are scanned to obtain images, which are then annotated using appropriate tools. Scanning can be done using flatbed scanners or camera-based scanners. To suit a wide spectrum of DIA applications, we digitize the document on a flatbed scanner at multiple resolutions – 200, 300, and 600 dpi. We also plan to have a smaller set of document images captured through cameras and similar digitizers. Most of the present-day DIA systems use flatbed scanners. Therefore, our data set is biased toward this. Image corpus is carefully built as explained below.

We scan individual pages to avoid the degradation at binding area. This sometimes requires removal of the binding of the books. However, this may not be feasible for some of the manuscripts and rare books. We set the page on the scanner and align it reasonably well. It helps in reducing the burden of skew or rotation modules. Skew angles are typically less than 3°. We also try to avoid dust on the scanner and backside reflections. However, they are not completely eliminated. Once a page is set for scanning, it is scanned in different resolutions. This help in propagating annotation in one image to other images more or less automatically. The file formats used for storing the digitized documents may also affect the quality of image. Many of the popular file formats like JPEG store the information in a compressed manner. It is advisable to store raw images without any compression for better performance of the DIA algorithms. We use uncompressed TIFF for the storage.

2.1.2 Processing and Storage

The original scanned document images are preprocessed to correct skew and thereafter for smoothing and thresholding using scanfix. A copy of every image after each preprocessing step is stored separately. The functional parameters of preprocessing like skew angle are stored since they are useful for automatic performance evaluation. Storing these individual images help in obtaining appropriate data for diverse tasks in document image analysis. Digitization and preprocessing produces a number of intermediate image files. Such images are integral part of the image corpora. After preprocessing, the original image may be required by the systems for evaluation purposes. Hence, the scanned and processed versions of the documents are stored in a consistent directory structure. There is no universally accepted correct image preprocessing algorithm. Therefore, while corpus building, we use a reasonably popular algorithm/tool to obtain the preprocessed image rather than worrying about the best preprocessing scheme. Since all the images are stored throughout, corpus can be improved at a later stage without re-annotation. This allows us to modify/replace any of these algorithms with minimal effort in future.

Our objective in the initial phase is to build an image corpus of more than 5000 pages in at least nine different Indian languages. Each of these pages will be stored in at least 12 different forms, resulting in more than 60000 images in each of the nine Indian languages.

2.2 Text Corpus

The content of the document images is required for performance enhancement of pattern classification algorithms. The textual content is also useful in development of language models for OCR development. Most of the post-processors need the textual content for building language models in order to improve the OCR performance. Content generation is one of the most time-consuming activity during data set generation, as it is completely manual. A possible alternative is to start with a reasonably accurate OCR and then refine the text manually or semi-automatically. However for Indic scripts, this is still only a remote possibility.

As explained in the next section, we align the text corpus with image corpus in a semi-automatic manner for efficiency in the annotation. To make the process highly automatic, the content generation should be systematic. Line and paragraph breaks in the original document are retained in the typed text. Text corresponding to each scanned image is stored in separate file. Alignment of the content in a page is done with the help of an annotation tool. This reduces the effort required for generation of the textual annotation. Generation of Indian language content also need some mention. There are no standard keyboards available for Indian languages. Typing on English keyboards is cumbersome. ITRANS can be used as an alternative which uses a Roman encoding for Indian scripts. Such text requires a converter to get the content finally in UNICODE for wider acceptability.

The data generated in these phases need consistent storage for efficient access [7]. Like the image corpus, the text corpus is stored in standard directory structure for easy and efficient access for annotation and other purposes. File naming conventions and storage hierarchy are maintained to accomplish that. Figure 1 shows an example of storage structure required for annotation of books.

2.3 Annotated Data Sets

Annotation of data has become central to the success of supervised and semi-supervised machine-learning algorithms. A number of approaches have been

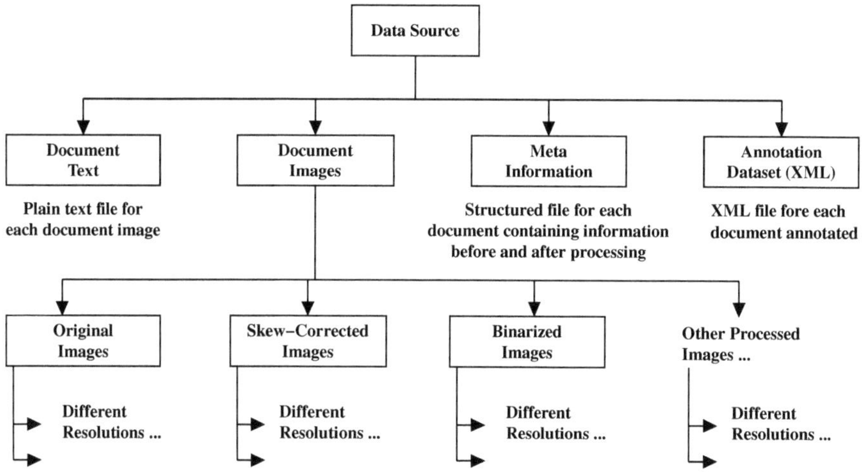

Fig. 1 Hierarchical storage of document image and text content in a directory structure

explored in the past for generation of data sets for different languages of the world. In a significant work for Indian languages, Setlur et al. [8] designed a truthing tool for manual annotation of words from document images of *Devanagari* scripts. Around 120,000 words from 400 scanned documents were annotated using this tool. For the languages with availability of reasonably good commercial OCRs, annotation has been concerned primarily on functional and structural layout information.

Our annotation methods are semi-automatic in nature. It uses scripts, tools, and manual interventions to achieve the objective. Many of the structural and functional tags are attached manually, while the content is annotated highly automatically. Content-level annotation is done by aligning the text with image.

Since our goal is to annotate large number of pages in multiple Indic scripts, innovative solutions are required to complete this annotation in limited time. We provide structural and functional annotation to the text and graphics blocks using a semi-automatic tool, we have developed. We then align image and textual content is parallel at word level. A model-based annotation on the lines of [9] is then employed for annotation at the character level. A set of tools with efficient algorithms in the back end achieve this. Annotated data are stored in an XML format that allows efficient access and incremental update [10].

3 Annotation

Annotation is the process of labeling image components (often using text) with additional details such as layout information, language, script, print conditions. Performance evaluation of document image analysis systems should be done on a variety

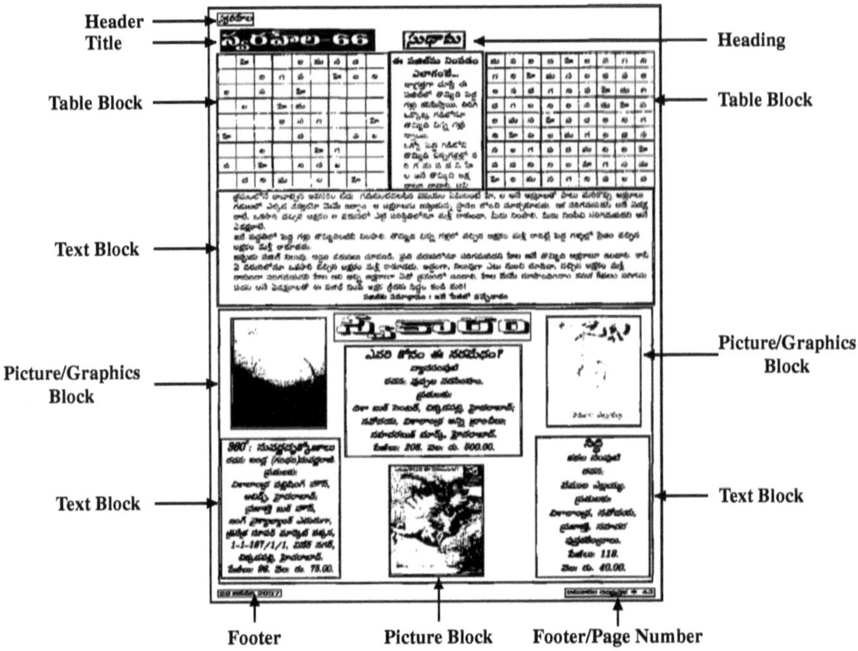

Fig. 2 An Indian language document image and annotation of the components

of large annotated data (obtained from diverse sources) to ensure the quality of algorithms and the robustness of the solution. This would require proper annotation with storage of every detail during the annotation. For example, meta details like source of document, quality of print could also become important parameters for evaluation of recognition engines. Figure 2 shows an example of an Indian language document image and some levels of annotation.

Our content-level annotation is primarily an alignment process of the document image with independently typed text. The problem of alignment of parallel handwritten and text corpora has been addressed in the context of segmentation of text lines to words by Zimmerman and Bunke [11]. Tomai et al. [12] proposed a similar approach to annotate words of historic handwritten data, where the recognizer is constrained to output the words in the transcript. Elliman et al. [7] presented annotation of documents containing cursive writing. Their data set consisted of around 900 sheets of cursive writing annotated at word level.

University of Washington data set, UW-I, consists of 1147 document page images from English scientific and technical journals [13]. Another data set, UW-II, consists of 624 English pages and 477 Japanese pages from journals [14]. These databases store text zone bounds, ground truth data for each zone, finer attributes and qualitative information useful for document image understanding tasks. Japanese Character Image Database [15] contains approximately 180,000 (0.18 M) Kanji, Hiragana, Katakana, alphanumeric, and symbolic characters extracted from a variety of machine-printed documents, with quality varying from clean to degraded. Indian scripts, with complex glyphs and poor commercial systems, immediately need annotated data at the character (*Akshara*) level. Our immediate goal is to annotate over 100 books in Indian languages. This large-scale annotation needs efficient algorithms and tools.

Performance evaluation of a document analysis system includes testing of modules like preprocessing, segmentation, layout analysis, and recognition. Testing each of these modules requires different types of annotation information. For example, the annotation requirements of segmentation task is different from that of a character/word recognition unit. Most of the Indian languages have their own scripts. This further complicates the annotation process. Performance of the image processing and segmentation algorithms vary across scripts [16]. It has been shown in [16] that the segmentation of text blocks into lines and words is non-trivial for many of the Indian scripts. Segmentation of words into characters (or basic unit which can be recognized) is difficult because of lack of a commonly accepted standard. In spite of this, segmentation and annotation of document images up to word level can be done with some level of human intervention.

3.1 Hierarchical Annotation

Document images are annotated at different hierarchical levels to capture structural and functional truth information that are required for different modules of the document analysis systems. The process and tools needed for this purpose could be manual, semi-automatic, or automatic.

3.1.1 Different Levels of Annotation

The process of annotation is classified mainly into three levels. In each level, components of the documents are labeled with truth information. The truth information is useful for deciding the next stage of processing or annotation.

Document-Level Annotation: Document-level annotation includes capturing meta information related to the document. Meta information includes mainly document type, publication details, other details of the source, and digitization details. Document type includes information like type of source from which document is obtained, document quality. Publication details include author, title, date, publisher and edition information. Digitization information includes information regarding the scanning process like the scanning resolution, image file formats, details of the preprocessing done on scanned images. The script-specific and font information (if available) are also part of the document-level truth information, which could also be useful for recognizers.

Layout and Structure Annotation: The structure of the document image is annotated by segmentation and labeling. The document image is segmented into different blocks that are marked with corresponding labels. The blocks are mainly labeled as text and non-text blocks. The text blocks contain only the textual parts of the image.

These could be further classified as title, headings, footer, table, caption, etc. The non-text blocks are classified as pictures, graphs, drawings, etc. These classifications help in further processing of the document. The actual content is not annotated here but the layout and structure are marked. Based on the annotation information at this level, the further processing steps and type of algorithms required could also be decided.

Content-Specific Annotation: The text blocks are processed further to annotate their content. The text blocks are segmented into lines, words, and characters, which are labeled with corresponding text information. The segmentation into different components is a challenging task due to complexities of Indic scripts. However, the difficulty increases when the documents are of complex prints with non-Manhattan layouts. Representation and storage complexities increase with Indic scripts and complex layouts.

3.1.2 Methods of Annotation

Annotation can be carried out in a number of ways depending on the quantity of data required and the target system that uses the annotated data. Selection of a particular method depends on the level of annotation, complexity of the script, and quality of the document [6]. A good annotation process should use the right combination of these methods at different levels so that the best result is achieved efficiently.

Manual Annotation: Manual annotation is the process of selecting each image component and manually labeling it with corresponding details. Labeling documents according to structural and layout characteristics can be achieved with manual annotation. It also helps to add a specific description to each detail. For example, when annotating a picture, the details in the picture can be added as attributes of label. But the task of marking each Akshara image with corresponding text is a tedious task. Therefore, manual annotation is not efficient and useful at all levels of document annotation process. As it needs human assistance in each and every step, efficiency of the method depends directly on the efficiency of the user of the program.

Semi-Automatic Annotation: Annotation speed is increased with semi-automatic process. The layout annotation is done manually using a tool. The automatically segmented blocks of the document are labeled and classified as text and non-text. The errors in block segments and corresponding text labels are manually corrected by editing. For Indian languages where scripts are complex, semi-automatic annotation is efficient. Semi-automatic processes are required to segment the text blocks into lines and words. The users have to correct the segmentation boundaries. We align the text with image automatically, and manually verify/refine the alignment with the help of an annotation tool.

Automatic Annotation: Another alternative is the automatic annotation. Here the document is labeled with corresponding details without any manual intervention. To get the best output for automatic annotation, accurate segmentation techniques are required along with correct label text. Also, the text labels should be available in advance. As human intervention in this process is minimal, it takes minimal time

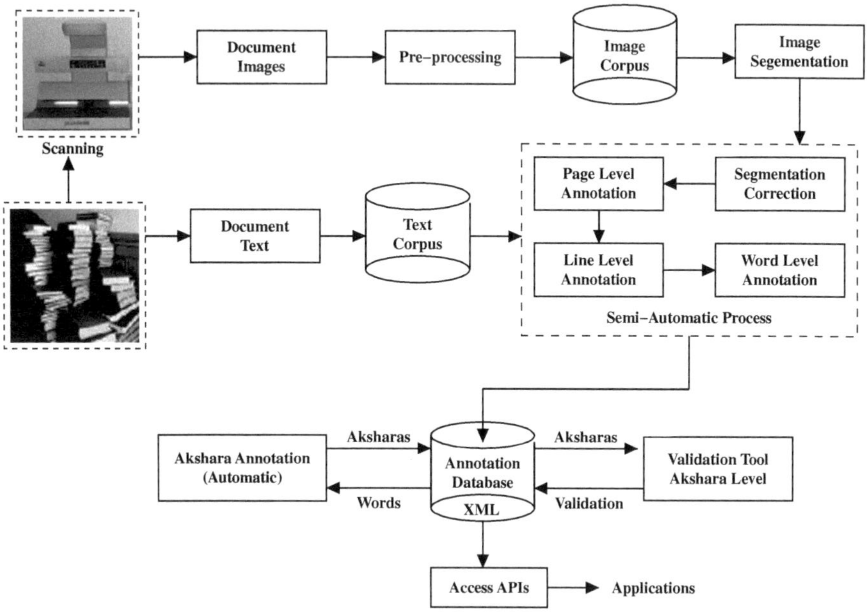

Fig. 3 The complete document image annotation process

for completion of the annotation process. The efficiency is truly dependent on the efficiency of the algorithms. However, with the use of any of the above-mentioned methods, the final annotation result should be validated to ensure the quality and correctness of annotation.

3.2 Annotation Process

The process of annotation is broadly divided into three steps: segmentation, labeling, and validation. Overall annotation process is presented in Fig. 3. The document is divided into different elements in a hierarchical fashion. This step is called segmentation. Labeling marks the segments with corresponding text or information. Correctness of the segments and their labels is verified in the validation phase. These steps can be performed by applying domain-specific techniques. The language, document quality, and layout complexity are important factors for choosing the appropriate techniques for the annotation [6].

3.2.1 Segmentation

Segmentation is the process of identifying meaningful elements in the document. At one level, these elements can be blocks of text or non-text content. At another level, these blocks may be split further to identify lines, words, and characters. The picture blocks may be classified further to identify different objects in it. Segmentation of text blocks is important from a recognizer's perspective. Different algorithms may be required for segmentation of variety of documents depending on their layout complexity, script, etc.

A detailed discussion on the popular segmentation methods is available in [17]. Most of these algorithms are designed and evaluated for Roman scripts [16]. For documents with correct valleys between blocks, lines, and words, X-Y Cut can perform reasonably. By adjusting the parameters, many of the existing algorithms can be adapted to a good extent to the documents with complex scripts. However, in the presence of gangling components, segmentation remains still a challenging problem. For many Indian language documents in Hindi, Telugu, Bangla, etc., need not have the well-defined structure suited for simple segmentation schemes. The specific characteristics will have to be used for obtaining accurate segmentation [16]. In our annotation tool, we have provided a plugin architecture for inserting script-specific segmentation algorithm.

3.2.2 Components Labeling

Once segments of document are identified during segmentation, the next step of annotation is labeling them with appropriate tags and information along with additional details. Different tools may be used for labeling at different segment levels. The selection of the type of tool is based on ease of use and the percentage of error from each method.

Functional-Level Annotation: At this level, the properties of the document are annotated and stored. Different details related to the documents and digitization process are stored in this level. These details are used to classify the data set according to different attributes in digitization, source metadata, and quality levels. It is stored as an attribute to each page of the data. This is done as manual process since the data related to each page are different and are not stored at any place but are entered directly. Other functional parameters could be generated automatically during processing the images.

Structure-Level Annotation: The layout structure of the document is represented by location of different elements or components. The boundaries of each block are marked with corresponding type of the block. Annotation of the different blocks is application and domain specific. Labeling of components is a semi-automatic process. The class of such segments is determined by users. Number of columns of text, their alignment, and block representation also determine the layout structure of the document. Hence, the labeling task at higher level is direct and is done either automatically or semi-automatically.

Content-Level Annotation: In block-level annotation, the text and non-text blocks of the document image are classified and labeled. The text blocks are further processed to obtain more granularity in annotation. The non-text blocks are also processed, but annotation is highly application domain specific. Figure 4 shows the block diagram of text annotation process. The annotation is carried out in a number of stages, generating data of different granularities at every level during these stages.

Fig. 4 Hierarchical Annotation: Different levels of document image segmentation and labeling

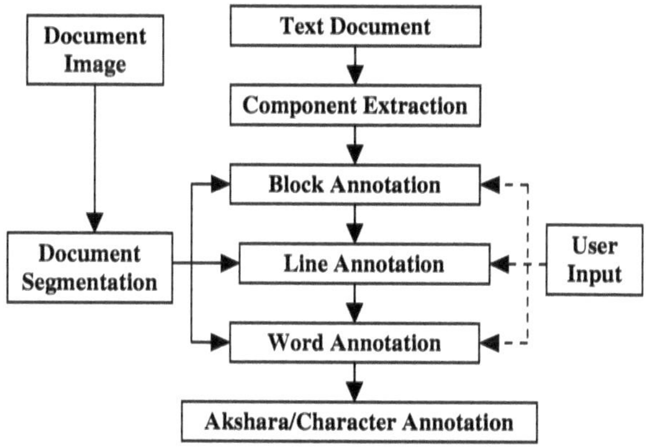

While keying in the unaligned parallel text, strict guidelines are followed. This makes the segmentation of text lines trivial and the alignment straightforward. However, due to errors in the image segmentation and noise in the textual content (spell errors), the method can fail and user interaction may be required. The detection and correction of segmentation errors can be modeled as an alignment problem.

Akshara annotation is the process of mapping a sequence of connected components from the word image to the corresponding text Akshara. Image of Akshara text is rendered for matching with components of the word image. Connected component matching module, which is similar to stroke matching module of [9], is used to come up with the best alignment of the Akshara components to the corresponding Aksharas of words. Figure 5 shows the process of Akshara-level annotation. Generally, it is assumed that each Akshara in the text corresponds to one or more connected components in the word image. However, computing the best assignment of connected components to Akshara is not trivial as multiple components can form an Akshara.

A modified version of the elastic matching or dynamic time warping (DTW) algorithm is employed to solve this problem of alignment. The alignment cost between two sets of connected components is measured by computing the distance between a set of features extracted from them. The total cost of DTW is used as similarity measure to group together components that are related to their root Akshara

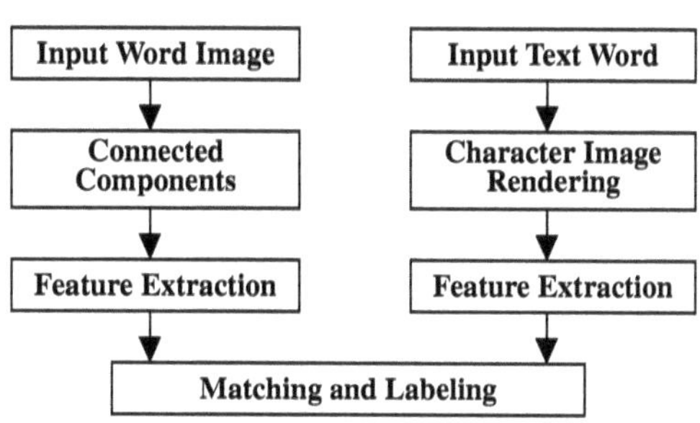

Fig. 5 Akshara-level annotation of the word images of text blocks

by partial match. Elastic matching is able to absorb the possible splits and breaks in the image segmentation. When components of two Akshara are merged, the algorithm assigns two Akshara as label, which can be corrected using a validation tool. With the assumption that multiple connected components might map to a single Akshara, we formulate the problem as follows: Find the best alignment between components and Aksharas using DTW matching score as the cost of grouping multiple components to form Akshara. More details of this alignment process may be seen in [9].

3.2.3 Annotation Tools

Annotation tools are essential for the generation of data sets [18]. The classification of tools is based on how they carry out the process of annotation [6].

Online and off-line Tools: The annotation tools are generally of two types: online tools and off-line tools. In an online tool most of the steps of annotation are carried out online. The components are labeled while correcting segmentation errors. These are mostly manual annotation tasks. Off-line tools use the labels already prepared and efficient algorithms align the components and the labels. Errors in the data or inputs are reported by the tool. Semi-automatic tools are used for such annotation. The advantage with off-line annotation tool is that the steps of annotation can be parallelized. For example, text-typing can be carried out separately while the process of digitization and processing is ongoing.

Semi-Automatic Annotation Tool: The document images consist of different layout varieties. An application-specific annotation tool is designed to work on fixed layout structure and content properties. When the layout structure is not stable different modules of the annotation tools may fail. For example, the segmentation routines may fail or generate errors in the segments. To fix the errors, manual correction should be facilitated. Hence, development of a general annotation process and tools is a challenging task. An example of such a tool is presented in [6]. A screenshot of a semi-automatic annotation tool for word-level annotation is shown in Fig. 6.

Automatic Annotation Tool: All steps of the annotation cannot be carried out manually due to time inefficiency. Semi-automatic tools also become inefficient when frequent user intervention is required. Hence, automatic annotation modules or tools are necessary. One such example is the segmentation of words into Aksharas or symbols and annotating them. Another example is to propagate the annotation across images scanned at different resolutions. Here, segmentation and labeling should happen together. The information from text labels would be helpful in segmenting the words properly. The complete process of Akshara annotation is explained in [6].

Validation: The annotated data are checked for errors to get high quality of truth information. This is carried out in the validation process. The validated data are very useful in building and evaluating OCR systems or any other research activity that needs huge data set of document images [6].

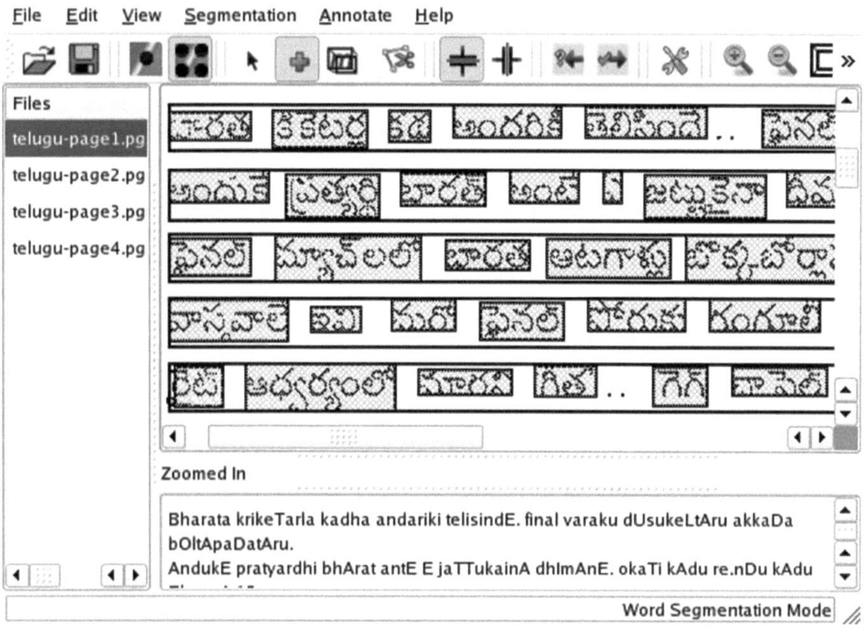

Fig. 6 Semi-automatic word-level annotation tool for Indian language document images

Manual creation of large data set of annotated document images is cumbersome and time-consuming process. The difficulties are solved by semi-automatic annotation tools that need little manual intervention. With the use of such tools, labeling of larger components, like paragraphs, lines, and words, of the document images would be easier but labeling down the word level would be again a time-consuming process. This step can be speeded up using automatic tools. There are possibilities of errors in the automatic annotation below word levels. If there are errors in the word-level annotation itself then the impact of it would be greater in the level below that. Performance measure of the system under evaluation depends on the correctness of the annotated data. One solution is to make manual corrections to wrongly annotated words by finding similar words and display them, check the list for errors, and correct the wrong ones. Hence, to make such corrections during automatic annotation validation tool is required. The prerequisites, expected functionality of the validation process, and the tool are explained below.

The major steps in the validation phase are (i) enumeration of distinct Aksharas or symbols present in a book or from specified number of pages from a media; (ii) displaying all occurrences of each Akshara on screen for checking; (iii) marking wrong Aksharas on the display screen for correction; and (iv) fetching word containing wrong Akshara and correcting the annotation and marking all Aksharas of the fetched word as valid.

4 Representation and Access

Once the corpus is created, we need effective and efficient methods to access the data sets. The recognizers may need the data in specific formats. Some require word-level segmentation information of the document images, whereas some others may need Akshara-level information or class identifier-level details of the Aksharas. Thus large data sets call for a standard representation that is independent of the script, and allows semantic interpretation of the print at various user-defined logical levels [10]. With the generation of large data, there is need for efficient access techniques. The data should be organized and stored in a structured way for efficient access. A standard is required to ensure the ease of access by a spectrum of communities that may need the data. XML provides an efficient method of data storage. It is easy to write applications on a standard data set. Even updation and changes to the data can be done easily in an XML storage standard. The representation should capture information about script, printing style, quality of printing, and truth. It should also capture information about source data providers and the data capture environment.

XML is accepted by all communities of the world for data representation. The data are represented in a hierarchy of XML tags. The schema has information that is broadly classified into four categories based on the type of meta information and annotation data to be stored. Figure 7 shows the block diagram of the schema. The categories of the schema are explained in the following sections.

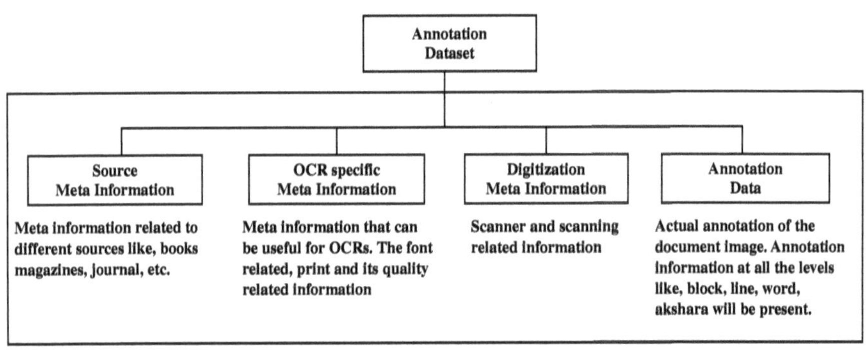

Fig. 7 The document image metainformation and annotation storage elements and sub-elements

4.1 Sources of Metainformation

The general information about the sources of document images is stored as metadata. The metadata schema gives information about the sources that are annotated. The source type, publication details, and other information essential for records are stored. Sources like postcards (mails), forms, newspaper clips. need different representation schemes. A source-specific schema has to be created for such document media.

4.2 Recognizer-Specific Metainformation

A recognizer need not recognize all types of documents. It needs additional information to adapt to a class of documents. Its performance often depends on functional information like font type, paper quality, layout complexity. Some of the details required are enumerated below.

1. Quality of the paper used in printing the source. We define four quality levels for representing the sources as listed below. This classification is specific to the application or data set.

   - *QA:* Good-quality print like laser print on a clean paper with resolution greater than 300 dpi.
   - *OB:* Moderate-quality print on ordinary paper with resolution around 100–300 dpi.
   - *OC:* Poor-quality print on an ordinary paper like typewriter prints.
   - *OD:* Very bad quality print on low-quality paper and low-quality ink in which the backside characters are also visible along with noise, cuts, and breaks.

   As it stands, the definition of quality is subjective. We may have more objective quality metrics defined based on (i) percentage of cuts and merges; (ii) popularity of font and printing style; (iii) interline and interword spacings; and (iv) performance of a base recognizer.
2. Type settings used in printing of the source.
3. Font-specific information like font name, font size, category (like TTF).

All of the above information may not be available in the source itself. An expert may have to predict some of the attribute values. In that case, based on the number of attributes mentioned in the source and predicted by an expert a reliability factor can also be specified for the meta information.

4.3 Digitization Meta Information

Document images are obtained from diverse documents under different settings. This information may be useful in applying specific type of algorithms in annotation and recognition. Information related to settings and types is also stored in the meta information of the schema in a separate digitization section. This information includes the following:

1. Type and properties of scanner used to capture the images from the sources.
2. Internal resolution of the scanner used to capture the images from the sources. Images are extrapolated to different resolution from the ones captured using the internal resolution. This information, if available from the manufacturer, is also stored.

3. Scanning platform and the default file format in which the scanner stores the scanned image.
4. Scanner settings like gray level, color information, black and white page, and bits per pixel information.
5. If the scanning is done using isolated pages or flattened pages (e.g., while scanning a book), this information is also stored.
6. Details of how the digitization and annotation is done (location, people involved).
7. Date of publication and details of the source.

4.4 Annotation Data

The annotation data are organized in a hierarchy to make updation or modification easier in future. Figure 8 shows the hierarchy in which the annotation data are stored. The annotation information are stored at different levels like blocks, paragraphs, lines, words, and Aksharas. For each of these levels the image information is stored in separate fields. The separation between the image data and the annotation information helps easier updates or modifications to the schema. The image data representation is changeable without affecting the annotation and its level information. Similarly, the annotation information is changeable without affecting the image

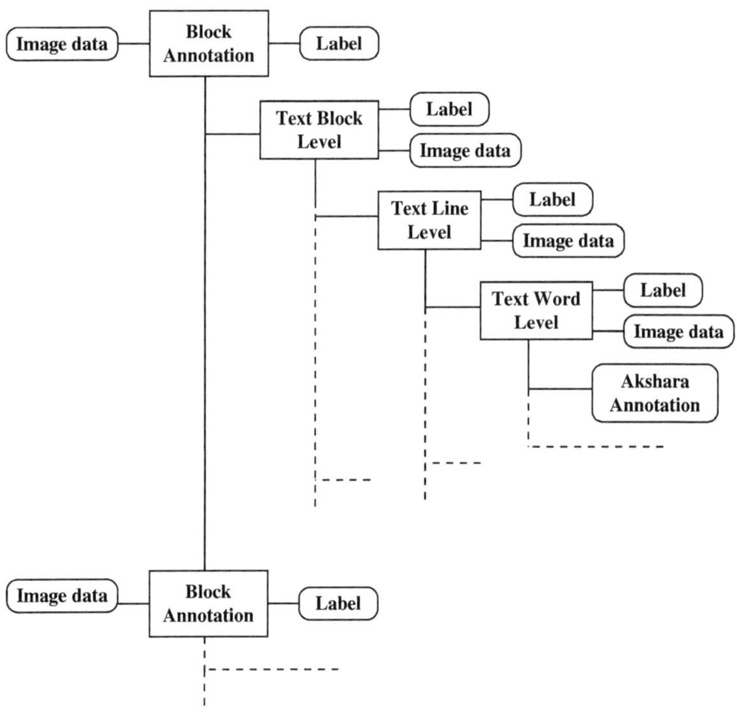

Fig. 8 Organizing the annotation data and image data in a hierarchy

data representation. The page structure information and other levels and sub-levels of the annotation information are explained in the following sections.

4.4.1 Page Structure Information

Page structure information contains the bounding box information of every block, text, and non-text obtained after segmentation, along with their labels after annotation. Storage of the bounding box information instead of its image saves storage space and separates the image data from the schema.

1. *Text block:* The blocks that contain only text are labeled as text paragraphs. Other blocks can be labeled as headings, picture captions, table captions, etc., based on the content. The bounding box information of these blocks is also stored in the schema. These text blocks may be further segmented as lines of blocks, words of lines, and Aksharas of words. The OCR may prefer to have information like font name, size, scan resolution which can be accessed from the metadata. To facilitate this, a reference to the metadata information file will be given in each page of the annotation. Sometimes, a single page of a collection may have different font style, font size, scan resolution, or print quality. In such cases additional fields providing such information, overriding the meta information, are added to that page. Such additional or special information is very useful in improving the performance of OCRs when applied on a huge collection.
2. *Non-text block:* The blocks remaining after the text block labeling are non-text blocks. Following are the non-text blocks that are annotated and represented in the XML schema:

   - mathematical equations;
   - figure/picture parts of the document image;
   - different types of graphs;
   - tables.

4.4.2 Text Block Structure Information

Text blocks obtained after page-level annotation of the document image are further segmented and annotated as lines and words. The line and word annotation information is stored hierarchically in the XML schema, which is further used for Akshara annotation by segmenting the words.

1. The segmentation information provided at page level is used in segmentation of text block into lines. Bounding box information is used to extract text blocks from document image. The bounding box and annotation information of the lines within text block of document image are stored in the annotation schema.
2. Bounding box provided in line annotation is used to extract the lines from document image. Similarly, the line annotation is used to extract the text words for

labeling. The extracted line is segmented into words and these words are annotated with the extracted text words. Finally, the annotation information is stored in the schema.

4.4.3 Akshara Structure Information

Bounding box representation may lead to errors in representing Aksharas due to overlapping of the character or part of characters. Therefore, when Akshara-level information is required to be accessed from the schema only Aksharas have to be returned.

Most classifiers require class identifiers (CIDs) of the components present in each Akshara. The CIDs used by each group of researchers or users can be different from one another. Therefore, unique CIDs cannot be decided at this stage. However, a mechanism can be provided to update the schema. In that case, the specific user or group will provide a segmentation module at Akshara level along with classes and CIDs, which are used by the schema generator to provide annotation along with the CIDs.

4.5 Representation Issues

Generally, the components of document image are represented with the help of bounding boxes. The bounding box information consists of coordinate values of two corners of the component. This representation model works for simple layouts and European language documents. Use of such model is not feasible for Indian language documents. The Aksharas of Indian language overlap one another in one of the two dimensions of the page. In the presence of such overlaps, segmentation itself is a challenging task. In such case, representation of overlapping bounding box becomes non-trivial. It necessitates adding extra information to the bounding box representation (for example, rank of the component of interest) or using another representation.

4.5.1 Complex Layout

Bounding box representation cannot be used for picture and text blocks that appear in oval shape. Such blocks are generally found in magazines and advertisements. The text and pictures are printed in zigzag manner and overlapping boundaries exist in such documents.

4.5.2 Indian Language Script Issues

- Some of the Indian language scripts have Aksharas that do not have UNICODE representations. When such Aksharas appear in the documents, the corresponding Akshara label cannot be entered. An alternative is required in such places.

– Characters in languages like Hindi [19], Bangla [20]. are connected by a headline called *Shirorekha*. Special representation scheme has to be used for annotation of *Shirorekha* within a word or Akshara. Special algorithm could be employed for *Shirorekha* removal before annotating Aksharas of words.

Some examples of the issues of Indian language scripts are shown in Fig. 9. The representational issues should be transparent to the user. User should be able to get an Akshara or word in the original gray or binary image. User can get pixels corresponding to the word or Akshara from binary image.

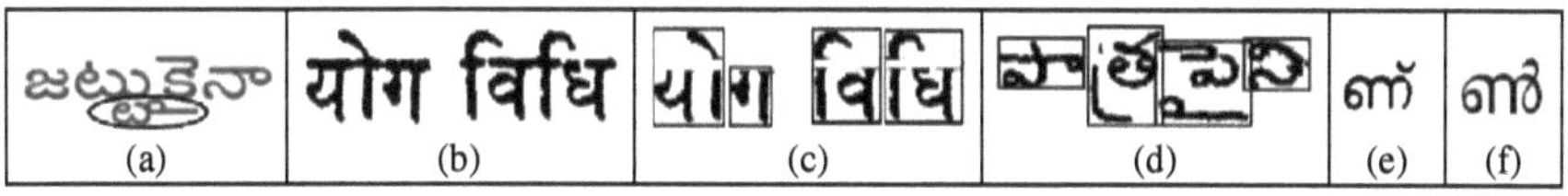

Fig. 9 Data representation issues of Indian language data sets: (**a**) touching components of two Aksharas of Telugu due to formatting errors in word processors, (**b**) Hindi words with Shirorekha, (**c**) multiple components after Shirorekha removal, and (**d**) Overlapping bounding boxes. Unavailable UNICODE representations for (**e**) and (**f**)

4.6 Data Access

A set of standard application program interfaces (APIs) are required for effective access to the data sets. They are aimed at developing automated applications in the document image analysis-related tasks. There are mainly two types of data that can be accessed from an annotated database.

– Image corpus data: Various images of the database based on layout complexity for layout analysis tasks.
– Annotation data: The text and image components required for development and performance evaluation of recognizers.

The data accessed from the database can be at any level of granularity starting from meta information to the lowest component level pixel details. The APIs should support access at all levels of the granularity. Some examples of the details that may be accessed by the users are as follows:

– Given specific font name, style, size, and quality of the required data return all Aksharas of that category.
– Given content (UNICODE) get all or part of the Aksharas with the font and quality specifications.
– Based on the number of Aksharas present in the database, retrieve statistics of Aksharas and distribution.
– Obtain the bounding box or representation and pixels of the gray or binary images.

5 Implementation and Execution

The task of annotation has to be carried out in a phased manner. Many of the associated tasks are manual and labour intensive. Some others are automatic or semi-automatic in nature.Image acquisition, text content typing, and labeling are the main tasks of the data generation process. In the last couple of years, we had worked toward building a data set useful for OCR development in Indic scripts. Though we have designed the whole process to suit a wide variety of document image analysis tasks; our present focus has been on content-level annotation of documents, primarily from books.

5.1 Organization of Tasks

Data generation from document images becomes more challenging when the documents are noisy and degraded. We started by identifying a set of books to suit the development and evaluation of character recognizers. This was also indirectly motivated by the recent successful digitization of large books as part of digital library of India. The books we have identified vary significantly in year of publication, fonts and print-styles, paper quality, etc. They were first digitized as explained in the earlier sections.

Since the parallel text is aligned with the word image, the textual content is created next. Annotation of Akshara requires image rendering from the text. Image processing softwares or applications are used to render or generate the images of word or Aksharas from text. The applications require standard UNICODE of the text. However, all Indian languages and fonts are not supported by these applications.

Complete data generation from large collection of documents is a time-consuming process. Some of the steps of this process can be executed is parallel to speed up the process. The image acquisition and text content typing can be carried out in parallel. It takes even more time for Indian language typing, as there are no standard keyboards available. These tasks can be carried out properly by following predefined set of guidelines as required by the application. After the digitization process, the images are preprocessed to obtain good quality of image corpus. Standard image processing tools are generally used for preprocessing. With the use of such tools, the functional parameters may not be captured. In such cases special algorithms are required for determining these parameters from the processed and original images.

The task of image acquisition, text typing, and labeling can be pipelined to speed up the data generation process. However, proper synchronization of the tasks becomes important. After preprocessing, the images are segmented by automatic process. Segmentation can be done in batch mode. The segmentation has to be checked for errors before labeling. This is done effectively in a tool that allows the user to check the segment boundaries, correct the errors. It also allows user to verify and correct the wrong text label before marking the segments. This manual verification task is simple till the word level of annotation.

5.2 Status of the Data Sets

A large collection of images are being generated and annotated to be used as data sets by Indian language researchers. These data sets which are intended for document analysis research comprise (i) comprehensive image corpus; (ii) text corpus; and (iii) annotated data of text at different granularities. The data sets have been made available to a consortium of prominent universities and institutions of India. The major focus is on printed document media for generation of the data sets. In addition to the details provided in Table 1, there is a plan to develop similar corpus for Nepali and Tibetan languages.

Table 1 Indian language data sets for OCR research. Size of the data sets being generated

	Image corpus size			Annotated corpus	
Language	Books	Pages	Images	Images	Words
Telugu	44	7585	91020	5083	5401908
Bangla	29	5330	63960	56	21347
Gujarati	28	6406	76872	1260	233674
Gurumukhi	35	5503	66036	1000	316426
Hindi	30	5134	61608	2324	573632
Kannada	30	5250	63000	1046	165776
Malayalam	40	5576	66912	2573	482645
Oriya	17	5272	63264	90	23232
Tamil	22	4573	54876	494	76672

Table 1 shows the status of data generation activity being carried out. The objective is to generate annotated data sets for 5000 pages in each of the above-mentioned Indian languages. Acquisition and processing of more than 5000 pages of eight languages are completed. Text content and annotation of these pages are being carried out as explained in this chapter.

Future work in this direction include (i) Akshara- and symbol-level annotation to aid the design and evaluation of classifier system independent of the segmentation modules; (ii) annotation of Indic documents with complex layouts to extend the applicability of these algorithms to a diverse category of documents; and (iii) to annotate documents obtained through cameras (in camera-based scanners, cellphone cameras, as well as natural text in broadcast videos).

6 Conclusions

In this chapter, we have outlined the process followed for the development of a corpus to help the Indian language OCR research. Some amount of automation is achieved by annotation tools and scripts for propagation of annotation. The present status of the annotation is also summarized. Development of huge corpus of document images is crucial to the successful use of machine learning algorithms in character recognition and document analysis. This demands corpus with significant diversity. Much more work is required to achieve this.

Acknowledgements Authors wish to acknowledge the financial support provided by Ministry of Communication and Information Technology, Govt of India. They also want to acknowledge the inputs from the members of the Indian language OCR consortia in formulating the annotation procedure. They also thank the members of the consortia for identification of the books to be included in the corpora and getting some of these books typed.

References

1. Henry Baird: Digital Libraries and Document Image Analysis. In: Proc. 7th International Conference on Document Analysis and Recognition (ICDAR) **1** (2003) 2–14
2. Digital Library of India. http://dli.iiit.ac.in
3. Vamshi Ambati, Lakshmipratha Hari, N. Balakrishnan, Raj Reddy and C.V. Jawahar: Process and Architecture for Digital Library of India. In: Proc. of ICDL (2006)
4. K. Pramod Sankar, V. Ambati, Lakshmi Hari and C. V. Jawahar: Digitizing A Million Books: Challenges for Document Analysis. In: Proceedings of Seventh IAPR Workshop on Document Analysis Systems (DAS) (2006) 425–436
5. U. Pal and B. B. Chaudhuri: Indian Script Character Recognition: A Survey. Pattern Recognition **37** (2004) 1887–1899
6. C. V. Jawahar and Anand Kumar: Content Level Annotation of Large Collection of Printed Document Images. In: Proc. of International Conference on Document Analysis and Recognition (ICDAR) (2007) 799–803
7. D. Elliman and N. Sherkat: A Truthing Tool for Generating a Database of Cursive Words. In: Proc. of 6th International Conference on Document Analysis and Recognition (ICDAR) (2001) 1255–1262
8. Srirangaraj Setlur, Suryaprakash Kompalli, Vemulapati Ramanaprasad and Venugopal Govindaraju: Creation of Data Resources and Design of an Evaluation Test Bed for Devanagari Script Recognition. International Workshop on Research Issues in Data Engineering: Multilingual Information Management (2003) 55–61
9. Anand Kumar, A. Balasubramanian, Anoop M Namboodiri and C.V. Jawahar: Model-Based Annotation of Online Handwritten Datasets. In: Proc. of 10th International Workshop on Frontiers in Handwriting Recognition (2006)
10. M. Agrawal, K. Bali, S. Madhvanath and L. Vuurpijl: UPX: A New XML Representation for Annotated Datasets of Online Handwriting Data. In: Proc. of International Conference on Document Analysis and Recognition (ICDAR) (2005) 1161–1165
11. M. Zimmermann and H. Bunke: Automatic Segmentation of the IAM Off-line Database for Handwritten English Text. In: Proc. of 16th International Conference on Pattern Recognition (ICPR) (2000) 35–39
12. C. Tomai, B. Zhang and V. Govindaraju: Transcript Mapping for Historic Handwritten Document Images. In: Proceedings of the 8th International Workshop on Frontiers in Handwriting Recognition (2002) 413–418
13. I. Guyon, R. Haralick, J. Hull and I. Phillips: Data Sets For OCR and Document Image Understanding Research. In: Proc. 2nd International Conference on Document Analysis and Recognition (ICDAR) (1993)
14. R. Haralick: UW-II English/Japanese document image database. Intelligent Systems Laboratory, University of Washington (1993)
15. Japanese Character Image Database. The Center of Excellence for Document Analysis and Recognition, State University of New York at Buffalo (1995)
16. K. Sesh Kumar, K. Sukesh Kumar and C. V. Jawahar: On Segmentation of Documents in Complex Scripts. In: Proc. of International Conference on Document Analysis and Recognition (ICDAR) **2** (2007) 1243–1247

17. Faisal Shafait, Daniel Keysers and Thomas M. Breuel: Performance Comparison of Six Algorithms for Page Segmentation. In: Document Analysis Systems VII (2006) 368–379
18. A. Bhaskarbhatla, S. Madhavanath, M. Pavan Kumar, A. Balasubramanian and C. V. Jawahar: Representation and Annotation of Online Handwritten Data. In: Proc. of 9th International Workshop on Frontiers in Handwriting Recognition (IWFHR) (2004) 136–141
19. Veena Bansal and R. M. K. Sinha: A Complete OCR for Printed Hindi Text in Devanagari Script. In: Proc. 6th International Conference on Document Analysis and Recognition (ICDAR) (2001) 800–804
20. B. B. Chaudhuri and U. Pal: A Complete Printed Bangla OCR System. Pattern Recognition *31*(5) (1998) 531–549

On OCR of Major Indian Scripts: Bangla and Devanagari

B.B. Chaudhuri

Abstract This chapter describes our work in the OCR of Bangla and Devanagari, two of the most widely used scripts of the Indian subcontinent. Due to their strong structural similarities, these two scripts can be tackled under a single framework. The proposed approach starts with character and symbol segmentation and employs three recognizers for symbols of different zones. For the middle zone, a two-stage approach with group and individual symbol recognizers is used. The main recognizer is a covariance-based quadratic classifier. The problem of error evaluation and creating ground truth for Indic scripts has also been addressed. A post-recognition error detection approach based on spell-checker principles has been proposed mainly to correct an error in a single position in a recognized word string. Encouraging results have been obtained on multi-font Bangla and Devanagari documents.

Keywords Bangla · Devanagari · OCR · Benchmarking · Error correction

1 Introduction

Optical character recognition (OCR) of machine-printed Roman scripts is a mature technology, and software vendors are currently competing to push the system accuracy toward 100%. Following years of intensive research, OCR of printed Chinese, Japanese, and Korean scripts has also reached a high degree of accuracy. However, south Asian, and in particular, Indian scripts, lag behind in OCR development.

Several reasons may be attributed to this situation. First, full-fledged Indic OCR development for scanned documents started as late as the mid-1990s. Second, from an OCR viewpoint, a majority of Indian scripts are more complex than their European counterparts. They are *abugida* or alphabetic-syllabic scripts, which can have

B.B. Chaudhuri (✉)
Indian Statistical Institute, Kolkata- 700108, India
e-mail: bbcisical@gmail.com

V. Govindaraju, S. Setlur (eds.), *Guide to OCR for Indic Scripts*, Advances in Pattern Recognition, DOI 10.1007/978-1-84800-330-9_2,

1000–1200 unique character shapes in a document of running text. The scripts generally have 50 basic characters. Additionally, there are vowel allographs and consonant compounds with distinct shapes created by the combination of two-, three-, and four-consonant compounds (there is even a five-consonant compound in a now-obsolete word), resulting in a large class space. Further increasing the shape complexity, in a script such as Bangla, some compounds and syllables are printed in more than one form (*transparent* and *non-transparent* group of fonts). Third, statistical language and script models, which are useful for developing a robust OCR system, are not well developed for most Indic scripts. Despite the complexity and technical hurdles associated with developing accurate Indic OCR, if several research groups work in parallel, the testing and evaluation of approaches will lead to rapid advances in the field. With the exception of Devanagari, serious attempts at OCR development in Indian scripts by multiple research groups have been rare (a survey is presented in [1]).

Most approaches to Indic script OCR involve the segmentation of the document image into characters and symbols which are then submitted to a recognition engine. We have not come across any segmentation-free approaches to word recognition for printed Indic text. Also, in order to reduce the shape complexity and hence the number of classes by a factor of 2 or more, the upper (ascender), middle, and lower (descender) zones of a text line are partitioned in most approaches [2–6]. While upper zone demarcation can be very accurate for scripts such as Devanagari, Bangla, Assamese, and Punjabi (due to the presence of the easily detectable horizontal line called *Shirorekha* above which lies the upper zone), detection of lower zone (portion below baseline) is highly prone to error. This is due to the fact that the lower zone is scarcely populated, and not only modifiers but also parts of basic characters may intrude into this zone. For south Indian scripts such as Telugu or Malayalam, the isolation of both upper and lower zones is more complicated. To avoid errors due to incorrect segmentation, some OCR systems do not demarcate the lower zone, sacrificing reduction in the number of pattern classes. Other researchers employ a recognition-driven segmentation in a feedback loop [7], which increases the time complexity.

While dividing characters into these zones helps to reduce the number of pattern classes, the recognition output for these zones must be combined into valid character–modifier combinations and then converted into ISCII or Unicode format. This is not a trivial process due to the alphabetic-syllabic nature of the scripts, where some vowel modifiers may consist of topologically separated parts, one lying to the left and the other to the right of a consonant/compound (e.g., for Bangla script). To form a word, a rule-based writing protocol and a reasonably accurate identification of symbol location all necessary. Errors in symbol/character segmentation or recognition, or detection of the location of modifiers with respect to the middle zone character, may result in erroneous Unicode strings. Such post-processing problems do not arise in the OCR of alphabetic scripts such as English.

In this chapter we describe our OCR module (including post-processing and error evaluation) for two Indic scripts – Devanagari and Bangla, which are challenging scripts for OCR [1]. The OCR engine described in Section 2 has some structural similarity with that of the Bangla OCR system detailed in [3]. However, there are major differences in the basic approach to classification and error correction. Due to the ortho-syllabic nature of Bangla and Devanagari scripts, the definition of an OCR error needs a fresh look, as described in Section 3. Error handling in an OCR system may work in one of two ways: (a) the error detection module can be used in a feedback loop to the classifier for re-classification/re-segmentation/correction or (b) the module can be serially connected after the recognition engine (without any feedback mechanism) to perform error detection and correction, and generate the final output. In this chapter we have employed the second scheme. This error-handling module, explained in Section 4, is based on two versions of the language dictionary.

2 Basic OCR System

The basic OCR system used in this work is illustrated in Fig. 1. The pre-processing steps include binarization and noise removal, skew detection and correction, layout analysis and text column separation, as well as line, word, character, and sub-symbol segmentation. For the pre-processing steps until layout analysis, we employ prior off-the-shelf techniques with some suitable modifications to adapt to Bangla and Devanagari document images. Text line detection is carried out by using projection profiles with a suitable threshold. The threshold is chosen so as to minimize the variance of ratio of text line height to the height of the inter-line white space. Based on line length and average inter-text gap height, allowance is made for the presence of black pixels in the inter-line space due to noise and strokes overlapping from neighboring lines. The document is thus divided into three fuzzy regions: (a) confirmed text line region, (b) text/non-text overlap region, and (c) confirmed inter-line gap region. The word segmentation module is trained with multi-font, multi-style script pages, using word gap ground truth from various documents. In Devanagari and Bangla, the headline or *shirorekha* connects the characters in a word. But there are occasional intra-word gaps, because some characters do not have a *shirorekha*. Analyzing the training data, a gap-width threshold is found such that gap detection errors (false identification of a gap causing word splitting and missed detection of a gap causing a combination of two words) can be minimized. During the test phase, a gap wider than this threshold is deemed as a word gap. Using these methods on a set of documents with single column text printed using different fonts and on different types of paper, a line segmentation error rate of 0.01% and word segmentation error rate of 0.23% were obtained.

The *shirorekha* is detected during the text line identification phase and is used to separate the upper zone from the other zones. Lower zone separation was not attempted in our system; lower and middle zones remain as a single mid-low zone. Next, mid-low zone characters of each word are separated primarily by identifying white vertical runs from the baseline region up to the headline. For Bangla script, we make use of the fact that any full character will have vertical extent from

Fig. 1 Basic OCR system

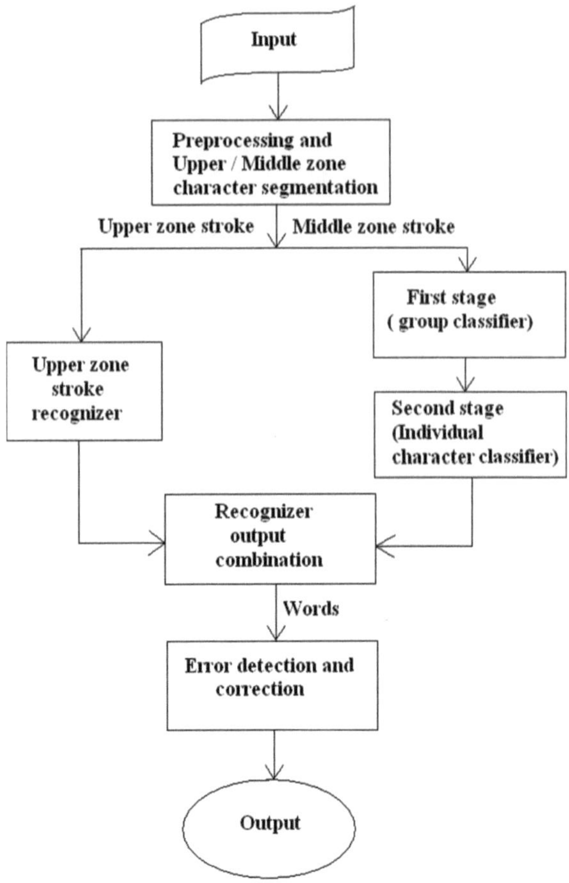

headline to baseline and a signature having a smaller vertical span (less than 75% of middle zone height) cannot be a full character. However, a Devanagari compound character may consist of *half-characters* that have a lesser vertical extent which may not touch the associated full character in the mid-low zone. For such conjuncts and for kerned character pairs, contour following is used for character segmentation. Adjacent characters may sometimes touch each other at points below the *shirorekha* due to scanning artifacts or poor print quality. Touching characters that are candidates for splitting can be identified by the large width-to-height ratio of the component. A second-stage segmentation procedure is invoked [6] on such components. About 98.3% of characters/symbols are correctly segmented using this combined approach. An alternative approach for touching character segmentation for Roman text by Song et al. [8] can also be used.

The output of the segmentation module consists of basic letters, compound characters, and vowel modifier parts in the middle zone as well as ortho-syllables that are then sent to the recognition engine. For the upper zone signatures, individual components above the headline are detected and stored along with their bounding box information.

Separate sets of recognizers are used for upper and mid-low zone symbols. First, some small signature shapes are separated using features such as normalized area, height, and width compared to mid-zone height, position within the middle zone, vertical lines, and left and right convexity. These signature shapes include the vertical line used as a period, exclamation sign, *visarg* sign, dot (*bindu*) in the upper zone, comma, and apostrophe. They are recognized using an approach similar to the shape-based method for the upper zone, described later in this chapter. The main classifier engine is used for the recognition of other symbols in the mid-low zone.

The main classifier consists of two stages. The first stage is a *group classifier* that exploits a high degree of shape similarity among some subsets of characters/syllables. The group classifier puts the input sample into one of several similarly shaped groups. In Bangla and Devanagari scripts, three types of shapes can be observed, which may be exploited to form similar-shaped groups. Some characters of the alphabet have signature shapes only in the middle zone while others extend up to the upper zone. Some character pairs are identical in the middle zone and differ only in the presence or absence of upper zone signature shapes. This is the first type of similarity. In the Devanagari alphabet, three pairs of vowels have this property, but in the Bangla alphabet, a couple of consonants also fall in this category (see first row of Fig. 2). In the second category, the characters have nearly identical shapes in the middle zone but differ only in the presence or absence of very small signature shapes as shown in the second row of Fig. 2. The third type of similarity arises due to syllabic form, generated by joining vowel modifiers like short *u*, long *U*, and *ri* below the basic consonant/compound characters. Since the consonant/compounds are much larger than these modifier markers, the overall shapes are highly similar except in the lower zone. The first subset of the third row of Fig. 2 shows some examples. These ortho-syllabic forms increase the number of shape classes by a factor of 3–4 that can be reduced by the same factor if put into small groups. However, groups may contain a single class as well. Single-class groups are created when accuracy does not improve by clubbing one class with another.

The task of the second stage *individual character classifier* is to distinguish and classify individual members from the multi-class groups. This two-stage approach has several advantages. First, it makes the number of classes in each stage small without the need for segmentation of descender symbols. Second, it significantly reduces the error of misclassification of similarly shaped character/syllable/symbols

(आ ओ), (इ ई), (ए ऐ)	(ই ঈ), (ঢ ট), (ড উ)
(क फ), (ड ङ ड़), (भ म)	(ড ড়), (য ষ য়), (ও ত)
(क कु कू), (ष्ट ष्ठ), (फ्ल क्ल)	(ক কু কূ), (জু জ্ব), (স্প স্প)

Fig. 2 Three types of shape similarity. *Left* – Devanagari, *right* – Bangla characters.

at the first stage. This is important because the first stage deals with a large number of classes. In the second stage, no group consists of more than 15 classes and it is easier to handle this small subset of classes.

2.1 Group and Individual Character Classifiers

For the group classifier, the group formation may be guided by visual shape similarity of classes, or learned through the reduction of overall group misclassification during the training phase. Starting with an initial condition wherein each group contains a single class (i.e., no effective grouping), the training data are run on the classifier and a recognition–confusion matrix is generated. To illustrate, let a character C_i be misclassified into class C_j with x_{ij} % error, and C_j be misclassified into C_i with x_{ji} % error. If C_i and C_j are in a single group, then the error $x_{ij} + x_{ji}$ will disappear in a group classification environment. To form groups which will substantially reduce such errors, we can use a conventional classifier at the training phase and rank the error sum of such pair-wise characters in decreasing order up to, say, the rth rank. The number of generated groups can be r or less, since the pairs (C_i ,C_j), (C_j ,C_k), and (C_k ,C_l) can further be grouped as (C_i ,C_j ,C_k ,C_l). By sufficiently increasing the group size and hence reducing the number of groups, we can greatly minimize misclassification at the group level. However, a very small number of groups reduces the discriminating power at the first stage. Groups should be such that individual members can be accurately classified in the second stage, thereby improving the overall recognition score. In our experiments, we have found that 200–250 group classes formed out of the nearly 1000 character classes provided the best results for the group classification stage for both Bangla and Devanagari scripts. For laser quality documents with low paper noise, 97.10–98.27% group classifier accuracy is achieved in a multi-font environment.

The classifier for the first stage uses one set of features which is based on run-lengths in four directions (horizontal, vertical, and two diagonal) using a 5×5 grid for each character candidate. Another set of features is derived from the white-to-black transitions scanning both rows and columns. For classification, a co-variance matrix-based quadratic classifier was used. The classifier was trained with the above features on size-normalized samples obtained from text documents containing five different fonts. In the group classification scheme, there is one quadratic classifier for each class of each group.

Therefore, for an input character image X, the quadratic discriminant function is computed for all symbol classes. If the character C is the top choice of the classifier, and C belongs to the group G, then X is classified into group G. If group G has only one member, then the second stage of classification is not invoked. If group G has multiple members, in the second stage, local shape features are generated for X in order to assign it a unique class of character/symbol. The shape features are font-independent signatures whose presence/absence indicates a particular class of G. For detecting this class, the algorithm concentrates on a small portion of the character where the distinctive shape is likely to be present. The dis-

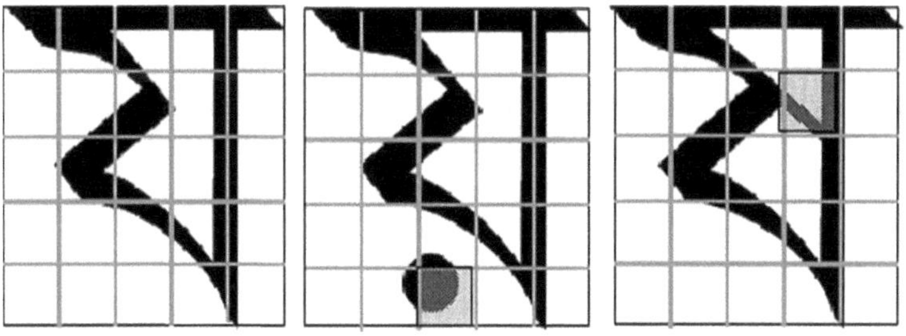

Fig. 3 Regions where shape dissimilarity is prominent

tinction can be curvature-based such as convexity, concavity, or region of inflection, or topologically based, like a small isolated circular component, or a hole (see Fig. 3). Park et al. [9] considered a hierarchical feature space for coarse-fine resolution binary feature vector for handwriting classification. On the other hand, we consider a small moving window and scan over the bounding boxes of characters in a group to identify areas with high mismatching scores. Pixel weights are set proportional to this score during training. In this manner, the region where shapes differ significantly is emphasized, and the region where the shapes are similar is suppressed in the test phase. In addition, we use topological features such as holes and isolated components during classification.

A third classifier is used for the recognition of upper zone signatures which are small in size and sometimes similar in shape. It can also be a neural net or shape-based classifier, where typical features are concave/convex regions, the location of the intersection of the signature shapes with the *shirorekha*, intersection of two or more curves, presence/absence of hole etc. For Bangla, about 24 different shapes may be found in the upper zone and a set of simple deterministic classifiers is used to recognize them. For Devanagari, the number of upper zone shapes is less than half of those in Bangla. Some typical upper zone shapes are shown in Fig. 4.

In all of the above stages, the recognizer reports a *reject* answer if the best classifier score is lower than a predefined threshold.

Next, the recognized characters and symbols in the upper and mid-lower zones are input to a syllable-generation module. This module consists of a set of rules for combining the recognition outputs from the two zones into full characters and modifiers and then into syllables. Positional information of the upper zone strokes plays a significant role here. For example, if a shape touches the *shirorekha* once at the left side (with respect to midpoint of its bounding box) "below" which there is a

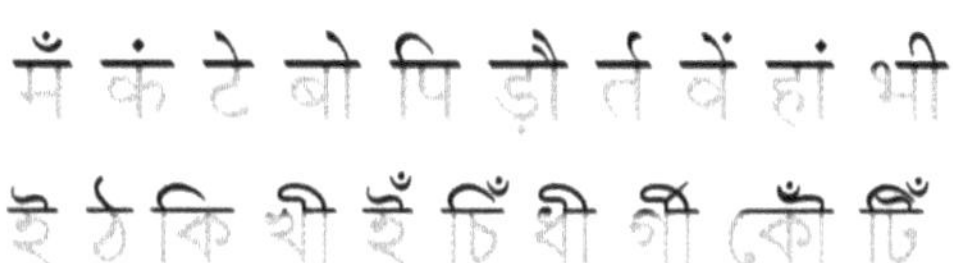

Fig. 4 Upper zone shapes in Devanagari (*upper row*) and Bangla (*lower row*) scripts

vertical line or *danda*, then the shape, along with vertical line, constitutes the vowel modifier of ই (i). This modifier is associated with the character X whose bounding box is "below" the bounding box of the signature. A measure is defined to characterize the attribute "below." However, due to inaccurate segmentation and recognition, the recognition results may not be able to generate a valid character/modifier combination based on the set of rules. In this case, an error in segmentation or recognition is assumed, and a *reject* result is reported for both zones. After the syllables are generated, the result is returned as Unicode values. The quantification of errors for Indic script OCR is addressed in the following section.

3 Quantification of Errors

A document page may have a complex geometric layout which needs partitioning into single column texts for the OCR engine. An error in doing this falls within the category of layout segmentation error. On a text column segmented by a layout analyzer, the OCR engine starts by identifying individual lines of text. The level of error made in line separation is normally not reported in OCR literature, although a high word recognition rate on a page document would indicate accurate line segmentation. Ground-truthing of lines and defining the metric to be used to evaluate line segmentation are difficult in handwritten documents or very noisy machine-printed documents due to touching between lines and uneven skew across the lines. It is an easier problem with clean machine-printed documents where the line mis-identification error rate may be computed as 1 – (no. of correctly identified lines)/(total no. of lines in the document column).

OCR systems usually report recognition error rates either at the word or character level. Word recognition error is defined as the average percentage of mis-recognized words in the script. At the character level, the error rate is the average percentage of mis-recognized characters. Word error is considered a pessimistic estimate since a single character error makes the entire word erroneous. Some OCR systems have a reject option, in which character rejection error and mis-recognition error rates are distinguished. In an alphabetic script like English, character-level error is a fair estimate.

For Indic scripts, word-level error computation can be done in the same way as for English script. Two types of errors can be computed, word segmentation error and word recognition error. If out of N_w words, N'_w are correctly segmented, then the word segmentation error is $E_{wi} = 1 - N'_w / N_w$. If out of N'_w words N''_w are correctly recognized by the system, then the recognition error E_{wr} may be defined either as $1 - N''_w / N_w$ or as $1 - N''_w / N'_w$.

The concept of character recognition error in OCR of Indic scripts is ambiguous. There are three categories of characters, namely (a) basic alphabet, (b) modifiers and other markers, and (c) compound characters. The vowel modifiers attached above/below the basic/compound characters together form an ortho-syllabic shape, called *Akshara* which is the linguistic character unit. Most Indic OCR methods segment these linguistic character units or Aksharas into smaller units for recognition. If the system misrecognizes an Akshara, how does a system count the error at the character level? Should it be two units or one unit of error? Vowel characters অ (*a*) versus আ (*A*);share primitives (*A* consists of a modifier sign *danda* after the shape for অ (*a*) but is traditionally considered another vowel character). The modifiers for ও (O) and ঔ (Ou) have two topologically separate components. Conjunct characters consist of two, three, or four consonants. Conjunct characters could also have modifiers. Should these be considered multiple units of error? Further, the recognition engines may separately recognize the symbols in upper- and mid-lower zones, but if the symbol combination module makes an error in combining the zone-specific results into the correct basic, modifier, and compound representation, then how do we account for the error?

We propose two approaches to address the problem. One is based on the concept of *ortho-syllabic (Akshara) error*, where each syllable consists either of a basic/compound character or of a basic/compound character connected with a vowel modifier. In word images of Bangla, Devanagari, and other scripts, syllables are phonetically and orthographically well represented in the left–right sequence so that we can segment them vertically and count their number in a word image. Now, if we assume that failure to recognize a complete syllable is one unit of error, then the ortho-syllabic error rate of the OCR system can be calculated from the corresponding syllable-level ground truth using a simplified version of minimum edit (ME) distance (because both are in left–right sequence).

The ortho-syllabic error is more fine-grained than word error but less fine-grained than character error. But the advantage is that the ortho-syllable is devoid of character definition complexity and is a natural and meaningful representation of Indic script/language. To examine relative granularity, we computed some primary statistics from a Bangla script corpus, according to which 100 characters correspond to about 22 words (a compound character with modifier is counted as the number of consonants plus one for modifier) on an average. So, if the OCR error for character primitives is 4%, the word-level error can be as high as 18%. Typically it will be lower since a fraction of words may have more than one error in its character primitives. These 100 character primitives constitute about 60–65 ortho-syllables. So, if the OCR error for character primitives is 4%, the syllabic error percentage will be about 6–7%.

The second approach we propose is to convert the recognized characters and symbols of a word into Unicode strings (the reject option may be given a code from one of the empty cells in the 2-D Unicode table). To compute the error, a Unicode representation of input text should also be maintained as ground truth. Again, the minimum edit distance between the OCR output and the ground truth can provide the character error rate of the system.

Note that the latest version of the Bangla Unicode (version 5.1) table has some drawbacks, though the Devanagari Unicode table is fairly complete. In Bangla, the compound formed by the character র(r) followed by য (j) can take two orthographic shapes, which currently need multiple code words for distinct representation. However, we can eliminate this problem by using the free Unicode cells, as stated above.

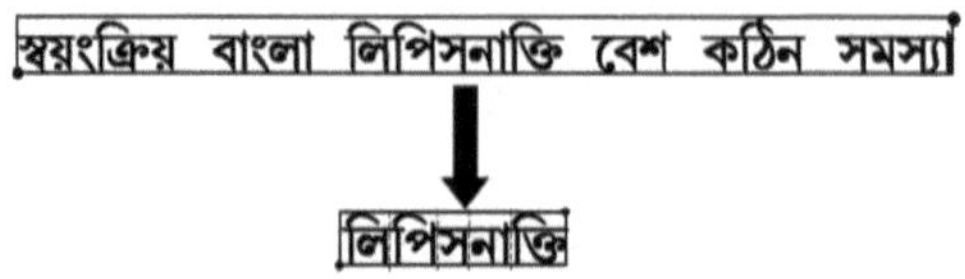

Fig. 5 Annotation of text line and words for ground truth: The bounding box co-ordinates are stored for lines, words, ortho-syllables, and corresponding Unicode values (ortho-syllables are shown using *dotted lines*)

Also, for error evaluation, the compounds formed by 2, 3, and 4 consonants should be counted as 2, 3, and 4 units of characters, while vowel modifiers of any topology should be counted as 1 unit.

For testing of OCR systems, ground truth up to the syllable level can be accurately generated in these scripts. Two aspects of ground truth, namely geometric location and the symbolic representation of the text in a document, are important in Indian scripts. The geometric layout may start at the text line level where the line is numbered and represented by its bounding box location within the document. This is followed by the number of words in the line. Then, each word position in the line is represented by their bounding box co-ordinates. The finest level division is the horizontal partitioning of the syllable boundary in the word, which can be semi-interactively generated. Next, the Unicode string for the word may be demarcated in terms of the strings for syllables (for example, see Fig. 5). Here, the third word of the line has five syllables and the Unicode representations of syllable 1 is 09B209BF, syllable 2 is 09AA09BF, syllable 3 is 09B8, syllable 4 is 09A809BE, and syllable 5 is 0995[09CD]09A409CF. The code within third bracket is a compound formation code and is not counted in error calculation. But the compound formed by the previous and following characters is considered as 2 units, even if the error occurs in only one character.

4 Post-recognition Error Correction

Corpus-based contextual information can be employed for detecting and correcting errors in OCR output [10,11]. The contextual information is incorporated in one of two approaches, namely (i) deterministic approach based on n-gram and (ii) probabilistic approach based on maximizing the sum of log of confusion probability and transition probability (in a Markovian framework). The second approach is efficiently implemented by the Viterbi algorithm. For an m-character string, this is equivalent to traversing through a trellis graph of N $\times$ m nodes, where N is the size of the alphabet. If negative of log of transition probability is the weight associated with edges of the trellis and negative of log of confusion probability is the weight associated with the nodes, then the path with minimum cumulative weight represents the desired correction output.

Among Indian scripts, a complete OCR system with post-recognition error correction reported by Chaudhuri and Pal [3] was later modified using confusion matrix-based frequency and dictionary-based error correction approaches as follows. The confusion matrix generated at the training phase represents mis-recognition of a character q as x with probability $p(q \Leftarrow x)$. Suppose that m different characters can be mis-recognized as x with finite probability estimates. When the OCR output string X does not have a match in the dictionary, character confusion probability is used to correct the error through substitution. To do so, a string X is generated by replacing x by q in X. Suppose m strings are generated by substitution of x in X. This process is repeated for all characters of X. The collection of all generated strings is checked in the dictionary and valid words among them are found. Among the valid words, the one in which character replacement has occurred with highest probability is chosen as the error-corrected word. If a valid word is not in the collection, the correction effort is abandoned.

Bansal and Sinha [12] proposed a post-recognition correction approach for Devanagari script by partitioning the dictionary in terms of number of middle zone characters, vertical bars, upper modifiers, lower modifiers, etc., to ensure that the search is made among a small subset of words. During correction, they did not employ any statistical information that could be gathered from the training phase. Kompalli et al. [7] have integrated multi-choice recognition with language n-gram and a dictionary-based model for improving the results of their Devanagari OCR system.

We propose a new dictionary-based forward–backward search scheme for error correction that is computationally attractive. The approach is motivated by spell-checking techniques used in word processors [13] combined with our previous studies in error pattern generation [14]. Of the errors made by our OCR system before post-processing, 86.71% erroneous words have error in a single character position while only 12.32% have an error in two positions. Our scheme focuses on correcting errors in a single position in words, and briefly describes an approach for two-position errors.

4.1 Forward–Backward Error Correction Scheme

The basic idea in the forward–backward correction scheme is as follows. Let the OCR system output a string S for an input word image. We assume that the original text is error free and contains either root or inflected (root words fused or concatenated with valid suffixes) words. Now, if the OCR does not make any error, the string S will be a valid root/inflected word. To check this, we can either have a dictionary of all surface words or can maintain two word lists: one for the root words and the other for the suffixes. In the second case, either a set of word morphological rules or a set of finite state automata (FSA) should be incorporated to check if the string S is a valid inflected word. If S is not accepted by this system, it goes to the correction module.

For OCR output error correction, it is better to keep all inflected words in the dictionary. In the proposed technique, two versions of the dictionary are used. One version is similar to a conventional dictionary and is called forward dictionary D_f. In the other, called reversed order or backward dictionary D_r, the character order of the word is reversed. For example, *word* will be reversed as *drow*. This is done to facilitate the search process starting from the end of the output string S and moving leftward. These reversed words are also alphabetically arranged and stored in the backward dictionary. For quick search, these dictionaries can be structured in the *Trie*form. The combined forward and backward dictionaries are used for error correction.

Let the OCR output a string S with an error at one character position. The error may be any type, such as substitution, insertion, or deletion. In the OCR environment, substitution errors occur most frequently, followed by insertion. The rejection (by classifier) may be considered as a deletion error (with certainty). For a single error, we can show that use of the two dictionaries can efficiently suggest both the position of the error and the correction candidate. The erroneous string generated by OCR will not have a complete match in any dictionary. Let us find the maximum number of character positions from the left in S that matches a word in D_f. This is an easy task in an alphabetically ordered or trie-structured dictionary. Let it be up to the k_1th character in S. For example, if the erroneous word is "forlune"(in case of "fortune") then we can match up to the first four characters "forl" in an English dictionary, since there is a valid word "forlorn." But a longer substring match is not possible since there is no word that starts with "forlu." In this case, we get $k_1 = 4$. Now, the following proposition is true for any string S having a single position error.

Proposition 1 If, for any erroneous string S, the longest substring match in forward dictionary occurs for the first k_1 characters, then the error must lie within the first $k_1 + 1$ characters of S. The rest of the characters of S are error free.

To prove the proposition, let it be false, i.e., let the error not lie in the first $k_1 + 1$ characters. Now, since the first $k_1 + 1$ characters are error free, then we could find at least one word in the dictionary where the first $k_1 + 1$ characters match with those of the string S. This is a contradiction, since the longest dictionary word string match occurred for the first k_1 characters, not for $k_1 + 1$ characters. Hence Proposition 1 is true.

Now, let us reverse the string S in the manner described above and get S'. We repeat the matching process with S' and reversed dictionary D_r. This is equivalent to leftward matching of the string from the back end. On D_r let us find a maximum match of say k_2 characters of the reverse string S'. Then following the same arguments as Proposition 1, we can say that the error must have occurred in $k_2 + 1$ characters of S'. In other words, the error must lie within the last $k_2 + 1$ characters, while the rest of S is error free. This reverse dictionary-based version of our proposition can be called Proposition 2.

Note that Propositions 1 and 2 provide some idea about where the error has occurred in S. If $k_1 = 0$, i.e., if there is no valid word in the conventional dictionary whose first character is the same as that of S, then the error has occurred at or contiguous with the first character of S. Hence, the detection of error location is very accurate. Now we can use D_r to suggest the correction candidates by finding the valid words in D_r whose characters all but the last one matches with those of S' and whose length is $|S| \pm 1$. The candidate list is small and the search is fast since the dictionaries are alphabetically ordered. There is no need of a costly dynamic programming algorithm for final selection of candidates. Similarly, if $k_2 = 0$, i.e., if there is no word in the dictionary whose last character matches with that of S, then too we have detected the location of error. It is at or contiguous with the last character of string S. All other characters belong to the intended word. So, we can use them as a key for selecting candidate words for correction using the conventional dictionary D_f. If k_1 or k_2 are small, then one of the above approaches will be very useful. But if the value of any of them is nearly half the length of S, then the method is less attractive. However, we can combine the two propositions into one and come up with a better way of locating the position of error.

Proposition 2 If for any erroneous string S, the largest match in forward dictionary occurs for the first k_1 characters and the longest match on the reversed word dictionary occurs for the last k_2 characters, then the error must have occurred in the intersection of the first $k_1 + 1$ and the last $k_2 + 1$ characters of S. The rest of the characters are error free.

To prove the proposition, we note that if the error is outside the intersection region, then we could get a longer match either in the conventional dictionary, or in the reversed word dictionary which is a contradiction. In Fig. 6, the error zone is shown with a darker background. The remaining portion is error free. For an illustration of the propositions with a Devanagari string, see Fig. 6.

Note that, as a corollary to the above arguments, the intersection region cannot be null given a single error in S. Also, this proposition allows us to locate the error position in S with reasonable accuracy. If the intersection region is narrow, the location is more precise. To get an idea about how broad this region can be, we conducted a simulation study. Five hundred valid Bangla words of lengths ranging from two characters to ten characters were chosen. Single deletion and insertion errors were

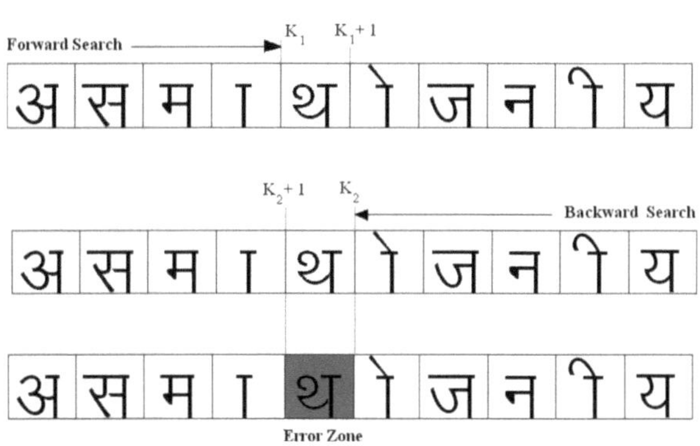

Fig. 6 Backward–forward error detection (the correct word is असमायोजनीय

Table 1 Error location in synthetic data

Error zone length (no. of characters)	% of words
1	41.36
2	32.94
3	16.58
4	07.10
5	01.78
6	00.24
Error located at either end of the error zone	90.77

randomly generated at arbitrary positions of the words and the resulting strings were subject to detection of error location using the approach guided by Proposition 3. The width of the intersection region described above is measured by the number of character positions. The results are shown in Table 1. In 74% of the samples, the width of this region is two characters or less. More interestingly, in about 91% of the samples, the error is located at either extreme of the intersection region. In other words, an attempt at dictionary matching terminates at the erroneous character in the string in about 91% of cases.

Now, let the error word string S be n character long. Using the above test, we can discern that its first n_1 and last n_2 characters are free from error. To generate the correction candidates, we use a conventional dictionary to check for words whose length lies between n + 1 and n −1, as well as whose first n_1 and last n_2 characters match with those of S (because these are error-free regions). Words having length outside this range are not considered because such words cannot be transformed into a string of n characters by a single error. Let the subset of words resulting from the above operation be W. Now we find only those words from W that can be formed by a single transformation like substitution, deletion or insertion. Single transformation is considered because this is a single error model. This subset, say W_1 , is normally smaller than W. Now, from this W_1 the word for which character replacement has occurred with highest estimated probability (computed during training phase) is chosen as the correct word.

Note that Propositions 1–3 do not hold for two errors in a word. For correcting two position errors, one possibility is to use a reverse edit distance-based approach. Here, all possible combinations of two position insertions, deletions, and/or substitutions are made on S to form a set of new strings. These new strings are then matched in the dictionary D_f to recognize valid words. Among the valid words, the one in which the a priori character mis-recognition probability is minimum may be accepted as the final OCR output.

In this work, we considered only the single error model described above. If this model could output a valid word, then it was accepted as a corrected word. If no valid word was obtained by the approach, the string was abandoned as uncorrectable.

In this manner, about 76.3% single error corrections could be made, out of which 72.1% were the correct document words. The recognition scores on our document

Table 2 Various recognition scores for laser quality documents in five fonts

Classifier output	% accuracy (Devanagari)	% accuracy (Bangla)
Group classifier	97.93	97.31
Symbol classifier	95.79	95.15
Ortho-syllable recognition	93.66	93.21
Unicode representation	95.41	95.07
Word recognition	83.77	82.18

set at different classification levels are given in Table 2. The performance numbers in the last three rows include the use of an error correction module.

5 Discussion

A system for OCR of Devanagari and Bangla documents has been described in this chapter. The system is based on segmentation of words into characters, sub-characters, and symbols which are then processed through multiple classifiers. The recognition results are then combined to obtain the output in Unicode. The issues of error evaluation and error correction of Indic script have been presented and ortho-syllabic error evaluation is advocated. The performance of the Devanagari OCR was found to be better than the Bangla OCR.

Combination of other types of classifiers (SVM, convolutional NN) with different features should be evaluated. Use of heuristic and statistical language models could also lead to better results. A segmentation-free approach to word recognition [15] can also be explored.

Acknowledgment Partial support from DIT, Govt of India, in the form of a sponsored project is acknowledged with thanks.

References

1. U Pal and B B Chaudhuri, Indian Script Character Recognition: A Survey. *Pattern Recognition*, Vol. 37, pp. 1887–1899, 2004.
2. B B Chaudhuri and U Pal, Printed Devnagari Script OCR System. *Vivek*, Vol. 10, pp. 12–24, 1997.
3. B B Chaudhuri and U Pal, A Complete Printed Bangla OCR System. *Pattern Recognition*, Vol. 31. No. 5, pp. 531–549, 1998.
4. V Bansal and R M K Sinha, Integrating knowledge sources in Devanagari Text recognition. *IEEE Transactions on Systems, Man and Cybernetics*, Part A, Vol. 30, No. 4, pp. 500–505, 2000.
5. H Ma and D Doermann, Adaptive Hindi OCR using generalized Hausdorff image comparison, *ACM Transactions on Asian language Information Processing*, Vol. 26, No. 2, pp. 198–213, 2003.
6. U Garain and B B Chaudhuri, Segmentation of Touching Characters in Printed Devanagari and Bangla Scripts using Fuzzy Multifactorial Analysis, *IEEE Transactions on Systems, Man and Cybernetics, Part C*, Vol. 32, No. 4, pp. 449–459, 2002.

7. S Kompalli, S Setlur and V Govindraju, Design and comparison of segmentation driven and recognition driven Devanagari OCR, *Proceedings of the 2nd International Conference on Document Image Analysis for Libraries (DIAL)*, pp. 96–102, 2006.
8. J Song, Z Li, M Lyu and S Cai, Recognition of merged characters based on forepart prediction, necessity-sufficiency matching and character-adaptive masking. *IEEE Transactions on Systems, Man and Cybernetics, Part B,* Vol. 35, pp. 2–11, 2005.
9. J Park, V Govindaraju and S N Srihari, OCR in a hierarchical feature space,*IEEE Transactions on Pattern Analysis and Machine Intelligence*, Vol. 22, No. 4, pp 400–407, 2000.
10. J J Hull and S N Srihari, Experiments in text recognition with binary n-grams and Viterbi algorithms.*IEEE Transactions on Pattern Analysis and Machine Intelligence*, Vol. 4, no. 5, pp 520–530, 1982.
11. R Singhal and G T Toussaint, Experiments in text recognition with modified Viterbi algorithm.*IEEE Transactions on Pattern Analysis and Machine Intelligence*, Vol. 1, pp. 184–192, 1979.
12. V Bansal and R M K Sinha, Partitioning and searching dictionary for correction of optically read Devanagari character strings. *International Journal of Document Analysis and Recognition*; Vol. 4, pp. 269–280, 2002.
13. K. Kukich, Techniques for automatically correcting words in text, *ACM Computing Surveys* , Vol. 24, No. 4, pp. 377–439, 1992.
14. P K Kundu and B B Chaudhuri, Error patterns in Bangla Text, *International Journal of Dravidian Linguistics.* Vol. 28, No 2, pp. 49–88, 2000.
15. J Rocha and T Pavlidis, Character recognition without segmentation. *IEEE Transactions on Pattern Analysis and Machine Intelligence*, Vol. 17, pp. 903–909, 1995.
16. S Mori, C Y Suen and K Yamamoto, Historical review of OCR research and development. *Proc IEEE,* Vol. 80, No. 7, pp. 1029–1058, 1992.

A Complete Machine-Printed Gurmukhi OCR System

G.S. Lehal

Abstract Recognition of Indian language scripts is a challenging problem and work towards the development of a complete OCR system for Indian language scripts is still in its infancy. Complete OCR systems have recently been developed for Devanagari and Bangla scripts. However, research in the field of recognition of Gurmukhi script faces major problems mainly due to the unique characteristics of the script such as connectivity of characters on a headline, characters pointing in both horizontal and vertical directions, two or more characters in a word having intersecting minimum bounding rectangles along horizontal direction, existence of a large set of visually similar character pairs, multi-component characters, touching and broken characters, and horizontally overlapping text segments. This chapter addresses the problems in the various stages of the development of a complete OCR system for Gurmukhi script and discusses potential solutions. A multi-font Gurmukhi OCR for printed text with an accuracy rate exceeding 96% at the character level is presented. A combination of local and global structural features is used for the feature extraction process, aimed at capturing the geometrical and topological features of the characters. For classification, we have implemented a multi-stage classification scheme in which the binary tree and k-nearest neighbor classifiers have been used in a hierarchical fashion.

Keywords OCR, Gurmukhi · Segmentation · Classification · Post-processing

1 Introduction

Although research on Devanagari, Tamil and Telugu optical text recognition technology started around the mid-1970s [1–4], the early research hadonly theoretical

G.S. Lehal (✉)
Department of Computer Science, Punjabi University, Patiala, India
e-mail: gslehal@gmail.com

V. Govindaraju, S. Setlur (eds.), *Guide to OCR for Indic Scripts*, Advances in Pattern Recognition, DOI 10.1007/978-1-84800-330-9_3,

importance and did not lead to the development of a practical OCR system. It was not until the mid-1990s that researchers started working on the development of complete OCR systems for Indian scripts such as Devanagari, Bangla and Telugu [5–9]. Such developments were followed by research work on OCR of Gurmukhi script, starting in the late 1990s. A complete OCR for Gurmukhi has been presented by Lehal and Singh [10].

Gurmukhi script is used primarily for the Punjabi language, which is currently the world's 12th most widely spoken language. The populace speaking Punjabi is not only confined to north Indian states such as Punjab, Haryana, Delhi, Rajasthan, and Jammu and Kashmir, but can be found all over the world. There is a rich body of literature in this language in the form of scripture, books, poetry, etc. In fact, Gurmukhi was the first official script adopted by the Punjab state and is the second language in many northern states of India. Given the script's rich history and widespread use, it is important to develop OCR technology. Such an OCR system will likely find many practical usages and applications in various areas. In this chapter, we present a complete OCR system for Gurmukhi script.

2 Characteristics of Gurmukhi Script

Like most Indian language scripts, Gurmukhi is written in a nonlinear fashion. The width of the characters is not constant. The vowels attached to consonants are not in one vertical or horizontal direction, but rather placed either on the top or at the bottom of consonants. This makes the use of the script on computers complicated to represent and process. Some of the major characteristics of the Gurmukhi script which present a challenge for OCR are: the character set; connectivity of symbols; word partitioning into zones; frequently touching characters; broken characters and headlines; and similarity of group symbols.

2.1 Character Set

Symbolic in nature, Gurmukhi script consists of 41 consonants called *vianjans*, 9 vowel symbols called *laga* or *matras*, 2 symbols for nasal sounds (◌ਂ , ◌ੰ), 1 symbol for reduplication of any consonant (◌ੱ) sound and 3 half characters (◌੍ਹ ◌੍ਵ ◌੍ਰ) which lie at the feet of consonants. The complete Gurmukhi character set is shown in Fig. 1.

2.2 Connectivity of Symbols

Most of the characters contain a horizontal line at the top, which mostly connects the characters of a word. Because of this headline, there is no vertical inter-character

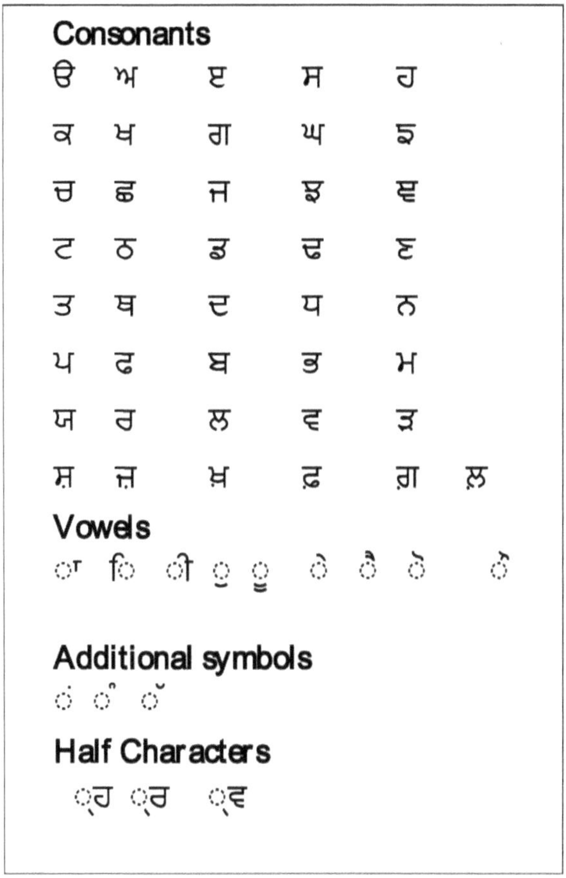

Fig. 1 Gurmukhi character set

gap in the letters of a word, and formation of merged characters is a norm rather than an aberration in Gurmukhi script.

2.3 *Word Partitioning into Zones*

A word in Gurmukhi script can be partitioned into three horizontal zones (Fig. 2). The upper zone denotes the region above the headline, where vowels reside, while the middle zone represents the area below the headline where the consonants and some sub-parts of vowels (ਾ ਿ ੀ) are present. The middle zone is the busiest zone. The lower zone represents the area below middle zone where the two vowels (ੁ ੂ) and half characters lie in the foot of consonants.

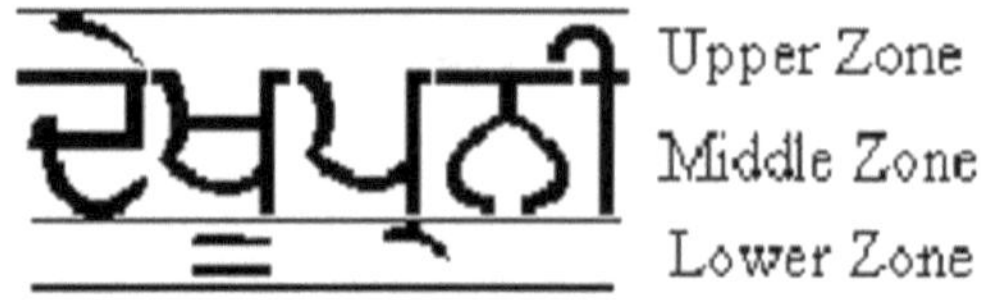

Fig. 2 Three zones of a word in Gurmukhi script

2.4 Frequently Touching Characters

Many of the characters in the lower zone of a text line frequently touch the characters in the middle zone. Additionally, upper zone characters are occasionally merged into a single component.

2.5 Broken Characters and Headlines

It is observed that in Gurmukhi texts printed before the 1990s, there are frequently broken characters and headlines. The broken characters in the middle zone have to be carefully joined so that the lower zone characters are not joined accidentally. Broken headlines have to be joined together to improve the word shape for recognition.

2.6 Similarity of Group of Symbols

There are many topologically similar character pairs in Gurmukhi script. They can be categorized as follows:

i. Character pairs which, after thinning or in noisy conditions, appear very similar (ਟ and ਦ, ਤand ਭ, ਬ and ਥ, ਤ, ੜ, ੋ and ੌ,).
ii. Character pairs which are differentiated by whether they are open or closed along the headline (ਸ and ਮ, ਧ, ਪ, ਥ and ਖ).
iii. Character pairs which are exactly similar in shape but are distinguished only by the presence/absence of a dot in the feet of the character (ਸ and ਸ਼, ਖ, and ਖ਼, ਜ and ਜ਼, ਫ, and ਫ਼, ਗ and ਗ਼).

3 System Overview

The overall system design of the Gurmukhi OCR system developed and implemented is shown in Fig. 3. As with most of the OCR systems, there are five main processing stages: *Digitization, Pre-processing, Segmentation, Recognition* and *Post-processing*.

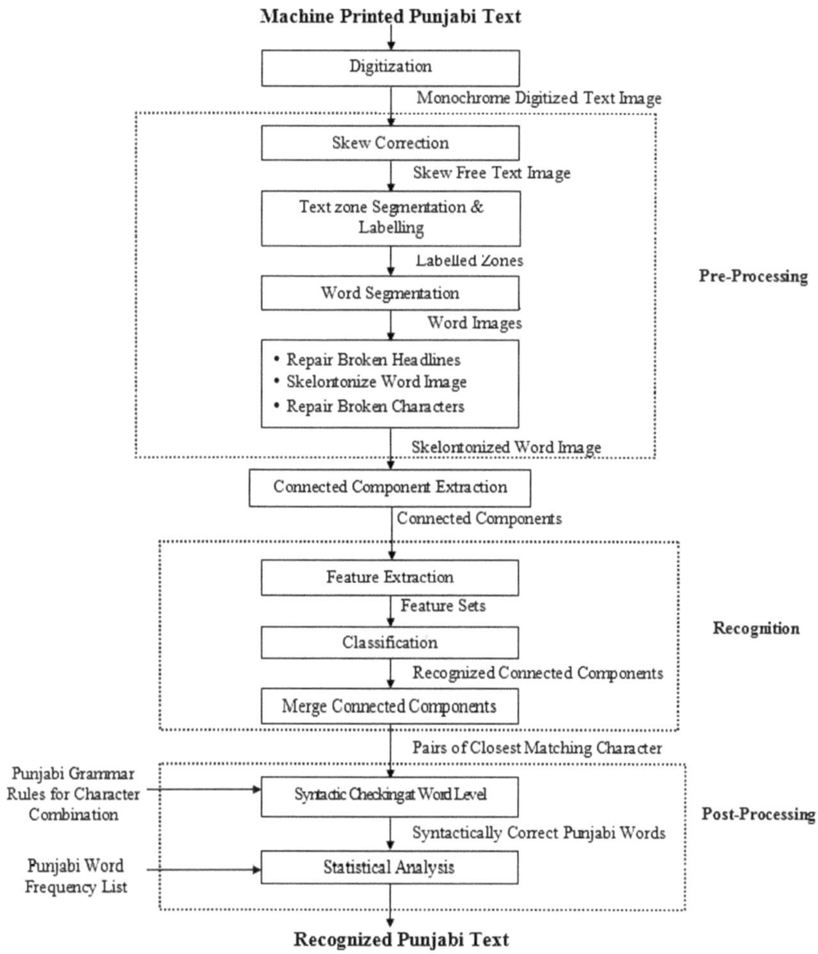

Fig. 3 An overview of the Gurmukhi script recognition system

4 Digitization and Pre-processing

The first step in recognizing a text document consists of converting the document into a numerically representable form. This conversion process is accomplished through the use of a digitizer, which can either be a scanner or a camera. The scanning resolution varies from 100 to 600 dots per inch (dpi). In our present work, we have used a scanning resolution of 300 dpi.

The pre-processing stage involves a number of operations that are applied successively to an image. In this process, raw images are improved by reducing noise and distortion, removing skew, and skeletonizing the pattern. In our current work we have performed the following pre-processing steps:

- Skew detection and correction
- Text zone segmentation
- Word segmentation
- Repairing the word shape
- Thinning
- Joining the broken characters
- Smoothening the headlines

For skew detection and correction, the algorithm developed by Lehal and Dhir [11] has been used.

Text segmentation of a script proceeds in three stages: line segmentation, word segmentation and character segmentation. Line segmentation is defined as the process of extracting the individual lines from words in a document. Word segmentation is the process of extracting words from a given line. Character segmentation is the process of extracting the individual characters that constitute the word unit. Since it is difficult to separate a cursive word directly into characters, a smaller unit than a character is preferred to simplify segmentation. In our current work, we have taken an 8-connected component as the basic image representation throughout the recognition process. Thus, instead of character segmentation, we have performed connected component segmentation. The representation of each connected component includes the coordinates and dimensions of the bounding box and a list of the individual runs of black pixels that make up the component.

5 Splitting Text into Horizontal Text Strips

Horizontal projection of a document image is most commonly employed to extract the lines from the document. If the lines are well separated and not tilted, then the horizontal projection will have well-separated peaks and valleys. These valleys are easily detected and used to determine the location of boundaries between lines (Fig. 4). But this simple strategy fails in many cases when applied to Gurmukhi script, resulting in over or under segmentation. Over segmentation occurs when the white space breaks a text line into two or more horizontal text strips. In printed Gurmukhi text, there are instances when one or more vowel symbols in the upper zone of a text line overlap with modifiers present in the lower zone of the previous line. In this scenario, white space no longer separates two consecutive text lines and two or more text lines may be fused together, resulting in under segmentation.

Thus, it is more appropriate to call the line segmentation stage the horizontal text strip segmentation stage, as the text strip is defined as a horizontal strip containing at least one black pixel in each row. The text image is broken into horizontal text strips using horizontal projection in each row. The gaps on the horizontal projection profile are considered as separators between the text strips.

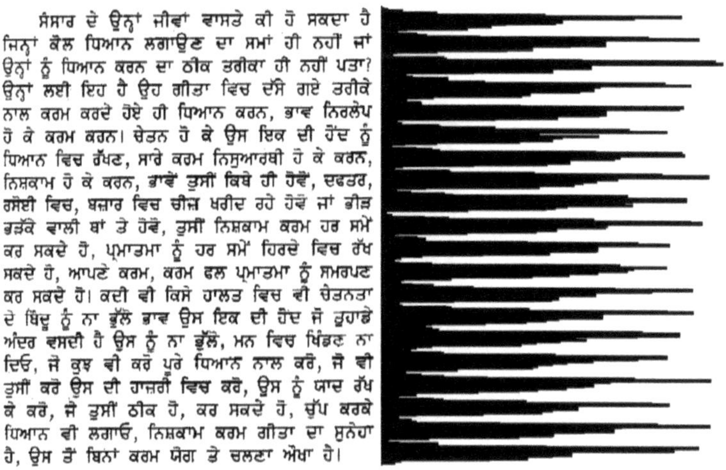

Fig. 4 Horizontal projection of a document image

Each text zone or strip could represent the

(a) Core zone of one text line consisting of the upper and middle zones, and optionally, the lower zone (core strip).
(b) Upper zone of a text line (upper strip).
(c) Lower zone of a text line (lower strip).
(d) Core zone of one text line and the upper or lower zones of the adjoining line (mixed strip).
(e) Core zone of more than one text line (multi-strip).

For example, the sample text image in Fig. 5, which consists of 9 text lines, is split into 10 horizontal strips after application of a horizontal projection profile. Strip nos. 2, 3, 4, 6 and 9 represent type a, strip number 1 is type b, strip number 7 is type c, strips 5 and 10 are type d, and strip no.8 is type e. The next task is to identify the type of each strip. For this purpose, a histogram analysis of the height of the strips is carried out using the following heuristics:

1. Calculate the estimated average height of the core strip. We cannot take it to be the arithmetic mean of all the strips, since the type b, c and e strips can greatly influence the overall figure. Instead, the median height of strips whose height is at least 10 pixels closely represents the average height of a core strip. We refer to this height as AV. Once the average height of the core strip is found, the types of other strips are identified. If the height of a strip is less than 33% of AV, then the strip is either type b or c. If the height is greater than 150% of AV, then the strip is a multi-strip. If the height of the strip is between 125–150% of AV, then the strip could represent a mixed strip. Otherwise, the strip is a core strip. To distinguish between type b and c strips, we look at the immediate next core strip.

Fig. 5 Text image split into horizontal text strips

We determine the spatial position of headline in the core strip, where the headline is found by locating the row with the maximum number of black pixels. If the headline is present in the upper 10% of the core strip region, then the previous strip is either type b or c.

2. Next, we determine the average height of a core strip (ACSH) by calculating the arithmetic mean of all core strips. This information will be used to dissect the multi-strip into constituent text lines. Also, the average consonant height (ACH) and average upper zone height (AUZH) are determined. This information is needed in the other segmentation phases.

The word images will be found in core, mixed and multi-strips. For segmentation of these strips into words, vertical projection is employed. Since all the consonants and the majority of the upper zone vowels are glued to the headline, theoretically, there is no inter-character gap and white space separates words. A vertical histogram of the text line is generated by counting the number of black pixels in each vertical line, and a gap of 2 or more pixels in the histogram is considered to be a word delimiter.

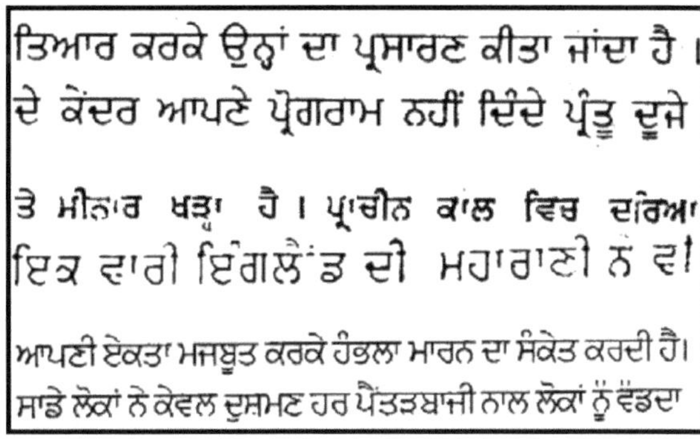

Fig. 6 Samples of text with varying word gaps

However, in reality, it is found that words are usually broken along the headline and a vertical white space of more than two pixels exists in a word image. This is particularly true for older documents. Based on experiments performed, the word delimiter was initially fixed as 15% of the average word height. Additionally, any group of connected pixels separated by word delimiter pixels at most, was treated as part of the same word. However, it was found that in some documents, the words were very tightly placed and the closely lying words were joined together, while in other cases, the consecutive characters in a word were vertically separated by more than word delimiter pixels. Depending on the inter-character and inter-word gap, we can classify the text documents into three categories:

- Type A – Normal inter-word gap and zero inter-character gap (first 2 lines of Fig. 6)
- Type B – Normal inter-word gap and in some cases non-zero inter-character gap (3rd and 4th lines of Fig. 6)
- Type C – Very small inter-word gap and zero inter-character gaps (last two lines of Fig. 6)

6 Word Segmentation

To take care of the problems which arise due to varying inter-character and inter-word gaps, it was decided that the value of the word delimiter must be determined in a dynamic fashion. The word delimiter was obtained by performing statistical analysis of the vertical pixel gap of the connected components lying in core and mixed zones. Vertical white gaps of more than 20 pixels were ignored. As an example, the values obtained from the analysis of three text pages containing type a, b and c texts are presented below (Fig. 7).

The word delimiter value can easily be found by analyzing the frequency of the vertical pixel gap graphs. For types a and c, there will be a single prominent peak corresponding to the inter-word gap as there is no inter-character gap. For type b, there will be two peaks. The first peak will represent the inter-character gap while

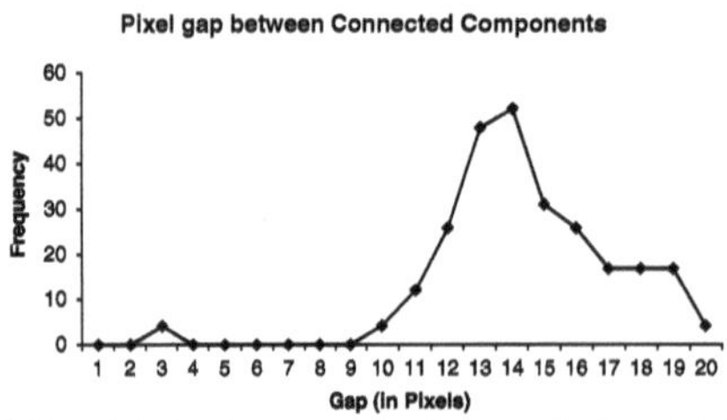

a) Vertical pixel gap between connected components of type A text

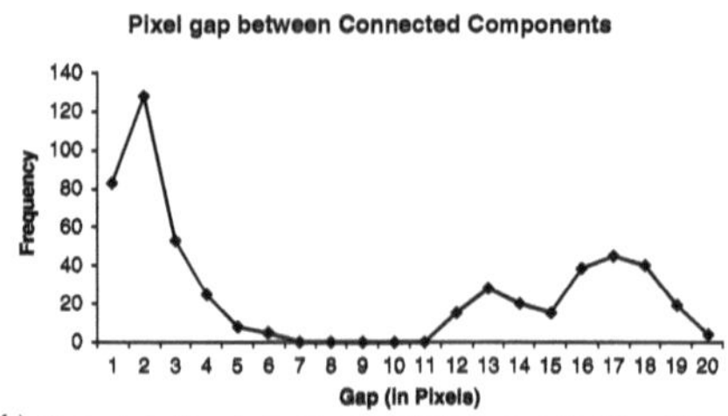

b) Vertical pixel gap between connected components of type B text

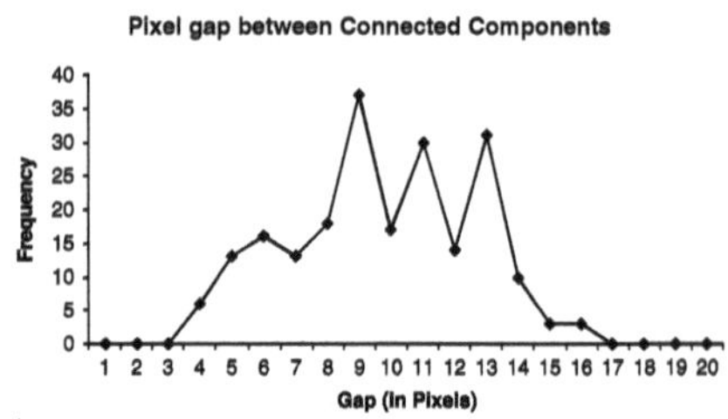

c) Vertical pixel gap between connected components of type C text

Fig. 7 Frequency graphs of the vertical pixel gap between connected components

the second peak will represent the inter-word gap. The word threshold (*wth*) value is taken as the first non-zero frequency in the peak corresponding to the word gap. Thus, in first graph *wth* is 10, while it is 12 in the second graph and 4 in the third graph. Also, from the analysis of Table 1, it can be observed that the standard deviation of pixel gap of connected components in type b documents is high when compared to those of type a and type c documents, while the median value is small.

Table 1 Statistics of inter-connected component gap

Type	Average gap	Median gap	Mode gap	SD of gap	Word delimiter
A	14.3	14	14	2.9	10
B	8.1	4	2	7.0	12
C	9.8	10	9	3.1	4

7 Sub-division of Strips into Smaller Units

In the next stage, all the text strips are processed from top to bottom in the order in which they occur in the text. Each strip is divided into smaller components, which could be characters or sub-characters in case of strips of type b or c, or words in the case of core strip and multi-strip. To simplify the segmentation, feature extraction, and classification steps, we have taken a connected component as our smallest unit. A connected component is a group of black pixels joined to each other in the viewpoint of 8-neighbor connectivity. If a zone is an upper or lower zone, then it is entirely made up of disconnected characters or sub-characters. These sub-characters can easily be isolated by scanning from left to right until a black pixel is found, and then using a search algorithm to find all of the black pixels connected to it.

The smallest component of a core strip is a word. The word may not contain all of the character images, as some of the characters or their parts may be present in the neighboring strips. Fig. 5 is an example of this, where the lower character (◌ੂ) of the third word in strip 6 is present in the next two strips. Similarly, the upper vowels of all the words of strip 2 are present in strip 1. For segmentation of the strip into words, vertical projection is employed. As already discussed in the previous section, a vertical histogram of the text line is generated by counting the number of black pixels in each vertical line, and a gap of *wth* or more pixels in the histogram is taken to be the word delimiter.

A multiple core strip is made of multiple overlapping text lines, which cannot be separated by horizontal projection. To segregate the text lines, the statistics generated in the first pass will be used. The zonal height is divided by the average core strip height (ACSH) which was obtained in step 2 of segmentation algorithm (explained in Section 5). This gives us an idea of the number of text lines present in the strip. To extract the first row, an imaginary cut is made at 0.75*ACSH. We have deliberately made a cut at 0.75*ACHS instead of ACSH, so that by chance, the line does not cross any character lying in next text row. The sub-strip is then split into words through vertical projection analysis using the same method as used in the segmentation of core strip. For the next sub-strip, a cut is made at ACSH height and the words are extracted in that sub-strip. This process continues until all of the sub-strips have been segmented into words. For the last sub-strip, the height is taken until the end of the strip.

8 Repairing the Word Shape

Some pre-processing operations must be performed on the word images before they are sent for character segmentation. In older texts, the word images are frequently broken along the headlines and at the character level. Therefore, it is necessary to repair the word shapes. In a Gurmukhi word, the middle zone characters are glued along the headline. The character segmentation algorithm expects the middle zone characters to be touching the headline, with no vertical inter-character gap. But sometimes, the headline is broken and the characters are not aligned along the y-axis and as a result, the word image is split into a group of single or multiple characters (Fig. 8a). This creates a problem for the character segmentation algorithm as it becomes difficult to identify the position of the headline and the components lying above and below it. Thus, it becomes necessary to join the broken headlines, aligning the headline of the characters of the word by displacing the character images along the y-axis (Fig. 8b). This is achieved as follows:

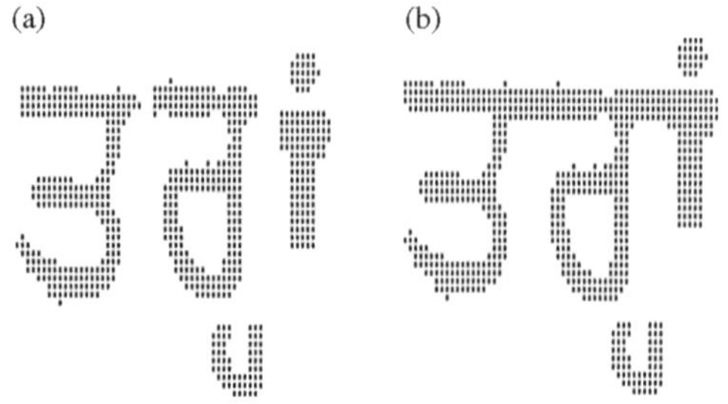

Fig. 8 (**a**) A word with broken headlines and (**b**) After repair

1. Determine the row in the word image corresponding to the word headline (*WHL*) in the upper half of the word image satisfying one or both of the following criteria:

   i. Row with maximum horizontal span of black pixels.
   ii. Row having maximum number of black pixel count.

2. Decompose the word image lying below *WHL* into connected components (*CCs*) separated by vertical white space. Each of these *CCs* could represent a group of one or more characters. It is to be noted that the pixels lying above and along *WHL* are ignored.

   For each component, determine the row corresponding to the position of headline (*CHL*) that satisfies one or both of the following criteria:

   i. Row with maximum horizontal span of black pixels.
   ii. Row having maximum black pixel count.
   iii. Row should be separated from *WHL* by at most *d* pixels where $d =$ 0.2∗height of *CC*
   Let $delta = WHL - CHL$
   Move all the pixels of *CC* by *delta* pixels along the *y*-axis.

3. Join all the *CCs* by drawing a horizontal line between the *CCs* along *WHL.*

In Fig. 9, we have samples of word images whose broken headlines were joined after applying the above algorithm. A side-effect of this algorithm is that, in some cases, the skewed word images are also corrected. One such skew-corrected sample image is shown in Fig. 10. The page containing the image was already skewcorrected, although some of the word images were still skewed due to the warping effect. Some of these images were also skew-corrected by the application of the above algorithm.

9 Thinning

Thinning is an essential step for many structural feature extraction methods. It reduces patterns to their skeletons or single-pixel width pattern. It is often an

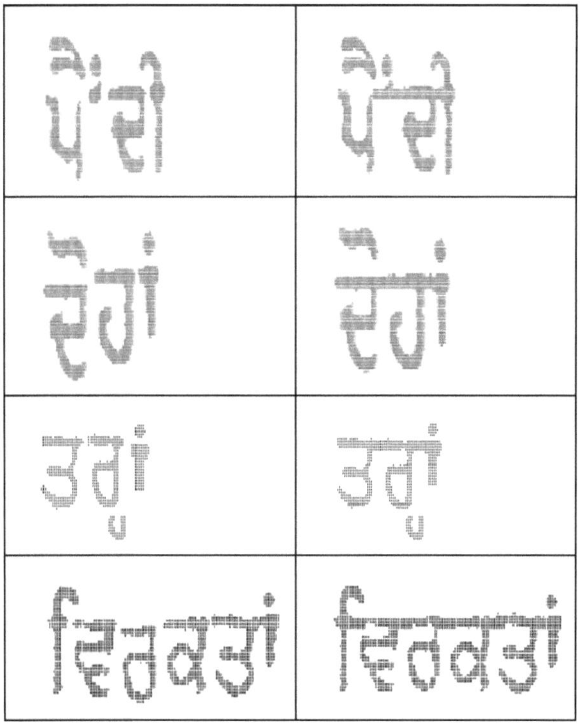

Fig. 9 Some samples of reconstructed broken headline word images

Fig. 10 Sample image after repairing headlines and thinning

efficient method for expressing structural relationships in characters as it reduces space and processing time by simplifying data structures. A typical thinning algorithm iteratively deletes points on the boundary of a pattern until it generates a one-pixel-wide connected skeleton. It deletes a point on the boundary that is neither an endpoint, nor a break point. This deletion does not cause excessive erosion, and at least one of its 8 neighbors cannot be deleted. In our present work, the segmentation and feature extraction stages have been greatly simplified by working on thinned images of text, though in some of the cases, the character shapes were slightly deformed.

Many thinning algorithms (or modifications of existing ones) have been proposed in recent years. Due to the proliferation of these algorithms, researchers in this area are often faced with the difficult question as to which algorithm is best suited for their application. We have used the thinning algorithm suggested by Abdulla et al.

[12] for skeletonization of the Gurmukhi text images. Figure 10 depicts a sample of original and thinned versions of images produced from the application of this algorithm. The original image, broken along the headline, is repaired and skew-corrected by applying the algorithm discussed in Section 8. The image is then thinned and smoothened along the headline to produce the final image shown in Fig. 10.

10 Repairing Broken Characters

Broken characters are commonly found in slightly older texts. An in-depth analysis was made of the common broken characters in Gurmukhi. For this purpose, about 2500 words containing broken characters scanned from old books were collected. The broken characters can be broadly categorized as

1. Characters broken from the headline.
2. Characters split vertically into non-overlapping parts.
3. Characters split horizontally into non-overlapping parts.
4. Character split into two or more overlapping parts.

Table 2 Categories of broken characters in Gurmukhi

Cat	Image
1	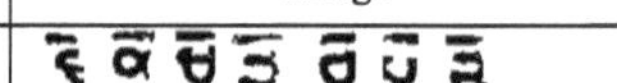
2	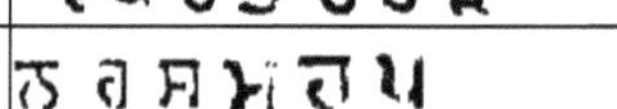
3	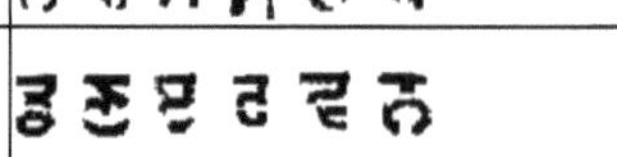
4	

Note that we ignore the headline while looking for overlapping regions.

As discussed above, a Gurmukhi word can be partitioned into three zones. We found that the majority of broken character segments are present in the middle zone. Also note that there are six multiple-component characters in the middle zone and care has to be taken that we do not join those components. Many times the characters in the lower zone are very closely placed near the middle zone characters, and therefore should not be treated as broken components of middle zone characters and joined with them. The broken components must be joined with the appropriate components to form the character. Decisions must be made in order to determine which connected component pairs will be joined and which will be ignored. A detailed study of the structure of Gurmukhi characters and words is needed while designing the algorithm.

The algorithm for handling broken characters is to be implemented after the thinning stage. Thus, our technique assumes that we have broken skeleton images of characters, which we then have to suitably join.

First, the position of the headline in the word image is noted and the headline is then rubbed off. The word image is then decomposed into connected components (CCs) and the relevant information about the CCs is extracted and stored. The closely lying CCs are determined. It is observed that in many cases, genuinely separated CCs lie very close to each other and care has to be taken so that they are not joined. We have categorized such closely lying CCs which should not be joined in Table 3.

Table 3 Closely lying Gurmukhi connected components to be ignored for joining

Category	**CC images with headlines removed**
1. CCs of middle zone characters containing dot-like symbol at feet of characters called *nukta*	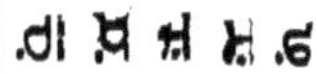
2. Closely-lying CCs of the characters in the middle and lower zone	
3. Vertically closely-lying or overlapping CCs	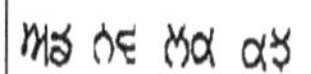
4. CCs which are vertically very close,with one of the CC a vertical line	

For the joinable pairs, their joining points are found. These joining points could be depending on the overlapping category, endpoints, bend points, joints or boundary points in the CC. We define the endpoint, joint, bend point and boundary point as follows:

1. *End Point*: A black pixel not lying on the y-axis corresponding to the headline and with only one black pixel in its 3×3 neighborhood.
2. *Joint*: A black pixel not lying on the y-axis corresponding to the headline and having three or more black pixels in its 3×3 neighborhood.
3. *Bend Point*: A white pixel where two or more lines meet at 90 or 45°.
4. *Boundary Point*: A black pixel lying on one boundary of the CC.

These points are extracted from the CCs and the point pairs (where the first point is from one CC and second point from the other CC) lying within the threshold value are collected. If no such pair is found, then the CCs are not joined. The decision to join the CCs is kept pending until all of the CC pairs have been processed. If any of the joining points have common points, then only the nearest pair is retained. The points are then joined by drawing lines between them. If there remain some CCs which are not touching the headline, then we must determine if they can be joined with any other CC or headline. To do this, we use the structural property of

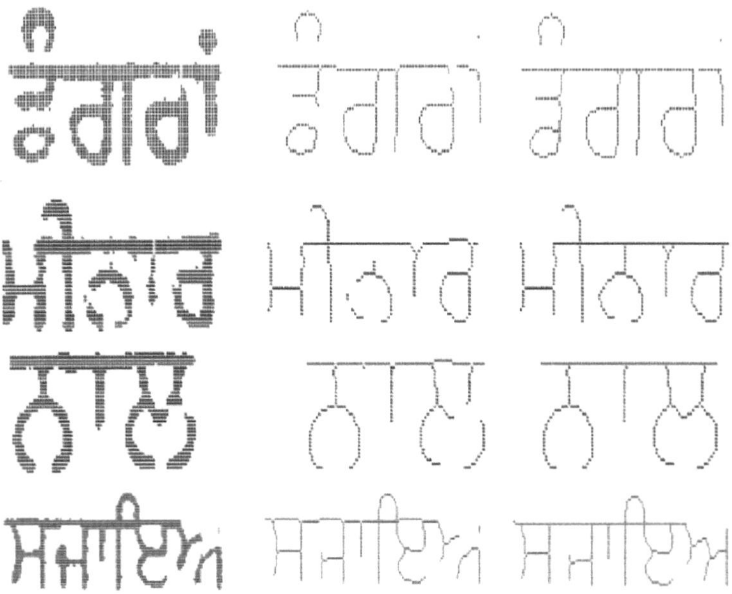

Fig. 11 Samples of broken images after thinning and reconstruction.

Gurmukhi script that all the characters in the middle zone touch the headline at least once, and increase the threshold value.

The algorithm was tested on a set of 2500 words containing broken characters. In 82.3% of cases, the broken components were correctly joined together to form a recognizable unit, while in 4.9% of cases the components were wrongly joined, and in 12.8% of cases the broken components were not joined with any other component. Some sample images are shown in Fig. 11. The first image in each row is the original binary image of the word. The second image is its thinned version while the third image is the image obtained after joining the broken components.

11 Character Segmentation

In Gurmukhi script, characters in a word are distributed along both the x-axis and the y-axis, unlike in Roman script where characters are distributed along the x-axis only. As mentioned, a connected component has been taken as the smallest unit, so it is more appropriate to call this phase "connected component segmentation" instead of "character segmentation". The segmentation stage breaks up a word and characters which lie above and below the headline into connected components and the classifier has been trained to recognize these connected components or sub-symbols. Table 4 lists all the connected components or sub-symbols derived from the Gurmukhi characters. It is to be noted that the headline is not considered a part of the connected component.

Table 4 sub-symbols of Gurmukhi script used for segmentation and recognition

Symbol	Sub-symbols	Symbol	Sub-symbols	Symbol	Sub-symbols
ਊ	ੳ and ⌒	ਖ਼	ਖ and .	ਿ	। and ⌒
ਗ	ਤ and ।	ਫ਼	ਫ and .	ੀ	। and ⌒
ਸ਼	ਸ and .	ਗ਼	ਤ, । and .	ੈ	‿ and ‿
ਜ਼	ਜ and .	ਲ਼	ਲ and .	ੳ	ੳ and ⌐
Gurmukhi characters in upper zone	Same shapes retained	Gurmukhi characters in lower zone	Same shapes retained	Rest of Gurmukhi characters in middle zone	Gurmukhi characters with their headlines stripped off

For type b and c strips, the segmentation of connected components is done in the previous step only. This phase is needed only for core, mixed and multi-strips. The connected component segmentation process proceeds in three stages. In the first stage, the connected components touching the headline and present in the middle and upper zones are isolated. In the second stage, the character sub-parts not touching the headline and lying in the upper zone are segmented. The characters in lower zones are isolated in the third stage.

The black pixels lying on the headline are not considered while calculating the connected components; otherwise, all of the characters glued along the headline would be treated as a single connected component. We refer to these connected components as sub-characters. Each sub-character represents either: (a) a single character or (b) a part of a character lying in one of the upper, middle or lower zones. For example, the connected components of strip 1 (Fig. 5) represent complete upper vowel characters, while the character ੀ is composed of connected components | and ⌒, where | is present in the middle zone and ⌒ is present in the upper zone. Similarly, the character ਗ is partitioned into connected components ਤ and |. For checking connectedness, the headline is not considered a part of the symbol and the sub-parts of a character connected by headline are considered unconnected, as in case of ਗ. The classification phase will classify the unknown symbols into one of the connected components. The zonal position of the connected components, the coordinate of the left-most pixel in the bitmap, and the amount of overlapping with other components in other zones are used to cluster the connected components into characters. Thus, instead of segregating a word into characters, each word is split into a group of connected components, so that each connected component represents the portion of a character lying in one of the zones.

The segmentation process begins with the left-most pixels on the headline. The headline is scanned from left to right until a black pixel above or below the headline is encountered. This signifies the start of a sub-symbol. A recursive contour trace is made for detecting the black pixels that make up the sub-symbol. This is facilitated through a depth-first search for all connected black pixels, marking each visited pixel. The search stops when there are no unvisited black pixels in the 3×3 neighborhood or when the headline is encountered. The advantage of this approach is that some of the features for recognition such as endpoints, joints, loops, left and right projection profiles are extracted and stored for classification during the segmentation stage only. This saves the computation time for the later feature extraction stage. The search then continues for the next black pixel adjacent to the headline by moving along the headline and looking for unvisited black pixels in its 3×3 neighborhood. Upon encountering such a pixel again, a recursive contour trace is made for extracting a sub-symbol. This process continues until the right-most pixel on the headline is reached, at which point all of the sub-symbols connected with the headline have been segmented. Some sub-symbols in the upper zone which are not touching the headline such as the ੱ and ਂ symbols in lower zone are not located. By systematically scanning the pixels in the space above the headline, all of the unvisited connected black pixels are compiled and sub-symbols are formed. Similarly, all of the connected black pixels in the lower zone are located by recursive contour tracing and the sub-symbols are isolated. We have used three classifiers for recognizing the subsymbols of the upper, middle and lower zones. Thus, a structure is associated with each word and contains information about the extent of the word and the zonal position of all the sub-symbols. The information related to each sub-symbol shape (i.e. the pixels that make up the sub-symbol), the features extracted, the zone in which the sub-symbol lies, and its position in the two-dimensional space are stored in an array of structures. This information is used in the later stage for classification and combining the sub-symbols to form Gurmukhi characters.

This image is then segmented. Connected regions of pixels (called segments) are located and organized into "blocks." Each block contains a set of pixels, the location of the segment in the original image, and a classification for the segment. It was found that, in some cases, a lower character from a previous text line was present in the upper zone of the next text line. For example, the word in Fig. 12 contains a character in its upper zone which is actually part of a word from the previous text line. For such cases, special precaution is necessary. The information about the average height of upper zone of a word is used. If it is found that the distance between connected components lying in the upper zone of a word with the headline is less than one third of the average height of the upper zone, then it is concluded that the component is part of the previous line and overlapping with the current line. The sub-symbol is then recognized as a sub-symbol from the lower zone and is passed onto the classifier for the lower zone. Also, the information from the recognized sub-symbol is passed onto the previous line, where the sub-symbol is inserted into the lower queue of the appropriate word.

Since we do not have overlapping text lines in the case of the multi-strip, it is very difficult to make horizontal cuts separating the text lines. So, a cut at 75% of the height of ACSH is made. This cut will be slicing most of the words into

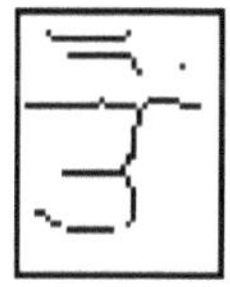

Fig. 12 Example of a lower vowel of a previous line intruding into the upper zone of a word in the next line

two parts, but that does not create a problem since we are looking for connected components only. A search is made for connected components in the same manner as with the core strip. Portions of the words which have been sliced and are lying in the next sub-strip will also be added to the connected component of the current word, since they are still physically connected. Next, the connected components present in the upper zone of the word are identified. The upper zone can also contain lower zone vowels of words lying in the previous line. So, a distinction is made using the distance of the minimum bounding rectangle with the headline. We do not search for connected components in the lower zone, since if a connected component of the upper zone of a word present in the next line is encountered, then the search will lead to words present in the next line and they will all be identified as lower zone symbols of the current word. For the same reason, the cut is made at 75% of ACSH, so that no pixel from a word in the next line is encountered in the current sub-strip.

11.1 Touching Characters

It has been observed that touching characters are frequently present even in clean machine-printed Gurmukhi texts. As mentioned, the segmentation process for Gurmukhi script proceeds on both x- and y-axes, and two or more characters of a word may be sharing the same x coordinate. Therefore, in order to segment touching characters in Gurmukhi script, merging points of characters must be determined both along the x- and y-axes. These touching characters can be categorized as follows:

(a) Touching characters in the upper zone
(b) Touching characters in the middle zone
(c) Lower zone characters touching the middle zone characters
(d) Lower zone characters touching each other

Figure 13 shows examples of touching characters within these categories. Statistics such as the average character width and height and certain heuristics were developed to solve the segmentation problem for Gurmukhi characters (the details of which are discussed elsewhere [13]). During experiments, it was found that 6.9% of upper zone characters, 0.12% of middle zone characters, 19.11% of lower and middle zone characters, and 0.03% of lower zone characters were touching with each other.

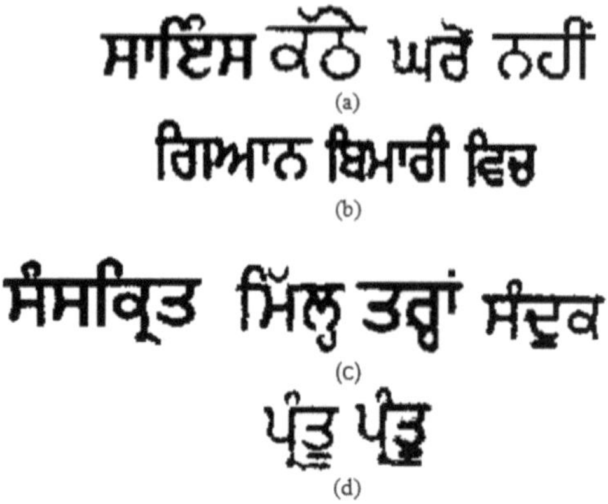

Fig. 13 Examples of touching characters (**a**) Touching characters in the upper zone (**b**) Touching characters in the middle zone (**c**) Touching characters in the middle and lower zones (**d**) Touching characters in lower zone

12 Recognition Stage

The recognition stage of Gurmukhi OCR mainly consists of the following processes: feature extraction; classification of connected components using extracted features and zonal information; and the combination and conversion of the connected components in order to form Gurmukhi symbols.

12.1 Feature Extraction

After a careful analysis of the shape of Gurmukhi characters using different fonts and sizes, two sets of features were developed. The first feature set, or the primary feature set, is made up of robust font- and size-invariant features. The purpose of this primary feature set is to precisely divide the set of characters lying in the middle zone into smaller subsets which can be easily managed. The cardinality of these subsets varies from 1 to 8. The Boolean-valued features used in the primary feature set are:

(i) *Number of Junctions with the Headline (P_1):* It can be noted that each character in Gurmukhi has either 1 or more than 1 junction with the headline. For example, the character ਢ has one junction while ਪ has 2 junctions. This feature has been used to divide the complete Gurmukhi character set into almost two equal subsets. This feature is true if the number of junctions is 1, otherwise it is false.

(ii) *Presence of Sidebar (P_2):* The presence or absence of a sidebar is another very robust feature for classifying the characters. For example, ਮ, ਘ, and ਹ have a sidebar while ਕ, ਙ, and ਛ do not. This feature is true if a vertical line is present on the right-most side of the sub-symbol, otherwise it is false.

(iii) *Presence of a Loop (P_3):* The presence of a loop in the sub-symbol is another important classification feature. The loop should not be formed along the headline. Thus, this feature is true for the sub-symbol of ਰ, but is false for the sub-symbol of ਘ, since no headline is involved in the loop.

(iv) *No Loop Formed with Headline (P_4):* This feature is true if the character is open at the top along the headline, or in other words, if there is no loop containing the headline as its subpart. Examples of characters with this feature are r and k, while it is absent in ਲ and ਘ.

The secondary feature set is a combination of local and global features which are aimed at capturing the geometrical and topological features of characters, and efficiently distinguishing and identifying characters from a small subset. While the primary feature set is used only for middle zone characters, this secondary feature set is used for the classification of all Gurmukhi script characters lying in any one of the three zones. The secondary feature set consists of the following features:

(v) *Number of Endpoints and their Location (S_1):* A black pixel is considered to be an endpoint if there is only one black pixel in its 3x3 neighborhood in the resolution of the character image. In order to determine the position of an endpoint within one of the nine quadrants, the character image is divided into equal zones within a 3x3 area that are numbered 1 through 9. Using these zones, the position of the endpoints in terms of their position in quadrants and their numbers are noted.

(vi) *Number of Junctions and their Location (S_2):* A black pixel is considered to be a junction if there are more than two black pixels in its 3x3 neighborhood in the resolution of the character image. The number of junctions as well as their positions in terms of 9 (3x3) quadrants is recorded. Junctions lying within a pre-defined radial distance are merged into a single junction and the junctions associated with the headline are ignored.

(vii) *Horizontal Projection Count (S_3)*: Horizontal Projection Count is represented as $\text{HPC}(i) = \sum_j F(i, j)$, where F(i,j) is a pixel value (0 for background and 1 for foreground) of a character image, and i and j denote row and column positions of a pixel, with the image's top left corner set to F(0,0). It is calculated by scanning the image row-wise and finding the sum of the foreground pixels in each row. To address the issue of variations in character sizes, the horizontal projection count of a character image is represented by percentage instead of an absolute value. In our present work, this is stored as a four component vector where the four components represent the percentage of rows with one pixel, two pixels, three pixels and more than three pixels.

(viii) *Left and Right Projection Profiles (S_4 through S_8)*: The next five features are based on projection profiles. Left projection of a character is derived by scanning each line of the character from top to bottom, from left to right, and by storing the first black pixel of the character in each row. Similarly, the right projection profile is found by scanning the character from top to bottom and from right to left. The pixels lying along the headline are ignored while deriving the projection profiles.

(ix) *Right Profile Depth (S_4):* The maximum depth of the right profile is stored as a percentage with respect to total width of the box enclosing the character image.

(x) *Left Profile Upper Depth (S_5):* The profile is computed from the left and the maximum depth of the upper half of the profile is stored as a percentage with respect to total width of the box enclosing the character image.

(xi) *Left Profile Lower Depth (S_6):* The maximum depth of the lower half of the left profile is stored as a percentage with respect to total width of the box enclosing the character image.

(xii) *Left and Right Profile Direction Code (S_7, S_8):* A variation of chain encoding is used on left and right profiles. The profile is scanned from top to bottom and local directions of the profile at each pixel are noted. Starting from the current pixel, the pixel distance to the next pixel in west, south or east directions is noted. The cumulative count of movement in the three directions is represented by a percentage of occurrences with respect to the total number of pixel movement. This information is stored as a three component vector, with the three components representing the distance covered in west, south and east directions, respectively.

(xiii) *Aspect Ratio (S_9):* Aspect ratio which is obtained by dividing the sub-symbol height by its width was found to be very useful for classifying the sub-symbols lying in the lower zone.

(xiv) *Distribution of Black Pixels about the Horizontal Mid-Line (S_{10}):* This distance is calculated by moving from left to right and at each column determining the distance between the nearest black pixel in that column and the horizontal middle line. This distance is then summed and normalized by dividing by the area of the character image and then converted into percentage. To take care of the distortions at the endpoints in some character images, we ignore 10% of the vertical regions at both the ends. The character image area is the product of its height and the truncated width.

12.2 Classification

In our present work, we have used a multi-stage classification scheme in which the binary tree and k-nearest neighbor classifiers have been used in a hierarchical fashion. The complete feature set used for classification using the k-nearest neighbor classifier is tabulated in Table 5. This classification scheme for the Gurmukhi characters proceeds in the following three stages:

(i) Using zonal information, we classify the symbol into one of the three sets, lying either in the upper, middle or lower zone.

(ii) If the symbol is in the middle zone, then we assign it to one of the 10 sets shown in Table 5 using primary features and the binary classifier tree. At the end of this stage, the symbol will be classified into one of 12 sets including the sets for characters in upper and lower zones.

(iii) Lastly, the symbol classified as 1 of the 12 sets of Table 5 is recognized using the k-nearest neighbor classifier and the secondary feature set assigned for that particular set.

Table 5 Secondary feature set for classification of character sets

Set #	Character set	Features for classification
1	C r	S_1 S_2 S_3
2	h j .	S_1 S_2 S_3
3	c L x T D Q f B	S_1 S_2 S_3 S_4 S_5 S_6 S_7 S_8
4	t N V d n v R	S_1 S_2 S_3 S_4 S_5 S_6 S_7 S_8 S_{10}
5	k	–
6	W b	S_5 S_8
7	a G p m	S_1 S_2 S_3 S_5
8	s Y y	S_1 S_2 S_3 S_5
9	u	–
10	e J M l	S_1 S_2 S_3 S_4 S_7 S_8
11	[illegible]	S_1 S_7 S_8 S_{10}
12	U H q	S_8 S_9

12.2.1 Design of the Binary Tree Classifier

We have designed a strictly binary decision tree with 10 leaf and 9 non-leaf nodes. The leaf nodes correspond to the classification of the character in one of the 10 subclasses. The height of the tree is 4. Only one feature is tested at each non-terminal node for traversing the tree. The decision rules are binary, i.e. the presence/absence of the primary feature. The features at the non-terminal nodes are chosen according to their robustness and tolerance to noise and remain invariant under font and image size. The most stable feature is used at the root node and divides the character set into two almost equal subsets. The complete binary tree classifier is shown in Fig. 14.

12.3 Merging Sub-symbols

In this last stage of character recognition, the information regarding the coordinates of the bounding box of sub-symbols and context is used to merge and convert the sub-symbols to Gurmukhi characters. For combining the sub-symbols, three queues are maintained for storing the sub-symbols lying in the upper, middle and lower zones (upper_queue, mid_queue, lower_queue). A fourth queue (char_queue) is used to store the recognized Gurmukhi characters of a word. The recognized sub-

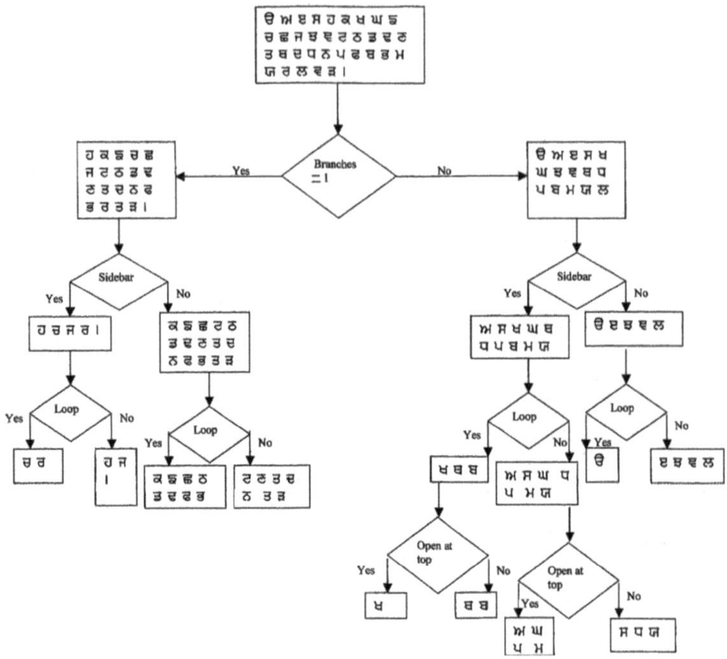

Fig. 14 Binary tree classifier

symbols are sorted in ascending order with respect to their position on the *x*-axis and then pushed into their respective Queues.

Note that most of the sub-symbols can be converted into equivalent characters (Table 5). It is only in some cases where a character may be broken into more than one sub-symbol and rules must be devised in order to merge these sub-symbols. For example, if the sub-symbol in the middle zone is ᑯ and the next sub-symbols in the middle and upper zones are | | and ∩, respectively, and if the upper sub-symbol is vertically overlapping with one or more of the middle zone sub-symbols, then these sub-symbols might represent one of the character combinations ਰੀ ਰਿ or ਗ*. In Fig. 15, we have the thinned images of characters ਰੀ, ਰਿ and ਗ* split into connected components (CCs). These CCs are images that are then separated according to their zonal position in the word. If seen in isolation without any other information, it is not possible to decide what character combinations can be formed from these CCs. The shapes of the upper zone CCs are nearly similar and they have been treated as the same in our current work. The information regarding the overlapping of the upper and middle zone CCs is used to identify the characters represented by the CCs. Thus, if ∩ is overlapping with both ᑯ and | then the CCs combine to form ਰੀ. If ∩ is overlapping with only |, then the CCs combine to form ਰਿ and if ∩ is overlapping with only ᑯ then the CCs combine to form ਗ* (Fig. 15).

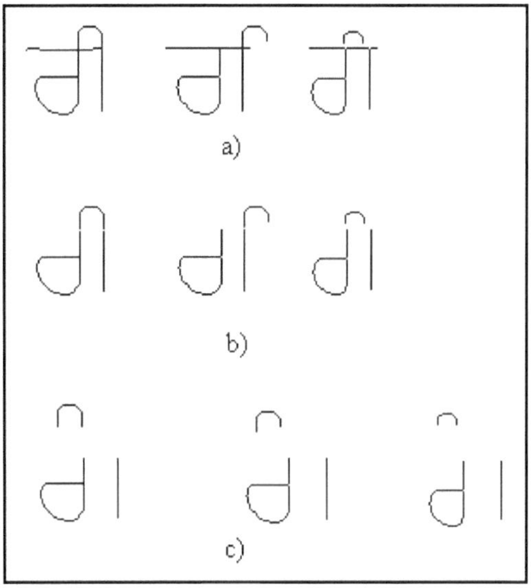

Fig. 15 (a) Thinned images of characters ਰੀ, ਰਿ and ਗ*, (b) word images segmented into connected components (c) and connected components separated according to zones

We have devised the following decision rules for combining and converting the sub-symbols:

1. If (sub-symbol ∩ is found in the upper zone) then
   If (the sub-symbol ਖ is found in vertically overlapping middle zone below ∩) then merge the 2 sub-symbols to form character ੳ.
   else
   If (the sub-symbol | is found in vertically overlapping middle zone below ∩) then
   if (.is present on the left end of ∩) then
   combine the 2 sub-symbols to form character ਿ
   else
   combine the 2 sub-symbols to form the character ੀ.
   else
   recognize the sub-symbol ∩ as character ਂ
2. if (sub-symbol ਰ is followed by sub-symbol | in the middle zone) then
   if (sub-symbol ∩ is the next sub-symbol present in the upper zone) then
   if (ਰ, ∩ and . are overlapping vertically) then
   combine the three sub-symbols ਰ, ∩ and | to form characters ਰ and ੀ
   else
   if (only ਰ and ∩ are overlapping vertically) then
   combine the three sub-symbols ਰ, ∩ and . to form characters ਗ and ਂ
   if (only . and ∩ are overlapping vertically) then
   combine the three sub-symbols ਰ, ∩ and . to form characters ਰ and ਿ
   else
   if (the sub-symbol . is present in the feet of ਰ) then

combine the three sub-symbols ਰ . and ~ to form character ਗ਼

else

combine ਰ and . to form character ਗ

else

convert sub-symbol ਰ to character ਰ

3. if two _ characters are found in vertically overlapping areas in lower zone, they are combined to form the character =
4. if the characters ਸ, ਜ, ਖ, ਫ, or ਲ have the sub-symbol . present in their lower zone then they are converted to characters ਸ਼, ਜ਼, ਖ਼, ਫ਼ and ਲ਼, respectively.
5. The rest of the sub-symbols can just as such be converted to equivalent characters.

13 Post-Processing

In order to rectify the classification errors, the output of the classification stage is fed to the post-processor. For the post-processing, we have used a Punjabi corpus which serves the dual purposes of providing data for statistical analysis of the Punjabi language and also for checking the spelling of a word. Punjabi grammar rules are incorporated into post-processing in order to check for illegal character combinations such as the presence of two consecutive vowels or a word starting with a forbidden consonant or vowel.

A word frequency list is created from the Punjabi corpus. The list stores the frequency of occurrence of all words present in the corpus. The list is then partitioned into smaller sub-lists based on the word size. We have created seven sub-lists corresponding to word sizes of two, three, four, five, six, seven and more characters. Further, in each sub-list, a list of visually similar words is generated. Two words are considered visually similar if each character in the corresponding position of the two words is visually similar.

The purpose of the word frequency list is twofold:

13.1 Check for the Existence of a Word in the Corpus

The recognized word is checked for its presence in the corpus by performing a lookup on the list. If the word is not present, then it is replaced with the nearest matching word provided that the distance of the recognized characters from the stored templates is greater than some preset threshold value. This is necessary to prevent accidental conversion of non-dictionary words such as proper nouns and abbreviations to a dictionary word.

13.2 Perform Holistic Recognition of a Word

All the forms of the recognized words are sorted in descending order of frequency of occurrence. If it is found that the first word in the list has a frequency of occurrence greater than some predefined value, then the recognized word, even though it may be present in the corpus, is converted to the higher probability word. Again, it is subject to the condition that the distance of the recognized characters from the stored templates is greater than some threshold value. The details are available in [14].

14 Experimental Results

We tested our OCR system extensively on more than 130 Gurmukhi text documents consisting of about 201,760 characters. The documents were pages from books printed over the last 40 years, magazines and laser print-outs in multiple sizes and fonts. We tested on font sizes 12, 14, 16, 20 and 24 on more than 20 different font faces used in the printouts, books and magazines. The overall recognition accuracy was 96.12%. In an earlier work [10], we had reported higher recognition accuracy, but it was carried out on good quality documents. When the same system was tested on slightly lower quality documents, the accuracy went down. The main sources of errors were identified and it was found that broken headlines and characters were one of the major sources of errors particularly in older documents. The algorithms developed to handle the broken headlines and characters resulted in an overall increase of 1.31% recognition accuracy.

Some other observations which were made during the experiments are as follows:

The upper zone characters, which account for 28.6% of character occurrences have recognition accuracy of 90.91%. The upper zone vowels, ਿ and ੀ), because of the similarity in shapes and large possible shape combinations were greatly confused

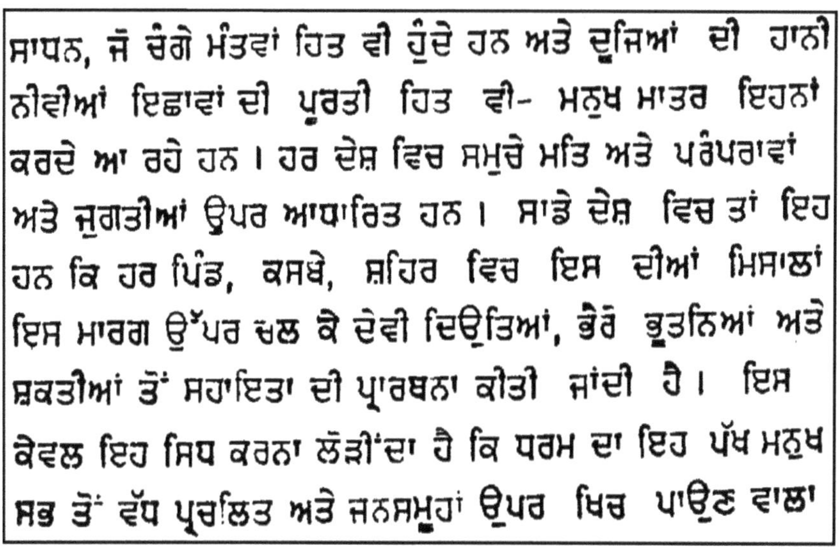
ਸਾਧਨ, ਜੋ ਚੰਗੇ ਮੰਤਵਾਂ ਹਿਤ ਵੀ ਹੁੰਦੇ ਹਨ ਅਤੇ ਦੂਜਿਆਂ ਦੀ ਹਾਨੀ
ਨੀਵੀਆਂ ਇਛਾਵਾਂ ਦੀ ਪੂਰਤੀ ਹਿਤ ਵੀ- ਮਨੁਖ ਮਾਤਰ ਇਹਨਾਂ
ਕਰਦੇ ਆ ਰਹੇ ਹਨ । ਹਰ ਦੇਸ਼ ਵਿਚ ਸਮੁਚੇ ਮਤਿ ਅਤੇ ਪਰੰਪਰਾਵਾਂ
ਅਤੇ ਜੁਗਤੀਆਂ ਉਪਰ ਆਧਾਰਿਤ ਹਨ । ਸਾਡੇ ਦੇਸ਼ ਵਿਚ ਤਾਂ ਇਹ
ਹਨ ਕਿ ਹਰ ਪਿੰਡ, ਕਸਬੇ, ਸ਼ਹਿਰ ਵਿਚ ਇਸ ਦੀਆਂ ਮਿਸਾਲਾਂ
ਇਸ ਮਾਰਗ ਉੱਪਰ ਚਲ ਕੇ ਦੇਵੀ ਦਿਉਤਿਆਂ, ਭੇਰੋ ਭੂਤਨਿਆਂ ਅਤੇ
ਸ਼ਕਤੀਆਂ ਤੋਂ ਸਹਾਇਤਾ ਦੀ ਪ੍ਰਾਰਥਨਾ ਕੀਤੀ ਜਾਂਦੀ ਹੈ । ਇਸ
ਕੇਵਲ ਇਹ ਸਿਧ ਕਰਨਾ ਲੋੜੀਂਦਾ ਹੈ ਕਿ ਧਰਮ ਦਾ ਇਹ ਪੱਖ ਮਨੁਖ
ਸਭ ਤੋਂ ਵੱਧ ਪ੍ਰਚਲਿਤ ਅਤੇ ਜਨਸਮੂਹਾਂ ਉਪਰ ਖਿਚ ਪਾਉਣ ਵਾਲਾ

Fig. 16 A Gurmukhi sample image

ਸਾਧਨ, ਜੋ ਰੰਗੇ ਮੰਤਵਾਂ ਹਿਤ ਵੀ ਹੁੰਦੇ ਹਨ ਅਤੇ ਦੂਜਿਆਂ ਦੀ ਹਾਨੀ
ਨੀਵੀਂਆਂ ਇਛਾਵਾਂ ਦੀ ਪੂਰਤੀ ਹਿਤ ਵੀ-ਮਨੁਖ ਮਾਤਰ ਇਹਨਾਂ
ਕਰਦੇ ਆ ਰਹੇ ਹਨ। ਹਰ ਦੇਸ਼ ਵਿਚ ਸਮੁਚੇ ਮਤਿ 'ਅਤੇ ਪਰੰਪਰਾਵਾਂ
ਅਤੇ ਜੁਗਤੀਆਂ ਉਪਰ ਆਧਾਰਿਤ ਹਨ। ਸਾਡੇ ਦੇਸ਼ ਵਿਚ ਤਾਂ ਇਹ
ਹਨ ਕਿ ਹਰ ਪਿੰਡ, ਕਸਬੇਂ, ਸ਼ਹਿਰ ਵਿਚ ਇਸ ਦੀਆਂ ਮਿਸਾਲ੍ਹਾਂ
ਇਸ ਮਾਰਗ ਉੱਪਰ ਚਲ੍ਹ ਕੇ ਦੇਵੀ ਦਿਉਤਿਆਂ, ਡੇਰੇ ਭੂਤਨਿਆਂ ਅਤੇ
ਸ਼ਕਤੀਆਂ ਤੋਂ ਸਹਾਇਤਾ ਦੀ ਪ੍ਰਾਰਥਨੱ◌ਾ ਕੀਤੀ ਜਾਂਦੀ ਹੈ। ਇਸ
ਕੇਵਲ ਇਹ ਸਿਧ ਕਰਨਾ ਲੋੜੀਂਦਾ ਹੈ ਕਿ ਧਰਮ ਦਾ ਇਹ ਪੱਖ ਮਨੁਖ
ਸਭ ਤੋਂ ਵੱਧ ਪ੍ਰਚਲਿਤ ਅਤੇ ਜਨਸਮੁਹਾ ਉਪਰ ਖਿਚ ਪਾਉਣ ਵਾਲ੍ਹਾ

Fig. 17 Output of recognition on image from Fig. 16

by the recognizer and the confusion was partially resolved by the post-processor. The other source of error in the upper zone is frequently touching characters and the character *bindi*, which resembles a dot as in i and j and is frequently merged with other upper zone characters.

The recognizer performed very well on the characters in the middle zone, which is the busiest zone. There are 42 characters in the middle zone and their combined frequency of occurrence is 68.2%. A majority of the errors in this zone were made in the recognition of the visually similar character pairs (ਬ and ਥ) and (ਚ and ਰ) and the characters with dots at their feet. The recognition rate of middle characters is 98.07%.

The lower zone, in which two vowels and three half characters reside, accounts for approximately 3.2% of all characters and has a recognition accuracy of 94.29%. Some of the causes of error are the similarity in shapes of the characters, small size of the characters and merging of the lower zone characters with the middle zone characters. Fig. 16 shows a sample image from our test set and the output of the recognition system is shown in Fig. 17.

15 Conclusion

In this chapter we have presented a complete multi-font and multi-size OCR system for Gurmukhi script. It has been tested on page images from various books printed over the last 40 years, magazines and laser print-outs in multiple sizes and fonts and has a recognition accuracy of more than 96% at the character level. The system still needs to be improved for handling degraded documents. To further improve the accuracy, additional features and more sophisticated classifiers are being explored.

References

1. V. K. Govindan, A. P. Shivaprasad, Character Recognition-A Review, *Pattern Recognition*, Vol. 23, 1990, pp. 671–683.
2. S.N.S. Rajasekaran, B.L. Deekshatulu, Recognition of Printed Telugu Characters, *Computer Graphics and Image Processing*, Vol. 6, 1977, pp. 335–360.
3. G. Siromoney, R. Chandrasekaran, M. Chandrasekaran, Machine Recognition of Printed Tamil Characters, *Pattern Recognition*, Vol. 10, 1978, pp. 243–247.
4. R. M. K. Sinha, H. N. Mahabala, Machine Recognition of Devanagari Script, *IEEE Trans on Systems, Man and Cybernetics*, Vol. 9, 1979, pp. 435–449.
5. B. B. Chaudhuri, U. Pal, A Complete Printed Bangla OCR System, *Pattern Recognition*, Vol. 31, 1998, pp. 531–549.
6. V. Bansal, Integrating Knowledge Sources in Devanagri Text Recognition, *Ph.D. thesis*. IIT Kanpur, 1999.
7. H. Ma and D. Doermann, Adaptive Hindi OCR Using Generalized Hausdorff Image Comparison, *ACM Transactions on Asian Language Information Processing*, Vol. 2, No. 3, September 2003, pp. 193–218.
8. A. Negi, B. Chakravarthy and B. Krishna, An OCR system for Telugu, *Proc. Of 6th Int. Conf. on Document Analysis and Recognition,* 2001, pp. 1110–1114.
9. U. Pal and B.B. Chaudhuri, Indian Script Character Recognition: A Survey, *Pattern Recognition*, Vol. 37, 2004, pp. 1887–1899.
10. G. S. Lehal and C. Singh, A Complete Machine Printed Gurmukhi OCR System, *Vivek,* Vol. 16, No. 3, 2006, pp. 10–17.
11. G. S. Lehal and R. Dhir, A Range Free Skew Detection Technique for Digitized Gurmukhi Script Documents, *Proceedings 5th International Conference of Document Analysis and Recognition,* 1999, pp. 147-152.
12. W. H. Abdulla, A. O. M. Saleh and A. H. Morad, A Pre-processing Algorithm for Handwritten Character Recognition, *Pattern Recognition Letters,* Vol. 7, 1988, pp. 13–18.
13. G. S. Lehal and C. Singh, Text Segmentation of Machine Printed Gurmukhi Script, *Document Recognition and Retrieval VIII,* Paul B. Kantor, Daniel P. Lopresti, Jiangying Zhou, Editors, Proceedings SPIE, USA, Vol. 4307, 2001, pp. 223–231.
14. G. S. Lehal and C. Singh, A Post Processor for Gurmukhi OCR, *SADHANA Academy Proceedings in Engineering Sciences,* Vol. 27, Part 1, 2002, pp. 99–112.

Progress in Gujarati Document Processing and Character Recognition

Jignesh Dholakia, Atul Negi and S. Rama Mohan

Abstract Gujarati is an Indic script similar in appearance to other Indo-Aryan scripts. Printed Gujarati script has a rich literary heritage. From an OCR perspective it needs a different treatment due to some of its peculiarities. Research on Gujarati OCR is a recent development as compared to OCR research on many other Indic scripts. Here, in this chapter we present a detailed account of the state of the art of Gujarati document analysis and character recognition. We begin with approaches to zone boundary detection, necessary for the isolation of words and character segmentation and recognition. We show results of various feature extraction techniques such as fringe maps, discrete cosine transform, and wavelets. Zone information and aspect ratios are also used for classification. We present recognition results with two types of classifiers, viz., nearest neighbor classifier and artificial neural networks. Results of experiments wherein various combinations of feature extraction methods with classifiers are also presented. We find that general regression neural network with wavelets feature gives best results with significant time saving in training. Since Indic scripts require syllabic reconstruction from OCR components, a procedure for text generation from the recognized glyph sequences and a method for post-processing is also described.

Keywords Gujarati OCR · Segmentation · Feature extraction · Neural networks · Discrete cosine transform · Wavelet transform

1 Introduction

Several Indian languages have a rich literary history with documents available in a printed or handwritten form. Gujarati-printed script also has its unique history which is tied to the work of M.K. Gandhi [1, 2] which was originally in Gujarati.

J. Dholakia (✉)
Department of Applied Mathematics, The M. S. University of Baroda, Vadodara, Gujarat, India
e-mail: jignesh.dholakia@gmail.com

V. Govindaraju, S. Setlur (eds.), *Guide to OCR for Indic Scripts*, Advances in Pattern Recognition, DOI 10.1007/978-1-84800-330-9_4,

Another interesting fact is that the oldest running published newspaper in India is a Gujarati daily, *Mumbai Samachar*, published since 1822 (first by Fardoonjee Marzban). However it is a pity that, very little of this wealth of Gujarati literature is available in an electronic form which can allow searching and indexing. The major obstacle to building up such a corpus is the complexity of script (described in the following section) that makes keyboard data entry to be time-consuming and prone to errors. The solution lies in building robust Optical character recognition systems for Gujarati script. Work in this regard is not so mature compared to OCR systems for other Indic scripts like Devanagari and Bangla. However the problems faced and the solutions we present here for Gujarati are useful and can be extended to some of the other Indic scripts which do not have a *shirorekha* (the distinctive headline present in Devanagari and Bangla scripts).

Gujarati OCR is a relative newcomer in comparison to the other Indic scripts like Devanagari, Bangla, Telugu, Tamil, and Punjabi. In India the work really started in earnest with the funding of projects during the years 2002–2003 by the Ministry of Communications and Information Technology, Government of India. Internationally, there is very little published work on Gujarati OCR. However, there seems to be a large demand of the OCR as a product. Present efforts are part of the research of a consortia mode project entitled *Development of Robust Document Analysis and Recognition System for Printed Indian Scripts*.

Here in this chapter we first give a detailed introduction to the script and then review difficulties in developing OCR systems for Gujarati script and show its distinctiveness from other Indic scripts. This is followed by a description of the overall recognition strategies for developing OCR systems. Here then we describe an algorithm which reduces the difficulties in recognition but as a trade-off requires a slightly complex segmentation method for finding zones in text lines and segmenting recognizable units. Recognition using a GRNN is described with conclusions and results.

2 Gujarati Script: OCR Perspective

Gujarati script (Fig. 1) is used to write the Gujarati language spoken by about 50 million people (also called Gujarati) in the western part of India. Apart from the native speakers of the state of Gujarat in India, Gujarati-speaking diaspora is across all parts of India and in almost any part of the world. Gujarati literature is not only of interest to the Gujarati but also to the researchers abroad [1, 2, 3].

Gujarati has 12 vowels and 34+2[1] consonants. Apart from these basic symbols, other symbols called "vowel modifiers" are used to denote the attachment of vowels with the core consonants. Consonant–Vowel combinations occur very often in most of the Indic languages including Gujarati. This is denoted by attaching a symbol, unique for each vowel, to the consonant, called a dependent vowel modifier or *Matra*. The *matra* can appear before, after, above, or below the core consonant.

[1] Two conjuncts /ksha/ and /jya/ are treated as if they are basic consonants in Gujarati script

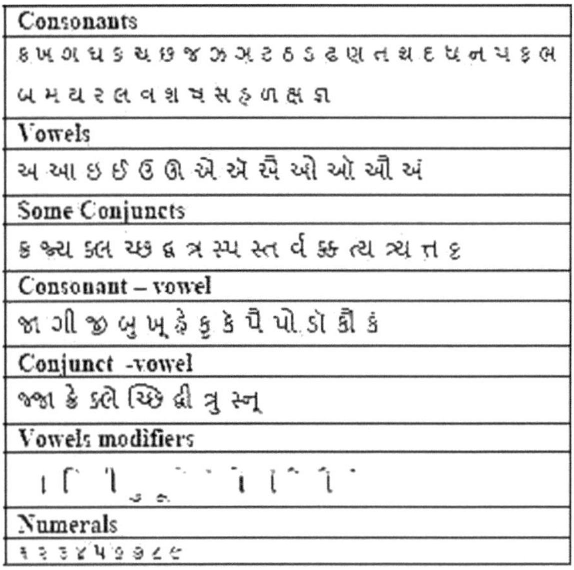

Fig. 1 Gujarati script

In addition to basic consonants, like most Indic scripts, Gujarati also uses consonant clusters (conjuncts). That is, consonants without the inherent vowel sound are combined and thereby leading to three possibilities for the shape of the resulting conjuncts:

1. Conjunct shape is derived by connecting a part of the preceding consonant to the following one:

   ક + ્ + ત = ક્ત , ટ + ્ + ટ = ટ્ટ

2. The conjunct can take completely different shape

   દ + ્ + ય = દ્ય , ક + ્ + ષ = ક્ષ , દ + ્ + વ = દ્વ

3. Addition of some mark indicating conjunct formation in upper/middle/lower zones (mainly conjuncts involving /r/)

   ક + ્ + ર = ક્ર , ર + ્ + વ = ર્વ , ટ + ્ + ર = ટ્ર

Moreover, conjuncts may themselves occur in half forms. Reference [3] gives detailed description on Gujarati script with the rules to form conjuncts and other modifications that might take place in the shapes of basic consonant symbols.

It can be seen that the shapes of many Gujarati characters are similar to those of the phonetically corresponding characters of Devanagari script. As in the case of

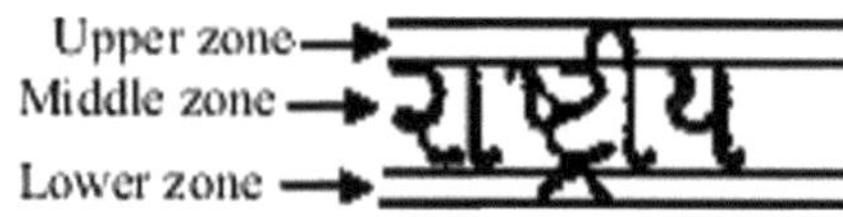

Fig. 2 Logical zones

other Indic scripts, Gujarati also does not have the distinction of lower and upper cases. In spite of these similarities with the Devanagari script, Gujarati script has many distinct characteristics and the most important of them is "absence of so-called *shirorekha(header line)*" in the script and differences in the shapes of many of the consonants and vowels, etc.

Similar to the text written in Devanagari or Bangla script, text in Gujarati script can also be divided into three logical zones: upper, middle, and lower as shown in Fig. 2.

Gujarati, due to its peculiar characteristics, needs to be treated differently from the other Indo-Aryan scripts like Devanagari, Bangla, Gurmukhi.

Research for developing Gujarati OCR started much later than the research-level attempts of developing OCR system for other Indian scripts like Bangla and Devanagari. Due to common roots of Indo-Aryan script and similarity due to that, the work that has been done for other script for various subtasks like line/word segmentation [5, 6], touching character segmentation [7], recognition [8, 5, 9] has been useful in the work described here. Some ideas from work in English hand-printed character recognition [10] are also used.

Our first exposure to Gujarati character recognition was from the work published in ICDAR 1999 [11]. An experiment to recognize 10 pre-segmented Gujarati characters using Hu-invariant moments as feature extractors and *k*-nearest neighbor classification was presented. The accuracy reported was very low and there was no systemic approach to the problem of Gujarati document analysis or recognition. Thereafter Dholakia et al. [12] contributed to Gujarati document analysis by an approach to zone boundary detection published in ICDAR 2005. There we show the application of basic concept of the slope of a line, to extract text information from the document image. There have been quite a few publications from the group at The M.S. University of Baroda, on use of wavelets as feature extractor and various neural network architectures for classification [13, 14]. We have also used an optimization technique (dynamic programming) to develop more robust methods for zone boundary identification [15]. The latest of all, [16] reports the study of designing easily trainable architecture of neural network which gives maximum recognition accuracy reported so far. In that work, we have also reported confusion character sets derived out of 119 symbols when they were classified using wavelet features and GRNN/nearest neighbor classifiers.

3 Segmentation

Segmentation, as we know, separates out various building blocks of the document. As it is well known the level of segmentation will constrain the choice regarding a

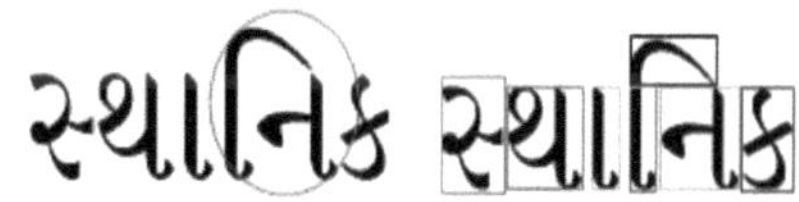

(a) (b)

Fig. 3 Two possible approaches for recognition: (a) CV combination and (b) symbols in three zones

recognizable unit. As Gujarati does not have *Shirorekha*, from the OCR perspective, it can be considered similar to certain south Indian scripts, like Telugu.

Now, for the level of segmentation, let us try to decide what should be our unit of recognition. There may be two different approaches to recognition (Fig. 3):

1. Recognizing a (C)CV combination as a whole (as explained in previous section).
2. First segmenting the consonants from dependent vowel modifier and then recognizing them separately. The recognized text has to be composed by reconstructing the (C)CV cluster based on combining the recognized glyphs.

Selecting first option will result into exorbitantly large number of symbols to be recognized. Total number of symbols to be recognized in this case would be

34 consonant + 5 vowel symbols + 34 consonants × 12 vowel modifiers + approximately 250 conjunct × 12 vowel modifiers = approximately 3500 symbols

Such a large number of symbols poses a great challenge of designing large class of classifier and it is known that designing a classifier to handle such a large number of classes is a very difficult task. Now, if we choose to recognize components in each zone separately, the total number of components to be identified are *middle zone components* (consonants + conjuncts + vowel modifier corresponding to /AA/ + half forms of consonants + half form of conjunct) + *upper zone symbols* (upper parts of the vowel modifiers corresponding to /i/, /ii/, /e/, *Anuswar*, *repha*, *Chandrabindu*) + *lower zone symbols* totaling to not more than 350.

Hence, it is clear that second option is more feasible as the number of classes reduces significantly. That means, if we want to avoid known complexities of designing classifier with large number of classes, we will have to carry out slightly complex process of zone boundary detection and then recognizing symbols in each zone. Since this is the choice we make, it is then necessary to have a robust zone boundary separator which can reliably identify zone separation boundaries. This is described in the following section.

4 Zone Boundary Identification

As explained in the previous section, we need to have a zone boundary locater to develop an OCR system for Gujarati script. The algorithm should be robust and reliable because it can easily be seen that a little oversegmentation may cut the character in middle zone and the residual component in middle zone may be similar to another valid symbol of the script.

(a)

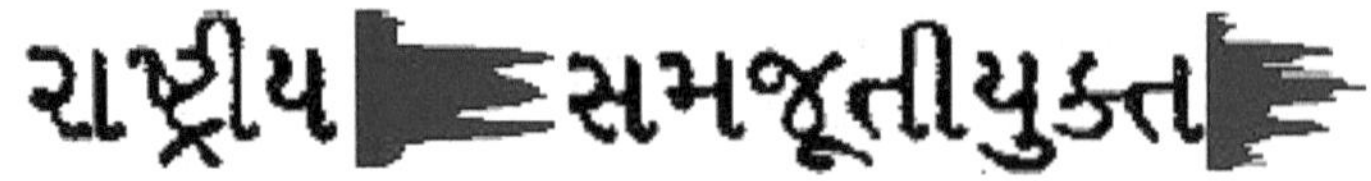

(b)

Fig. 4 Horizontal projection: (a) Devanagari text and (b) Gujarati text

Zone boundary identification is also required in other Indo-Aryan scripts like Devanagari and Bangla and sufficient work is done in this area for these scripts [5, 9]. Looking at the similarity of these scripts an obvious choice was to use the same algorithm as used by these scripts for Gujarati. But, the algorithms for these scripts use *shirorekha* as an important parameter to decide the upper zone boundary, since it gives a prominent peak in the horizontal projection [5] of line/word (Fig. 4(a)). Unlike these scripts Gujarati does not have shirorekha, hence no prominent peak in its horizontal projection (Fig. 4(b)) and hence we cannot use the technique used for identifying zone boundaries in scripts with *shirorekha* Gujarati script.

It may be argued, after analysis of horizontal projections of Gujarati texts (Fig. 4(b)), that instead of peak there is a trough at the boundary positions. But, it may also be noted that trough is not as prominent and detecting rising/falling edges is not easy. Following are some of the instances in which this may not work to the required accuracy:

1. In the case where the number of modifiers is significantly large this trough will not be very prominent.
2. A slight misalignment of text may lead to cutting off of a significant part of a glyph in the middle zone (e.g., a small arc at the top left corner of the letter /ya/) which can effect the recognition accuracy (in case of previously sited example of /ya/ the shape after removal of that curvature would be similar to alphabet /va/).
3. When the number of modifiers are less, the trough is shallow and hence almost undetectable.

Hence, we need a novel approach for Gujarati which is not using the projection profiles for finding zone boundaries. The following two sections describe two attempts by us for the same.

4.1 Using Slopes of the Imaginary Lines Joining Top Left (Bottom Right) Corners

In order to overcome the problems posed by the above-mentioned situations, we devised a new algorithm to determine the zone boundaries [12]. The pseudo-code of the algorithm for detecting the zone boundaries is described below. In our algorithm first we consider all the potential connected components (CC) within a text line and compute the slopes of all the imaginary lines that join top left corners of all possible pairs of CC. The row coordinate of the CC that are end points of the maximum number of lines having the least slope would identify the row of separation between the upper zone and the middle zone. Similar procedure for the bottom right coordinates of the connected components would indicate the location separating the middle and the lower zones. **Algorithm 1** gives step-by-step procedure for the same.

Algorithm 1 To find zone separation boundary

Input: Image of a line of Gujarati text
Output: Row numbers of the two lines that separate upper and lower modifiers from the middle zone.
Step1: Extract the connected components in the line with the information about their bounding boxes.
Step2: For each pair of distinct connected components, compute the following:

1. Identify the coordinates (u_1, v_1) and (u_2, v_2) of the top left corners of the bounding boxes of the two components.
2. Identify the coordinates (l_1, m_1) and (l_2, m_2) of the bottom right corners of the bounding boxes of the two components.
3. Find the absolute values *S1* and *S2* of the slopes of the lines connecting (u_1, v_1) to (u_2, v_2) and (l_1, m_1) to (l_2, m_2)

$$S1 = \frac{|u_2 - u_1|}{|v_2 - v_1|}$$

and

$$S2 = \frac{|l_2 - l_1|}{|m_2 - m_1|}$$

Step4: Identify the lines that give the minimum of slopes $S2$. Those lines that fall in the region between 15 and 40% of line height above the bottom of the text line are candidates for being considered as separators of lower zone from the middle zone. If there is more than one line that satisfies this criterion, choose the line that occurs maximum number of times as the zone separator.
Step3: Identify the lines that give the minimum of slopes $S1$. Those lines that fall in the region between 15 and 40% of line height below the top of the text line are candidates for being considered as separators of upper zone from the middle zone. If there is more than one line that satisfies this criterion, choose the line that occurs maximum number of times as the zone separator.

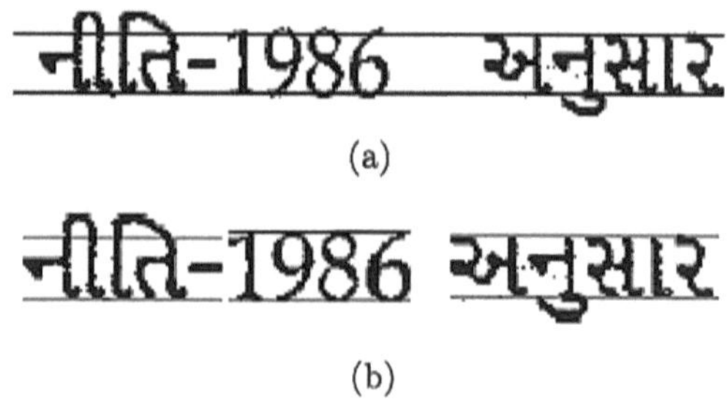

Fig. 5 Zone boundary detection: (a) line-level zone detection (notice oversegmentation) and (b) world-level improvement

Doing this process only at line level may not be sufficient, because it still leaves the possibility of errors in the situations where words are not horizontally aligned. Figure 5(a) illustrates this case for a sample line of text.

Due to this problem, the process mentioned above for a line needs to be repeated for the connected components of individual words also for determining the zonal boundaries. Here, there is a possibility of disagreement between the boundaries detected at word level and line level. In such cases, if a new location for any of the two separators is detected then those are considered to be valid, but if the word-level execution removes a zone detected in the line-level execution then the line-level decision is considered to be valid. Figure 5(b) shows the correction after calculating the zone boundaries at word level.

Table 1 gives details about the testing.

Table 1 Result of zone boundary detection using slope of imaginary lines

No. of books	No. of pages	No. of lines	Success (no. of lines)
5	43	935	858 (91.76%)

4.2 Dynamic Programming Approach

The algorithm in previous section gives reasonably good results; however, it has some limitations as follows:

1. It assumes the connected components of a word to be vertically aligned.
2. It assumes the zone separation path to be a straight line.

These assumptions together lead to the problem when the connected components of a word are not aligned, as shown in Fig. 6.

It can easily be seen that for robust and reliable zone segmentation, the assumption made in the above method needs to be relaxed, i.e., any general path can be zone separator and the selection of the path should depend only on the connected component under consideration and it should not refer to any other connected

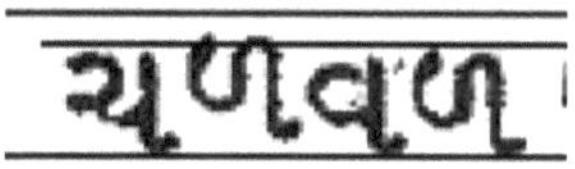

Fig. 6 Problem due to straight line zone separator

component in the word or line. An obvious question that anyone can have in mind is, how to find this general path which can be a reliable zone separator?

In search of an appropriate method, we have gone through many papers wherein researchers have tried myriad approaches for different kinds of segmentations [17, 10, 7, 18, 6]. Following text gives details about the method that we have selected to find a path as mentioned above with justifications wherever needed.

A careful analysis of the Gujarati script revealed the following facts:

1. We can assume upper zone separation boundary just above a horizontal stroke.
2. There is a zone constraint – viz., the zone boundary falls in the region from 15 to 40% of the line height below the top of the text line.

Similar assumptions can be made for lower zone also. In this section, we explain an approach for upper zone only since a similar approach may be devised for the lower zone with appropriate modification.

Now, finding the location of a zone separator is dependent on the existence of a horizontally oriented portion at the top and bottom of the middle zone component. This assumption is true for most of the Gujarati symbols that fall into middle zone. The exceptions are listed in Fig. 7(a). Zone boundary in such cases can be identified by joining the neighboring ends of zone separator by a straight line, without loss of precision (Fig. 7(b)).

Exceptions
ન ત ની નિ

(a)

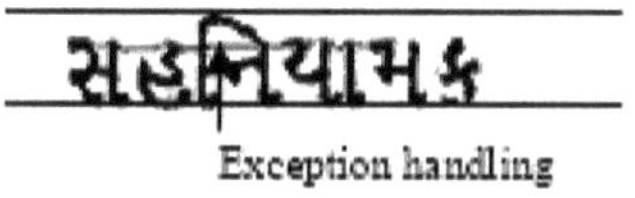

(b)

Fig. 7 Exception: (a) illustrations and (b) exception handling

We know that in conventional setup the term touching glyphs means the glyphs which are part of two different characters touching horizontally. If we refer to this as a *horizontal touching* then on the same lines we can look at the joint between glyphs in two different zones as *vertical touching* (Fig. 8).

Fig. 8 Touching example

The advantage of defining this concept is that now we can use the rich knowledge of touching character segmentation for zone separation.

Breuel [10] has described an approach to segment hand-printed characters, which allows the cuts to be curved (*curved pre-stroke cuts* (CPSC)). From the observations made above and the analysis of the script, it is clear that this approach can be adapted to find a zone separating path. We assume our image to be of the size $w \times h$.

The adapted version of the algorithm is as follows: We find the optimal path as described in [10] with only difference being our path will be horizontal unlike vertically oriented paths in [10], i.e., if the path P is a sequence of pixels (x_i, y_i) then the cost C assigned to the path can be modified to be

$$C = \sum_{i=1}^{w} c_s(y_i - y_{i-1}) + c_i(x_i, y_i; I), \tag{1}$$

where

$$c_s(\Delta y) = \begin{cases} 0 & \text{for } |\Delta y| = 0 \\ 1 & \text{for } |\Delta y| = 1 \\ \infty & \text{for } |\Delta y| = 1 \end{cases} \tag{2}$$

$$c_i(x_i, y_i; I) = \begin{cases} -5 \text{ if } (x_i, y_i) & \text{is above horizontal edge} \\ 2 \;\text{ if } (x_i, y_i) & \text{is in a stroke} \\ 1 \;\text{ if } (x_i, y_i) & \text{is an intermediate background pixel.} \end{cases} \tag{3}$$

The process starts by finding the connected component of a text line and for each component we try to find cut locations. We compute the centroid of the connected component say (x_c, y_c) and then we calculate $c(y)$ for all the path passing through point (x_c, y), for all $y = 0,1,2,\ldots,h$.

The constraint that we put on the coordinates of the pixel is also altered from $y_i = i$ in [10] to $x_i = i$ due to similar reasons as described in [10]. In addition to this, we put some more constraints on the points of the optimum path to form cut which will be described later in this chapter.

In order to compute $c(y)$ efficiently, we use dynamic programming in two stages: first by finding optimal path passing through each point (x_c, y) between 0 and x_c and then finding it between w and x_c. Algorithm proceeds in the same way as in [10], the only difference is the row operations there are replaced by column operations in our case. After calculating the cost we find out local optima at the line $x = x_c$. Then the optimal cut though the point (x_c, y) is obtained by following the content of the source array as in [10].

Here we need to enforce some more constraints on selection of the point that would be the member of the segmenting path due to the observation we made regarding the location of the zone separator.

- Point (x, y) can be member of upper zone separator of a line with line height Lh if and only if $0.15Lh \leq y \leq 0.4Lh$.

– Similarly, point (x, y) can be member of lower zone separator of a line with line height Lh, if and only if $(Lh - 0.40Lh) \leq y \leq (Lh - 0.15Lh)$.

Application of these constraints will prevent the algorithm from producing the zone separator in case of exceptional glyphs listed in Fig. 7(a). Such cases can be handled by producing path by joining end points of the neighboring zone separators (right end point of the left neighbor and left end of the right neighbor). If these characters occur as the first (last) character of the line then the segmenting path from the right (left) is extended up to the left (right) boundary of the text line. In other words, if for any part of the line, if any of the zone separators are not identified after executing this algorithm, then that region is assumed to have a straight line joining the ends of neighboring paths as its zone separator (Fig. 7(b)).

This approach gives the zone separator which is not a straight line and hence prevents oversegmentation. However, it is very time-consuming and work is needed to improve it further. The basic problem with this algorithm is that it assumes centroid to be located in the touching area [10], which need not be true in all the cases for Gujarati script and hence, in the case where it is outside touching area, the algorithm might fail to identify a correct zone separator.

5 Extracting Recognizable Units

Once the segmentation and zone boundary identification is done, the connected component extracted earlier is analyzed for separating out modifiers that might have been attached with the middle zone glyph in connected components. Thus we get the minimum unit which then needs to be recognized. Figure 9 shows an example of a word and its recognizable units.

Fig. 9 Zone marked word and connected components

6 Recognition

Task of recognition can be divided into two subtasks, viz., feature extraction and classification. If we look at the task performed by two processes, they are in contradiction to each other. As we know the goal of feature extraction is to find distinct characteristics of an object to be recognized, which makes it different from the other object. Unlike this, the job of classification is to group objects having similar features. In other words, feature extraction is a specialization task and classification is a generalization. For the best recognition, we must have the right combination of feature extractor(s) and classifier(s) and which is properly tuned. If we take extremely localized features it may result in a situation where each sample in the training set starts representing a class. Hence, two samples of the same class in the training set will represent two different classes and then it becomes difficult for classifier as the samples of same class fall into two different classes. On the other hand, if we take a weak feature extractor then it may generate very similar features for object belonging to two different classes.

It can be said from the above discussion that any good feature extractor should offer two properties in the feature generated by it:

1. The features of the objects belonging to the same class should have maximum similarity.
2. The features of the objects belonging to different classes will be least similar or have significantly large dissimilarity.

Further, it is clear from the script description that even after zone boundaries are identified properly, we are left with around 350 symbols to be recognized. In addition to the number of classes, there are several script characteristics which adds to the problem. A few of them are as follows:

1. similar looking glyphs, e.g., /ka/ /da/ /tha/ , /gha/ /dha/ /dya/, later half of /la/ and /na/
2. almost same shapes for alphabet /pa/ and numeral 5
3. more than one way in which basic glyphs of an *akshara* [19] combine, e.g., /la/ /ha/
4. nonuniform behavior of vowel modifiers
5. touching and broken characters
6. accurate identification of zone boundary absence of *shirorekha*

As mentioned above, the first recorded attempt for Gujarati character recognition, though a very limited subset, is published in ICDAR'99 [11]. Thereafter, there have been several efforts to find the right combination of feature extraction and classification technique [13, 14, 16]. A detailed description of all the feature extraction and classification techniques that are used for Gujarati character recognition is given in the following section.

6.1 Feature Extraction

Three different feature extraction methods have been tested for their feature extraction capabilities: (1) fringe map; (2) discrete cosine transform; and (3) wavelet transform. It may be noted that the earlier effort [11] was using Hu-invariant moments as features.

6.1.1 Fringe Map

Template-based recognition is a known method and fringe map has been used as template earlier for Telugu script recognition [9]. Here the template is generated by replacing each pixel by its distance from nearest black pixel. We consider distance of a pixel from its four neighbors. Figure 10(a) shows an example of fringe map for character /tha/.

As can be seen from the method of template generation, this feature is not size invariant. Hence, we scale all our recognizable components to a common size of 32×32.

```
2 1 1 0 0 0 0 0 1 1 1 1 2 3 4 5 5 4 3 2 1 1 1 2 2 3 4 5 6 7 8 9
1 0 0 0 0 0 0 0 0 0 0 0 1 2 3 4 4 3 2 1 0 0 0 1 1 2 3 4 5 6 7 8
1 0 0 0 0 0 0 0 0 0 0 0 0 1 2 3 4 3 2 1 0 0 0 0 0 1 2 3 4 5 6 7
0 0 0 0 0 0 1 1 1 1 1 1 0 0 1 2 3 3 2 1 0 0 0 0 0 1 2 3 4 5 6 7
0 0 0 0 0 1 2 2 2 2 2 1 0 0 0 1 2 3 3 2 1 0 0 0 0 1 2 3 4 5 6 7
0 0 0 0 0 1 2 3 3 3 2 1 0 0 0 1 2 3 2 1 0 0 0 0 0 1 2 3 4 5 6 7
0 0 0 0 0 1 2 3 3 2 1 0 0 0 0 0 1 2 3 2 1 0 0 0 0 1 2 3 4 5 6 7
1 1 0 0 0 0 1 2 2 2 1 0 0 0 0 0 1 2 3 2 1 0 0 0 0 1 2 3 4 5 6 7
2 1 0 0 0 0 1 1 1 1 0 0 0 0 0 0 1 2 2 1 0 0 0 0 0 1 2 3 4 5 6 7
3 2 1 0 0 0 0 0 0 0 0 0 0 0 0 1 2 3 3 2 1 0 0 0 0 1 2 3 4 5 6 7
4 3 2 1 0 0 0 0 0 0 0 0 0 0 0 1 2 3 3 2 1 0 0 0 0 1 2 3 4 5 6 7
4 3 2 2 1 1 0 0 0 0 0 0 0 0 1 2 3 4 3 2 1 0 0 0 0 1 2 3 4 5 6 7
3 2 1 1 1 0 0 0 0 0 0 0 0 1 2 3 4 4 3 2 1 0 0 0 0 1 2 3 4 5 6 7
2 1 0 0 0 0 0 0 0 0 0 0 1 2 3 4 4 3 2 1 0 0 0 0 0 1 2 3 4 5 6 7
1 0 0 0 0 0 0 0 0 0 0 1 2 3 4 5 5 4 3 2 1 0 0 0 0 1 2 3 4 5 6 7
1 0 0 0 0 0 0 0 0 1 1 2 3 4 5 6 5 4 3 2 1 0 0 0 0 1 2 3 4 5 6 7
1 0 0 0 0 0 0 0 1 2 2 3 4 5 5 5 4 3 2 1 0 0 0 0 0 1 2 3 4 5 6 7
1 0 0 0 0 0 1 1 2 3 3 4 4 4 4 4 3 2 1 0 0 0 0 0 0 1 2 3 4 5 6 7
2 1 0 0 0 1 2 2 3 3 3 4 3 3 3 3 2 1 0 0 0 0 0 0 0 1 2 3 4 5 6 7
3 2 1 0 0 0 1 2 2 2 2 3 2 2 2 2 2 1 0 0 0 0 0 0 0 1 2 3 4 5 6 7
4 3 2 1 0 0 0 1 1 1 1 2 1 1 1 1 1 0 0 0 0 0 0 0 0 1 2 3 4 5 6 7
5 4 3 2 1 0 0 0 0 0 0 1 0 0 0 0 0 0 0 0 0 0 0 0 0 1 2 3 4 5 6 7
6 5 4 3 2 1 0 0 0 0 0 0 0 0 0 0 0 0 0 0 0 0 0 0 0 1 2 3 4 4 5 6
7 6 5 4 3 2 1 1 1 0 0 0 0 0 0 0 0 0 0 1 1 0 0 0 0 1 2 3 3 3 4 5
8 7 6 5 4 3 2 2 2 1 1 1 1 1 1 1 1 1 1 2 1 0 0 0 0 1 2 3 2 2 3 4
9 8 7 6 5 4 3 3 3 2 2 2 2 2 2 2 2 2 2 2 1 0 0 0 0 1 2 2 1 1 2 3
0 9 8 7 6 5 4 4 4 3 3 3 3 3 3 3 3 3 3 2 1 0 0 0 0 1 2 1 0 0 1 2
11 10 9 8 7 6 5 5 5 4 4 4 4 4 4 4 4 4 3 2 1 0 0 0 0 1 2 1 0 0 0 1
12 11 10 9 8 7 6 6 6 5 5 5 5 5 5 5 5 4 3 2 1 0 0 0 0 1 1 0 0 0 0 0
13 12 11 10 9 8 7 7 7 6 6 6 6 6 6 6 5 4 3 2 1 0 0 0 0 0 1 0 0 0 0 0
14 13 12 11 10 9 8 8 8 7 7 7 7 7 7 7 6 5 4 3 2 1 0 0 0 0 0 0 0 0 0 1
15 14 13 12 11 10 9 9 9 8 8 8 8 8 8 8 8 7 6 5 4 3 2 1 1 0 0 0 0 0 1 1
```

(a)

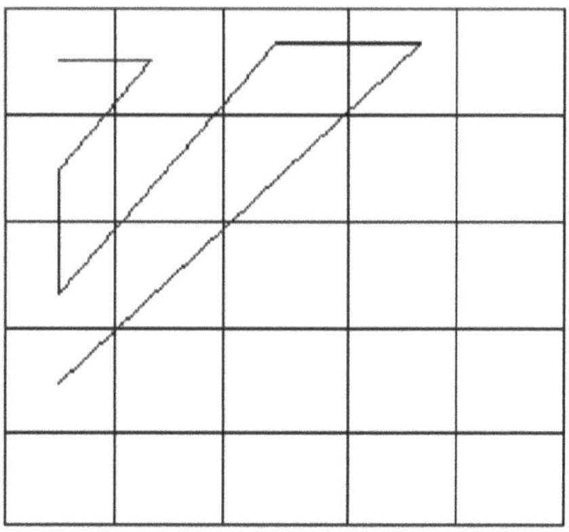

(b)

Fig. 10 Features: (a) template (fringe map) and (b) zigzag direction for DCT

6.1.2 Discrete Cosine Transform

Discrete cosine transform (DCT), $D(u, v)$, of an image, say $I(x, y)$ is given by Eq. (4). It is a very important tool in image compression [20] where reduction of the memory requirement is the main goal. In the case of recognition also we try to reduce the number of elements in feature vectors as it directly implies faster calculation at the time of classification with less storage required. Considering this fact we have selected this as feature extractor:

$$D(u,v) = \frac{2}{\sqrt{nm}} C(u)C(v) \sum_{y=0}^{m-1} \sum_{x=0}^{n-1} I(x,y) \cos \frac{(2x+1)u\pi}{2n} \cos \frac{(y+1)v\pi}{2m} \quad (4)$$
$$u = 0, 1, 2, \ldots, n-1,; \quad v = 0, 1, 2 \ldots, m-1.$$

It is clear from the theory of DCT that it is also not scale invariant and the process of calculating DCT can be optimized in terms of time and space if the dimensions of input matrix are some power of 2. Hence, here too we scale the images to the size of 32 × 32 before subjecting them to DCT. Again, it is well known that the low-frequency coefficients stores most of the information regarding the original data and hence the original data can be approximated by considering only a few low-frequency coefficients. In case of 2-D DCT of an image, such coefficients lie on the top left corner of the matrix. Therefore we select a few top left coefficient as the feature vector in the zigzag order as shown in Fig. 10(b).

6.1.3 Wavelet Transform

A spatially localized basis for expressing a signal is useful in signal processing because it provides a local analysis of the signal. As wavelets are known for their time and frequency localization, they are used by many researchers for feature extractor [21, 13, 14, 22].

Families of wavelet basis vectors by Ingrid Daubechies are very well localized in space as well as in frequency. In [23] authors have shown Daubechies D-4 wavelets give better results for handwritten Chinese character recognition than the other wavelets. It is also shown that D-4 gives better results than other statistical methods used for feature extraction. Further, the results in [13, 14] encouraged the use of Daubechies D-4 wavelets as a feature extractor in this experiment.

Figure 11 gives binary representation of the image after scaling it to the size of 32 × 32 and the binary image obtained by thresholding low–low coefficients of Daubechies D-4 wavelet transform after first level of decomposition. It can be seen

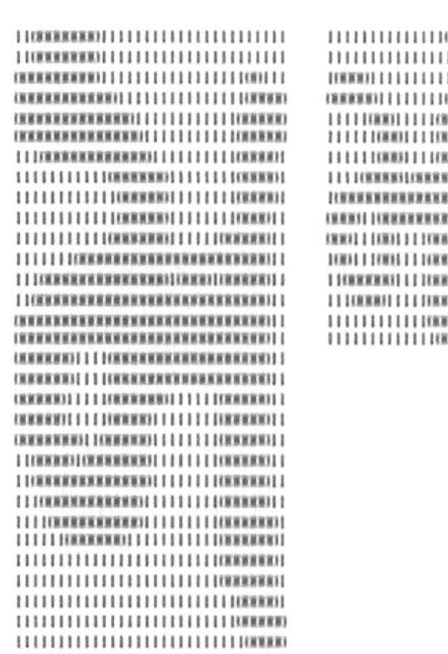

Fig. 11 Wavelet reconstruction

from right-hand side reconstruction in Fig. 11 that all the important features are preserved. This makes wavelets a strong contender for feature extraction.

6.1.4 Zone Information

We use zone information as one of the features to reduce the search and confusion. This also reduces the complexity of classifier design as classification of upper and lower zone glyphs will involve less than 10 classes. Also, for middle zone glyphs search will be limited to only features of middle zone glyphs. In other words, we will build three classifiers, one for classifying glyphs from each of the three zones.

6.1.5 Aspect Ratio

One of the most frequently occurring glyphs in Gujarati is a bar (vertical line) sign corresponding to vowel modifier for /AA/. The aspect ratio of this glyph is very much different from other glyphs and also the scaled version of this glyph will cover entire 32×32 matrix with black pixel and it can generate match for any random glyph when compared using any of the conventional features. Hence, for each of the glyph we calculate aspect ratio and we use this information to classify glyph corresponding to vowel modifier /AA/.

6.2 Classification

In the history of OCR researchers have attempted various types of classifier to get the best classification. The range covers the simplest classifiers like nearest neighbor classifier to the complex ones like neural networks, hidden Markov models.

Two types of classifiers are used for Gujarati character recognition: nearest neighbor-based classifier and neural network-based classifier. The first paper on Gujarati character recognition reports use of k-nearest neighbor classifier with Hu-invariant moments as features [11]. A brief description of these methods is given below.

6.2.1 Nearest Neighbor Classifier

Nearest neighbor classifier or 1-nearest neighbor classifier, one of the oldest and simplest classifiers, was selected as the other classifier to be used in this experiment. This can briefly be described as follows [24].

This rule classifies x in the category of its nearest neighbor. More precisely, we call $x'_n \in (x_1, x_2, \ldots, x_n)$ a nearest neighbor to x if

$$min \;\; d(x_i, x) = d(x'_n, x), \qquad \text{where, } i = 1, 2, \ldots, n.$$

The nearest neighbor rule chooses to classify x to the category n, where x_n is the nearest neighbor to x and x_n belongs to class θ_n. A mistake is made if θ_n is not the same as θ.

6.2.2 Artificial Neural Networks [25, 26]

Artificial neural networks (ANN) are popular and well-recognized tools for classification due to their learning and generalization capabilities. They have been used in building OCR systems [27, 13, 14, 16].

Out of various architectures, multi-layer perceptron (MLP), radial basis functions network, and general regression neural network have been studied for Gujarati character recognition [13, 14, 16].

6.2.3 Multi-layer Perceptron (MLP) [25]

Multi-layer perceptron (MLP) is the most commonly used of all the ANN architectures used for pattern recognition. In our experiments we have used MLP with linear activation function at the output layer. A detailed description of a general MLP can be found in [25]

The MLP is fully connected in the sense that every neuron in any layer is connected to each and every neuron in the subsequent layer by a weighted link through which the state of the neuron is transmitted. The weights on the links constitute the information stored by the network. The training of the network for reflecting a set of input–output patterns is a process of adjusting the weights on the network connections such that the resulting network captures the desired input–output behavior.

6.2.4 Radial Basis Functions (RBF) networks

Radial basis function neural networks are three-layered (one input layer, one unsupervised hidden layer of usually high dimensionality, and one supervised output layer) feed-forward network [25]. These networks basically involve passing of the inputs through a nonlinear transformation followed by a linear mapping. Each hidden layer neuron applies a nonlinear transformation from the input space to the hidden space. This transformation does not involve the weights of the connections from input to the hidden layer and only depends upon a nonlinear function called the radial basis function, with two parameters called the center (μ) and the spread (σ). These functions can be chosen from a class of functions characterized by Micchelli's theorem. We have adopted Gaussian functions for this purpose as they have the desirable properties of being localized and nonsingular interpolation matrices as shown below:

$$h_i = exp[-(x-\mu)^T(x-\mu)/(2\sigma^2)], \tag{5}$$

where h_i is the output of the ith hidden neuron, x is the n-dimensional input vector, μ is the n-dimensional center vector, and σ is the n-dimensional spread (standard deviation) vector of the radial basis neuron. The hidden layer is fully connected to the input layer and the receptive field (the region of space over which the neuron has appreciable response) of each neuron is controlled by its center (μ) and spread

(σ). Each hidden layer neuron is connected to each of the output layer neurons by links that have trainable weights. The actual output of each unit of the output layer is produced using the function

$$y_i = \frac{h_i w_{ij}}{\Sigma h_i}, \tag{6}$$

where w_{ij} is a weight vector. The output of each output layer neuron is the linear weighted summation of the hidden layer outputs h_i. The actual output of the neuron is obtained by dividing this output with the sum of all hidden layer outputs (σh_i).

Training of RBFNN involves the minimization of errors observed at the output layer by adjusting the centers and spreads of the hidden neurons and the weights of the output layer. First, each hidden neuron's center (μ) and spread (σ) must be assigned a value. Second, the weight matrix w must be trained. The center and spread of each hidden neuron are chosen using the K-means clustering algorithm. The weights of the output layer are optimized using a supervised training method. The weight matrix is adjusted in a direction that reduces the difference between the actual and target outputs of the network. The following gradient descent algorithm is used for the weight adjustment:

$$w_{ij}(n+1) = w_{ij}(n) + (t_j - y_i)x_j,$$

where w_{ij} is the weight of the link between hidden layer neuron j and output layer neuron i, t_j is the target output of neuron j, y_i is the actual output of the output layer neuron i, and x_i is the input.

6.2.5 General Regression Neural Network (GRNN)

Most of the researchers employ neural network architectures using iterative learning techniques like back propagation [22, 13, 14], RBF [27], dynamic neural networks (DNN) [21]. The basic disadvantage of these techniques is that the algorithms take a large number of iterations to converge to desired solution. GRNN, in comparison, is single-pass neural network architecture and converges much faster to the desired solution. General regression neural network (GRNN) was first proposed for speech recognition [28, 29] and used there with good success. However, it is for the first time that we had used it as a classifier for Gujarati character recognition.

GRNN can briefly be described as follows [26].

Let w_{ij} be the desired output corresponding to input training vector X_i and *jth* output. Then,

$$y_j = \frac{\Sigma_{i=1}^{n} w_{ij} h_i}{\Sigma_{i=1} n h_i}, \tag{7}$$

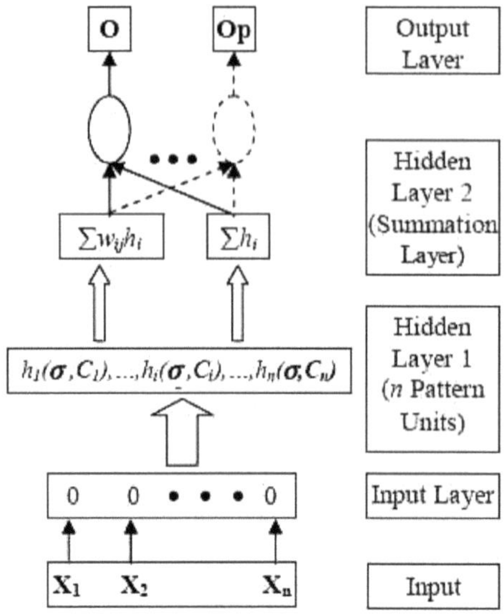

Fig. 12 GRNN architecture [29]

where

$$h_i = \left(-\frac{D_i^2}{2\sigma^2} \right), \tag{8}$$

$$D_i^2 = (X - X_i)^T (X - X_i), \quad \sigma = spread \ .$$

The estimate y_j can be visualized as a weighted average of all the observed values, w_{ij}, where each observed value is weighted exponentially according to its Euclidean distance from input vector X and n is the number of patterns available in the input space.

According to Eqs. (7) and (8) the topology of a GRNN consists of (Fig. 12) the following:

- The input layer (input cells), which is fully connected to the pattern layer.
- The pattern layer which has one neuron for each pattern. It computes the pattern functions which is expressed in (8).
- The summation layer has two units N and D corresponding to numerator and denominator of Eq. (7), respectively. w_{ij}, the desired output of *jth* output neuron of *ith* training pattern, is multiplied with corresponding exponential term $h_i(\sigma, C_i)$, C_i is a center for *ith* training pattern X_i. Value of N for *jth* output neuron is computed by summing this multiplication for all training patterns. Denominator D is computed by considering $w_{ij} = 1$ in the procedure used for computing N.
- Finally the output unit divides N by D to provide the result.

6.3 Experimental Setup and Results

While searching for best combination of feature extractor and classifier, researchers have tried various combinations of the above-mentioned techniques. In most of the cases, due to lack of scale invariance property in the feature extraction techniques we have to scale the component to some fixed size. In most of the experiments so far, researchers have resized the recognizable components to size of 32×32 pixels and then the features were extracted from these scaled components.

It is obvious to get connected components that are very small due to residual noise or broken characters in the document, which are easily confused with other valid character. Hence, components having less than three rows or less than three columns are not considered for recognition purposes and are just discarded. Remaining components are then subjected to various feature extraction and classification methods. Further, it may be recalled that vowel modifier corresponding to /AA/ has very distinct aspect ratio and it appears quite often, because this symbol not only is used to depict vowel modifier corresponding to /AA/ sound but also appears as part of some basic consonants like /ga/, /sha/, /Na/ and also middle zone component that results from vowel modifier of /i/, /I/, /o/, /O/, /Au/, /Au/, after zone separation is of the same shape. Hence to speed up the recognition process we do not subject the connected components to feature extraction and classification only when it is vowel modifier of /AA/ and it is identified using its distinct aspect ratio.

Tables 2–5 give the details regarding experiments carried out by various researchers: (for further details readers are directed to the original published paper).

Table 2 Hu -moments and k-NN classifier [11]

Zone	No./type of symbols	Features	Classifier	Recognition accuracy
Middle	10 consonants	Hu-invariant moments up to order 7	K-nearest neighbor	67

Table 3 Data set details for EXPERIMENT 3 [16]

S. No.	Category	No. of fonts	Font sizes	Style
1	Consonants (37 symbols)	4	11–15	Regular, bold, italic
2	Independent vowels (5 symbols)	3	11–15	-do-
3	Conjuncts (67 symbols)	2	11–15	Regular, bold
4	Numerals (10 symbols)	3	11–15	Regular, bold italic

Table 4 DCT and nearest neighbor classifier

Zone	No./type of symbols	Features	Classifier	Recognition accuracy
Middle	10 numerals	80 zigzag DCT coefficients	1-NN classifier (Euclidean distance)	88.43%

Table 5 Wavelets and neural network

Zone	No./type of symbols	Features	Classifier	Recognition accuracy	Remarks
		EXPERIMENT 1			
Middle	10 numerals	256 low–low wavelet coefficients after first-level decomposition Wavelet: D-4	Multi-layer perceptron (error backpropagation) Input neuron: 256 Hidden neuron: 12 Output neurons: 10	93.75%	[13]
Middle	10 numerals	256 low–low wavelet coefficients after first-level decomposition Wavelet: D-4	RBF network Input neuron: 256 Hidden neuron: 200 Output neurons: 10	93.33%	
		EXPERIMENT 2			
Middle	10 numerals 34 consonants 3 conjuncts 5 vowels **total 52 classes**	256 low–low wavelet coefficients after first-level decomposition Wavelet: D-4	Multi-layer perceptron (error backpropagation) Input neuron: 256 Hidden neuron: 50 Output neurons: 10	94.46%	[14]
Lower	5 vowel modifiers	256 low–low Wavelet coefficients after first-level decomposition Wavelet: D-4	Multi-layer perceptron (error backpropagation) Input neuron: 256 Hidden neuron: 20 Output neurons: 4	96.32%	
		EXPERIMENT 3			
Middle	119 symbols of Consonants Vowels Conjuncts Numerals	256 low–low wavelet coefficients after first-level decomposition Wavelet: D-4	GRNN Input neuron: 256 Output neurons: 119	97.59%	[16]
			Nearest neighbor classifier	96.71%	

7 Text Generation

The ultimate goal of any OCR system is to generate editable text. It is clear from the description so far that from the OCR design proposed here Gujarati possesses some similar characteristics to the south Indian script and hence we have taken connected component-based approach [9]. Hence, the system recognizes connected components and it is clear from Table 2, Fig. 5 and description of Indian scripts in [19] that there need not be one-to-one mapping between connected components and *Akshara*

[19]. In Gujarati, one consonant may be made up of two or three connected components and in case of some *akshara* the number of connected components varies with font and quality of the paper and printing; /la/, /ha/, /Na/ are a few examples of such cases. Also zone boundary detection and segmentation due to that also result into segmentation of one connected component into many (Fig. 5). Hence to form an *Akshara* from its constituent connected components, it is necessary to find all the connected components of each and every *akshara*.

This is done using the script grammar [19]. It is obvious that components from two different syllables are similar and hence one component may be recognized as the other. This can lead the text generation engine to generate wrong sequence or non-deterministic state. Following are a few illustrations of it:

- The first part of /la/ is recognized as lower part of /ha/ or first component of /la/ and vice-versa.
- The rotated T like part of /la/ is confused with /na/ and vice versa.

Such confusions need to be removed before starting text generation by analyzing neighboring connected components.

As described in [19], Indian scripts have a well-defined script grammar which guides and controls the formation of *akshara*. We also follow simple automata-based technique to analyze connected components of a word and make clusters of connected component based on their relative positions, which correspond to different *aksharas* in that word. The final output is a sequence of Unicode characters for each of the clusters.

8 Post-processing

Post-processing of recognized text is not taken up so far for Gujarati OCR system. The required resources for the task are still under development. An N-Gram analysis-based post-processing is planned with an OCR-specific spell checker.

9 Conclusion

Gujarati script shares many common features with other Indo-Aryan scripts such as Devanagari, Bangla. However, the absence of *shirorekha* makes it different from all other Indo-Aryan scripts and hence document analysis and recognition techniques used for other scripts of this family cannot be readily applied to Gujarati. In fact, from OCR purposes Gujarati can be treated in the same lines as other South Indian scripts. The absence of *shirorekha* also poses additional challenges in segmentation.

Recognition of (C)CV combination results in large number of classifiers and hence zone boundary detection becomes mandatory. Methods used for detecting upper zone boundary in other Indic script depends heavily on existence of *shirorekha* and as Gujarati script is not written with *shirorekha* those techniques cannot be applied with the desired accuracy. Two different approaches have been described here to carry out this task. First one assumes that connected components of a word will be vertically aligned. It uses a simple mathematical concept of slope of a line and identifies zone boundaries. This method gives quite satisfactory results but the limitation of this and many other methods of zone boundary detection is that they assume straight line as a zone separator and it may result into an oversegmentation of some of the connected components in word/line. Hence, a dynamic programming-based approach to find zone boundary was also proposed by us in the past. But a thorough testing and optimization is needed to overcome the difficulties mentioned in Section 4.2.

Various feature extractors and classifiers have been tried for finding the best combination. MLP with backpropagation and RBF networks gave promising results, but they were tried for only a small subset of total number of classes. The main reasons for that were training takes a lot of time and there is no method to decide optimum number of hidden neurons in case of MLP. Hence, a large number of iterations are required to decide the number of hidden neurons and each iteration takes a lot of time. GRNN, being a single-pass neural network architecture, straightaway offers solution to the large training time and also eliminates number of iterations to decide the number of hidden units. It can be concluded that wavelet features with GRNN classifier gives best results reported so far. GRNN also reduces the off-line processing time of training the network. This chapter also gives some confusion resolution techniques and describes methods used to collect all the components of an *akshara* and generating text out of it.

Work is required to build a suitable post-processing engine and required linguistics resources for the same so that OCR can become usable. However, it can be concluded that despite a delayed start in this area, Gujarati OCR development has come a long way.

Acknowledgment Most of this work was supported by the grants from the Ministry of Communications and Information Technology, Government of India, under *Resource Center for Indian Language Technology Solutions* project and *Development Of Robust Document Analysis And Recognition System For Printed Indian Scripts* project.

References

1. Gandhi, M. K.: Hind Swaraj (Indian Homerule). Navjeevan Publishers
2. Gandhi, M. K.: Satya-na Prayogo–Atmakatha (My Experiments with Truth - Autobiography). Navjeevan Publishers
3. Dwyer, R.: The poetics of devotion: the Gujarati lyrics of Dayaram. (2000)
4. Mehta, S. Y., Dholakia, J.: Gujarati Script. Vishwabharat@TDIL **April**(2004)
5. Bansal, V., Sinha, R. M. K.: A Complete OCR for Printed Hindi Text in Devanagari Script. Proc. 6th ICDAR (2001)
6. Pal, U., Chaudhuri, B. B.: Automatic Separation of Machine-Printed and Hand-Written Text Lines. Proc. of 6th ICDAR (2001) 645–648
7. Pal, U., Belaid, A., Choisy, C.: Touching Numeral Segmentation Using Water Reservoir Concept. Pattern Recognition Letters **24** (2003) 261–272
8. Chaudhuri, B.B., Pal, U.: An OCR System to Read Two Indian Lanague Scripts : Bangla and Devanagari. Proc. 4th ICDAR (1997) 1011–1015

9. Negi, A., Bhagvati, C., Krishna, B.: An OCR System for Telugu. Proc. 4th ICDAR (1997) 1110–1114
10. Breuel, T.: Segmentation of Hand printed Letter Strings using a Dynamic Programming Algorithm. Proc. of 6th ICDAR (2001) 821–826
11. Antani, S., Agnihotri, L.: Gujarati Character Recognition. Proc. 6th ICDAR (1999) 418–421
12. Dholakia, J., Negi, A., S., Ramamohan: Zone Identification in Printed Gujarati Text. Proc. ICDAR (2005) 272–276
13. Ramamohan, S., Yajnik, A.: Gujarati Numeral Recognition Using Wavelets and Neural Network. IICAI (2005) 397–406
14. Yajnik, A., Rama Mohan, S.: Identification of Gujarati Characters Using Wavelets and Neural Networks. ISTED Conference on Artificial Intelligence and Soft Computing (2006) 150–155
15. Dholakia, J., Negi, A., Pathak, V. D.: A Novel Approach To Model Zone Separation Problem In Printed Gujarati Text And Its Solution by Application Of Dynamic Programming. Proc. Of International Conference of Advanced Computing and Communication (2007)
16. Dholakia, J., Yajnik, A., Negi, A.: Wavelet Feature Based Confusion Character Sets for Gujarati Script. ICCIMA (2007)
17. Bloomberg, D., Minka, T., Popat, K.: Document Image Decoding using Iterated Complete Path Search with Subsampled Heuristic Scoring. Proc. of 6th ICDAR (2001) 344–349
18. Popat, K.: Decoding of Text Lines in Grayscale Document Images. Proc. Of ICASSP (2001) 1513–1516
19. Negi, A., Murthy, K. N., Bhagvati, C.: Issues of Document Engineering in Indian Scripts and Telugu as a Case Study. Vivek (2003)
20. Gonzalez, R. C., Woods, R. E.: Digital Image Processing. Addison-Wesley (1993)
21. Pujari, A. K., Naidu, D. C., Sreenivasa Rao, M. Jingara, B. C.: An Adaptive Character Recognizer for Telugu Scripts using Multiresolution Analysis and Associative Memory. Image Vision Computing **22**(14) (2004) 1221–1227
22. Bhattacharya, U., Parui, S. K., Sridhar, M., Kimura, F.: Two-stage Recognition of Handwritten Bangla Alphanumeric Characters Using Neural Classifier. Proc. Of IICAI (2005) 1357–1376
23. Chaudhuri, A. R., Mandal A. K., Chaudhuri B. B.: Page Layout Analysis for Multilingual Indian Document. Proc. of LEC (2002) 24–32
24. Duda, O., Heart, P., Stork, D.: Pattern Classification. 2nd. edn. J. Wiley (2001)
25. Haykin, S.: Neural Networks, A Comprehensive Foundation. Pearson Education Asia (2002)
26. Specht, D. F.: A General Regression Neural Network. IEEE Transactions on Neural Networks **2**(6) (1991) 568–576
27. Kumar, V. B., Ramakrishnan, A. G.: Radial Basis Function and Subspace Approach For Printed Kannada Text Recognition. Proc. Of ICASSP **5** (2004) 321–324
28. Amrouche, A., Rouvaen, J. M.: Efficient System for Speech Recognition using General Regression Neural Network. International Journal Of Intelligent Technology **1** (2) (2006) 183–189
29. Amrouche, A., Rouvaen,J. M.: Arabic Isolated Word Recognition Using General Regression Neural Network. Proc. of the 46th IEEE International Midwest Symposium on Circuits and Systems **2** (2003) 689–692.
30. Huang, L., Huang, X.: Multi Resolution Recognition Of Off line Handwritten Chinese Characters With Wavelet Transform. Proc. 6th ICDAR (2001) 631–634
31. http://www.omniglot.com
32. Pal, U., Chaudhuri, B. B.: Automatic Separation of Machine-Printed and Hand-Written Text Lines Proc. 6th ICDAR (1999) 645–648
33. Wang, K. Y., Casey, R. G., Wahl, F. M.: Document Analysis System. IBM J. Res. Development **26** (1982) 647–656

Design of a Bilingual Kannada–English OCR

R.S. Umesh, Peeta Basa Pati and A.G. Ramakrishnan

Abstract India is a land of many languages and consequently one often encounters documents that contain elements in multiple languages and scripts. This chapter presents an approach towards designing a bilingual OCR that can process documents containing both English and Kannada scripts which are used by the Kannada language of the southern Indian state of Karnataka. We report an efficient script identification scheme for discriminating Kannada from Roman script. We also propose a novel segmentation and recognition scheme for Kannada, which could possibly be applied to many other Indian languages as well.

1 Introduction

India is a multilingual nation and many of its people communicate in multiple languages. There is often a mix of English or the language of a neighbouring state with the local language. This is also true of many printed documents such as forms, school text books, certificates and official orders of the state or central governments. Thus, for an OCR to be widely useful in the Indian milieu, we feel that it must necessarily be at least bilingual, capable of handling both the regional language and English. Interestingly, many a times, the script changes at the level of the word within the same sentence or a text line in such printed documents. This chapter, therefore, reports an approach for a bilingual OCR that can recognize both Kannada and English words from the same printed document.

In general, the design of a bilingual OCR might proceed by first segmenting the words from the document image, after the necessary initial steps of noise cleaning, page layout analysis and text segmentation. After identifying the script of a word, the characters of the word may be recognized using a single OCR engine that

R.S. Umesh (✉)
Department of Electrical Engineering, Indian Institute of Science, Bangalore 560 012, India

V. Govindaraju, S. Setlur (eds.), *Guide to OCR for Indic Scripts*, Advances in Pattern Recognition, DOI 10.1007/978-1-84800-330-9_5,

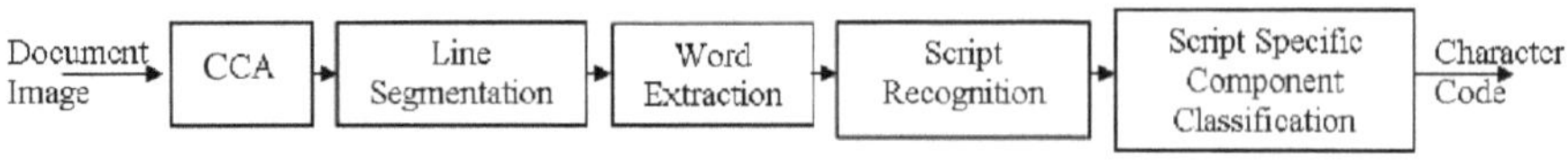

Fig. 1 A schematic of the proposed bilingual Kannada–English OCR

employs two sets of training samples, one for English and the other for the Indian script. In our case, the idea is to recognize the script of each word, and accordingly send it to the Kannada or English recognition engine, as appropriate. This is because, the technology of English OCR is well developed and one could easily use a commercially available OCR for English. Figure 1 shows a schematic of our system.

Here, we report an efficient script recognition scheme that is more than 99% accurate in discriminating Kannada from Roman. We also propose a novel segmentation and recognition scheme for Kannada, which could possibly be applied to many other Indian languages as well.

2 Kannada Script

Kannada is the official language of the south Indian state of Karnataka. It has its own script derived from Bramhi script. Modern Kannada alphabet has a base set of 52 characters, comprising 16 vowels (called as swaragalu) and 36 consonants (vyanjanagalu). There are two more consonants used in old Kannada, namely lla and rra, taking the total number of consonants to 38. Further, there are consonant modifiers (vattaksharas or conjuncts) and vowel modifiers. The number of these modifiers is the same as that of base characters, namely 52. Compound characters called aksharas are formed by graphically combining the symbols corresponding to consonants, consonant modifiers and/or vowel modifiers using well-defined rules of combination. The script has its own numerals too. In addition to the base set of characters and numerals, the script includes special symbols used in poetry, shlokas (prayer chants), Kannada grammar. Thus, the number of possible consonant–vowel combination aksharas is $38 \times 16 = 608$. Similarly, the number of possible consonant–consonant–vowel aksharas is $38 \times 38 \times 16 = 23104$. While designing a character recognition system, if we consider each akshara as a separate class, the number of classes becomes prohibitively high. However, in Kannada, consonant modifiers and some of the vowel modifiers are mostly printed separately from the base character. So, if we treat each connected component as a different class, the number of classes in recognition can be reduced by a great extent. Figure 2 shows the vowels, consonants, all the consonant–vowel combinations and some of the consonant–consonant–vowel aksharas of the letter ka, all the conjuncts and the Kannada numerals.

3 Segmentation

The task of segmenting a document image into text and non-text, lines, words and eventually into individual characters is of fundamental importance for optical

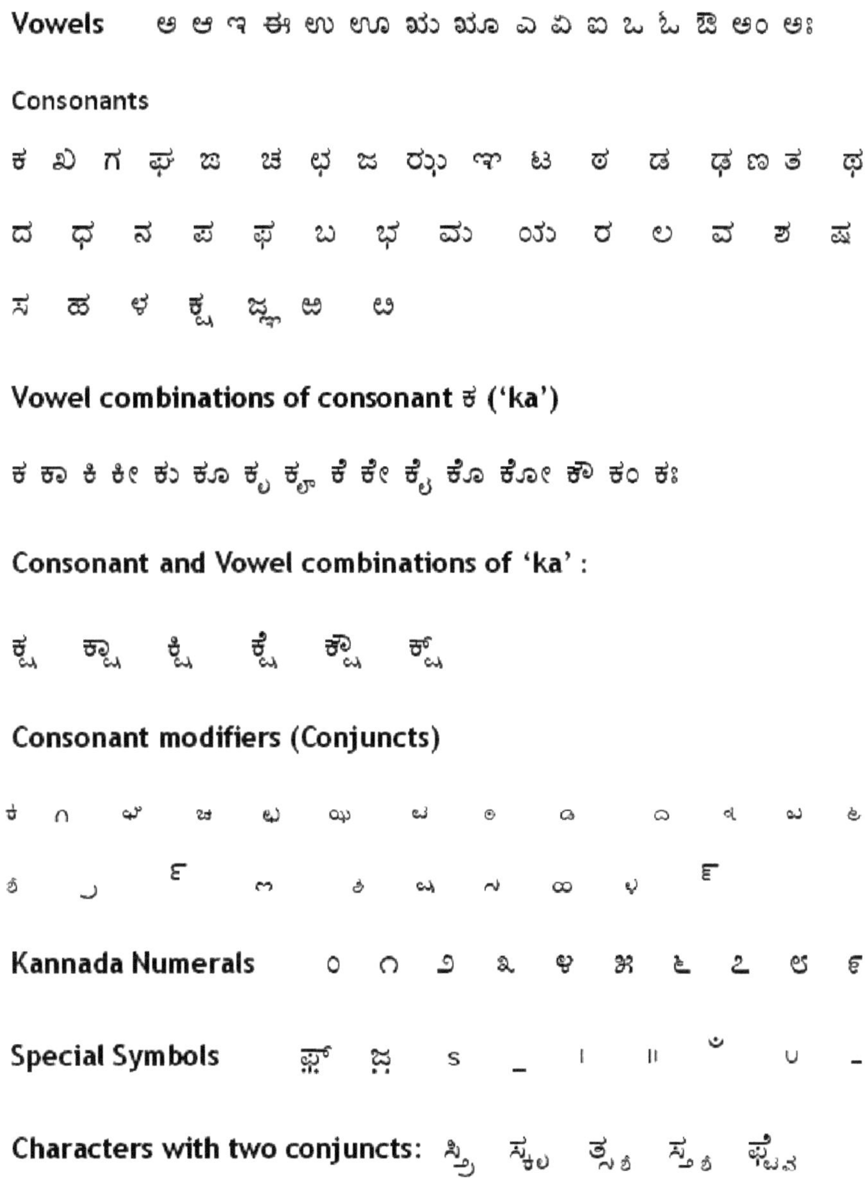

Fig. 2 Kannada character set

character recognition. This chapter does not address the problem of separation of text from non-text. The input to this scheme is the bounding box information of various independent connected components in the skew-corrected, de-noised, component-labelled image. We propose a set-theoretic approach based on the bounding box information for segmenting the text lines from the document image.

This method is distinct from the ones proposed is [1, 2] which are based on the horizontal projection profiles.

3.1 Line Segmentation Based on Connected Components

This can be seen as the task of identifying unique non-intersecting sets of image components that form various text lines. Every component in the image needs to belong to only one text line. Figure 3 shows two text lines of a Kannada document using only the bounding boxes of the connected components. Rows 1, 2, 3 and 4 denote particular rows of pixels. Labels a, b, c, etc. denote bounding boxes of specific connected components.

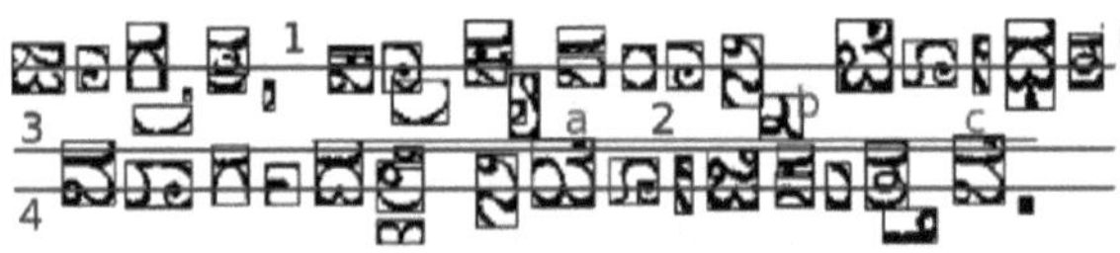

Fig. 3 Two text lines of a Kannada document. The bounding boxes of some of the connected components of successive lines intersect the same scan line, preventing line segmentation using horizontal projection

To detect and delineate text lines, we consider all the connected components intersected by each horizontal scan line. We compute the inter-component distances and look for close neighbours. If the distances of close neighbours are below a predefined threshold, then the set of intersected components is considered to belong to the same text line. Thus, the components intersected by scan lines 1 and 4 in Fig. 3 form distinct text lines, while those intersected by scan line 2, namely *a*, *b* and *c* do not, since they lie far spread apart. Similarly, scan line 3 also fails this test. At the end of this procedure, we are left with disjoint sets of components, and their spans (heights) decide the extent of these lines. A few isolated, left out components either fall within the span of one of the lines already found, or are assigned to the line containing their nearest component. Figure 4 presents the proposed line segmentation algorithm schematically. Let the labelled image be denoted as $L_{m \times n}$. Let the components in L be denoted by c_i, $i = 1 \ldots p$. Let each pixel row of L be denoted by $R_j, j = 1 \ldots m$. Then, set-theoretic segmentation can be described by the following steps:

- Form $S_j = \{c_i | c_i \cap R_j \neq \phi\}$, $j = 1 \ldots m$, $i = 1 \ldots p$ (form sets of components intersected by each pixel row)
- If $S_j \subset S_k$, set $S_j = \phi$,j, $k = 1 \ldots m, j \neq k$ (remove proper subsets of components; their supersets contain the same information)
- $\forall S_j \neq \phi, j = 1 \ldots m$ if $F(S_j,\gamma) =$ FALSE, $S_j = \phi$. F is a binary function based on the inter-component distances of elements of S_j and a threshold γ

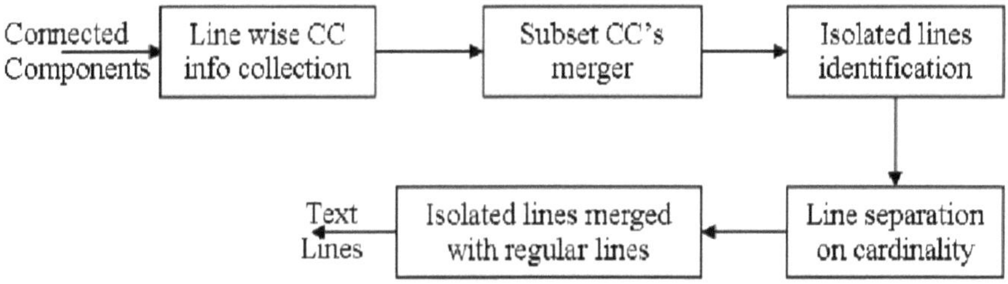

Fig. 4 A schematic of the proposed line segmentation algorithm

- $\forall S_j \neq \phi$ if $S_j \cap S_k \neq \phi,\ j,\ k = 1 \ldots m,\ j \neq k,\ and\ (S_j - S_k) \cap S_i = \phi,\ \forall i \neq k,\ S_j = \phi$ (merge sets that have some common components and the rest, unique components)
- $\forall c_k \in \left\{\{c_i, i = 1 \ldots p\} - \{\bigcup_{j=1}^{m} S_j\}\right\}$ (components not associated with any of the sets), find $min\|c_k - c_l\|,\ c_l \in \left\{\bigcup_{j=1}^{m} S_j\right\}$. Let the minimum occur at c_q. If $c_q \in S_t$, then $c_k \in S_t$ (associate the component with the set containing its nearest connected component)
- $S_k \neq \phi,\ k = 1 \ldots m$ will now be disjoint sets of components. Each set comprises components that form a text line

3.2 Word and Character Segmentation

Following line segmentation, one normally obtains information on the columns, which do not pass through any bounding box on a given line. By studying the distribution of the spacing information so obtained from all the lines of the document, one can threshold the distances to obtain word and character separation information.

However, we propose an alternative weighted distance spacing measurement which may give better results in case of documents containing multiple font sizes. Whenever the font size increases, so do the word and character spacing. So, if the spacing between any two adjacent components is weighted as a function of the sizes of the components across the gap (average of heights), one may obtain a more meaningful information about the spacing. This is effectively performed by using the bounding box information we employed for line segmentation. Thus, it turns out to be an additional benefit of using connected components to start with.

4 Script Recognition

Our recognition mechanism is based on separate engines for Kannada and English. Thus, once the document is segmented into text lines, words and components, we perform script recognition. Lot of research has been reported on script recognition

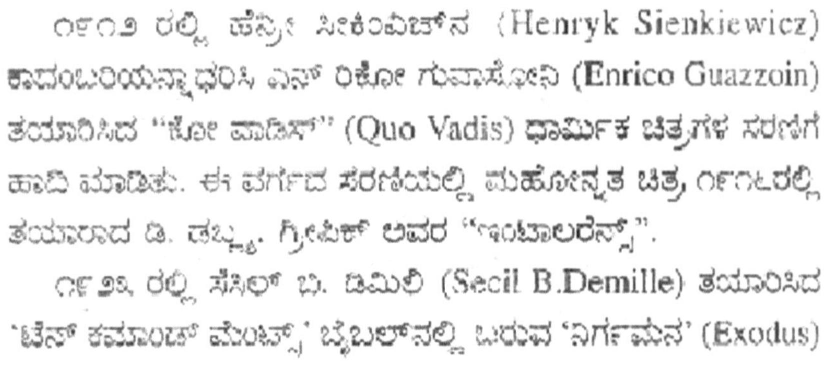

Fig. 5 Sample bi-script document showing interspersed Kannada and English words, necessitating script recognition at the word level

at a paragraph/block or line level. While the former assumes that a full document page is of the same script, the latter imagines documents to contain text from multiple scripts but changing only at the level of the line. Though the latter is a realistic assumption in some cases, many Indian language documents have the script changing from one word to the next. In Fig. 5, we show a bi-script document, where the presence of interspersed English words in a Kannada document is clearly seen.

Script identification acts as a preliminary level of filtering to reduce the search complexity. Here, efficacy of various combinations of two different features and three different classifiers is evaluated for the bi-script recognition task. An initial design of a filter bank that generates good accuracy for various script identification tasks, followed by a feature selection algorithm to choose the minimal best subset of these features to deliver the best output is reported.

4.1 Gabor and DCT-Based Identification

Pati [3] studied the structural properties of 11 Indian scripts before designing an identifier for these scripts. Based on that study, we decided to employ features that are both frequency and direction sensitive. This, in our opinion, would be best able to discriminate between the scripts. Thus, we employ a multi-channel filter bank, using Gabor functions [4, 5]. We have used a radial frequency bandwidth of one octave. This is because, the cortical cells in the visual cortex V1 of primates are observed to have that bandwidth and the coding of natural images is best attained at this bandwidth [6]. An angular bandwidth of 30° is chosen for this experiment. After a careful evaluation of the various radial frequencies and angles for their usefulness for this application [4], we decided to use three radial frequencies and six angles. The radial frequencies chosen are 0.125, 0.25 and 0.5 rads, while 0°, 30°, 60°, 90°, 120° and 150° are the angles chosen.

Discrete cosine transform (DCT) concentrates the information content in relatively fewer coefficients. For natural signals and images, the data compaction of DCT is close to that of the optimal KL transform. But unlike KLT, DCT is not dependent on the data. The symmetry of its transform matrix is exploited to obtain efficient hardware and software implementations [7]. Most image and video coders employ DCT. It has also been employed for other applications such as pitch modification for speech synthesis [8]. Pati [9] has used DCT coefficients for machine recognition of printed Odiya characters.

For an image f(x,y), the DCT coefficient matrix F(u,v) is given by

$$F(u,v) = \sum_{i=0}^{M-1} \sum_{j=0}^{N-1} f(x,y) \cos\left(\frac{\pi u(2x+1)}{2M}\right) \cos\left(\frac{\pi v(2y+1)}{2N}\right)$$

where M and N are the number of rows and columns of the image matrix; u and v are the frequency indices along the x- and y-directions, respectively. Figure 6(a) and (b) demonstrates the feature extraction mechanisms using Gabor and DCT functions for recognizing Roman from the Kannada script.

We have used three different classifiers to decide about the script of the test words: (i) the nearest neighbour classifier (NNC), (ii) linear discriminant classifier (LDC) and (iii) the support vector machines (SVMs). Nearest neighbour has been a standard and time-tested classifier. This classifier has proven to deliver good output, when we have a class representative training set. Here, Euclidean distance of the test pattern is evaluated in the feature space, with each of the training patterns. The class value of the nearest neighbour is assigned to the test pattern. A linear discriminant function partitions the feature space using a hyperplane. The two sides of this plane represent the two classes. The class value of the test pattern is decided based on which side of the plane it lies.

Among the discriminant approaches for classification, the most recent is the support vector machine [10], where the optimal hyperplane decides the separation between individual classes of patterns. The creation of a unique model to represent a class, derived by training the model with prototypes of each class, aids in maximization of the correct classification rate. We have used the SVMTorch – II, a toolbox designed and developed by Collobert and Bengio [11]. Of the various kernel functions this toolbox provides, we have used the Gaussian function with the total variance of the data set, in a case-by-case basis, chosen as the standard deviation of the kernel function.

4.2 Results of Script Identification

Images are scanned from bi-script documents, such as books, newspapers and magazines. Variations in printing style and size are ensured. About 100 scanned pages are segmented by an automated process [9]. From this collection of word images,

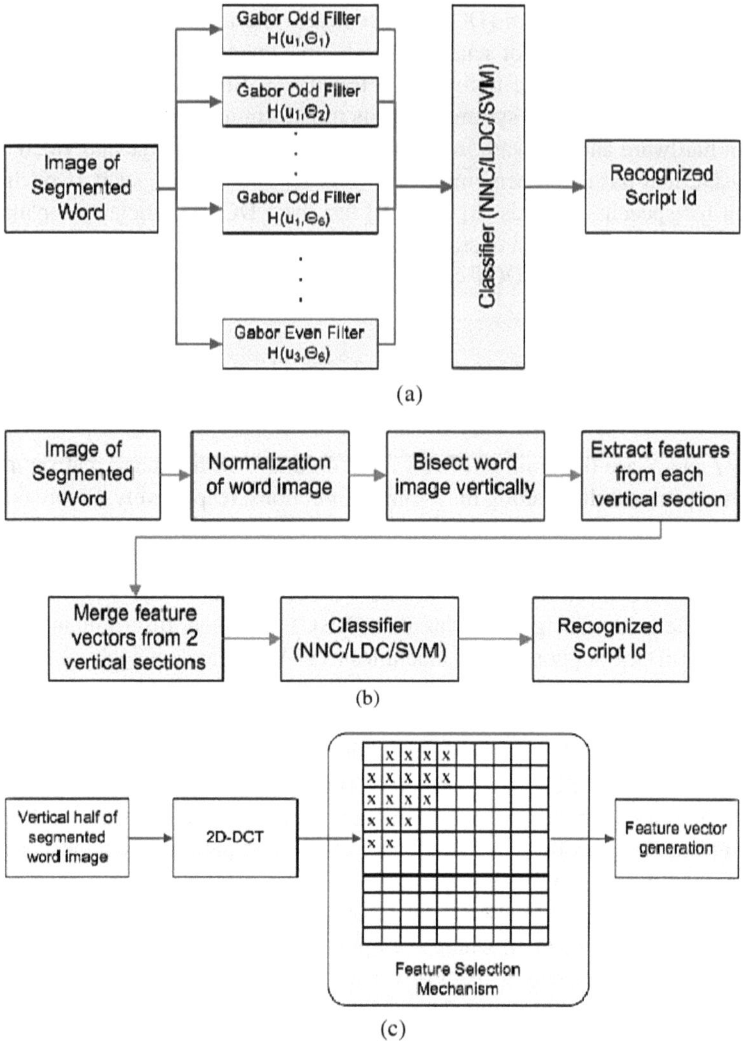

Fig. 6 Extraction of feature vectors from word images for script recognition: (**a**) shows the extraction of Gabor features, while (**b**) demonstrates that of DCT features. (**c**) indicates those DCT coefficients that are included as part of the feature vector, to make the dimension same as that of Gabor

20,000 distinct words each are selected for both Kannada and English. Of these, 7000 are used for training and the balance 13,000 word images are used for testing.

The performance is presented in percentage (%), which gives the average recognition accuracy for both the involved scripts. Table 1 presents the results separating Roman from Kannada script with different feature–classifier combinations. The recognition rate we have achieved equals or exceeds 99% with Gabor transform

Table 1 The recognition accuracies of the various feature–classifier combinations for the bi-script case involving English and Kannada words

GT-NNC	GT-LDC	GT-SVM	DCT-NNC	DCT-LDC	DCT-SVM
99.9	99.0	99.7	98.2	90.3	97.5

features for any classifier. The best result of 99.9% is obtained with the nearest neighbour classifier.

5 Component Classification

5.1 Introduction

The problem of recognizing printed Kannada characters has been studied in [1, 2]. As we find, it is one of being able to distinguish data from a large number of classes, typically around 450. This we find is the case with many Indian scripts [12]. The problem of classifying data from a large number of classes has been studied in [13]. The study shows a steep increase in computational costs with increase in the number of classes. Hence, most attempted solutions reduce the classes one needs to distinguish, by breaking characters into smaller subunits, usually using a script-dependent segmentation technique [1, 2]. Each subunit is individually recognized, and a conclusion is drawn about the character based on the recognized subunits. However, the rules for segmenting the characters are usually script specific, and entail many assumptions. This makes it hard to adapt any such technique to other scripts. In what follows, we report a novel and effective strategy to solve this problem and discuss its merits and limitations. In Kannada and many other Indian scripts, a character can contain more than one eight-connected independent image components (which we shall refer to as "components"). In this study, we report only about component classification, since it plays a central role in the whole recognition task. Recognition of characters from components is an important task that may need considerable attention but is not the focus of this study.

The proposed strategy is based on the fundamental observation that distinct component classes differ usually either in the number or kind of strokes or junctions they are composed of, or in the nature of stroke interconnections. In this study, we cast this inherent property into a graph-theoretic framework by associating thinned (single pixel wide) form of each component with a planar graph. The strokes are mapped to the edges of the graph, and the stroke junctions are mapped to vertices. A component can thus be associated with the incidence matrix of its graph representation. We report here our study on how this mapping can be used for the task of component classification.

We introduce our graph-based processing of components through the illustration in Fig. 7, which depicts a planar graph with $\{a,b,c,d\}$ as vertices and $\{1,2,3,4,5,6\}$ as edges. The signed incidence matrix for the graph is given by the centre part of the

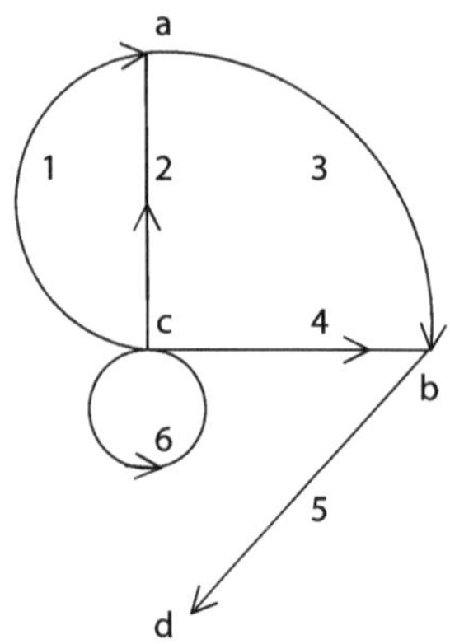

	a	b	c	d	hp	
1	1	0	−1	0	0	2
2	1	0	−1	0	0	2
3	−1	1	0	0	0	2
4	0	1	−1	0	0	2
5	0	−1	0	1	0	2
6	0	0	1	0	1	1
vp	1	1	−2	1		
	3	3	4	1		

Fig. 7 A sample graph and its signed incidence matrix

table in Fig. 7. We adopt a systematic way to assign directions to edges. If the edge has a horizontal alignment, we assign the left end with a positive sign. Similarly, a vertically aligned edge has a negative sign associated with the lower end. When an edge has a mix of both the alignments, we give priority to the alignment that has a larger distance. In case of equal alignments in both the directions, we give preference to the height over width. Assigning directions to the loops is based on the relative position of the vertex with respect to the loop (left/right or above/below, etc.). The column named hp denotes the sum of the entries of the corresponding row in incidence matrix. The final column gives the sum of the absolute values of the row entries. Similarly, the row vp denotes the sum of the corresponding column entries of the incidence matrix, whereas the last row gives the degrees of the vertices (sum of absolute values of column entries). Later, we use these entities to represent a component.

5.2 Graph Representations for Components

Some OCRs use thinned versions (single pixel width representations) of components in classification, since it renders the task robust to font thickness and style variations. In the proposed scheme, we use thinning to obtain information about junctions and strokes in the character.

A 2D convolution of the binary image of a thinned component with a 3×3 mask of ones yields different values at junctions and edges. Pixels anywhere on any edge get a value of 3; pixels that define terminal vertices get a value of 2 and pixels that belong to vertices of order 3 and higher get a value above 3. Thus, one can segregate edges from vertices and map the component to a planar graph. We adopt a systematic way to assign directions to edges and associate a signed incidence matrix with the component.

We can expect some of the components belonging to different classes to have same incidence matrices. Also, due to font variations, we can expect a single

Table 2. Statistics of various kinds of objects collected from 113 scanned Kannada document pages

Object kind	1	2	3	4
Number of samples (%)	1781 (1.5)	4958 (4.3)	33806 (29.3)	74661 (64.8)

component class to have multiple graph representations. Besides, visually similar looking components could end up having very different matrix representations. Before we proceed further, we see whether the number of edges and vertices in the graph representation of components alone can be used to subdivide the component classes.

This segregation leads to four important categories of character components, which we call "object kind i", $i = 1 \ldots 4$. These categories denote those components which can be mapped to a point ($i = 1$), closed loops ($i = 2$), simple edges joining two vertices ($i = 3$) and objects with more than one edge/vertex ($i = 4$), respectively. It is interesting to know the prevalence of each of these categories in a general document of a script. Such an analysis is shown for Kannada script in Table 2, wherein the number of components of various kinds found in 113 images obtained from three different books scanned at 300 dpi is shown in relative and absolute terms. Observe that about 30% of the samples were simple edges connecting two terminal vertices. It is interesting to note that if we segregate the learning process into three distinct branches (excluding objects which map to a single point), based on the kind of object we are dealing with, we would have already achieved one level of simplification of the problem we started with (one of classifying from about 450 classes). Thus, we begin to see the advantages of simple graph-based features that we have defined. However, this still leaves us with the major task of segregating complex objects of kind 4, which form the major chunk of the data we get (nearly 65%). The rest of the chapter is dedicated to solve this problem.

Before obtaining incidence matrices, we need to order the edges and vertices in a manner that remains invariant under normal font variations. However, since vectors do not have a natural ordering, any spatial ordering scheme can produce a different incidence matrix for very small changes in the position of the vertices or edges. To circumvent this problem, we order the edges based on their relative lengths. However, since vertices do not have such an attribute, we resort to the notion of "vertex significance", wherein we consider the sum of the lengths of the edges incident at a vertex as an attribute to rank the vertex, i.e. a vertex at which longer and/or more edges are incident has a higher ranking than the vertex with fewer and/or shorter edges. An incident matrix with edges and vertices ordered in this manner yields a robust representation for a component under normal font variations. Ties can either be broken arbitrarily (as we did), or systematically, based on factors like position. We next explore ways in which we can use the incidence matrix information for the task of classification.

Every classification scheme inherently uses a distance measure to compare patterns and this plays a decisive role in determining classification efficiency. We build such a notion from the signed incidence matrices.

5.3 Distance Measures

The area of graph and sub-graph matching addresses the problem we are faced with, and has been a subject of intense study [14]. However, we report a simple, yet useful strategy for this purpose. We resort to a few discrete, qualitative notion of distance, instead of quantitative ones. It is needless to say that this is not the best we can do with the information we have.

Let I and I_u be the signed and the unsigned incidence matrices, respectively, of a component. The rows of I are ordered in the descending order of relative edge lengths. The columns of I are stored in the rank of "vertex significance". From the graph, we collect the information in four separate row vectors, which we call R_i, $i = 1 \dots 4$ and define as follows:

- $R_1 = [no.ofedges \quad no.ofvertices]$
- $R_2 = [Eulerno. \quad no.ofnonzeroelementsinI]$
- $R_3 = [vert.proj.ofI_u \quad horz.proj.ofI_u]$
- $R_4 = [vert.proj.ofI \quad horz.proj.ofI]$

where "vert proj" and "horz proj" stand for vertical and horizontal projections, respectively, as defined in the context of Fig. 7.

Clearly, R_1 and R_2 contain information about the gross features of the graph. R_3 contains partial information from the unsigned incidence matrix I_u and R_4 contains partial information from the signed incidence matrix in a condensed form.

Given two representations R_i^m and R_i^n $i = 1 \dots 4$, for samples numbered m and n, we define the qualitative distance between them as follows:

– if $R_i^m = R_i^n$ *for* $i = 1 \dots j$, then they are said to *match at level j*
– if $R_1^m \neq R_1^n$, then they are said to be *unrelated*

Based on this notion of distance, we define the kinds of relationships the various component classes may develop, from the observations of graph representations of the training samples. Let the training samples belong to classes C_k, $k = 1,2 \dots w$. Let $R_i^{a,m}$, $m = 1 \dots, p$ and $R_i^{b,n}$, $n = 1 \dots, q$, $i = 1 \dots 4$ be the representations of training samples (p and q in numbers) associated with classes C_a and C_b, respectively:

– for some samples r and s, if $R_i^{a,r} = R_i^{b,s} \forall i$, and $a \neq b$, then, C_a and C_b are said to be in *conflict at level 4*

- for some samples r and s, if $R_i^{a,r} = R_i^{b,s}$, $i = 1,2,3$ *and* $i \neq 4$, and $a \neq b$, then C_a and C_b are said to be in *conflict at level 3* (similarly, we can define *conflicts at levels 2 and 1*)
- classes in conflict are said to be *related*
- if for no samples r and s, $R_1^{a,r} = R_1^{b,s}$, then classes C_a and C_b are said to be *unrelated*
- for some samples r and s, if $R_i^{a,r} = R_i^{a,s}$, $i = 1 \ldots j < 4$ and $R_{j+1}^{a,r} \neq R_{j+1}^{a,s}$, then r and s are *equivalent representations of class C_a up to level j*

Equipped with these qualitative distance measures between patterns and classes, we proceed with the classification strategies we use.

5.4 Classification Strategy

The classification strategy we have adopted combines both deterministic and probabilistic decision making. First, using training samples, we try to learn the various *conflicts* among classes and *equivalent representations* for every class. After this learning, given a test pattern, we use the graph features R_i to see if we can assign a unique class label. In case of *conflicts*, this will not be possible. However, in this process of finding a unique class label, the graph-based features effectively narrow down the bigger classification task into a smaller one of classifying a sample to one among the conflicting classes. From here, we use probabilistic classification to assign a label to the test pattern. The important point to observe here is the switch to conflict resolution can happen at any level (from 1 to 4), since conflicts can be defined at various levels. Usually this will be dictated by certain trade-offs between accuracy and computational cost, as we show later. The classifier we use to resolve conflicts is the support vector machine (SVM) [15]. Though it is not mandatory to use SVMs, their utility in character recognition has been well documented [2, 13]. We have chosen RBF kernel, and the SVM formulation "support vector classification" for multi-class classification, for reasons elaborated in [13, 15].

5.5 Training

During learning, we build a table of representations that can guide us through the deterministic phase of classification. The table is grown by incrementally adding every new representation that we come across in the training set. A representation here denotes values of R_i, $i = 1 \ldots 4$ along with the class label. Every class will retain only its unique representations in the table. All *conflicts* and *equivalent representations* will be stored in the table. We also keep a count of repetitions of all representations. These can be used to obtain estimates of prior probabilities of equivalent representations of a particular class and also the prior probabilities of a particular representation belonging to conflicting classes, which can be used later for prediction.

Also, we collect features (moment and 2D spline) of components belonging to different classes in different files. Thus, we generate as many feature files as the number of classes. For every conflict at every level, we use features from conflicting classes to build an SVM classifier, e.g. suppose we find components from three different classes are in conflict at level 1 (share the same representation, say $R_1(m)$). They can also be in conflict again at level 1 with some other $R_1(n)$. Each of these is a distinct conflict. For each such conflict at each level, we build a separate SVM classifier, leading to a huge chest of classifiers. We maintain a table to help us pick the right classifier when a conflict arises during testing. We call this as classifier pointer table. We are now equipped to tackle any conflict that arises during testing.

5.6 Prediction

Figure 8 shows a schematic of the classification strategy for the components. Given a test pattern, we obtain its graph representation and look up in the representation table to find whether such a representation exists in it (a simple string comparison with existing representations). If a unique match is found (no conflicts), we decide that the test pattern belongs to the corresponding class. This classification is completely deterministic and dictated by the graph structure.

In case of conflicts, we use the classifier specifically trained with samples from the conflicting classes at the highest level of representation, to classify the pattern, e.g. given a test pattern, if it so happens that we do not find a match for R_4 of the test pattern in the representation table, but find that conflicts exist at level 3, then it is obvious that conflict exists at levels 2 and 1 also (due to the very nature by which the representation table is generated). Though we can choose a classifier trained to resolve conflicts at any of the levels 1, 2 or 3, we choose the classifier trained to resolve conflicts at level 3, i.e. we narrow down the conflicts as much as possible using the graph-based representation. This, as we show later, reduces the computational complexity by a great extent compared to trying to resolve conflicts at lower levels. When we do not find any match based even at level 1 (i.e. the sample is *unrelated* to any training data), we can declare that the test pattern does not belong to any of the given classes. Thus, this scheme provides an opportunity for decision making at many levels.

5.7 Experiments, Results and Discussion

5.7.1 Data Sets

Synthetic Data Set: This data set contains computer-generated character components, digits and punctuations from 21 different Kannada fonts, including a few decorative ones. The font size is varied in the range 50–100 in steps of 10 and the characters are printed at 100 dpi. A total of 446 component classes are found in the

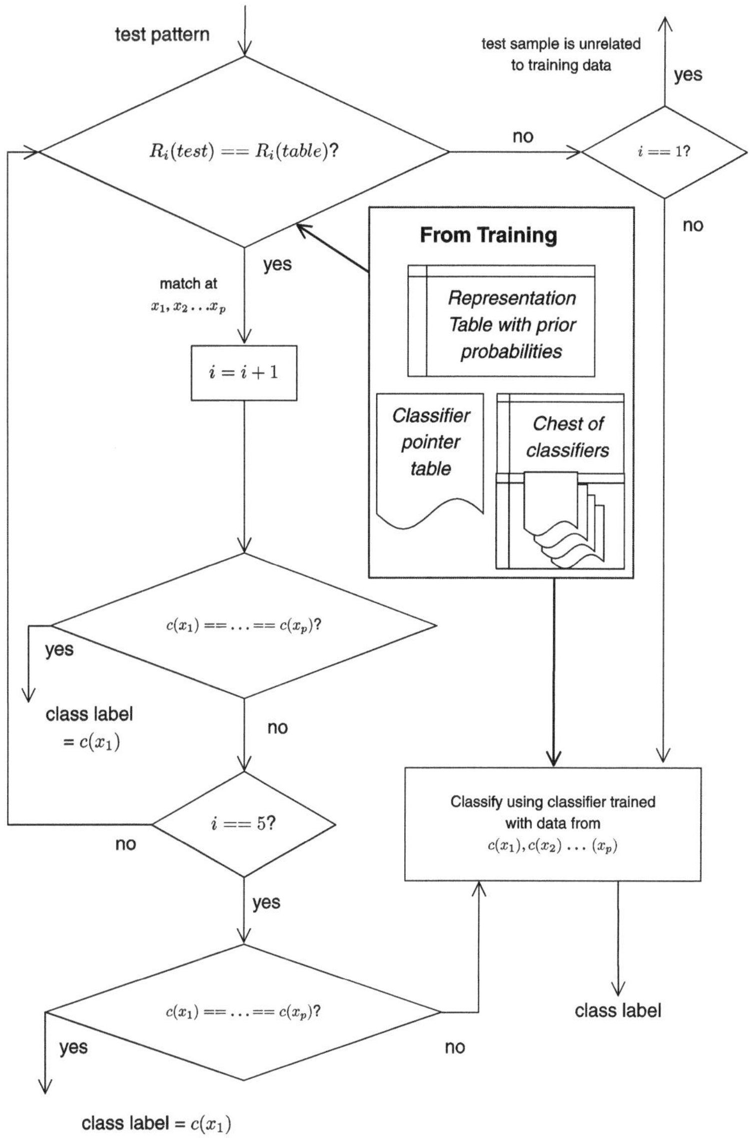

Fig. 8 The strategy for classifying the connected components. x_i denotes the ith entry in the representation table and $C(x_i)$ denotes its class label

whole script, including the ones in multiple-component characters. We have 33,552 samples in all, providing, on an average, about 75 samples for each class. The factors that influenced the choice of this data set are font shape and size variations and the availability of samples from all possible components in fairly uniform numbers. The size variation in the data set mimics the usual sizes of components in documents scanned at 300 dpi and higher.

Table 3 Statistics regarding objects of kind 4 in synthetic and real data sets. Values of component height and width are given in number of pixels

	Comp. ht.	Comp. wd.	No. of test samples/class
Synthetic data set (406 classes, 26,851 samples)			
Mean	55.4	76.4	66
Std	71.1	34.6	45
Real data set (281 classes, 50,316 samples)			
Mean	48.9	47.6	179
Std	14.0	18.0	579

Real Data Set: This data set contains 50,316 objects of kind 4, obtained from three different books with pages randomly chosen from scans performed at 300 and 600 dpi. The components in this data set belong to 281 classes, leading to around 179 training samples per class.

Table 3 shows the composition of the synthetic and real data sets. While the real data set contains only objects of kind 4, the synthetic data set contains components of every kind. However, Table 3 shows information regarding only the objects of kind 4 in both the data sets, obtained after extracting bounding boxes of the components. As can be observed, the real data set has fewer classes but more average samples per class than the synthetic data set.

Figure 9 shows the histogram of the number of classes as a function of the logarithm of the number of samples per class. We observe that a large number of classes in the synthetic data set (about 180) have more or less similar number of examples (about 90). We can also observe that there are few classes that have less samples per class. But, it is evident that the synthetic data set is better than the real data set in representing various classes. From Fig. 9b, we see that there are huge variations in the number of samples per class. This is substantiated by the figures in Table 3, where the standard deviation is higher than the mean. We observe that more than half the classes have far fewer samples per class than the synthetic data set, while a few classes had too many, leading us to conclude that this real data set is biased. All the results that we present in this section need to be interpreted taking into account this observed bias. For this reason, we believe that the results from the synthetic data set better represent the general properties of the proposed scheme.

5.7.2 Features for SVM Classifiers

We choose features that do not require image scaling. Thus, we use normalized central moment features [16] and 2D least-squared B-spline features [17]. Though moment features have been extensively studied and used, the use of 2D B-splines

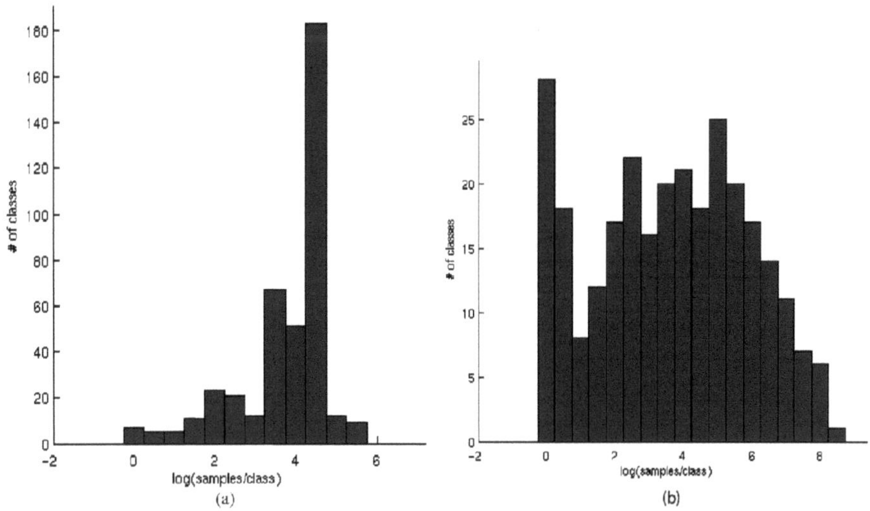

Fig. 9 Statistics on the number of samples per class in the data sets. x-axis: ln(#samples/class), y-axis: no. of classes. (a) synthetic data set and (b) real data set

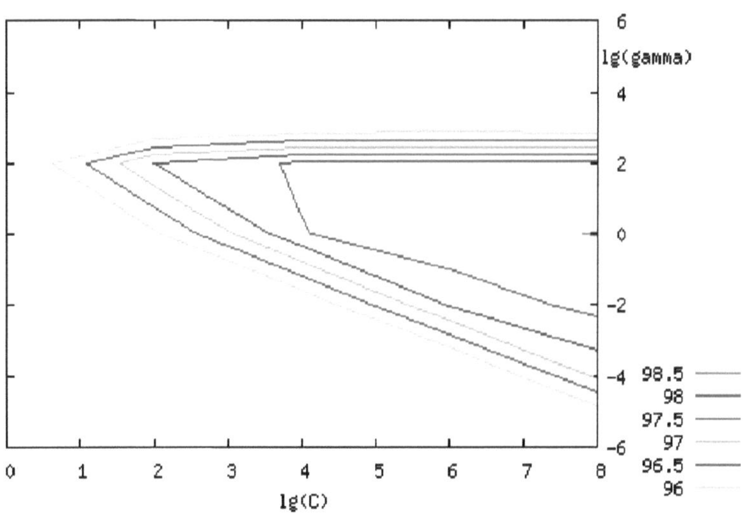

Fig. 10 Cross-validation results obtained using a multi-class SVM (RBF kernel) for objects of kind 4, with 25 2D-spline features. The log scales of the axes are in base 2 (see also Plate 1 on page 315 in the Color Plate Section)

for this purpose has received relatively little attention. Since these are solutions to sets of linear equations, they are not computationally very expensive. Our limited comparative studies seem to show that 2D least-squared B-spline coefficients can be effectively used as features for component recognition. Figure 10 shows the eight-fold cross-validation results on the synthetic data set obtained from libsvm [15] using an RBF kernel with 25 B-spline features on objects of kind 4.

5.7.3 Pre-processing

Real OCR data can have holes in edge strokes as a result of noise and binarization. Thinning is extremely sensitive to the presence of holes. If spurious holes are not filled, they can lead to unwanted thinned characters, and thereby to wrong graphs. This, by far, seems to be the biggest challenge to graph-based representation of noisy components. A good morphological pre-processing step can probably mitigate this problem to a great extent. We found morphological majority, followed by spurring to be sufficient to overcome most of these effects in synthetic data. However, we find that this may not be sufficient to tackle effects of noise in real data. It is needless to say that the efficacy of the proposed method would improve by adding more sophisticated morphological preprocessing and script-specific processing steps that can render graph representations robust to noise and font variations.

5.7.4 Results and Discussions

We segregated the synthetic data set into the four kinds of objects discussed in Section 5.2. The first column of Table 4 gives details regarding the components of various kinds in the synthetic database. The term without brackets is the object kind. The first term in brackets is the number of classes contributing to this object kind and the second term in brackets is the number of samples of the particular object kind found in this database and the last term in brackets gives the proportion of the particular kind of object in the database. Note that a single class can turn out to belong to different object kinds due to variations in fonts.

These statistics differ from the statistics obtained from real data shown in Table 2, since these were synthetically generated. We can observe that 14 classes contribute to objects of kind 2 (closed loops) and 76 classes contribute to objects of kind 3 (simple edges). The fact that we can efficiently classify objects of kinds 2 and 3 using dedicated classifiers is shown in column 4 of the same table.

However, objects of kind 4 have contributions from 414 classes. As we can observe, the relative cost of computation rises steeply for classifying objects of kind 4. The table shows that if we use 16 moment features, time to classify a pattern

Table 4 Cross-validation results for synthetic data set, obtained using SVM (rbf kernel) alone. mnts, moment features; spl, 2D least-squared spline features; Dim., dimensionality; (C,γ), values of C and γ for best accuracy; cost, relative cost of classification

Obj. kind	features	Dim.	Best(%) Accu.	C,γ	SVs	Cost
2 (14)	Mnts	16	98.35	16, 1	261	1.0
(977) (3.0%)	Spl	25	98.26	16, 0.0625	170	1.0
3 (76)	Mnts	16	98.67	64, 4	1701	6.5
(5178) (15.7%)	Spl	25	98.82	64, 0.0625	1927	11.5
4 (414)	Mnts	16	97.09	256, 16	17261	66.1
(26851) (81.4%)	Mnts	25	97.38	256, 4	17360	103.9
	Spl	25	98.51	256, 1	17669	105.8

of kind 4 will be about 66 times more than the time needed to classify an object of kind 2, and with 25 spline features, it could be nearly 106 times longer. This is the difficulty we encounter when we try to classify objects of too many classes and particularly so, as the dimension of the feature vector increases. Hence, objects of kind 4 will be the focus of our study in the rest of this chapter. As can be seen from the last row of the same table, the spline features outperform the moment features at nearly the same computational cost.

We have built two separate classifiers on the lines of the proposed scheme to segregate objects of kind 4 in synthetic and real data sets. We have performed eightfold cross-validation on each of the data sets. During each cross-validation run, (7/8)th of the data samples are used for training, using which, we build a representation table and derive features to build models to classify conflicting classes at various levels using SVMs. The rest of the data are used for testing. We have run two experiments, one with 16 moment features and the other with 25 spline features on the synthetic data set, while we used only 16 moment features in the real data set, since we observed similar trends with both features in the synthetic data set. We report results from both the classifiers and corresponding features. Since the results from the deterministic part of the strategy are invariant to the chosen features (we used the same representation tables for both the features), they are reported only once for each classifier. In our discussions, we mostly quote results obtained with moment features from the synthetic data set and the corresponding results from the real data set are quoted in brackets.

We have chosen a strategy to obtain useful C and γ for training the SVMs for every conflict, since this is critical for obtaining good results. In order to achieve this, we have performed threefold cross-validations across a wide range of C ($2^0 - 2^6$ in powers of 2) and γ ($2^{-8} - 2^2$ in powers of 2) values. If the peak performance occurred at a unique pair of C, γ value, we have used the same for training the SVM. If many pairs of C, γ give the same performance, we have used the average values, since as we see from Fig. 10, the regions of similar performance are nearly convex and hence, we expect the means to lie within these regions. However, the values so obtained need not be optimal. In reporting the results, for ease of reading, wherever appropriate, we have rounded the mean values of number of classes, support vectors and conflicts to the nearest integer.

Table 5 shows the statistics obtained from the eight representation tables generated by the cross-validation experiments. As expected, there are fewer unique strings at lower levels of representations. A fact that is clearly evident from Table 5 is the relatively high variation observed in the real data set, in terms of graph representation. This is borne out by the fact that the total number of representations in the table is on an average, nearly half the size of the training data, while for the synthetic data set, it was only about a quarter. We believe that the main reason for this is that we have far few samples for many classes, as seen in Fig. 9b, and invariably, nearly all of them have to end up in the representation table, thereby increasing the table length. What is interesting is the fact that nearly 62% ($UR_4/\sum UR_i$) (86% for real data set) of all the variations occur only at level 4, i.e. if the representation table construction were to be truncated at level 3, on an average, the number of representations in our

Table 5 Statistics from the representation tables. # Tr., no. of training samples; Reps., total representations in the table; UR_i,$i = 1 \ldots 4$, "unique representations at level i" in the tables; (% total), the means as a percentage of # Tr

	# Tr.	Reps.	UR_1	UR_2	UR_3	UR_4
Synthetic data set (26,851 samples)						
Mean	23550	6274	71	332	2356	4425
(% Tr.)	100.0	26.6	0.3	1.4	10.0	18.8
Std	2.2	16.2	0.7	5.0	9.9	11.1
Real data set (50,316 samples)						
Mean	43924	24677	107	237	3275	21705
(% Tr.)	100.0	56.2	0.2	0.5	7.5	49.4
Std	16.4	19.6	2.3	1.5	5.8	33.9

tables would be only about 12% (8%) of the overall training samples. This could be a pointer to the fact that we might not have had enough samples in both real and synthetic data sets for learning, especially at levels 3 and 4.

Table 6 shows information about the conflicts found in the tables. It shows that conflicts increase as the level of representation increases. Though this may seem counterintuitive, we need to observe that the number of unique representations at every level also increases, as shown in Table 5, thus bringing down the number of classes per conflict. Table 6 points to the important fact that we must expect the training times to be huge if we want to use the proposed scheme. As described in Section 5.4, each conflict is eventually resolved using an SVM. We need to cross-validate and find optimal parameters for each of these SVMs. Thus, in total, we need to cross-validate and train on an average about 1477 SVMs

Table 6 Number of conflicts and classes per classifier at various levels

	Level 1	Level 2	Level 3	Level 4
Conflicts at each level				
Synthetic data set				
Mean	61	233	618	565
Std	1.0	2.9	5.2	4.1
Real data set				
Mean	93	153	1148	1139
Std	1.0	2.5	8.0	12.3
Classes per classifier				
Synthetic data set				
Mean	46	16	5	4
Std	48.7	22.5	8.6	4.7
Max	182	123	119	50
Real data set				
Mean	43	27	7	3
Std	37.1	34.2	9.9	1.7
Max	118	117	92	14

(61+233+618+565) for synthetic data and 2533 SVMs (93+153+1148+1139) for real data. Although the number of training samples per SVM goes down as we go to higher levels of representation (which we shall see shortly), it still looks like a daunting task. However, given that the training is usually a one time job in the case of OCR engines, the highest importance is accorded to the classification time and accuracy. We shall shortly show that this exorbitant cost we incur in training pays off well during testing, and hence should not be a matter of concern in developing OCR engines on these lines.

The crucial information about what happens to computational costs is captured in the number of classes per conflict, since this determines the number of support vectors and hence the cost of computation. Table 6 shows this statistics too. As we can observe, the number of classes per conflict (hence classifier) varies drastically, e.g. for level 4, the average number of classes per conflict is 4 (3). But the maximum number of classes is found to be 50 (14) for a particular SVM, thereby hinting that there should be many SVMs which distinguish only three or two classes. Hence, the average computational cost could be much lower than what we perceive from this table. Similar is the case with other levels too.

Table 7 shows the average number of support vectors per classifier, which is a better estimate of how the computational need will go down, as we go to higher

Table 7 Number of support vectors per classifier (denoted as SVs/Cfr) and mean relative computational cost (mean. rel. cost) at various levels. M-SVM stands for the single multi-class SVM trained with samples from all classes

SVs/Cfr	M-SVM	Level 1	Level 2	Level 3	Level 4
Synthetic data set					
Normalized central moments (16 features)					
Mean	15949	1598	445	99	84
Std	33	2007	838	272	157
Max	15983	8326	5218	4197	1883
Mean. rel. cost	**189.9**	**19.0**	**5.3**	**1.2**	**1.0**
2D least-squared splines (25 features)					
Mean	16178	1584	467	137	101
Std	28	2023	878	319	176
Max	16229	8324	5426	4449	1926
Mean. rel. cost	**160.2**	**15.7**	**4.6**	**1.4**	**1.0**
Real data set					
Normalized central moments (16 features)					
Mean	9554	1978	1204	222	61
Std	62	1951	1764	522	75
Max	9596	6161	6074	5458	995
Mean. rel. cost	**157.2**	**32.6**	**19.8**	**3.7**	**1.0**
2D least-squared splines (25 features)					
Mean	8050	1762	971	199	61
Std	59	1742	1518	470	68
Max	8114	5607	5568	4803	617
Mean. rel. cost	**132.0**	**28.9**	**15.9**	**3.3**	**1.0**

levels of representations. It shows that classifying data at level 4 could be nearly 19 (32) times quicker on an average (using moments), compared to classifying it at level 1. However, as we could have guessed by the huge deviations in the number of classes per classifier, the number of support vectors per classifier has a huge variance too. What is clear from the results of Table 7 is that the computational cost of classification using the proposed scheme at various levels is much lower than the cost of classification using a single multi-class SVM (M-SVM), whose results are shown in Fig. 10. However, this gain does not take into consideration the cost involved in searching the representation table and obtaining graph-based features, which we shall mention shortly. Assuming that these costs are relatively small, we see that classifying a component using the proposed scheme can give us acceleration factors of nearly 10 (5), 36 (8)), 162 (43) and 189 (157), respectively, as we go to higher levels of representation using moment features. This makes a huge difference to testing time, which is very crucial for OCR applications. This can make a big difference in practically being able to use a classifier for the task. Though results shown in Fig. 10 are very attractive, such a classifier can seldom be used in real-life applications, due to this single factor.

The lower speedup factors for real data set, observed in Table 7, can be attributed to the fact that far fewer classes are being classified in the real data set compared to the synthetic one. We believe that a real data set with a large number of classes would show results similar to the synthetic data set, since an increased number of classes would relatively increase the support vectors in the single multi-class SVM by a huge margin compared to the increase in support vectors in classifiers trained to resolve conflicts.

To know the true gain in speed, we must factor out the time spent on obtaining graph-based features and in traversing the deterministic path of the scheme, wherein we employ string matching to narrow down to higher levels of representation. Some OCR algorithms thin or skeletonize the data to remove certain font-based dependencies. Getting to graphs from this stage involves only binary morphological filtering, and simple calculations which can be implemented efficiently. Thus, we can safely exclude the role of this while estimating computational costs. In the deterministic part of the algorithm, we perform exact binary string search over small strings (maximum length being around 150 bytes). The search can be made quicker by building a heap structure from the representation table during training [18], leading to search times of $\theta(\ln(n))$, n being the number of entries in the representation table. This computation is much smaller than $\theta(s \times d)$ multiplications, where s and d represent the number of support vectors and their dimension, respectively. This is especially true at lower levels of representations, where the strings are only a few bytes in length, but the number of support vectors is relatively large. The deterministic and probabilistic computational costs may become comparable only at higher levels (3 and 4), in which case, we see that the acceleration factors are above 100. Factoring out the computational needs for the deterministic part still leaves us with huge acceleration factors. Hence, we see that the SVM classification is the only major computational cost we incur at lower levels of representation. This behaviour

Table 8 Classification accuracies when classification is restricted to a particular level of graph-based features

Classification accuracy (%)	Level 1	Level 2	Level 3	Level 4
Synthetic data set				
Normalized central moments (16 features)				
Mean	94.8	93.2	88.3	90.1
Std	0.3	0.6	0.9	0.6
Min	94.3	92.0	86.9	89.2
Max	**95.4**	**94.0**	**90.1**	**90.8**
2D least-squared splines (25 features)				
Mean	95.8	94.3	88.6	90.7
Std	0.3	0.3	0.6	0.5
Min	95.5	93.8	87.5	89.8
Max	**96.2**	**94.7**	**89.1**	**91.1**
Real data set				
Normalized central moments (16 features)				
Mean	96.3	95.9	87.4	82.8
Std	0.2	0.2	0.6	0.6
Min	96.1	95.6	87.1	82.3
Max	**96.4**	**96.1**	**87.8**	**83.2**
2D least-squared splines (25 features)				
Mean	96.7	96.3	87.7	83.1
Std	0.2	0.2	0.3	0.6
Min	96.4	96.0	86.7	82.4
Max	**97.0**	**96.6**	**88.2**	**84.1**

becomes particularly useful when one would like to increase the number of features being used by the SVMs to resolve conflicts.

Moreover, the total entries in the representation table should logically reach a saturation limit as the number of training samples increases. Thus, as the size of the training set increases, the string search part of the algorithm may need relatively less and less time compared to SVM classification. In all, we can safely conclude that we can indeed realize large acceleration factors by resorting to the proposed scheme.

Though the proposed scheme looks computationally attractive, the performance of this scheme in terms of classification accuracy is also important. Table 8 shows the results obtained from the cross-validation study. The classification accuracy at a particular level refers to the accuracy obtained by restricting conflict resolution to that level, e.g. if we do not use the representations beyond R_1 and instead resolve conflicts by using classifiers trained to resolve conflicts at level 1, we get results tabulated in the second column of Table 8. However, if we let the algorithm use the full extent of representation, we get results up to level 4 (last column). Due to lack of matching representations at higher levels, some decisions may have to be taken at lower levels, i.e. results at level 4 could have contained results obtained at lower levels. We observe that the classification accuracies obtained at levels 1 and 2, though slightly lower, are comparable to the ones shown in Fig. 10, thereby making

Table 9 Contribution from each level for the total classification

Contribution (%)	Level 1	Level 2	Level 3	Level 4
Synthetic data set				
Mean	0.12	3.98	4.97	90.07
Std	0.05	0.50	0.45	0.61
Real data set				
Mean	0.17	3.43	33.36	63.01
Std	0.03	0.09	0.42	0.43

a clear case in favour of this strategy by virtue of its classification speed. Table 8 also shows that decision making at lower levels (1 and 2), irrespective of whether we could make decisions at higher levels, can yield better accuracy. However, this comes at an increased computation cost, as shown in Table 7. We see a trade-off between accuracy and computational cost coming into picture at this juncture. But classifying at level 2 is still about 36 (8) times faster than what we would have done with a single SVM classifier, as we can infer from Table 7. Also, as expected, we observe that the classification accuracies obtained with splines is better than those obtained with moment features with both the synthetic and real data.

It is instructive to see what the contribution of each of the levels is to the total classification. Table 9 shows such a break-up. We see that nearly 90% (63%) of the data can be classified at level 4, which is a very good prospect from the point of view of computational cost. However, from Table 8, we find that we may have to sacrifice accuracy in this case. We observe that in the case of real data, about 30% of the components have no match with existing representations at level 4, clearly indicating that the learning of representations at level 4 is at its very early stages. As we find, it is better in the case of synthetic data, where only 10% needs to be classified at the lower levels.

We now try to analyze the various errors leading to relatively poor performance at higher levels of representation. It is also important to note the fact that in the proposed graph-based scheme, there are two kinds of errors that can be committed at each level. First, the errors due to the deterministic part of the algorithm based on graph features. Second, the errors committed by individual SVMs. It is instructive to know which of these errors dominates at each level. This can provide insights to improve upon the achievable classification accuracy. Table 10 shows such statistics. We can split the errors that arise due to graph features into three types, referred to as types 1, 2 and 3. Type 1 errors are those for which no match could be found even at level 1. Type 2 errors denote those instances where, though a unique string match is found, the label assigned based on graph features is wrong. Type 3 errors occur when the classifier pointer table associates a wrong classifier for the test pattern.

As we find from Table 10, most of the errors are indeed due to reliance on the graph-based representation, especially of types 2 and 3. We also observe that errors due to SVMs are much less in the case of splines than in the case of moment features. We observe that at levels 1 and 2, most errors are of type 3, whereas errors of type 2

Table 10 Relative (%) errors when classification is restricted up to a particular level

Rel. errors (%)	Level 1	Level 2	Level 3	Level 4
		Synthetic data set		
Graph	**Normalized central moments (16 features)**			
Type 1	0.5	0.4	0.3	0.5
Type 2	2.1	3.2	42.8	36.7
Type 3	61.5	72.8	44.5	43.5
Total	**64.1**	**76.4**	**87.6**	**80.7**
SVM	35.9	23.6	12.4	19.3
Graph	**2D least-squared splines (25 features)**			
Type 1	0.7	0.5	0.3	0.6
Type 2	3.4	4.1	48.6	39.7
Type 3	74.9	82.4	44.0	48.5
Total	**79.0**	**87.1**	**92.9**	**88.8**
SVM	21.0	12.9	7.1	11.2
		Real data set		
Graph	**Normalized central moments (16 features)**			
Type 1	0.7	0.6	0.2	0.4
Type 2	1.5	5.3	22.4	54.7
Type 3	69.0	68.4	71.1	43.0
Total	**71.2**	**74.4**	**93.7**	**98.1**
SVM	28.8	25.6	6.3	1.9
Graph	**2D least-squared splines (25 features)**			
Type 1	1.1	1.0	0.3	0.5
Type 2	3.0	6.0	23.9	55.1
Type 3	81.6	80.5	72.5	42.7
Total	**85.7**	**87.5**	**96.7**	**98.3**
SVM	14.3	12.5	3.3	1.7

are very low. This indicates that we have been able to learn the existence of conflicts or patterns that lead to conflicts, but have been unable to capture all the conflicting classes for various representations.

This is in contrast to the case of levels 3 and 4, where we observe that errors of type 2 are significant, indicating that the learning is oblivious to the fact that multiple classes share a common representation, let alone know which of them. This also explains the large contribution of errors of type 3 at these levels. This indicates that the algorithm has not seen enough training samples at these levels and is still at a very early stage of learning. Theoretically, errors of types 2 and 3 should be absent (or saturate to some value in practice) with larger training sets, since this is a deterministic strategy. Hence, to realize the true value addition provided by the proposed graph-based scheme, we may need to use huge training sets.

Moreover, the representation of characters based on R_i is a very simple reduction of the information actually present in the signed incidence matrix. We can employ graph matching/comparison algorithms [14, 19], and/or other graph features, which may better the performance of the deterministic part of the scheme.

We can see that there is scope for improvement on the SVM front too (especially in the case of synthetic data). We attribute the errors committed by SVM to sub-optimal parameter selection and training. As mentioned earlier, we train each SVM based on an average of a set of best parameters obtained from three-fold cross-validation over a coarsely sampled, wide range of parameters [15]. This we should expect by no means to lead to best possible results with SVMs. Moreover, we had too few samples to train the SVMs. An increase in the number of training samples might yield better classification accuracy for each individual SVM. These observations make us believe that we can improve the performance here too. So, a better parameter criterion to choose the training parameters combined with search on a much finer parameter grid should definitely improve the results. A particular aspect that could perhaps be helping SVM classification is the fact that a set of conflicting classes need not necessarily have components that look visually alike, since the grouping is based on graph features. This can make the classification task easier when features that capture visual information are chosen. So, perhaps fewer and simpler features can suffice for the task on hand. We can even probably choose a different set of features to classify at different levels.

We now analyze other possible causes for the observed poor performance at higher levels. We believe the degradation in performance can be attributed to three main causes apart from the size of the training data set. The first is the inherent variation in real data. Perhaps we can try to alleviate this effect by using script-specific pre-processing schemes, e.g. discarding very small terminal edges, closing looping edges and coalescing very small non-terminal edges with vertices. The second contributor to the malperformance could be noise leading to holes in component images during binarization. Presence of holes can dramatically alter graph representations, thereby mixing up representations, and increasing representations per class. This can also be minimized by better pre-processing techniques. However, the third and a more subtle factor to note is the effect of scanning resolution. Since the deterministic part of the algorithm depends heavily on edge junctions, a coarse scan can lead to loss of junction information. This can make graph representation less effective. A component scanned at different resolutions can have very different graph representations. Thus, a relatively high scanning resolution (depending on the font size) may be needed in order to extract best results from the graph-based schemes. This further emphasizes the need to use features that do not need image scaling for use with classifiers, since as images get larger, resizing gets costlier. From Table 3, we observe that the components in the real data set have significantly different statistics compared to the synthetic data set and are on an average smaller especially in width. This could probably be due to particular classes being completely missed out in real data set. However, if indeed small-sized components exist in the data set, they could lead to more conflicts at higher levels, as evidenced by Table 6, thereby making learning harder. Combinations of these factors need to be accounted for, during training and testing, for the graph-based scheme to be effective.

From the above results and discussions, we see that there is a large scope for improvement in the whole methodology. The results mentioned here are only conservative estimates of what is potentially achievable with this scheme.

Extensions: In the experiments we discussed, we have not used the prior information about which we mentioned in Section 5.4. Using prior information can help us identify insignificant conflicts, which can be omitted in training, thereby reducing the training time. In conjunction with SVMs that can give probabilistic outputs [15], it can also help to improve the classification accuracy of the SVMs.

We could continue to use the strategy outlined here and use other graph features to further sub-divide the problem. A particularly useful extension could be to use edge labels obtained from an edge classifier (mapped to edge weights in graphs) to disentangle possibly merged components. The proposed method also seems to be potentially useful in online character recognition, where we can replace edge information by stroke information. In this case, we will not have the problem of ordering edges and vertices, since we obtain time information with each stroke. This may make this strategy very suitable for online character recognition.

6 Conclusion

A bilingual OCR system has been presented, with a robust segmentation strategy that does not depend on projections. We have demonstrated the use of graph-based features in building fast and efficient classification engines for Kannada script. This can easily be extended to other scripts, since this is a script-independent strategy. Though the scheme involves a highly taxing learning phase, we have shown that it can yield a high speedup in testing, a key factor in designing OCR engines. We have discussed the scalability of the scheme and shown that it is well suited for learning from very large data sets. Similar ideas could be used to develop bilingual OCRs involving other Indian scripts.

References

1. B. Vijayakumar and A. G. Ramakrishnan, Machine recognition of printed Kannada text, Document Analysis Systems V, D. Lopresti, J. Hu, and R. Kashi (Eds.), Lecture Notes in Computer Science 2423, Springer Verlag, Berlin, 2002 pp. 37–48.
2. T. V. Ashwin and P. S. Shastry, A font and size independent ocr system for printed kannada documents using support vector machines, Sadhana. 27(1): 35–58, February 2002.
3. P. B. Pati, Analysis of multi-lingual documents with complex layout & content, PhD Thesis, Indian Institute of Science, Bangalore, INDIA, 2007.
4. P. B. Pati and A. G. Ramakrishnan, Word level multi-script identification, Pattern Recognition Letters, 2008, doi:10.1016/j.patrec.2008.01.027
5. P. B. Pati, S. S. Raju, N. K. Pati, and A. G. Ramakrishnan, Gabor filters for document analysis in Indian Bilingual Documents, Proceedings of First International Conference on Intelligent Sensing and Information Processing (ICISIP-04), IEEE Publications, Chennai, India, 2004, pp.123–126.
6. D. J. Field, Relation between the statistics of natural images and the response properties of cortical cells, Journal of Optical Society of America A. 4(12): 2379–2394, 1987.
7. K. R. Rao and P. Yip, Discrete Cosine Transform: Algorithms, Advantages, Applications. Academic Press, New York, 1990.

8. R. Muralishankar, A. G. Ramakrishnan, and P. Prathibha, Modification of pitch using DCT in the source domain, Speech Communication. 42:143–154, 2004.
9. P. B. Pati, Machine recognition of printed Odiya text documents, Master's thesis, Indian Institute of Science, Bangalore, INDIA, 2001.
10. C. J. C. Burges, A tutorial on support vector machines for pattern recognition, Data Mining and Knowledge Discovery. 2(2): 955–974, 1998.
11. R. Collobert and S. Bengio, On The convergence of SVMTorch, an algorithm for large scale regression problems, Tech. Rep., Dalle Molle Institute for Perceptual Artificial Intelligence, Martigny, Switzerland, 2000.
12. Peeta Basa Pati and A. G. Ramakrishnan, OCR in indian scripts: A survey, IETE Technical Review. 22(3): 217–227, May–June 2005.
13. Chih-Wei Hsu and Chih-len Lin. A comparison of methods for multiclass support vector machines. IEEE Transactions on Neural Networks. 13: 415–425, March 2002.
14. Bruno T. Messmer and Horst Bunke, Efficient subgraph isomorphism detection: A decomposition approach, Transactions on Knowledge and Data Engineering 12(2): 307–323, 2000.
15. Chih-Chung Chang and Chih-Jen Lin, *LIBSVM*: A Library for Support Vector Machines, Software available at http://www.csie.ntu.edu.tw/cjlin/libsvm
16. J. Flusser, Moment invariants in image analysis. In Proceedings of World Academy of Science, Engineering and Technology. 11: 196–201, Feb 2006.
17. C. De Boor. A Practical Guide to Splines. Springer-Verlag, 1978.
18. R. L. R. Thomas H. Cormen, and Charles E. Leiserson. Introduction to Algorithms. MIT Press/McGraw-Hill, 1990.
19. D. Lopresti and G. Wilfong. A fast technique for comparing graph representations with applications to performance evaluation. International Journal on Document Analysis and Recognition. 6(4): 219–229, April 2003.

Recognition of Malayalam Documents

N.V. Neeba, Anoop Namboodiri, C.V. Jawahar, and P.J. Narayanan

Abstract Malayalam is an Indian language spoken by 40 million people with its own script. It has a rich literary tradition. A character recognition system for this language will be of immense help in a spectrum of applications ranging from data entry to reading aids. The Malayalam script has a large number of similar characters making the recognition problem challenging. In this chapter, we present our approach for recognition of Malayalam documents, both printed and handwritten. Classification results as well as ongoing activities are presented.

1 Introduction

Malayalam is an Indian language spoken by 40 million people mostly in the south-western state of Kerala. In this chapter, we take a look at Malayalam, specifically from the point of view of the problems of OCR and handwriting recognition. The primary goals of this chapter are to

- introduce the language and script to the reader and present the opportunities in Malayalam OCR to the research community
- explore the primary challenges in building an OCR for Malayalam and point out the possible solutions along with comprehensive results on character classification
- present the problem of Malayalam handwriting recognition, its challenges, possibilities, and potential approaches
- point out some fruitful directions for future research in the area and its applicability to other Indian languages

N.V. Neeba (✉)
Centre for Visual Information Technology, International Institute of Information Technology, Hyderabad, India
e-mail: jawahar@iiit.ac.in

V. Govindaraju, S. Setlur (eds.), *Guide to OCR for Indic Scripts*, Advances in Pattern Recognition, DOI 10.1007/978-1-84800-330-9_6, © Springer-Verlag London Limited 2009

1.1 The Malayalam Language

Malayalam is one of the five major languages of the Dravidian language family, which also includes Tamil, Telugu, Kannada, and Tulu. It is the principal language of around 40 million people of the state of Kerala and the union territories of Lakshadweep and Mahe. The Malayalam speakers – referred to as *Malayalis* – have been strongly peripatetic. Hence, the language is heard widely all over India as well as in the Persian Gulf countries, Europe, Australia, and the North America.

1.1.1 Origin

Malayalam is closely related to the languages of Tamil and Sanskrit. The language started as a variant of Tamil that was spoken in regions of Kerala, and evolved its own form, grammar, and vocabulary by 500 CE [1]. A significant transition from Tamil happened with the introduction of a form of literature called *Manipravalam*, which freely mixed words from Sanskrit into the language. Most words in traditional Malayalam has its roots in either Tamil or Sanskrit. Due to its lineage to both Sanskrit and Tamil, the Malayalam alphabet has the largest number of letters among the Indian languages.

Kerala had a flourishing spice trade with Europe, Middle East, and Egypt for over 2000 years. This long-standing exposure led to words and expressions being borrowed from a variety of languages such as Arabic, Hebrew, Latin. The most significant influence in the recent past has been English, which has contributed a large number of words in everyday use, mostly in its original form.

1.1.2 Literary Culture

Malayalam has a strong literary history, which is centuries old and is very rich in several genres of literature [4]. The earliest known literary composition in the language is from the 13th century. Notably, the work *Ramacharitam* by Cheeraman is recognized by scholars as the first book in Malayalam. The first Malayalam grammar/literary treatise, *Leelathilakam*, was compiled in the 14th century. Malayalam also has a rich vocabulary, with around 90,000 words listed in the dictionary, *shabdathArAvali*. The word *M*alayalam (*m*ala:mountain + *a*Lam:place) used to refer to the land itself, and later became the name of the language spoken by the people there.

The literature started in a form close to Tamil in the beginning of common era (Sangam Age), which took a quick deviation with the introduction of *Manipravalam*. The verse and poetry forms dominated the literature; prose forms are available only from the late 19th century. The script and the linguistic structure of Malayalam was formalized by Thunchathu Ramanujan Ezhuthassan, who lived in the 16th century. He is regarded as the father of modern Malayalam language. The intermediate development of the literature was primarily through the lyrics for performing art forms of Kathakali, Koothu, and Thullal and translations of the mythological stories. In fact, one of the first works in the language, *Bhashakautilyam*, from the 12th century is a translation of *Arthashastra* from Sanskrit. A variety of literary styles in prose and poems, including mythical, satirical, fictional, narrative, and travelogue, were created in Malayalam before the 18th century. The literary journals such as *Bhasha Poshini* and *Vidya Vinodini*, which came into existence toward the end of the 19th century, played a critical role in popularizing the literary culture and criticism in the language. The modern day literature in Malayalam is as evolved and complex as that of any other languages in the world.

1.1.3 Word and Sentence Formation

The influence of Sanskrit has not been limited to the words, but has contributed to the grammar and word formation as well. The agglutinative nature of Sanskrit words in poems has been borrowed by Malayalam and is common in speech and writing. This allows one to combine multiple words into a single compound word using morphological rules. Its usage is so popular that one often encounters compound words formed from four or five words in common use. For example, the words *nizhal* (shadow), *pAva* (puppet), and *kootthu* (play) combine to form a single word: *nizhalppAvakkootthu*. There are examples of sentences formed from a single compound word. The first word in the sentence *mazhayundAyirunnengilennavanAr-OdANAvO paranjathu* is formed from nine separate root words. Note that this is not just a juxtaposition of multiple words, but a single word formed by fusing the component words according to the *sandhi* rules of the grammar.

Another form of variation of words in Malayalam is from verb inflections. It is interesting to note that unlike most Indian languages, Malayalam has low variation of verbs and adjective forms based on the number, gender, or person of the subject. For example, the verb *paranju* (said) remains the same whether the subject is I, you, she, he, or they. However, quite a large set of variations result from inflections based on tense, mood, aspect, etc. Like other Dravidian languages, such inflections are always formed from suffixes to the root word and not prefixes or infixes (*parayuka, parayum*). All prefixed verb forms are derived from Sanskrit and are not inflections, but variations in meanings (*samhāram, parihāram*), which in turn can have inflectional forms (*pariharikkum, pariharicchu*).

Inflections of subject or object also create word form variations making the possible set of legal words, extremely large (e.g., *rāmanāl* (by rama) and *rāmanōdu* (to rama)). Interestingly, such inflections reduce the restrictions on the order of words in a sentence to a large extent, making the modeling of sentence structures quite difficult. For example, the sentence: ‘ram told sita’ is usually written as *rāman sitayōdu paranju*. However, any permutation of the three words in the sentence would leave the meaning unchanged.

1.2 The Malayalam Script

Although most Indic scripts – Devanagari, Tamil, Gurumukhi, Telugu, Kannada, Gujarati, Oriya, Bengali, and Malayalam – vary greatly visually, they share some important similarities. The scripts of Indian languages have the same origins (Brahmi script from 3rd century BCE) and are founded on the same principles. Urdu, written in the Perso-Arabic script, is an exception. The scripts are all defined as "syllabic alphabets" in that the unit of encoding is a syllable. The languages share the majority of the syllable set as well as their order, and the primary difference is in the glyphs used to represent the syllables. Also, the Indian languages are phonetic in nature. The basic graphical unit is called an *akshara*, which represents a unique phonetic syllable. Each script has a large *akshara* set formed from combinations of consonants and vowels.

Until around 16th century, Malayalam used a script named *vattezhuthu*, while *grandhakshara* was used to write Sanskrit. Two minor variants of *vattezhuthu*, named *kolezhuthu* and *malayanma*, were also used in different regions of the state. Around 16th century, a consolidated set of 51 symbols from *vattezhuthu* and *grandhakshara* emerged as a unified script for writing Malayalam. The present-day Malayalam script (*aksharamala*) consists of 52 characters including 16 vowels and 36 consonants (see Table 1). In addition to this basic set, the script contains a large number of conjunct characters and special symbols.

The Malayalam script (or *lipi*) is primarily syllabic in nature and transcribes the sequence of syllables in a word. Each syllable is represented using a unique combination of consonants and a vowel. The orthography consists of the symbols for each consonant and vowel, rules for combining them, and exceptions where the combination of multiple consonants and vowels results in a new glyph. The predominant

Table 1 Aksharamala: The basic set consists of 16 vowels and 36 consonants

Vowels	അ	ആ	ഇ	ഈ	ഉ	ഊ	ഋ	ഌ		ൠ
	എ	ഏ	ഐ	ഒ	ഓ	ഔ	◌ം	◌ഃ		ൡ
Consonants	ക	ഖ	ഗ	ഘ	ങ	ച	ഛ	ജ	ഝ	ഞ
	ട	ഠ	ഡ	ഢ	ണ	ത	ഥ	ദ	ധ	ന
	പ	ഫ	ബ	ഭ	മ	യ	ര	ല	വ	ശ
	ഷ	സ	ഹ	ള	ഴ	റ				
Half-Cons.	ൺ	ൻ	ർ	ൽ	ൾ	ൿ				
Vowel and Consonant Modifier s	◌ാ	◌ി	◌ീ	◌ു	◌ൂ	◌ൃ	െ◌	േ◌	ൈ◌	െ◌ാ
	േ◌ാ	◌ൗ	◌്	്ല	്വ	്യ	്ര			
Conjuncts (examples)	ക്ക	ങ്ങ	ച്ച	ഞ്ഞ	ട്ട	ണ്ണ	ത്ത	ശ്ധ്യ	ശ്ശ്രു	മ്മ
	ന്റ	റ്റ	ന്ധ	ണ്ഡ	ള്ഭ	ന്മ	ദ്ധ	ജ്ഞ	ഞ്ച	ത്ര
Numerals	൦	൧	൨	൩	൪	൫	൬	൭	൮	൯
Others	൰	൱	൲	൳	ൾ	ൺ	ൻ			

orthographic unit is a consonant ending in a vowel, referred to as an *akshara*. The canonical structure is (C)V, where V represents a vowel, and the optional C represents one to three consonants. The system follows the principles of phonology and the writing corresponds to the pronunciation with very few exceptions.

Table 1 shows the basic vowel and consonant symbols. The two vowels at the top-right of the table are used for writing Sanskrit words only. The script also contains symbols for half-consonants, known as chillu, and symbols for vowels, when they appear together with consonants (consonant modifiers in Table 1). The complexity of the script, in terms of recognition, primarily comes from the similarity between different symbols and the large number of symbols that are present in the script. In addition to the above symbols (around 75), there is a very large set of symbols for specific combinations of (C)V or conjunct characters, as mentioned before. A small set of conjunct characters are shown in Table 1. The last two rows of Table 1 shows symbols that are present in the script, but not in common use anymore. *Arabic* numerals are used in practice instead of the script-specific numeral symbols. The last row shows special symbols for units of *ten*, *hundred*, *thousand*, *quarter*, *half*, and *three-quarters*, and for denoting *dates*.

The most frequent consonants in the language are *ka*, *ra*, *la*, and *va*, and the most frequent independent vowel is *a*.

1.2.1 Script Revision

The large number of symbols complicated manual typesetting and keying of Malayalam. A simplified or reformed version of the script (*lipi*) was introduced in 1971. The reform aimed to reduce the complexity of two particular aspects of Malayalam script. First, it recommended the replacement of a large number of irregular ligatures by a predictable sequence of basic glyphs. Specifically, this involved single consonant syllables ending in *u*, *uu*, *Ru* and those combined with the consonant *ra*. It also recommended the conversion of complex CCV and CCCV combinations to the corresponding sequence of consonant symbols, joined by the vowel suppressor. Table 2 shows examples of both modifications. Thus, the *new lipi* of Malayalam is supposed to use consonants and diacritics separately, rather than as complex

Table 2 Script revision: modified consonants and conjunct characters in both old and new lipis

Old	കു	കൂ	ക്ര	കൃ	വു	വൂ	വ്ര	വൃ
Revised	കു	കൂ	ക്ര	കൃ	വു	വൂ	വ്ര	വൃ
syllable	ku	kuu	kra	kRu	vu	vuu	vra	vRu
Old	ദ്ധ	ശ്ച	ത്മ	ക്ഷ	ക്ത്ര	സ്ക്രൂ	പ്പു	ഞ്ജു
Revised	ദ്ധ	ശ്ച	ത്മ	ക്ഷ	ക്ത്ര	സ്ക്രൂ	പ്പു	ഞ്ജു
syllable	da+dha	sha+cha	ta+ma	ka+Sha	ka+ta+ra	sa+ka+ra+uu	pa+pa+u	nja+ja+u

combined symbols. This new script reduces the number of distinct letters for typeset from around 900 to about 90. While it has had some effect on daily practice, this reform has only partially changed the well-established traditional approach, especially in writing. By the arrival of modern word processors, which removed the limitations on the number and complexity of glyphs, many of the old lipi characters re-emerged in print. However, there is no common agreement on the set of conjunct characters among different fonts. As a result, the modern script is often a mixture of traditional and simplified characters. Even in the same book, one could find the same compound character written in both old and new lipi.

1.3 Evolution of Printing and Publication

Printing in Malayalam started in 1821, when Benjamin Bailey created the first metal types of around 660 symbols and published a Malayalam dictionary from the press in Kottayam. Even before that, a Malayalam edition of the *New Testament* was published from Bombay in 1811. The CMS Press established by Benjamin Bailey in Kottayam in 1821 and the Basel Press by Hermann Gundert in Thalassery in 1838 paved the way to a revolution in literary publications in Malayalam. Currently, numerous books and publications are produced in Malayalam every year. In Kerala alone, around 70 daily newspapers, 235 weekly magazines, and 1560 monthly periodicals are published. This introduces a substantial opportunity for an OCR in Malayalam to enable search of scanned documents as well as to convert them to a textual representation.

The documents vary considerably in the quality of paper and the printing process that is used. Initial documents were mostly created using letter presses in low-quality paper. Another major source of printed documents were typewriters, which was introduced in the 1970s. These documents use the simplified script that was mentioned before. With the introduction of offset printing, which involves electronic typesetting, printing houses developed fonts with large number of complex characters, and the quality of printing improved considerably. Modern day documents are all electronically typeset, but the quality of paper used is often poor to make the publications affordable to a large portion of the population. The reproduction process also varies from high-quality offset printing to screen printing or photocopying from laser-printed originals for low-volume publications.

Until the introduction of printing, literary works were mostly preserved as handwritten manuscripts in palm leaves. Even today, handwriting continues to be popular in Malayalam, as (i) the societal factors have pushed the literacy rates in the state of Kerala close to 100%, allowing most people to read and write and (ii) the difficulty in designing keyboards with large numbers of characters, making it difficult for the common man to store data electronically in Malayalam. Availability of an online handwriting recognition system will allow a large portion of the population to use handwriting as a medium of input to store and communicate information in the digital form.

1.4 Challenges in Malayalam Recognition

The recognition of printed or handwritten Malayalam has to deal with a large number of complex glyphs, some of which are highly similar to each other. However, recent advances in classifier design, combined with the increase in processing power of computers have all but solved the primary recognition problem. The challenges in recognition come from a variety of associated sources:

- *Non-standard Font Design:* The fonts used in Malayalam printing were mostly developed by artists in the individual publishing houses. The primary goal was to map the ASCII codes to glyphs useful to typeset the language, and no standards were adopted in both the character mapping and glyph sizes or aspect ratios. This introduced the problem of *touching glyphs non-uniform gaps* (see Fig. 1) for many character pairs in the electronic document itself, which gets transferred to the printed versions. This makes the problem of word and character segmentation extremely difficult and error prone, and the errors are passed on to the recognition module. The introduction of Unicode has standardized the font mappings for newly developed fonts. However, the problem of standardizing glyphs still remains.

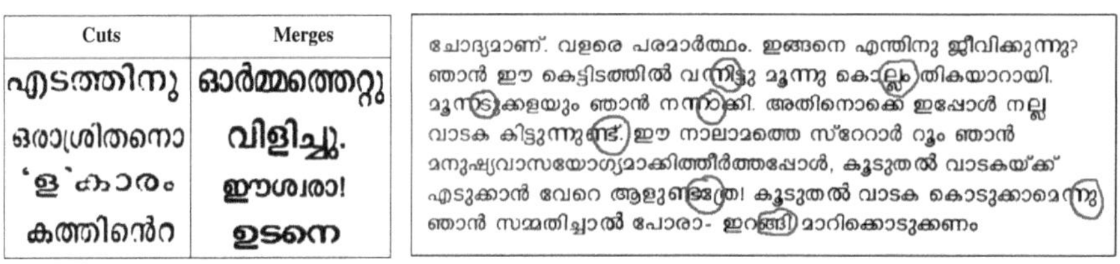

Fig. 1 Examples of cuts and merges in Malayalam printing: (**a**) words with cuts and merges and (**b**) merges in electronic typesetting

- *Quality of Paper:* To make the publications affordable to large portions of the society, publications often use low-quality paper in the printing process, even with offset printing. The presence of fibrous substances in the paper used changes its ability to absorb ink, resulting in large number of broken characters in print. The issues of touching and broken characters are very difficult to handle for the recognition module.
- *Script Variations:* As mentioned in the previous section, the script in Malayalam underwent a revision or simplification, which was partly reversed with the introduction of electronic typesetting. This results in a set of documents that could contain either the old lipi, the new lipi, or a mixture of the two. Any recognition system has to deal with the resulting variety intelligently, to achieve good performance.
- *Representation Issues:* Another related problem is that of limitations in the initial versions of Unicode that prevented textual representations of certain glyphs. Unicode did not have separate codes for chillus and they were created from non-vowel versions of the consonants using "ZWNJ" symbols. This causes substitu-

tion of one with the other in certain fonts, and can create significant differences in meaning of certain words. However these issues have been resolved up to certain extent in Unicode 5.0 onward.

- *Compound Words and Dictionaries:* A characteristic of the Malayalam language as mentioned before is the common usage of compound words created from multiple root words, using the *sandhi* rules. This creates a combinatorial explosion in the number of distinct words in the language. Hence, word-based post-processing or dictionary lookup cannot be employed in Malayalam.
- *Challenges in Handwriting Recognition:* In addition to the language-specific challenges mentioned above and the traditional problem of writing style variations present in all languages, the recognition of handwritten characters in Malayalam has to deal with additional problems. One of the primary issues is the complexity of certain glyphs, which gets simplified to various levels when people write them. This reduces the inter-class variability and increases the intra-class variability. Moreover, as the complexity of characters increase, the level of variations in writing them also increase, especially for online handwriting, which captures the temporal sequence of writing.

2 Character Recognition

The primary structure of the Malayalam OCR includes pre-processing stages such as noise removal, thresholding, skew correction, and layout analysis. This is followed by segmentation at various levels such as block, paragraph, line, word, and components. The classification stage recognizes each input symbol (component) from the features computed, and a language-dependent post-processing unit integrates the recognition results into characters and words.

2.1 Overview of the Approach

Figure 2 gives the overall design of the OCR system. We will take a quick look at the pre- and post-processing modules and then explore the core recognition engine in further detail.

- *Binarization:* The first step in recognition is the conversion of the input image into a binary one and removal of noise. Popular approaches such as adaptive thresholding and median filtering work well with most documents.
- *Skew Correction:* Popular techniques for skew detection in English documents such as component distribution-based estimates do not work in the case of Malayalam due to the complexity of its glyph distribution. Instead, horizontal projection profile-based approaches yield better results, although they require multiple lines of text to function well.
- *Page Segmentation:* The segmentation module divides the text regions into blocks, lines, words, and connected components. The recognition module assumes that the

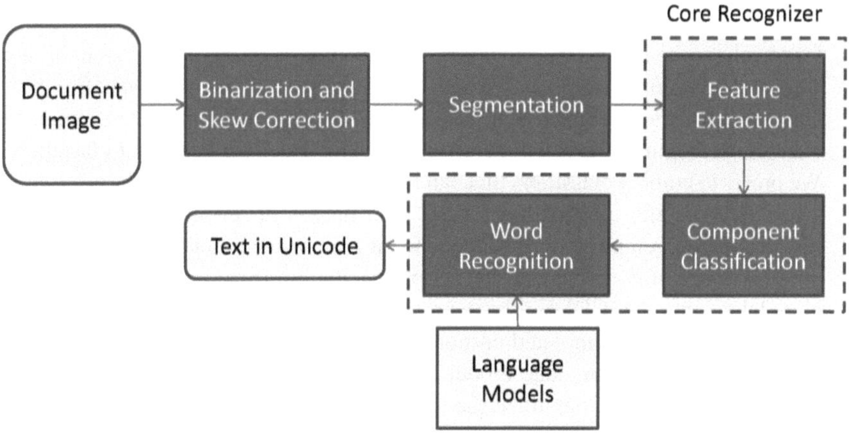

Fig. 2 The overall architecture of the OCR system

input is a set of components corresponding to a single word. Many efficient algorithms are known for identification of connected components in binary images.

- *Component Recognizer:* The component classifier is designed to develop a hypothesis for the label of each connected component in a given word. The goal is to make it efficient and accurate in the presence of noise. However corruptions of connected components due to cuts and merges are difficult to handle at this point and is often handled in the word recognizer or the post-processor.
- *Word Recognizer:* The task of the word recognizer is to combine the recognition results of the individual components and generate the most likely hypotheses regarding the underlying word. Language models of various complexities are often employed at this step.

One might note that the overall structure of the OCR is quite similar to those used for languages with Roman script. The differences arise in the design of the base classifier as well as the integration of results of the component classifier, to handle the cuts and merges. We will now take a closer look at the component classifier as well as the word classifier that integrates the results.

2.2 Design Guidelines

We follow the broad directions listed below:

1. Discover features rather than defining features. We prefer to derive a statistical feature extraction suitable for the script from examples, rather than defining intuitive features from the experience. This allows us to address the classification problem in a high-dimensional space.

2. Build the recognizer out of modules which can be analyzed or predicted. We prefer to follow the pattern classification and machine-learning principles in all the stages of recognition. This makes sensitivity and performance analysis feasible.
3. Use trainable modules as much as possible. Popular trend in Indian language character recognition is to handcraft the decision rules for design of classifiers. We prefer to employ classifiers that can be trained with a reasonably large corpus.
4. Use script-specific information for the final phases of recognition. Our recognition approach employs script-independent features and methods for the initial phases of recognition, and uses the script-specific information for converting the class labels into UNICODE. This uses script and language model.
5. Our design uses the annotated corpora extensively for training as well as learning. The script and language model is also computed out of this corpora. Our design principle is to maximize the recognition accuracy on the corpora which is used for training and testing. We also use the corpus for finding the popular degradations present in the word images.

2.3 Features for Component Classification

A variety of features for recognition of characters or components have been reported in the literature [9]. They could be structural features such as lines, loops, cups and crossings, moment features that capture the overall distribution of pixels, frequency domain representations. Each class of features has its own strengths and weaknesses. Performance of classifier systems that are based on specific set of features might vary considerably as the nature of fonts and the noise levels vary.

An alternate approach is to learn the features automatically from large quantities of training data. Classification algorithms that work in very high dimensions such as SVMs are good at extracting the most discriminative information from the raw pixels themselves. Hence we scale the component images to a fixed size, 20×20, and stack the rows of the image to form a 400-dimensional binary feature vector.

One could either use the raw feature vector directly or try to reduce the dimensionality of the raw vector by projecting it to a lower dimension. Once again, we use techniques such as PCA or LDA that automatically computes an optimal low-dimensional representation from large number of training samples. We argue that with a significantly large feature space, character classification can be solved with reasonable accuracy as demonstrated in Section 4. We prefer statistical methods for feature extraction and selection. Choosing a learning-based approach and utilizing large quantities of training data enable us to achieve robustness to noise and other degradations as well as font variations.

2.4 Classifier Design

The design approach to classifiers can be based on two different philosophies. The first one uses complex classifier models such as neural networks for direct classification of a sample into one of the n classes possible, resulting in an efficient classifier that is trainable. The second approach uses the divide-and-conquer strategy, where an ensemble of simple binary classifiers are integrated to form the final n-class classifier. Our classifier needs to handle a large number of classes, with close similarities between certain component pairs. Hence we prefer the latter approach for the problem of Malayalam OCR, as the individual classifiers can be independently trained and analyzed for improving the overall performance.

One could choose from a large set of classification algorithms for the binary classifiers. We have experimented with a variety of algorithms and found that support vector machines (SVMs) offer the best performance for this problem in most cases. A multi-class classifier can be built using different combination strategies from the individual classifiers, such as majority voting, one vs rest classifiers. Decision-directed acyclic graphs or DDAGs, which is a generalization of a decision tree is found to be quite effective in balancing the complexity of evaluation and the resultant accuracy.

An example of a DDAG for a 4-class classification problem is given in Fig. 3(a). At each node, a binary classification a vs b is performed and if the result is a, we interpret it as the sample does not belong to class b. The training of a DDAG requires ${}^nC_2$ classifiers to be trained. However, the classification of a sample requires only n classifications. A sample goes through N levels down the DDAG, before a final decision is made at the lowest level of the graph.

There are other potential organizations of binary classifiers that can result in faster recognition times. An efficient form of combining binary classifiers is a binary hierarchical decision tree (BHDC) [17]. The BHDC is essentially a binary tree structure, where each node separates a set of classes into two non-overlapping subset of classes (see Fig. 3(b)). The evaluation time in a BHDC is considerably lower than that of a DDAG ($O(logN)$). However, each binary classifier could be more complex, as it has to handle a decision boundary that is formed between two sets of classes. BHDC performs well when the classes are better separated.

For the problem of Malayalam OCR, we have found that a DDAG of binary SVM classifiers forms the best compromise of speed and accuracy (see experimental results). Our classification architecture is shown in Fig. 4. The base classifier, which

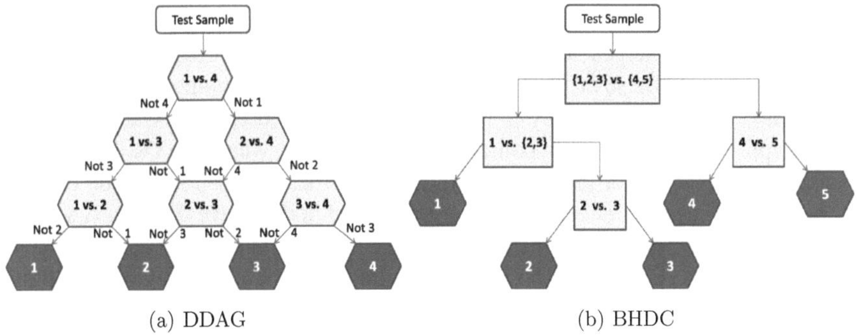

Fig. 3 DDAG (**a**) and BHDC (**b**) arrangements of binary classifiers

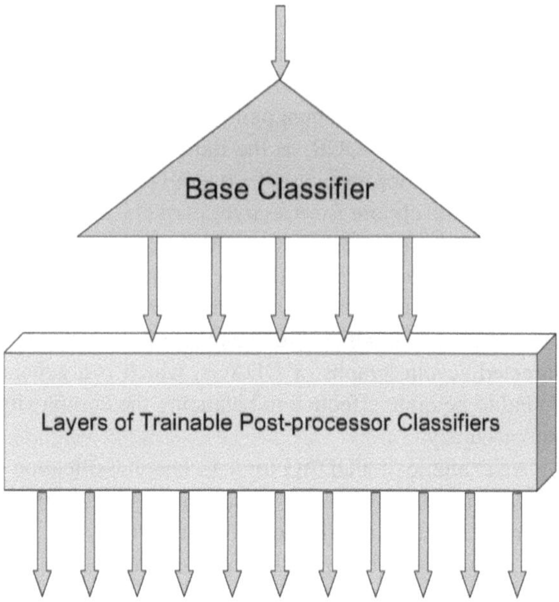

Fig. 4 Overall architecture of the classification scheme

is an SVM-DDAG classifies the component images in a common feature space. Then, a set of trainable post-processor classifiers are employed for addressing the confusions in similar pairs of classes. These classifiers employ highly discriminative class-specific features.

2.5 Beyond Recognition of Isolated Symbols

There are a variety of issues that have not been described in the design of the OCR till now. We will take a quick look at the most important ones, and possible directions of solutions. We have verified these approaches on the annotated corpus.

- *Dealing with Cuts and Merges:* As noted in the challenges, cuts in the connected components and merges between adjacent components affect the component segmentation itself. These problems cannot be handled at the component recognition level, and need to be solved by considering the word in its entirety. One of the possible approaches is that of hypothesis and verification, where the OCR generates a set of hypotheses for the input word, and a verification module can be used to compare the recognition result and the input word in the image domain. A second option would be to try merging or separation of potential cuts and merges to find the most probable word. In short, the basic approach for addressing degradations is to create hypotheses and find the one which best suits the script and language model. Hypotheses are generated by looking into the statistics of degradations (popular cuts and merges), details available in the gray images, etc.

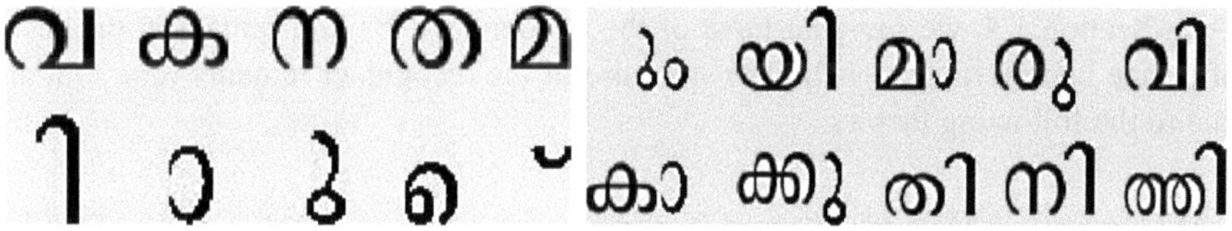

(a) (b)

Fig. 5 Popular symbol level unigrams and bigrams in Malayalam: (**a**) popular symbols and (**b**) popular co-occurring symbols

- *Word Segmentation of Complex Scripts:* We assumed that the input to the recognizer is a segmented word. However, document segmentation is not a trivial task, especially for Indian languages with complex scripts [18]. In many cases, one is required to segment pages that come from a homogeneous document collection, such as a book. In such cases, one can employ learning-based approaches to improve the word segmentation results considerably [19]. For documents with simple layout and reasonable line spacing, traditional segmentation schemes based on X–Y cuts will suffice.
- *Adapting to a Document Collection:* As mentioned before, the documents often come from a homogeneous collection. A potential approach to improve the classification accuracy is to utilize the similarity of styles across pages, and retrain the classifier as you go. We have employed this approach to the recognition of Malayalam documents with considerable success [20].
- *Using Word-Level Language Models:* One of the potential problems that remain unsolved for the recognition of printed as well as handwritten Malayalam text is that of using a dictionary. As we mentioned in the introduction, the number of legitimate words in Malayalam is potentially infinite due to inflections and combination of multiple words into a single one using *sandhi* rules. This means that one cannot use a fixed dictionary for Malayalam. However, it might be possible to develop a verification routine that uses a core dictionary and a set of rules to decide whether a recognized word is legal according to the language or not. Since the definition of character (or UNICODE) is different from that of symbol (or component) for Malayalam (as also for many Indian scripts), we compute the language and script model in terms of recognizable symbols. Figure 5 shows some of the popular symbols and co-occurring symbols in the language.

3 Recognition of Online Handwriting

Online handwriting is recorded as a sequence of strokes, where each stroke represents the sequence of points through which the pen moves from a pen-down to the pen-up. The strokes form the basic component of writing, and they capture both spatial and temporal information in the process of writing.

In Section 1.4, we saw that most of the challenges for OCR remain in the case of online handwriting as well. The structure of the recognizer remains very similar due to the following factors:

- The writing of Malayalam script is non-cursive as the pen is always lifted while moving from one akshara to the next. Hence one can split the problem into recognition of the strokes, and combination of the results to recognize a word.
- The strokes of a character form the primitives for recognition, which is similar to the connected components in the case of OCR. The problem is to combine the recognition results of the individual strokes to form a word recognizer.
- Problems such as cuts and merges in OCR have their counterpart in online handwriting, where different users write the same character using different number of strokes.

The recognition of online handwriting is much more challenging than printed symbols arising from the additional variability that is introduced by (i) writing style, (ii) writing speed, and (iii) writing direction. Due to this, the word recognizer has to deal with higher levels of uncertainty and needs to employ more powerful methods to achieve satisfactory results. We will now take a look at the specific issues in the stroke and the word recognition algorithms.

3.1 Stroke Recognition

The primary concerns in stroke recognizer are that of efficiency and accuracy. The stroke is represented as a sequence of points, which are the positions of the pen tip sampled at regular intervals in time. Hence, the number of points in two instances of the same stroke can vary considerably. A recognizer for such data can either convert it into a fixed-length representation or use models that can handle variable length representations such as hidden Markov models (HMMs) or dynamic time warping (DTW) based comparison. The first class is considerably more efficient than the second, while both have specific cases, where they are superior in terms of recognition accuracy.

The efficiency is extremely important for online handwriting due to the expectations of real-time performance, and the requirement to handle large number of classes. The number of stroke classes in online Malayalam handwriting is around 150. One could employ a two-stage approach (see Fig. 6(a)), where a fast classifier employing a fixed-length representation of the stroke, such as a neural network or SVM-DDAG, is used to perform the initial classification. The top-N results of this preliminary recognizer are considered as potential candidates and a discriminating classifier is employed that refines the potential class labels. Note that the accuracy of the stroke recognizer is expected to be low even after the two-stage approach. Hence it is important to compute the top-k results with confidence measures that can be used by the word recognizer to find the most likely word. The coarse classifier can employ a variety of popular features such as moments and frequency domain

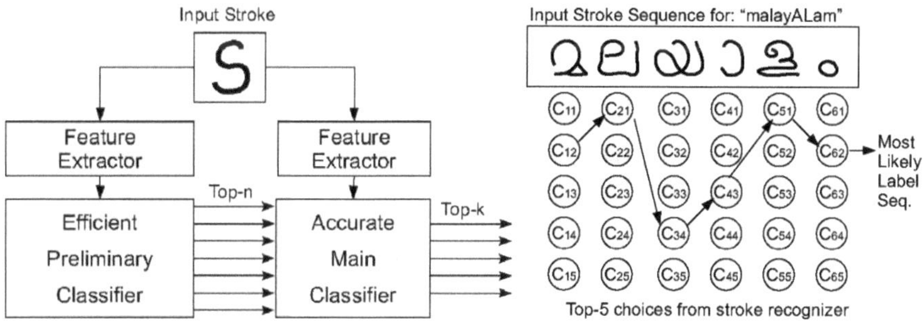

(a) Stroke Recognizer (b) Word Recognizer

Fig. 6 The stroke recognizer (a) employs two-stage architecture for efficiency. The word recognizer (b) uses the top-k choices from (**a**) to infer the most likely word. Word recognizer uses the options provided and find the best possible word (as in (**b**))

representations. However, computation of discriminative classifiers for time-series data is not well understood.

3.1.1 Dealing with Similar Strokes

Many stroke classes in Malayalam have very similar shapes, while differing in a specific part of the stroke. A discriminative classifier would give varying importance to different parts of the stroke, while looking at specific pairs of stroke classes. Consider two sequences of points representing any pair of similar characters as seen in Fig. 7. Fixed-length representations that lend to traditional discriminant analysis characterize the overall shape of the strokes and hence will be unable to concentrate on specific portions of the handwriting where the difference is present. Karteek et al. [21] present a DTW-based mechanism to get over this problem that aligned two strokes to obtain a fixed-length representation corresponding to each pair. The mechanism aligns corresponding parts of the strokes, and one can learn the relative discrimination capability of each sub-stroke using traditional discriminant analysis techniques.

Another potential approach to improving the stroke recognition accuracy is the combination of online and off-line characteristics. One could compute these independently for each stroke and combine the result. An interesting alternative would be to represent a stroke as a sequence of sub-strokes, where the number of sub-strokes employed would decide the amount of online information that is preserved. By varying the sub-stroke length, one can continuously move from the online to the off-line domain [25].

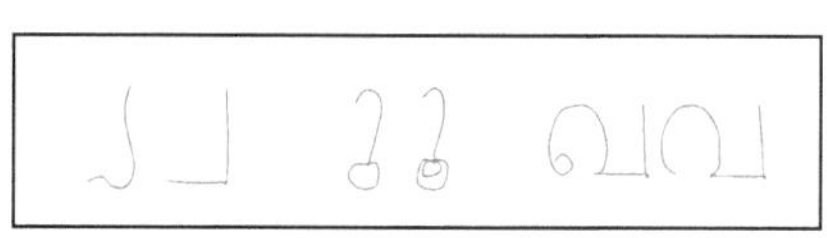

Fig. 7 Example of pairs of stroke classes that look similar in Malayalam

3.2 Word Recognizer

The stroke recognizer returns the top-k results with confidence values for each of the input stroke. One could attempt to segment a word into individual aksharas, and then recognize the aksharas independently. However, such a segmentation is not possible by inter-stroke spacing alone in the case of Malayalam, as the distance between strokes in an akshara is often equal to the inter-akshara spacing. For example, the word "malayALam" written in Fig. 6(b) contains four aksharas, while the strokes are almost equally spaced. The word recognizer should hence come up with the most likely interpretation of the stroke sequence as a sequence of aksharas. This is extremely difficult, as the number of possible interpretations for a sequence of N strokes, with top-k recognition results is k^N. Each of these interpretations need to be evaluated for consistency and likelihood to arrive at the most likely interpretation of the word (see Fig. 6(b)).

However, one can reduce the number of computations required by employing a dynamic programming approach, assuming that an akshara can have at most p strokes in it. The time complexity then reduces from exponential to $O(N * k^p)$, which is linear in N.

The dynamic programming (DP) formulation has the added advantage that it can incorporate low-level language models, while computing the most likely sequence of labels. As part of the DP algorithm, one needs to check the likelihood and validity of a sequence of interpretations for the last q strokes encountered ($q \leq p$), at every point of the input. This check can incorporate the recognition confidences, spatial layouts, as well as bigram statistics.

4 Experimental Results

In order to measure the effectiveness of the different features and classifiers mentioned before, one needs to carry out extensive experiments on real-world data that are sufficient in size to get statistically significant results. We will take a look at the design and outcome of several such experiments that measure various aspects of the recognizer.

4.1 Overview of the Data Set

One of the primary requirement to have experimental results of significance is to have a large annotated corpus of data that capture the variations that are encountered in real world. The development of such a corpus is extremely challenging and interesting (Fig. 8).

Document image annotation is done at a hierarchy of levels such as block level, line level, word level, akshara level, and component level. The annotated corpus provides quantized performance metrics for various stages of the classification process,

Fig. 8 Example images from annotated corpus

Table 3 Details of the books used for the experiments

Al.No.	Book No.	# Pages	# Words	# Symbols
1	Book 1	96	11,404	74, 774
2	Book 2	119	20,298	147,652
3	Book 3	84	10,585	83,914
4	Book 4	175	21,292	152,204
5	Book 5	94	12,111	92,538

including word and component segmentation. Table 3 provides a brief overview of the complete data set, which consists of five Malayalam books. The books were chosen to span a period of 50 years in printing, as well as to incorporate variations in fonts and paper quality.

4.2 Classifier and Feature Comparisons

We noted that there are a large number of features and classifiers that have been reported in the literature. We first look at an extensive experiment that covers nine different features from various categories and seven different classifiers operating on each of the feature set. The features used are central moments (CM), discrete fourier transform (DFT), discrete cosine transform (DCT), Zernike moments (ZM), projections of the image vector using PCA, LDA and on to randomly selected vectors (RP), distance transform (DT), and the raw image pixels themselves (IMG). The set of classifiers included multi-layer perceptron (MLP), k-nearest neighbor (KNN), approximate k-nearest neighbor (ANN), support vector machines combined using majority voting (SVM-1) and using DDAG (SVM-2), and decision tree classifier (DTC). Table 4 gives the error rates in percentage for each of the feature–classifier combinations.

The second column of the table gives the number of dimensions in each feature vector. We note that the compact representations such as the moments DCT work well with traditional multi-class classifiers such as MLP and with KNN. These types of features are classifiers that are traditionally employed in many pattern classification systems. However, with the use of rich feature sets such as the raw image pixels or their projections, the error rates decrease considerably, and more importantly, the large margin classifiers (SVMs) starts outperforming the others. Among the two

Table 4 Error rates on Malayalam data set with various classifiers and features

Feat	Dim.	MLP	KNN	ANN	SVM-1	SVM-2	NB	DTC
CM	20	12.04	4.16	5.86	10.04	9.19	11.93	5.57
DFT	16	8.35	8.96	9.35	7.88	7.86	15.33	13.85
DCT	16	5.43	5.11	5.92	5.25	5.24	8.96	7.89
ZM	47	1.30	1.98	2.34	1.24	1.23	3.99	8.04
PCA	350	1.04	1.14	2.39	0.37	0.35	4.83	5.97
LDA	350	0.55	0.52	1.04	0.35	0.34	3.20	4.77
RP	350	0.33	0.50	0.74	0.34	0.34	3.12	8.04
DT	400	1.94	1.27	1.98	1.84	1.84	4.28	2.20
IMG	400	0.32	0.56	0.78	0.32	0.31	1.22	2.45

options for combining the SVMs, the DDAG is far more efficient than the one using majority voting.

In the second experiment, we investigate the resilience of the different feature sets to various types of noise that are seen in document images. We consider different levels of boundary erosions (D1–D3), blobs, cuts, and Shears. Blobs are introduced in documents due to bloating of ink, while cuts are introduced due to non-impression on low-quality paper. Shear is most commonly seen, not as a degradation but in the form of italics in text. We carry out all of the experiments using the SVM-2 classifier (Table 5).

We note that once again, the projection-based features and the raw image pixels are the most resilient to all degradations. The primary reason for the above advantage is that features that are automatically derived from the data, such as PCA and LDA, are much more robust and significant when large quantities of annotated data are available for training. We note that shear is the most difficult type of noise to handle, as it changes the overall shape of the component.

In the next two experiments, we look at two different aspects of scale and their effect on performance of classifiers. The first one looks at the dimensionality of the feature space and the information that is captured by different features, as the number of dimensions increase. Classifiers such as SVMs are adept at handling

Table 5 Error rates of degradation experiments on Malayalam data, with SVM-2 classifier

Feature	D-1	D-2	D-3	Blob	Cuts	Shear
CM	9.45	9.46	10.97	16.28	12.33	30.07
DFT	7.89	7.93	7.98	26.70	8.73	18.90
DCT	5.71	5.72	6.07	19.80	7.93	16.46
ZM	1.96	1.98	2.10	8.41	4.35	17.75
PCA	0.30	0.31	0.32	2.17	0.64	8.59
LDA	0.39	0.39	0.40	2.01	0.61	7.32
DT	1.75	1.98	2.21	10.33	5.07	12.34
RP	0.48	0.67	1.04	3.61	0.71	6.75
IMG	0.32	0.33	0.33	2.78	0.66	6.84

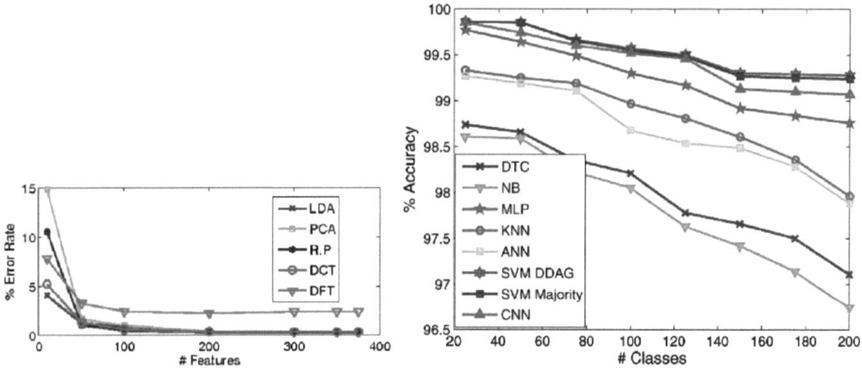

(a) (b)

Fig. 9 Classifier performance with varying number of **(a)** features and **(b)** classes (see also Plate 2 on page 316 in the Color Plate Section)

very high-dimensional feature vectors. Hence we expect to get an increase in the performance as the number of features increase, as more information is being captured. Figure 9(a) shows the error rate in classification as the number of features is increased for PCA, LDA, RP, DCT, and DFT features. The trend is clear and with the number of features increasing beyond 100, the error rate converges to a value less than 1%.

In the second experiment, we look at the ability of different classifiers to handle large number of classes. We randomly select a subset of n classes from our data set and perform classification with each of the following classifiers: MLP, KNN, ANN, DTC, SVM DDAG, SVM majority. We add two more classifiers, convolutional neural networks (CNN) and naive Bayes classifier (NB), to the experiment as the first one has proven its ability in classifying handwritten digits, and the NB classifier is a simple classifier that has provable optimal behavior under restrictive assumptions. We note that SVMs and CNN hold up their performance very well as the number of classes increase. Naive Bayes and decision tree classifiers prove to be the worst for our problem.

The third experiment is related to the idea of adaptation that was presented in Section 2.5. We use a random subset of the samples that are obtained from the verification process for retraining the classifier [20]. As we note from Fig. 10, the performance on all the books increase considerably over iterations. In the result below, we have used a sampling rate of 0.1 for selecting the training samples from the verified set.

4.3 Recognition of Online Handwriting

Experiments on online handwriting recognition on a set of 12,000 words collected from 100 writers were conducted to verify the effectiveness of the two-stage approach. The strokes are represented as a sequence of sub-strokes and a frequency

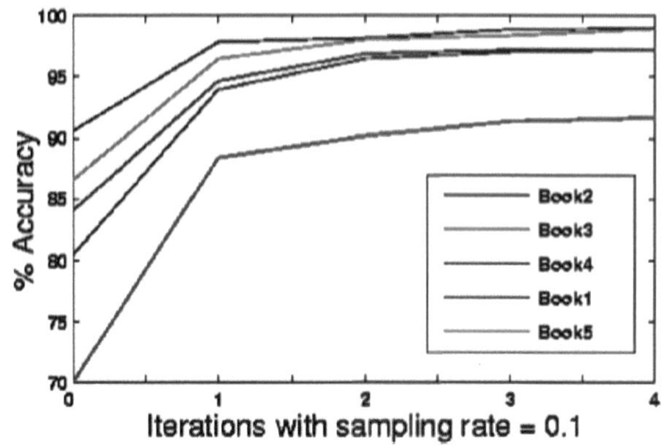

Fig. 10 Improvement in the performance of recognition of a book over iterations (see also Plate 3 on page 316 in the Color Plate Section)

Table 6 Top-k accuracy for initial stroke classifier

k	1	2	3	4	5
Top-k	0.885	0.940	0.9666	0.983	0.991

domain representation, using short-term fourier transform (SFT). The top five accuracies obtained are shown in Table 6. These results are obtained on a set of 3500 strokes from 32 writers, using an MLP classifier on fourfold cross-validation. The top one accuracy improves to 93.2% with the discriminating classifier.

The overall classifier achieves an accuracy of 93.5% at the character level in the 12,000 word database. Note that these results are based on the SFT-based features only and one could further improve it using additional features. Note that human accuracy on recognition of handwritten characters is estimated to be around 96%, without the use of contextual information. Hence, the potential for improvement at the word level is more if one uses language models such as bigrams to incorporate the context.

5 Conclusions

Malayalam is a language that has an active literary culture with a large number of publications. This combined with the high literacy rate of the people makes the problem of OCR and handwriting recognition relevant, and solutions immediately useful. The problem of Malayalam OCR and handwriting recognition is very challenging, and we have seen an initial attempt at understanding the challenges and exploring possible solutions to these problems. A large number of issues still remain to be solved and active research in this area is required to take this potential problem to useful levels, when products using the solutions would become available to the common man.

References

1. Bishop Robert Caldwell: Comparative Grammar of Dravidian Languages (1875).
2. Nagy, G. and Seth, S.C.: Hierarchical Representation of Optically Scanned Documents. Proceedings of the 7th International Conference on Pattern Recognition, Montreal (1984) 347–349.
3. Ulichney, R.: Digital Halftoning. The MIT Press, Cambridge, MA, (1987).
4. Ulloor S Parameswara Iyer: Kerala Sahitya Charitram, Vol 1–5 (in Malayalam) Kerala University Press, Trivandrum, 1953.
5. Fujisawa, H., Nakano, Y., and Kurino, K.: Segmentation Methods for Character Recognition: From Segmentation to Document Structure Analysis. in Proceedings of the IEEE **80**, (1992) 1079–1092.
6. Haralick, R.M.: Document Image Understanding: Geometric and Logical Layout. in Proceedings of the IEEE International Conference on Computer Vision and Pattern Recognition, Seattle, WA (1994) pp. 385–390.
7. Jain, A.K. and Yu, B.: Document Representation and its Application to Page Decomposition. IEEE Transactions on Pattern Analysis and Machine Intelligence **20**, (1998) 294–308.
8. Nagy G.: Twenty Years of Document Image Analysis in PAMI. IEEE Transactions on Pattern Analysis and Machine Intelligence **22**, (2000) 38–62.
9. Trier, D., Jain, A.K., and Taxt, T.: Feature Extraction Methods for Character Recognition – A Survey. Pattern Recognition **29(4)**, (1996) 641–662.
10. Bagdanov, A.D. and Worring, M.: First Order Gaussian Graphs for Efficient Structure Classification. Pattern Recognition **36**, (2003) 1311–1324.
11. Yamashita, A., Amano, T., Takahashi, I., rand Toyokawa, K.: A Model-based Layout Understanding Method for the Document Recognition System. in Proceedings of the International Conference on Document Analysis and Recognition, Saint-Malo, France (1991) pp. 130–138.
12. Kreich, J., Luhn, A., and Maderlechner, G.: An Experimental Environment for Model-Based Document Analysis. in Proceedings of the International Conference on Document Analysis and Recognition, Saint-Malo, France (1991), pp. 50–58.
13. Niyogi, D. and Srihari, S.N.: Knowledge-Based Derivation of Document Logical Structure. in Proceedings of the International Conference on Document Analysis and Recognition, Montreal, Canada (1995), pp. 472–475.
14. Mao, S. and Kanungo, T.: Empirical Performance Evaluation Methodology and its Application to Page Segmentation Algorithms. IEEE Transactions on Pattern Analysis and Machine Intelligence **23** (2001), 242–256.
15. Artires, T.: Poorly Structured Handwritten Documents Segmentation using Continuous Probabilistic Feature Grammars. in Workshop on Document Layout Interpretation and its Applications (DLIA2003).
16. Namboodiri, A.M. and Jain, A.K.: Robust Segmentation of Unconstrained On-line Handwritten Documents. in Proceedings of the Fourth Indian Conference on Computer Vision, Graphics and Image Processing, Calcutta, India (2004), 165–170.
17. Chalasani, Tejo Krishna, Namboodiri, Anoop, and Jawahar, C.V.: Support Vector Machine based Hierarchical Classifiers for Large Class Problems. in Proceedings of the sixth International Conference on Advances in Pattern Recognition, Kolkata, India (2007).
18. Sesh Kumar, K.S., Kumar, Sukesh, and Jawahar, C.V.: On Segmentation of Documents in Complex Scripts. in Proceedings of International Conference on Document Analysis and Recognition, Brazil (2007), 1243–1247.
19. Sesh Kumar, K.S., Namboodiri, Anoop M., and Jawahar, C.V.: Learning Segmentation of Documents with Complex Scripts. in Proceedings of the Indian Conference on Computer Vision, Graphics and Image Processing, Madurai, India (2006), pp. 749–760.
20. Neeba, N.V. and Jawahar, C.V.: Recognition of Books by Verification and Retraining. in Proceedings of the International Conference on Pattern Recognition, Tampa, Florida (2008).

21. Alahari, Karteek, Lahari, Satya P., and Jawahar, C.V.: Discriminant Substrokes for Online Handwriting Recognition. in Proceedings of the International Conference on Document Analysis and Recognition, Seoul, Korea (2005), 499–503.
22. NIST : NIST Scientific and Technical Databases, http://www.nist.gov/srd/.
23. LAMP: Documents and Standards Information, http://documents.cfar.umd.edu/resources/database/
24. Anand Kumar, A. Balasubramanian, Anoop M. Namboodiri and C.V. Jawahar: Model-Based Annotation of Online Handwritten Datasets. in Proceedings of IWFHR-2006, October 23-26, 2006, La Baule, France.
25. Karteek Alahari, Satya Lahari Putrevu, and Jawahar, C.V.: Learning Mixtures of Offline and Online Features for Handwritten Stroke Recognition. in Proceedings of International Conference on Pattern Recognition, Hong Kong, Aug 2006, Vol. III, pp.379-382.

A Complete OCR System for Tamil Magazine Documents

Aparna Kokku and Srinivasa Chakravarthy

Abstract We present a complete optical character recognition (OCR) system for Tamil magazines/documents. All the standard elements of OCR process like de-skewing, preprocessing, segmentation, character recognition, and reconstruction are implemented. Experience with OCR problems teaches that for most subtasks of OCR, there is no single technique that gives perfect results for every type of document image. We exploit the ability of neural networks to learn from experience in solving the problems of segmentation and character recognition. Text segmentation of Tamil newsprint poses a new challenge owing to its italic-like font type; problems that arise in recognition of touching and close characters are discussed. Character recognition efficiency varied from 94 to 97% for this type of font. The grouping of blocks into logical units and the determination of reading order within each logical unit helped us in reconstructing automatically the document image in an editable format.

Keywords Tamil · OCR · Neural networks · De-skewing · Segmentation · Gabor features

1 Introduction and Background

The value of optical character recognition (OCR), the technology that converts hard copies of documents into editable electronic form is well appreciated (see Nagy [1] for a comprehensive survey). Manual conversion of documents is too slow and expensive. Several commercial software firms like Abbyy, Scansoft have developed OCR systems for English and other European languages. OCR systems have also been developed for some of the Asian languages like Chinese, Japanese. OCR in Indian languages makes word processing a more pleasant experience considering the large sizes of Indian alphabet systems. Since the modern keyboard is designed

A. Kokku (✉)
Department of Biotechnology, IIT-Madras, Chennai 600036, India

V. Govindaraju, S. Setlur (eds.), *Guide to OCR for Indic Scripts*, Advances in Pattern Recognition, DOI 10.1007/978-1-84800-330-9_7,

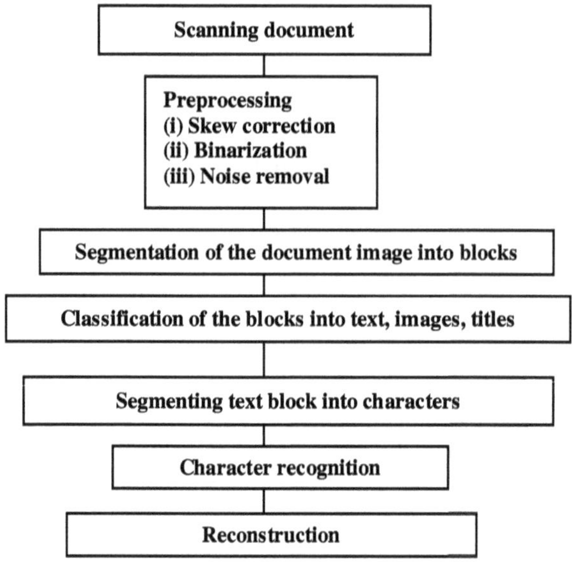

Fig. 1 Steps involved in OCR process

for English, a single Indian language character is often mapped onto a sequence of keystrokes making typing cumbersome. The rapid spread of computer literacy and usage in the 1990s in India had resulted in a growing interest in OCR. In Indian languages, complete printed OCR systems have been developed for Devanagari (Hindi) and Bengali scripts [2]. Pure text OCR systems have been developed for a few other languages like Telugu [3] and Tamil [35]. Presently, most of the currently available OCR systems for Tamil, the fourth widely used and spoken language among Indian languages, are designed for pure text. In a pure text OCR system, the text blocks have to be manually selected and should be given as an input. This forms the motivation for this work: to develop a complete OCR system for Tamil without any manual intervention.

The main components in OCR process are depicted in Fig. 1.

A review of some of the methods that are proposed in the literature for different steps in the development of the OCR system is given below.

1.1 Preprocessing

Preprocessing generally involves a series of image-to-image transformations. This is essential for other steps in document image analysis (DIA).

1.1.1 Skew Estimation

Techniques for skew estimation involve a wide range of approaches including projection profile analysis [4], Hough transform [5-7], clustering [8-10], cross-correlation [11], morphological transforms [12,13], and subspace line detection [14].

1.1.2 Binarization

Since characters are naturally binary entities, most of the commercial systems work on binarized text images. Ostu [15] proposed a nonparametric and unsupervised method of automatic threshold selection, which we have used in this work. A binarization method based on texture features was proposed by Liu and Srihari [16]. Trier and Taxt [17] and Abak et al. [18] evaluate various binarization methods.

1.2 Page Segmentation and Classification

Approaches to page segmentation and classification are divided into two categories:

1. Segmenting the image into blocks and then classifying them
2. Segmenting and classifying in the same step

1.2.1 Page Segmentation

Some techniques for segmenting a document image into homogeneous regions like text blocks, graphics are described below.

Smearing-based techniques: Wong et al. [19] introduced the run length smearing algorithm (RLSA) which is widely used as a preprocessing step for finding text. Though not for page segmentation, we used this method in overcoming the problem of text/non-text merging to be discussed in Section 3.2. Another popular approach to page segmentation is the recursive X–Y cuts (RXYC) algorithm. It is applied to clean, de-skewed binary input images. The RXYC algorithm recursively splits the document into two or more smaller rectangular blocks, which represent the nodes of a tree structure.

Several authors make use of modified versions of RXYC algorithm. Wang and Srihari [20] compare the RLSA and RXYC approaches. The RXYC algorithm is selected as being more suitable for the newspaper segmentation task. Nagy et al. [21] and Krishnamoorthy et al. [22] present a top-down approach that combines structural segmentation and functional labeling. Segmentation is based on the RXYC procedure and is guided by knowledge of the features of the document layout. We made use of projection profile methods in grouping the image blocks into logical units discussed in Section 5.1.

Segmentation algorithm presented by Pavlidis and Zhou [23] deals with a class of techniques based on smeared run length codes that divide a page into gray and nearly white parts. Segmentation is then performed by finding connected components either by the gray elements or by the white, the latter forming white streams that partition a page into blocks of printed material. Our approach to page segmentation into blocks, discussed in Section 3.1, is a modified version of the above method.

Jain and Yu [24] used a traditional bottom-up approach based on connected component extraction to implement page segmentation and region identification. Jain and Bhattacharjee [25] viewed text/non-text segmentation as a texture segmentation problem and presented a multi-channel filtering approach to texture segmentation.

1.2.2 Block Classification

Once a document page is classified into blocks, the blocks must be classified into text, non-text, etc.

Linear discriminant classifiers: The classification algorithm described by Wong et al. [19] computes some basic features from the blocks produced in the segmentation step that makes use of a smearing technique. It then discriminates between text and images by means of a linear classifier that adapts itself to varying character heights. Wang and Srihari [20] point out some limitations of the approach proposed by Wong et al. [19] related to the needed information about the geometric characteristics of the text lines. Their approach was based on statistical textural features and feature space decision techniques. In the work of Pavlidis and Zhou [23], blocks are classified into three classes: text, halftone images (produced with dithering or error diffusion techniques), and diagrams; this classification is based on across scan-line correlation function computed on the binary image.

Neural network classifiers: Le et al. [26] presented a method for classification of blocks extracted from binary document images. The authors compared four different neural network approaches for classification of blocks into two classes: text and non-text.

1.3 Optical Character Recognition (OCR)

OCR converts the individual word or character images into a character code like ASCII or Unicode. The stages of OCR process consists of character segmentation, scaling, script, language and font recognition and finally character recognition.

1.3.1 Character Segmentation

Different character segmentation algorithms are surveyed by Casey and Lecolinet [27]. Lu [28] also reviews techniques for dealing with segmenting uniformed or proportional fonts, broken or touching characters and also techniques based on text image features and recognition results.

Tsujimoto and Asada's [29] character segmentation approach was based on recognition results. Hoffman and McCullough [30] propose two algorithms, quasi-topological segmentation and topological segmentation, for segmenting uppercase serif characters based on character features. A method of segmenting merged characters by using neural networks and shortest path analysis was proposed by Wang and Jean [31].

1.3.2 Character Recognition

In their review of OCR research and development, Mori et al. [32] categorized character recognition approaches into two types: template matching and structure analysis.

Gray-scale character recognition methods proposed by Lee and Kim [33] used direct extraction of topographic features from gray-scale character images. Lee et al. [34] proposed a methodology for gray-scale character segmentation and classification. This uses projection profiles and topographical features for character segmentation and then a non-linear character segmentation path in each character segmentation region is found by using multi-stage graph search algorithm.

When it comes to character recognition in Indian languages, Siromoney et al. [35] proposed a method for recognition of printed Tamil characters. Here each character is represented as a binary matrix and encoded into a string using two different methods. The encoded strings form a dictionary. A given text is presented symbol by symbol and information from each symbol is extracted in the form of a string and compared with the strings in the dictionary. When there is an agreement, the letters are recognized and printed out in Roman letters following a special method of transliteration.

Sinha and Mahabala [36] proposed a method for recognition of Devanagari script. Recognition involves a search for primitives on the labeled pattern based on the stored description. Sinha [37] proposed a post-processor that corrects the Devanagari symbol string involving script composition syntax rules and symbol substitution rules.

The above methods work on printed, isolated characters. Chaudhuri and Pal [2, 10] used a tree classifier followed by a template-matching approach for recognizing Bangla and Devanagari scripts. These are the first complete OCR systems developed in Indian languages.

1.4 Logical Structure

Finally, for document reconstruction, the logical structure of a document has to be determined, which involves classifying different printed blocks, grouping them into logical units (e.g., stories), and determining the reading order of text blocks within each unit.

Tsujimoto and Asada [38] proposed a system in which tree transformation is performed with a set of deterministic rules, possibly repeated, which label the blocks and define their reading order. Niyogi and Srihari [39] developed a computational model for document logical structure derivation, in which a rule-based control strategy utilizes the data obtained from analyzing a digitized document image and makes inferences using a multi-level knowledge base of document layout rules.

1.4.1 Document Models

Complete document models should include logical as well as physical properties of documents. These models include licensed formats like Microsoft's RTF (rich text format) and free models such as SGML (standard generalized markup language and ODA (open document architecture).

The standard generalized markup language, or SGML, is an international standard to prescribe a format for embedding descriptive markup within a document, which controls the structure of a document. Open document architecture (ODA) is also an ISO document format for storing and exchanging documents. Documents stored in ODA format are independent of the program version and the platform on which the original document was created. Some other editable formats for reconstructing include LATEX, PDF, XML, and HTML.

In the sections to follow the description of various algorithms we use in different steps in the complete OCR system is given. This chapter is organized as follows. The preprocessing steps of the document image are described in Section 2. Section 3 explains the segmentation of the page into blocks and classification of the blocks into text, images, and titles. Text segmentation and Tamil character recognition are described in Section 4. Section 5 describes the reconstruction of the document image. Finally a discussion of results is presented in Section 6.

2 Preprocessing

A document image is obtained by optically scanning a hard copy magazine document as a black and white photograph using a flatbed scanner. It is represented as a two-dimensional array in which each element of the array is a pixel, whose value represents the intensity of the corresponding point in the hard copy page. A document of size 8.27 $\times$ 11.69 in. scanned at 300 dpi would yield an image of 3324 $\times$ 2466 pixels.

Preprocessing stage consists of four steps: compression, skew correction, binarization, and noise removal.

2.1 Image Size Reduction

Some of the image analysis techniques of text recognition, skew detection, page segmentation, and classification are applied on scaled down images. Such reduction not only increases speed of processing but also gives more accurate results for specific tasks. For scaling down, the nearest neighbor interpolation method is used. The image obtained by scaling down the original document image by ¼ is referred to as *doc1by4*.

2.2 Skew Correction

The algorithm we use for skew estimation aims at determining the orientation of the text line, which gives the document skew. So the process of skew correction involves two steps:

(i) Text part recognition
(ii) Skew estimation

2.2.1 Text Recognition

For finding the text part we use the radial basis function neural network (RBFNN) [40, 41]. The network is trained to distinguish between text and non-text (includes graphics, titles, line drawings). The input patterns for training the RBF neural networks are 20 Gabor filter [42] responses taken from different text and non-text windows of dimension 40×40, with five each in horizontal, vertical, and on both diagonal directions (Fig. 2 shows 20 Gabor filters). The neural network has 80 hidden nodes and two outputs, one for text and the other for non-text.

Now when a *doc1by4* image of Fig. 3(a) is sent to the trained RBFNN, the parts of the document labeled as text is shown in Fig. 3(b).

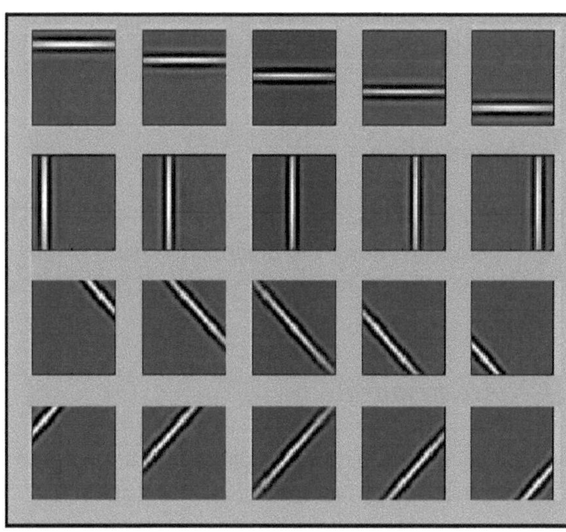

Fig. 2 20 Gabor filters

(a) (b)

Fig. 3 (**a**) *doc1by4* image and (**b**) the corresponding text-recognized image (76% of text is*INTbreak; recognized)

From Fig. 3(b), it is evident that although most of the text part is recognized correctly there are a few spaces where text is recognized as non-text and vice versa. Therefore, for a perfect text, non-text classification we will perform further processing on the above result in later stages.

2.2.2 Skew Estimation

For skew angle detection, cumulative scalar products (CSP) of windows of text blocks with the Gabor filters at different orientations are calculated. Orientation with maximum CSP gives the skew angle. Alignment of the text line is used as an important feature in estimating the skew angle. The skew angle for the document in Fig. 3(a) is found to be 0.5°.

2.3 Binarization

The threshold for binarizing the *doc1by4* image is calculated using Ostu's method [15]. Figure 4(a) shows the binarized version of the document of Fig. 3(a). After this step, the inked regions are represented by 1 and background by 0.

2.4 Noise Removal

The document is scanned for noise using a moving 5×5 window. If all non-zero pixels in the window are confined to the central 3×3 section, all those pixels are set to 0.

3 Segmentation and Classification

In the segmentation process the de-skewed, binarized, and noise-removed *doc1by4* image is segmented into rectangular blocks of isolated regions. And in the classification process the blocks are classified as text, titles, and images.

3.1 Page Segmentation

Our approach to page segmentation is a slightly modified version of segmentation method of Palvidis and Zhou [23]. When the skew-corrected binarized image of the compressed document is observed, we find that if all the wide and long white spaces are removed (excluding the white spaces between text lines) the page can be segmented into blocks. Figure 4(b) shows the document image segmented into blocks. Each white region represents a block. The contour coordinates of all the blocks are stored.

(a) (b)

Fig. 4 (**a**) Binarized document image of Fig. 3(**a**) and (**b**) image with all the long and wide white spaces removed

3.2 Classification of the Blocks

Classification of blocks into text and non-text involves comparing each block of the block-segmented image of Fig. 4(b) with the corresponding region of the textrecognized image of Fig. 3(b). The ratio of amount of text present in the region to the total area of the block is used to classify the block into text or non-text. The ratio ranges used for this classification are given in Table 1.

The second classification in Table 1, of text/non-text merge, is solved by the technique of run length smearing algorithm (RLSA), which smears off the merge

Table 1 Ratio ranges for text/non-text classification

Classification	Ratio
Text	0.5–1
Text/non-text merge	0.3–0.5
Non-text	<0.3

part thus segmenting it into independent text and non-text. Now, the non-text is segmented into titles and images based on the property that the height-to-width ratio of a title block is smaller than that of an image block. All the title and image blocks are stored as separate image files, which are used in reconstruction. All the segmented and recognized blocks of Fig. 3(a) are shown in Fig. 5.

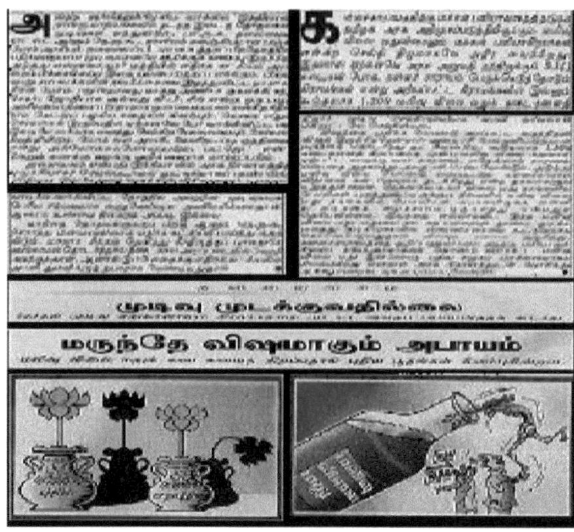

Fig. 5 All the segmented blocks of Fig. 3(a)

4 Optical Character Recognition

The text blocks have to be segmented into lines, words, and characters. For text block segmentation and character recognition the inverted binarized document (i.e., 0 for background and 1 for foreground) is taken. For character recognition the original document (without any size reduction) is used.

4.1 Line, Word, and Character Segmentation

The text blocks are first segmented into lines, lines into words, and then into individual characters. For segmentation of text blocks into lines the horizontal projection on the y-axis is used. The best threshold value for segmentation is chosen by trial and error, using the information of the height of the text block and the approximate line height.

Since the font used in Tamil newsprint is typically italic-like, with characters slanting at 79.21° with respect to the horizontal, for segmenting the line into words and characters inclined projection is taken on the text line. The segmentation is accurate if we have enough space between characters. If the characters are too close to each other or touch each other, segmenting becomes difficult.

For extracting characters that are too close but non-touching, connected component extraction method is employed, in which components are segmented not by horizontal separation but based on their connectedness. Segmentation and recognition of touching character string require segmenting the string at different intervals followed by recognition.

4.2 Recognition of Characters

A radial basis function neural network (RBFNN) is trained for the recognition of characters. The full set of 157 characters which includes isolated Tamil characters, English numerals, and punctuation marks are taken for training the neural network.

The characters are placed at the center of a 52×52 window and the input patterns to the RBF neural network are obtained from the response of 40 Gabor filters with 10 along each of four directions. The RBF neural network has 300 hidden nodes and 157 outputs, each output corresponding to a character.

The trained neural network is used for the recognition of the segmented characters.

Figure 6 shows the text part given for recognition and the output of the neural network for character recognition in HTML format. Ninety-six percent recognition *rate is* obtained for the text block in Fig. 6. In general, the recognition rate varied from 90 to 97%.

5 Reconstruction of the Document Image

5.1 Logical Structure Derivation

Derivation of logical structure of a document involves finding the relationship among various blocks of the document and grouping document blocks into logical "units," each unit representing an article or a story. The next step involves finding the reading order of the blocks within each unit.

For finding the logical units, it seems to be reasonable to assume that the magazine document page is represented in the form of a tree of nested rectangular logical units. We use X–Y cuts for grouping blocks into logical units; title information is also used in this process. We also assume that surrounding an article we have a suf-

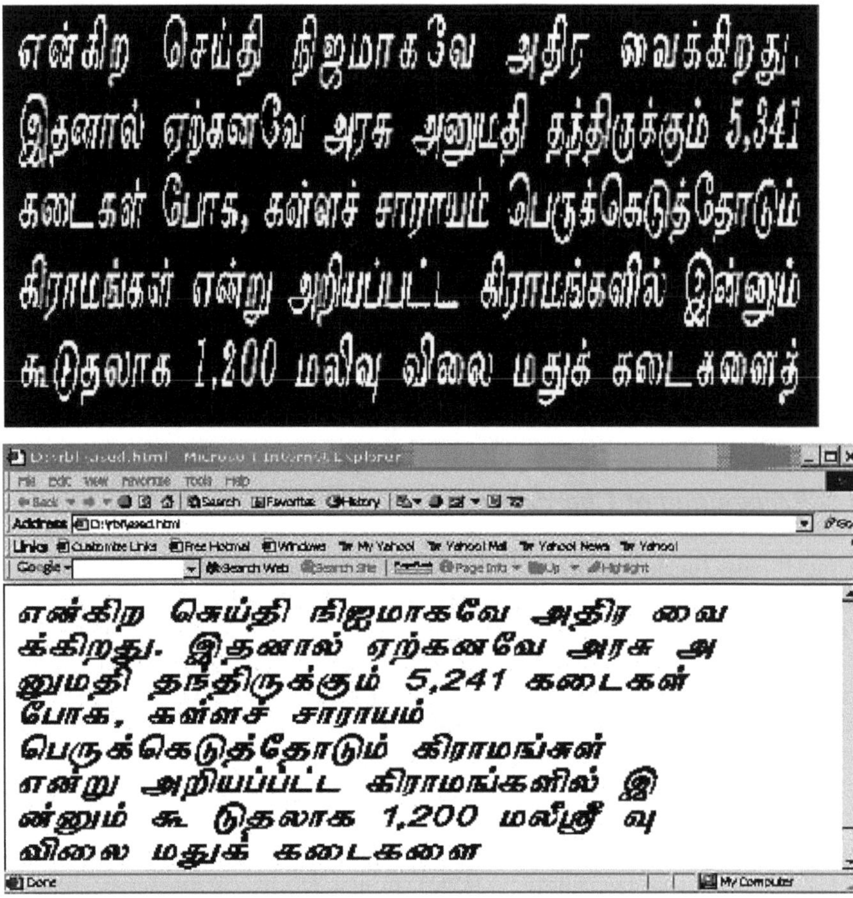

Fig. 6 Recognized text part (in HTML format)

ficiently wide white space, which separates it from other articles. Within a logical unit, the read order starts at the top left corner block and goes from top to bottom and moves left to right covering all the blocks.

5.2 Reconstruction into HTML Format

The final step involves translation of the blocks and unit information into an editable symbolic description of the logical structure of the document. For this, we choose the HTML (hyper text markup language) format. The feature of CSS (cascade style sheets) is used for placement of the recognized text and images. Figure 7 shows the reconstructed HTML image of Fig. 3(a).

Fig. 7 Document image of Fig. 3(a) reconstructed in HTML format

6 Results and Conclusions

6.1 Results

We tested the OCR system described in 25 document pages scanned from *India Today* (Tamil) magazine (more examples are shown in [43]). The page background was restricted to plain monochrome. Documents with a variety of layouts were selected.

Table 2 shows the variation of efficiency and time taken for various processes.

Table 2 Performance table (per page)

Process	Accuracy	Time taken
Text recognition	75–90 %	10–15 s
Skew estimation	92%	2–3 s
Segmentation and classification	96%	50–55 s
Character recognition	94–97%	5–20 min (varies linearly with the amount of text present)

Maximum errors in text recognition arise at the borders between text and non-text. For example, in some cases, when there is a caption in close proximity to an image, it may not be possible to delineate the white streaming space. Errors arise in delineating the border between text and non-text in such cases.

The system is implemented in MATLAB. Implementing in C considerably reduces the processing time.

6.2 Conclusions

We present a complete OCR system for Tamil newsprint. The system includes the full suite of processes from skew correction, binarization, segmentation, text and non-text block classification, line, word and character segmentation and character recognition to final reconstruction. Neural networks are applied to two subtasks: (1) text identification and (2) character recognition. Our approach of using RBF neural network gave fairly good results in recognition of text part and also in character recognition. The text-recognized image is effectively used in two situations: (a) skew estimation and (b) classification of the blocks.

Gabor filters played an important role in the extraction of features from the document image as well as from characters. These Gabor features are given as input to the RBF neural network. Gabor filter response is also used in the estimation of skew angle.

In the entire OCR process, the toughest challenges are faced in document segmentation and character recognition. Document segmentation is recognized as a hard problem and it may not be possible to formulate a single algorithm, which works with all kinds of documents. Our approach gave reasonable segmentation results with the class of document images chosen in this work. The error in segmentation of merging text/non-text regions, which occurs when the text and non-text are too close, is solved by the technique of RLSA.

Currently, characters of only a single font and font size are being recognized. We assume that font type used in a given newsprint sample is known as prior knowledge. The case of touching characters presents a serious difficulty in character segmentation. Our method of touching character segmentation worked for characters that are barely touching; it failed for complicated overlapping characters.

An important step in document image analysis is development of a suitable document model. A method for converting the physical structure of the magazine document into its logical structure is proposed. While reconstructing the logical structure, the read order is used in composing the document items. This helped to automatize the reconstruction process of converting into HTML format.

The algorithms developed can be easily made applicable to a larger class of documents and other Indic scripts:

- By training the RBF neural network for that particular text in text recognition
- Setting the appropriate dimensions of horizontal and vertical windows to pick the white spaces in segmentation of the document image into blocks
- Training the RBF neural network for recognizing the characters of that particular style

References

1. Nagy, G.: Twenty years of document image analysis in PAMI. IEEE Transactions on Pattern Analysis and Machine Intelligence, 22(1), 2000, pp. 38–62.
2. Chaudhuri, B.B. and Pal, U.: An OCR system to read two Indian language scripts: Bangla and Devanagari (Hindi). Proceedings of Intl' Conference on Document Analysis and Recognition, Ulm, Germany, pp. 1011–1015, 1997.
3. Rajasekharan, S.N.S. and Deekshatulu, B.L.: Generation and recognition of printed Telugu characters, Computer Graphics and Image Processing 6, 1977, pp. 335–360.
4. Bagdanov, A. and Kanai, J.: Projection profile based Skew estimation Algorithm for JBIG compressed images. Proceedings of Intl' Conference on Document Analysis and Recognition, Ulm, Germany, 1997, pp. 401–405.
5. Srihari, S.N. and Govindaraju, V.: Analysis of textual images using the hough transform. Machine Vision and Applications, 2(3), 1989, pp. 141–153.
6. Pal, U. and Chaudhuri, B.B.: An improved document skew angle estimation technique. Pattern Recognition Letters, 17(8), 1996, pp. 899–904.
7. Yu, B. and Jain, A.K.: A robust and fast skew detection algorithm for generic documents. Pattern Recognition, 29(10), 1996, pp. 1599–1629.
8. Hashizume, A., Yeh, P.S. and Rosenfeld, A.: A method of detecting the orientation of aligned components. Pattern Recognition Letters, 4, 1986, pp. 125–132.
9. O'Gorman, L.: The document spectrum for page layout analysis. IEEE Transactions on Pattern Analysis and Machine Intelligence, 15(11), 1993, pp. 1162–1173.
10. Chaudhuri, B.B. and Pal, U.: A complete printed Bangla OCR system. Pattern Recognition, 31(5), 1998, pp. 531–549.
11. Yan, H.: Skew correction of document images using interline cross correlation. CVGIP: Graphical Models and Image Processing, 55(6), 1993, pp. 538–543.
12. Chen, S. and Haralick, R.M.: An automatic algorithm for Text Skew estimation in document images using recursive morphological transforms. Proceedings of First IEEE International Conference on Image Processing, 1994, pp. 139–143, Austin, Texas.
13. Chen, S. and Haralick, R.M.: Recursive erosion, dilation, opening and closing transforms. IEEE Transaction on Image Processing, 4(3),1995, pp. 335–345.
14. Aghajan, H.K. and Kailath, T.: SLIDE: Subspace-Based line detection. IEEE Trans on Pattern Analysis and Machine Intelligence, 16(11), 1994, pp. 1057–1073.
15. Ostu, N.: A threshold selection method from gray scale Histograms. IEEE Transactions on Systems Man Cybernet, 8, 1979, pp. 62–66.
16. Liu, Y. and Srihari, S.N.: Document image binarization based on texture features. IEEE Transactions on Pattern Analysis and Machine Intelligence, 19(5), 1997, pp. 540–544.
17. Trier, O.D. and Taxt, T.: Evaluation of binarization methods for document images. IEEE Transactions on Pattern Analysis and Machine Intelligence, 17(3), 1995, pp. 312–315.
18. Abak, A.T., Baris, U., and. Sankur, B.: The performance evaluation of thresholding algorithms for optical character recognition. Proceedings of 4th International Conference on Document Analysis and Recognition, 1997, pp. 697–700, Ulm, Germany
19. Wong, K.J., Casey, R.G., and Wahl, F.M.: Document analysis system. IBM Journal of Research and Development, 26(6) 1982, pp. 647–656.
20. Wang, D. and Srihari, S.N.: Classification of newspaper image blocks using texture analysis. Computer Vision, Graphics and Image Processing 47, 1989, pp. 327–352.
21. Nagy, G., Seth, S., and Viswanathan, M.: A prototype document image analysis system for technical journals. IEEE Computer, 25(7), 1992, pp. 10–22.
22. Krishnamoorthy, M., Nagy, G., Seth, S., and Viswanathan, M.: Syntactic segmentation and labeling of digitized pages from technical journals. IEEE Transactions on Pattern Analysis and Machine Intelligence, 15(7), 1993, pp. 737–747.
23. Pavlidis, T. and Zhou, J.: Page segmentation and classification. CVGIP 54(6), 1992, pp. 484–496.
24. Jain, A. K. and Yu, B.: Document representation and its application to page decomposition. IEEE Transactions on Pattern Analysis and Machine Intelligence, 20(3), 1998, pp. 294–307.

25. Jain, A.K. and Bhattacharjee, S.: Text segmentation using Gabor filters for automatic document processing. Machine Vision and Applications, 5(3), 1992, pp. 169–184.
26. Le, D.X., Thoma, G.R., and Wechsler, H.: Classification of binary document images into textual or nontextual data blocks using neural network models. Machine Vision and Applications, 8, 1995, pp. 289–304.
27. Casey, R.G. and Lecolinet, E.: A survey of methods and strategies in character segmentation. IEEE Transactions on Pattern Analysis and Machine Intelligence, 18(7), 1996, pp. 690–706.
28. Lu, Y.: Machine printed character recognition – An overview. Pattern Recognition, 28(1), 1995, pp. 67–80.
29. Tsujimoto, S. and Asada, H.: Resolving ambiguity in segmenting touching characters. Proceedings of First International Conference on Document Analysis and Recognition, 1991, pp. 701–709.
30. Hoffman, R.L. and McCullough, J.W.: Segmentation methods for recognition of machine printed characters. IBM Journal of Research and Development, 1971, pp. 153–165.
31. Wang, J., and Jean, J.: Segmentation of merged characters by neural networks and shortest path. Pattern recognition, 27(5), 1994, pp. 649–658.
32. Mori, S., Suen, C.Y. and Yamamoto, K.: Historical review of OCR research and development. Proceedings of IEEE, 80(7), 1992, pp. 1029–1058.
33. Lee, S.W. and Kim, Y.J.: Direct extraction of topographic features for gray scale character recognition. IEEE Transactions on Pattern Analysis and Machine Intelligence, 17(7), 1995, pp. 724–729.
34. Lee, S.W., Lee, D.J., and Park, H.S.: A new methodology for gray-scale character segmentation and recognition. IEEE Transactions on Pattern Analysis and Machine Intelligence, 18(10), 1996, pp. 1045–1050.
35. Siromoney, G., Chandrasekaran, R., and Chandrasekaran, M.: Machine recognition of printed Tamil characters. Pattern Recognition, 10, 1978, pp. 243–247.
36. Sinha, R.M.K., and Mahabala, H.: Machine recognition of Devanagari script. IEEE Transactions on Systems Man Cybernet, SMC-9, 1979, pp. 435–441.
37. Sinha, R.M.K.: Rule based contextual post-processing for Devanagiri text recognition. Pattern Recognition, 20, 1987, pp. 475–485.
38. Tsujimoto, S. and Asada, H.: Major components of a complete text reading system. Proceedings of IEEE, 80(7), 1992, pp. 1133–1149.
39. Niyogi, D. and Srihari, S.N.: Knowledge-based derivation of document logical structure. International Conference on Document Analysis and Recognition, 1995, pp. 472–475, Montreal, Canada
40. Moody, J.E. and Darken, C.J.: Fast learning in networks of locally tuned processing units. Neural Computation 1, 1989, pp. 281–294.
41. Haykin, S.: Neural networks: A comprehensive foundation. Prentice Hall, 1999
42. Daugman, J.G.: Uncertainty relation for resolution in space, spatial frequency, and orientation optimized by two-dimensional visual cortial filters. Journal of the Optical Society of America A, 2(7), 1985, pp. 1160–1169.
43. Aparna, H.K.: "Document image analysis: A complete OCR system development for Tamil magazine documents", M.S. Thesis, Department of Electrical Engineering, Indian Institute of Technology, May, 2003, Madras.

Experiments on Urdu Text Recognition

Omar Mukhtar, Srirangaraj Setlur, and Venu Govindaraju

Abstract Urdu is a language spoken in the Indian subcontinent by an estimated 130–270 million speakers. At the spoken level, Urdu and Hindi are considered dialects of a single language because of shared vocabulary and the similarity in grammar. At the written level, however, Urdu is much closer to Arabic because it is written in Nastaliq, the calligraphic style of the Persian–Arabic script. Therefore, a speaker of Hindi can understand spoken Urdu but may not be able to read written Urdu because Hindi is written in Devanagari script, whereas an Arabic writer can read the written words but may not understand the spoken Urdu. In this chapter we present an overview of written Urdu. Prior research in handwritten Urdu OCR is very limited. We present (perhaps) the first system for recognizing handwritten Urdu words. On a data set of about 1300 handwritten words, we achieved an accuracy of 70% for the top choice, and 82% for the top three choices.

Keywords Optical character recognition · Urdu · Indic scripts

1 Introduction

Urdu is a major language of south Asia spoken by an estimated 130–270 million speakers. It is the national language of Pakistan and one of the 23 official languages of India. Urdu is an Indo-Aryan language of the Indo-Iranian branch and belongs to the Indo-European family. It is related to Arabic, Persian, and Hindi. An Urdu speaker can understand spoken Hindi and vice versa given that they share the Indic language grammar and some of its vocabulary. Thus, at the phonological and grammatical levels, Urdu and Hindi can be even considered as dialects of the same language. The differences arise because of the influence of Persian and Arabic on Urdu

O. Mukhtar (✉)
Centre for Unified Biometrics and Sensors, Department of Computer Science and Engineering, University at Buffalo, Amherst, NY 14228, USA
e-mail: omukhtar@cubs.buffalo.edu

V. Govindaraju, S. Setlur (eds.), *Guide to OCR for Indic Scripts*, Advances in Pattern Recognition, DOI 10.1007/978-1-84800-330-9_8, © Springer-Verlag London Limited 2009

Table 1 Urdu and Arabic characters

Arabic	خ	ح		ج	ث		ت		ب	ا
Urdu	خ	ح	چ	ج	ث	ٹ	ت	پ	ب	ا
Arabic	ص	ش	س		ز		ر	ذ		د
Urdu	ص	ش	س	ژ	ز	ڑ	ر	ذ	ڈ	د
Arabic	ل		ك	ق	ف	غ	ع	ظ	ط	ض
Urdu	ل	گ	ک	ق	ف	غ	ع	ظ	ط	ص
Arabic			ي		ه		و		ن	م
Urdu		ے	ی	ھ	ہ	ء	و	ں	ن	م

and the influence of Sanskrit on Hindi. This is reflected in Urdu being written in the Persian–Arabic Nastaliq script and Hindi being written in Devanagari script.

Urdu is written from right to left and uses a modified set of Persian alphabets and Arabic alphabets. It has 37 letters in the alphabet, 28 of which are taken from Arabic (Table 1). Like Arabic, the shapes of characters in Urdu are determined by their position in the word. The same letter can have different shapes when written in isolation, in the initial part, in the middle, or as the final letter of a word. It too does not have the notion of lowercase and uppercase, does not use space as boundary between words, has many diacritics, and uses similar rules for joining characters (ligatures).

Characters are grouped into joiners and non-joiners (Fig. 1). The non-joiners or separators can only acquire two types of shapes corresponding to the isolated and final positioning. Unlike Arabic, in addition to the four basic shapes (initial, medial, final, and isolated), characters can also have context-sensitive shapes.

There are some other significant differences between Urdu and Arabic (Table 2) writing as well. Arabic writing is more cursive and flowing, as it is mostly written in the Naskh calligraphic style whereas Urdu is generally written in the Nastaliq style. Urdu also has more character classes than Arabic and the shapes of the ligatures are quite different. Connected characters do not follow a baseline because the joined characters in Urdu are positioned according to their preceding, succeeding, and vertical justification of the ligature.

Urdu has 10 numerals (Fig. 2) that are taken from the eastern Arabic numerals. These are written from left to right, opposite to the direction of the text (Fig. 3) unlike Arabic.

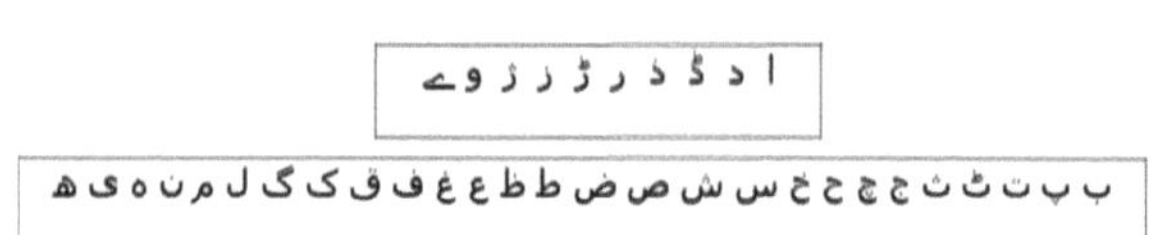

Fig. 1 Joiners (*bottom row*) and non-joiners (*top row*) in Urdu

Table 2 Comparison of Urdu with Arabic and Hindi

Characteristic	Urdu	Arabic	Hindi
Writing order	Right to left	Right to left	Left to right
Vertical justification	Center	Base	Top
Cursive	Yes	Yes	Yes
Diacritics	Yes	Yes	Yes
# Letters	39	28	40

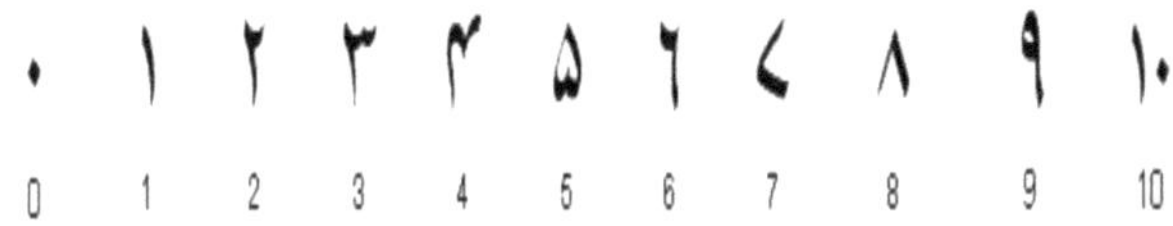

Fig. 2 Urdu numerals and their equivalent numerals

Fig. 3 The number is read as 1947 and not 7491 in Urdu

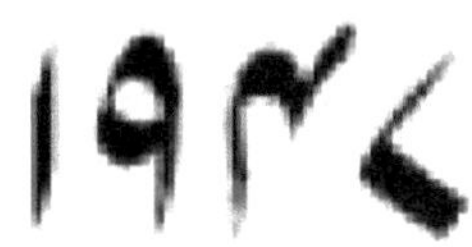

While there is a significant body of research in Arabic OCR, there has been relatively little available in Urdu OCR. Based on the similarities between Arabic and Urdu it would seem that an Arabic OCR would work quite well on Urdu text. However, Urdu presents unique challenges because of the context-sensitive variations of character shapes, differences in styles, absence of a reliable baseline, and additional alphabets and ligatures. Most importantly, in Urdu, space is not used as boundary between adjacent words and it is not possible to separate the words without semantic knowledge of the words.

There are some letters in Urdu that share the same basic shape but differ in the placement of the dot(s) or nuqta(s). In a word with multiple characters with dot(s), the only way to differentiate between two characters is through association of the dot(s) to the basic shape. This is further complicated when adjoining characters in a word have dot(s) Table 3.

In Urdu diacritics act as dependent vowels and are used along with consonants and independent vowels to prolong or stress their sounds. The diacritics (Aerabs) are optionally used in writings. Native speakers can figure out the correct pronunciation of a word by looking at its context or by virtue of their knowledge of Urdu (Table 4).

Table 3 Letters with similar shapes

Characters with similar base forms	
ت پ ٹ ث ب	ب
ح چ خ	ج

Table 4 Diacritics in Urdu

In machine-printed Urdu, gaps between words are connected. The dots are written as a rhombus whereas in handwritten Urdu, a single dot is written as a point, two dots are often written as tilde (~), and the three-dot group is written as a tilde over or under a single dot (Table 4). Many characters share the same basic shape and it is only through these dots that one can correctly identify two similar looking but different characters. Thus, correct recognition and association of these dots to the basic shape is very important in handwritten Urdu recognition.

2 Urdu Language Resources

There has been relatively little research in Urdu OCR in part because of paucity of corpora and image datasets. One of the first initiatives in making Urdu corpus available for research was the EMILLE Project, initiated by Lancaster University [16]. The project has released 200,000 words of English text translated into Bengali, Gujarati, Hindi, Punjabi, and Urdu, creating parallel corpus across these languages. The corpus also has 512,000 words of spoken Urdu, from BBC Radio. It also contains 1,640,000 words of Urdu text. These resources are also annotated with a large morphological syntactic tagset [7].

The Center for Research in Urdu Language Processing (CRULP) at the National University of Computer and Emerging Sciences in Pakistan has also been developing corpora and associated tools for Urdu text processing [10]. The following tasks have been undertaken:

(i) Collected a raw corpus of 19 million words of Urdu text (mostly from the newspaper – Jang News)
(ii) Developed a syntactic tagset similar to PENN Treebank tag-set
(iii) Manually tagged a corpus of 100,000 POS (parts of speech) words
(iv) Developed a 230 spelling error corpus based on typographical errors in newspapers and student term papers [17]
(v) Developed a corpus of Urdu names taken from telephone directories from all major cities of Pakistan
(vi) Created the Online Urdu Dictionary (OUD) which contains 120,000 entries, with 80,000 words annotated
(vii) XML tagged the OUD containing about 20 parameters per word
(viii) Translated 12,000 words in English
(ix) Developed a corpus-based lexicon of 50,000 words with frequency data and annotation [11]

3 Prior Work in Urdu Recognition Systems

In this chapter, we will provide an overview of the previous research in written Urdu OCR which was primarily limited to machine-printed text. Given the similarities between Arabic and Urdu, we will explore the extension of Arabic OCR to Urdu script. This will also be the first report on recognition of handwritten Urdu. Both Arabic and Urdu text recognition systems have to address similar challenges, thus it would be informative to first review how Arabic text recognition research evolved. We base our survey on [14], which provides a recent survey of off-line Arabic handwriting recognition as well as Arabic character recognition.

Machine print recognition is a simpler task than handwritten Arabic recognition. In 1980, [19] proposed a standard Arabic character set. Around the same time, the standard digitized Urdu character set, Noori Nastaliq, was developed by [12]. The following year, [23] presented an approach to Arabic OCR on newspaper headlines. This system used concavities, loops, and connectivity as features for machine print recognition. Amin and Masini [1] proposed a system for segmentation and recognition that used horizontal and vertical projections and shape-based primitives to recognize Arabic machine print in the presence of font variation. On a dataset of 100 multi-font words, their system achieved a character recognition rate of 85% and a word recognition rate of 95%.

Like Urdu, the characters in Persian are also taken from Arabic with some extra alphabets. A Persian OCR system proposed in [8] used a segmentation algorithm that traced word contours to separate disconnected overhanging characters and used a sliding window approach for most characters. BBN developed a script-independent OCR [2, 3, 15, 18] that has been tested on English, Arabic, Chinese, Japanese, and other languages. Their system uses a hidden Markov model (HMM) with the features based on image frames. The lexicon, language model, and the training data are language dependent.

Handwritten text is characterized by the changes in font, shape of letters or words, errors such as missing placement of dots, slant of line, overlapping adjoining words, and other issues that make handwritten text recognition much more difficult. Issues such as change in font, shape, errors, absence of uniform spacing between words and slanting of line is common to text written in any languages by a single writer. On top of these we have the variability in writing styles between individual people. These issues are further complicated in Arabic (and Urdu) because of the inherently cursive script as well as the change in shape of a character based on its position in the word.

Urdu OCR research is a relatively new, and the focus has been mostly on machine-printed Urdu text. While limited research has been conducted in individual printed character recognition, printed numeric recognition, line segmentation, individual character segmentation, layout analysis, and skew correction no work exists in Urdu word recognition.

Character recognition is the task of correctly identifying a single isolated character. In 2003, Pal and Sarkar present an approach for recognizing printed Urdu characters and numerals [22]. They use a binary-tree classifier in which eachdecision node (non-terminal nodes) uses coarse-grained water-reservoir features to classify similar looking characters into subsets. They report an accuracy of 97.8% on 3050 characters and numerals (the ratio of characters to numerals is not mentioned). Most of the errors in their experiments are due to segmentation failure. Shamsher et al. proposed another system based on neural network classification to recognize individual machine-printed character and numerals [25]. They train their system on Urdu text written in a 72-pt Ariel font and achieve accuracy of 98.3% on the test set (size is not mentioned).

Pal and Sarkar have tested their system on 3050 printed characters which contains numerals as well as characters [22]. Topological features, contour features, and water reservoir features are used to achieve an accuracy of 97.8%. Shamsher et al. also tested their system on printed Urdu numerals in Ariel font [25] and report achieving an accuracy of 98.3%.

4 Prior Work in Urdu Document Preprocessing

Shafait et al. present *geometric layout analysis* of Urdu documents [24] to segment the document image into homogeneous zones, each consisting of only one physical layout structure, and to identify their spatial relationship (e.g., reading order or line segmentation). They apply an existing Roman script layout analysis system to Urdu documents by incorporating textline models for Urdu as well as modifying the reading order (since Urdu is written from right-to-left). The algorithm they modify is based on the area Voronoi diagram [13]. They look at text line segmentation and reading-order accuracy on five types of typed documents: books, poetry, digest, magazine, and newspaper. The accuracy of their line segmentation system on a test set of 25 images on the five classes of document ranges from 72% on newspapers to 92% on poetry. They do not report the accuracy on the reading-order determination. Pal and Sarkar have also studied line segmentation in printed Urdu text [22]. First, they perform skew detection and correction followed by line segmentation using horizontal projection profiles. Hough transform-based technique is used to estimate and correct skew [22]. Skew is corrected to within $+/-0.5\%$ in 97.4% of the cases. Husain also performs skew detection and correction in the preprocessing step but does not mention the algorithm used and the accuracy achieved [9].

A *compound character* or a ligature is a group of two or more characters written so that there is no space between the characters, i.e., all the characters in the group are connected to each other. This phenomenon is not seen in machine-printed English but is seen in machine-printed Arabic, Urdu, Persian, and Hindi. Husain proposed a system for the recognizing machine-printed Urdu compound characters (ligatures) written in Nastaliq font [9, 27]. The Urdu language has about 20,000 ligatures (defined in the Noori Nastaliq font), counting the frequent ones for training and testing [6]. In his research, the similarity between Arabic and Urdu text recognition is noted and is used to aid in recognizing Urdu characters. A neural network is used to separate special ligatures from base ligatures, and in the second stage, the minimum centroid-to-centroid distance is used to associate special ligatures. Each of 200 test ligatures is classified into 45 output classes with 100% accuracy.

The *character segmentation* algorithm used by Pal and Sarkar uses a combination of component labeling and vertical projection profile method [22]. After the page of text has been segmented into lines, each individual text line is scanned vertically. If in one vertical scan two or less object pixels are encountered then the scan is denoted by 0, else the scan is denoted by the number of object pixels in that column. Thus a vertical scanning histogram is constructed. If there exists a run of at least K1 (empirically determined) consecutive 0's then the midpoint of that run is considered as the boundary of a character. Because of kerned characters (those that overlap with neighboring characters) of Urdu script some characters may not be segmented properly by the projection profile method. The authors report an accuracy of 96.9% on a private data set of unknown size.

Durrani provides a comprehensive overview of the *word segmentation* problem in Urdu [4]. As noted before, the presence of spaces do not indicate word boundaries in Urdu text. Ambiguity arises when Urdu words can be used in isolation as well as compound words, analogous to toothache and "tooth ache." He uses unigram and bigram matching on a set of 2367 words based on the CLURP collection which has 221 cases of space insertion and 183 cases of deletion. Accuracy of 95.7% is reported (Fig. 4).

Fig. 4 *Arrows* indicate possible segmentation of the words. The correct segmentation is the *arrow*, incorrect segmentation is the *lines*

5 Experiments

To the best of our knowledge, no handwritten Urdu data set exists. We chose 100 Urdu words, and asked two different writers (one native and the other non-native) to write each of the words, eight times, thus yielding 1600 handwritten words. The separate training and testing sets were ensured to have words which were made of Urdu characters (and not Arabic characters). Binarization was done using the thresholding algorithm in [21]; slant normalized was performed by a moment-based algorithm. GSC features are computed from the normalized character images (Fig. 5).

GSC features [5, 26] include local, intermediate, and the global features from the image. The gradient features capture stroke shape on a local neighborhood of pixels. The gradient features are computed by convolving two Sobel operators on the binary image. These operators approximate the x- and y-derivatives in the image. The gradient is a vector with magnitude and direction, but only the direction is used in the computation of the feature vector. The direction of the gradient can range from $0°$ to $359°$. This range is split into 12 non-overlapping regions of $360°/12°$.

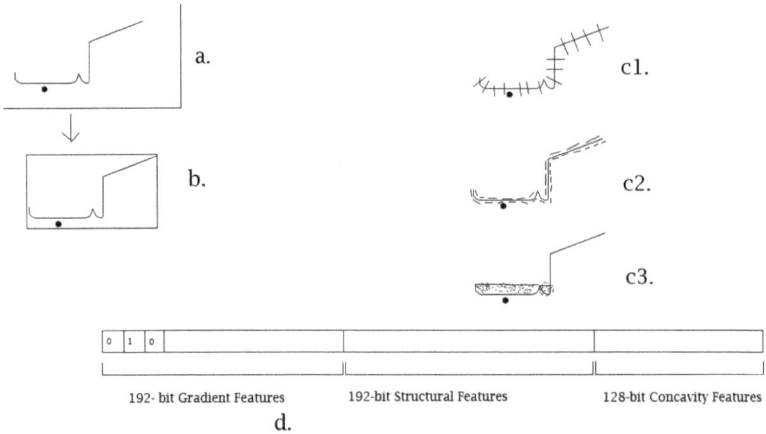

Fig. 5 Feature extraction from a Urdu word: **(a)** raw image; **(b)** slant correction and bounding box; **(c1)** gradient features; **(c2)** structural features; **(c3)** concavity features; and **(d)** total 512-bit GSC feature vector

Table 5 Preliminary results

Classifier	Accuracy			Training images	Testing images	Writers
	Top-1	Top-2	Top-5			
k-NN	70%	80%	84%	612	657	2
SVM	75%			612	657	2

Structural features are computed from the image by examining the gradient direction in a slightly larger neighborhood of each pixel. These structural features capture the curvature in an approximate fashion. Concavity features are global features of the image like pixel density, horizontal and vertical strokes in image, and concavity. Concavity features capture the image density and stroke information. A 512-bit binary vector represents the GSC feature.

With a k-NN classifier, we obtained an accuracy of 70% for the top-1 choice and 80% for the top-2 choices. With an SVM classifier, the accuracy was 75% for the top choice (Table 5). We point out that our word-level accuracy can be considered reasonable when compared with [22] where 97.8% is reported as character-level accuracy on 3050 individual characters and numerals.

References

1. Amin A, Masini G (1986) Machine recognition of multifont printed Arabic texts. Proc. Int. Conf. Patt. Recogn., Paris, pp. 392–395
2. Bazzi I, Schwartz R, Makhoul J (1999) An Omnifont Open-Vocabulary OCR system for English and Arabic. IEEE Trans. Pattern Anal. Mach. Intell. 21:495–504

3. Decerbo M, Natarajan P, Prasad R, MacRostie E, Ravindran A (2005) Performance improvements to the BBN BYBLOS OCR system. Proc. Int. Conf. Doc. Anal. Recogn., pp. 411–415
4. Durrani N (2007) Typology of Word and Automatic Word Segmentation in Urdu Text Corpus. NU
5. Favata JT, Srikantan G, Srihari SN (1994) Handprinted Character/Digit Recognition using a Multiple Feature/Resolution Philosophy. IWFHR 1994
6. Gulzar A, Shafiq-ur-Rahman (2007) Nastaleeq: A Challenge Accepted by Omega. EuroTex, Bachotek, Poland, 2007.
7. Hardie A (2003) Developing a tagset for automated part-of-speech tagging in Urdu. Proc. Corpus Linguist. 16
8. Hashemi MR, Fatemi O, Safavi R (1995) Persian Cursive Script Recognition. Proc. Int. Conf. Doc. Anal. Recogn., pp. 869–873
9. Husain, SA (2002) A multi-tier holistic approach for Urdu Nastaliq recognition. INMIC 2002, Islamabad pp. 528–532
10. Hussain S (2008) Resources for Urdu Language Processing, In the proceedings of the 6th Workshop on Asian Language Resources, IJCNLP'08, IIIT Hyderabad, India.
11. Ijaz M, Hussain S (2007) Corpus based Urdu Lexicon development. Proc. Conf. Lang. Technol., Peshawar
12. Jamil AM (1982) Noori Nastaliq: Computerized Urdu Calligraphy, Elite Publishers, Karachi.
13. Kise K, Sato A, Iwata M (1998) Segmentation of page images using the area Voronoi diagram. Comp. Vis. Image Underst. 70(3):370–382
14. Lorigo LM, Govindaraju V (2006) Off-line Arabic handwriting recognition: A survey. PAMI doi: 10.1109/TPAMI.2006.102
15. Makhoul J, Schwartz R, Lapre C, Bazzi I (1998) A script-independent methodology for optical character recognition. Patt. Recogn. 31:1285–1294
16. McEnery A, Baker J, Gaizauskas R, Cunningham H (2000) EMILLE: towards a corpus of South Asian languages. Br. Comput. Soc. Mach. Trans. Spec. Group.
17. Naseem T, Hussain S (2007) Spelling error trends in Urdu. Proc. Conf. Lang. Technol., Peshwar
18. Natarajan P, Decerbo M, Keller T, Schwartz R, Makhoul J (2003) Porting the BBN BYBLOS OCR system to new languages. Proc. Symp. Doc. Image Underst. Technol. pp. 47–52
19. Nouh A, Sultan A, Tolba R (1980) An approach for Arabic characters recognition. J. Eng. Sci., Univ. Riyadh 6:185–191
20. Nouh A, Sultan A, Tolba R (1984) On feature extraction and selection for Arabic character recognition. Arab Gulf J. Sci. Res. 2:329–347
21. Otsu (1979) A threshold selection method from gray-level histograms. IEEE Trans. Syst. Man Cybern. 19:62–66
22. Pal U, Sarkar A (2003) Recognition of printed Urdu script. ICDAR doi: http://doi.ieeecomputersociety.org/10.1109/ICDAR.2003.1227844
23. Parhami B, Taraghi M (1981) Automatic recognition of printed Farsi texts. Patt. Recogn., 14:395–403
24. Shafait F, Adnan-ul-Hasan, Keysers D, Breuel TM (2006) Layout Analysis of Urdu Document Images. INMIC 2006, Islamabad
25. Shamsher I, Ahmad Z, Orakzai JK, Adnan A (2007) OCR for printed Urdu script using feed forward neural network. Proc. Acad. Sci. Eng. Technol.
26. Srikantan G, Lam SW, Srihari SN (1996) Gradient-based contour encoding for character recognition. Patt. Recogn. 29(7), 147–1160
27. Wali A, Hussain S (2006). "Context Sensitive Shape-Substitution in Nastaliq Writing System: Analysis and Formulation" International Joint Conferences on Computer, Information, and System Science, and Engineering (CISSE2006), 53–58.

The BBN Byblos Hindi OCR System

Prem Natarajan, Ehry MacRostie, and Michael Decerbo

Abstract The BBN Byblos OCR system implements a script-independent methodology for OCR using hidden Markov models (HMMs). We have successfully ported the system to Arabic, English, Chinese, Pashto, and Japanese. In this chapter, we report on our recent effort in training the system to perform recognition of Hindi (Devanagari) documents. The initial experiments reported in this chapter were performed using a corpus of synthetic (computer-generated) document images along with slightly degraded versions of the same that were generated by scanning printed versions of the document images and by scanning faxes of the printed versions. On a fair test set consisting of synthetic images alone we measured a character error rate of 1.0%. The character error rate on a fair test set consisting of scanned images (scans of printed versions of the synthetic images) was 1.40% while the character error rate on a fair test set of fax images (scans of printed and faxed versions of the synthetic images) was 8.7%.

Keywords Hidden Markov Models · Hindi · OCR · Trainable · Script independent

1 Introduction

1.1 Background

The BBN Byblos OCR system is a trainable, HMM-based OCR system that has been demonstrated on multiple languages, scripts, and domains. All language-specific parameters are derived automatically from training data without modifying the fundamental system. Furthermore, the HMM modeling paradigm implicitly segments connected characters allowing the system to naturally process noisy data or

---

P. Natarajan (✉)
BBN Technologies, Cambridge, MA 02138, USA
e-mail: prem@bbn.com

V. Govindaraju, S. Setlur (eds.), *Guide to OCR for Indic Scripts*, Advances in Pattern Recognition, DOI 10.1007/978-1-84800-330-9_9,

languages with connected scripts such as Arabic. We have reported on the results of our efforts in porting our OCR system to Arabic, Pashto, English, and Chinese in earlier papers [1,2,5]. Porting the Byblos OCR system to a new language is a three-step process: character-set identification and data collection, model training, and system optimization. In this chapter we describe these steps in detail as they were applied to new Hindi data.

1.2 Review of Basic OCR System

In this section we briefly review the BBN Byblos OCR system. For a more detailed description the reader is referred to [1]. A pictorial representation of the system is given in Fig. 1 In the figure, knowledge sources are depicted by ellipses and are dependent on the particular language or script. The OCR system components themselves are identified by rectangular boxes and are independent of the particular language or script.

At the top level, the OCR system can be divided into two basic functional components: training and recognition. Both training and recognition share a common pre-processing and feature extraction stage in which we first de-skew the scanned image and then locate the regions (bounding boxes) of individual text lines. The feature extraction program computes a feature vector as a function of the horizontal position within each of these line regions (see Fig. 2) For each line of text, we apply a sliding analysis window that moves along the direction of writing by a step size that is less than the width of the analysis window. Each position of the analysis

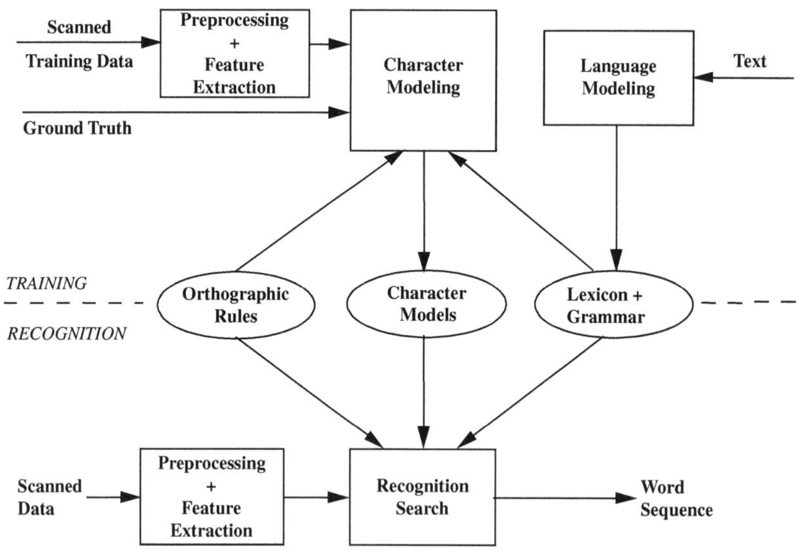

Fig. 1 Block diagram of the Byblos OCR system

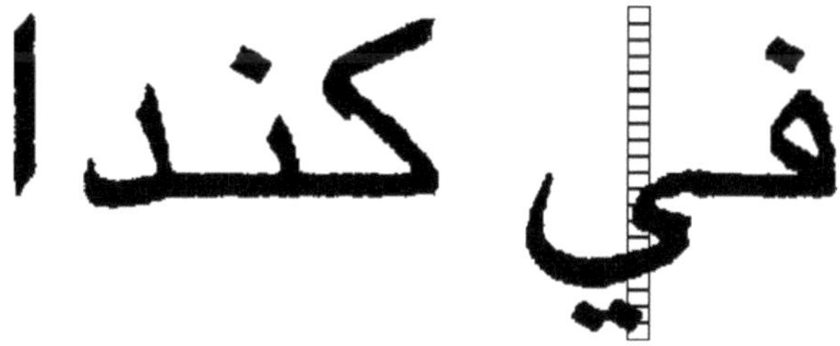

Fig. 2 Feature extraction on a line of Arabic text

window is referred to as a frame. For each frame we compute a language-independent, feature vector that is a numerical representation of the pixel content of the frame. In summary, this process can be thought of as scanning the line of text from left to right with a fixed-width window and measuring observations from that window at regular intervals.

The OCR system models each character with a multi-state, left-to-right HMM. Each state has an associated output probability distribution over the features. The number of states and the allowable transitions are system parameters. For our full-character experiments we use 14-state, left-to-right HMMs with the topology shown in Fig. 3 The number of states per model and the number of models per character have an impact on the overall performance vs speed metric and is in fact one of the primary variables in our experiments. The basic topology, however, is the same for all configurations and all languages.

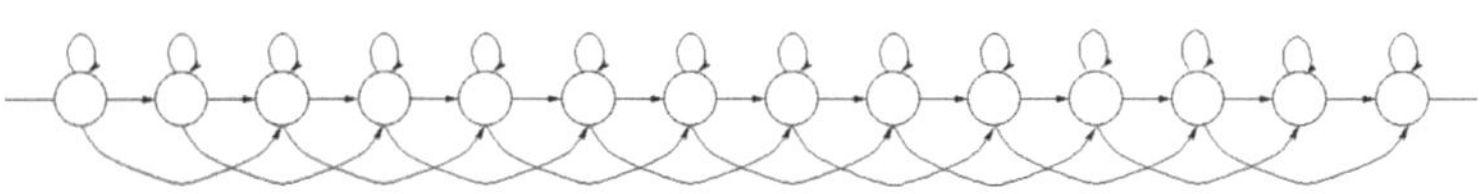

Fig. 3 HMM model topology – 14-state, left to right

1.3 Model Training and Recognition

Training is performed using the Baum–Welch or forward–backward algorithm, which aligns the feature vectors with the character models to obtain maximum likelihood estimates of HMM parameters. For our system the HMM parameters are the means and variances of the component gaussians in the gaussian mixture model of the state output probabilities, the mixture component weights, and the state transition probabilities. During recognition we search for the sequence of characters that is most likely given the feature-vector sequence and the trained character models, in accordance with the constraints imposed by a lexicon and/or a statistical grammar. The use of a lexicon during recognition is optional but its use generally results in a lower character error rate (CER). The lexicon is estimated from a suitably large text corpus. Typically the grammar (language model), which provides the probability of any character or word sequence, is also estimated from the same corpus.

A significant advantage of HMM-based systems is that they provide a language-independent framework for training and recognition. At the same time, they do not require the training data to be segmented into words or characters and can be automatically trained on non-segmented data [6,7]. Because the HMM modeling paradigm is primarily data driven, the parameters of the HMM, namely the transition probabilities between the states and the means and variances of the Gaussian mixture associated with each HMM, are derived purely from the training data. Consequently, the performance of the trained model is fundamentally dependent upon the nature and quality of the training data. It is important that the training data set be adequately large and diverse – especially when the nature of the test data (i.e., fonts, sizes, quality, source, etc.) is not predictable. When the test set domain is relatively predictable, the system can be retargeted for optimal performance simply by training on an adequate corpus of data from that domain.

2 DATA

2.1 Hindi Character Set

Hindi is written in the Devanagari script which is also used by many other south Asian languages such as Marathi and Sanskrit. The Devanagari script is a phonetic script consisting of a set of character glyphs that represent basic speech–sounds (i.e., similar to phonemes). And, as with any phonetic script, the orthography of a word dictates the pronunciation of the word. Devanagari can be encoded in the Unicode standard as well as several other encoding schemes such as ISCII 91 (Indian Script Code for Information Interchange) and PC_ISCII. For our OCR system, we have decided to use the Unicode standard for all languages because it is widely supported and covers a wide variety of scripts.

The Unicode standard for Devanagari contains 76 basic Devanagari glyphs including consonants and vowels. In Devanagari, many vowels take on a different shape based on whether they occur by themselves or in combination with a consonant. In addition, each combination of a vowel and a consonant produces a "new" ligature glyph. As a result, where needed, the Unicode standard includes two code points for a vowel – one for the independent vowel form and another for the dependent form.

For example the consonant "ra" (र), the vowel "e" (◌े) and the diacritic anusvara (◌ं) combine to form रें. The consonant "ra" (र) can also be combined with the vowel "i" (ि◌) to form "ri" – रि. Notice in the last example that the vowel "i" is rendered before the consonant even though it is pronounced after it. In addition to vowels forming alternate glyph shapes, combinations of consonants can form even more severe alterations to the component glyphs sometimes reducing glyphs to short strokes or diacritic-like marks.

In our current system, based on the available training data set, we model 50 of these basic glyphs and the associated ligatures with separate HMMs for each basic glyph and for each ligature. In addition we also include 30 basic Latin characters which occur in training – mostly digits and punctuation. In particular, for the results reported in this chapter, we modeled 800 ligatures representing combinations of different glyphs. We have included here a list of the basic glyphs that constitute the Devanagari script and the glyphs that were used in our experiments. Also shown is the process by which the basic glyphs are combined to form ligatures.

Basic Devanagari (Hindi) character (glyph) Set

◌ँ ◌ं ◌ः ऄ अ आ इ ई उ ऊ ऋ ऌ ऍ ऎ □

ऐ ऑ ऒ ओ औ क ख ग घ ङ च छ ज झ ञ ट

ठ ड ढ ण त थ द ध न ऩ प फ ब भ म य

र ऱ ल ळ ऴ व श ष स ह ◌□ऽ ◌ा ◌ि

◌ी ◌ु ◌ू ◌ृ ◌ॄ ◌ॅ ◌ॆ ◌े ◌ै ◌ॉ ◌ॊ ◌ो ◌ौ ◌्

ॐ ◌॑ ◌॒ ◌॓ ◌॔ क़ ख़ ग़ ज़ ड़ ढ़ फ़ य़

ॠ ॡ ◌ॢ ◌ॣ । ॥ ० १ २ ३ ४ ५ ६ ७ ८ ९

Basic Hindi glyphs used in our experiments

◌ः अ आ इ ई उ ऊ ऋ □ ऐ ऑ ओ औ क ख ग घ

च छ ज झ ट ठ ड ढ ण त थ द ध न प फ ब भ म

य र ऱ ल व श ष स ह ◌ा ◌ी ◌ॉ ◌ो ◌ौ

How ligatures (compound glyphs) are formed

क + ◌् + ट + ◌् + र + ◌ि = क्ट्रि

च + ◌ि + ◌ं = चिं

फ + ◌□+ ◌् + र + ◌े + ◌ं = फ़्रें

स + ◌् + त + ◌् + र + ◌ि = स्त्रि

ग + ◌् + र + ◌े = ग्रे

ज + ◌□+ ◌ि + ◌ं = ज़िं

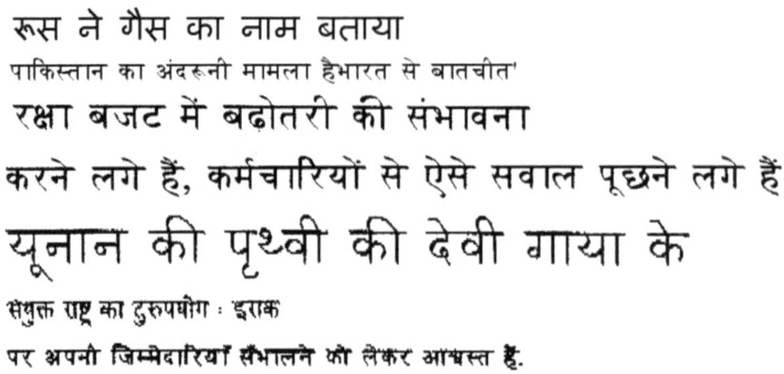

Fig. 4 The lines of text are sample Hindi images from our corpus. The first two lines are examples of synthetic images, the next two lines are examples of scans of printed documents, and the final three lines are examples of scans of faxed documents

2.2 Corpus

For our initial experiments in Hindi OCR we used a corpus of computer-generated (synthetic) images of Hindi text. The synthetic images were generated from Hindi text data that were collected from various Hindi language web sites. The corpus was also augmented with degraded versions of the synthetic images. We considered two types of degradations: (1) printing the synthetic images and then scanning the printed versions and (2) faxing the printed versions and then scanning in the faxed copies of the documents. The first type of images we refer to as the print version and the second is referred to as the fax version (Fig.4).

The training set consisted of 1773 pages containing a total of 904,067 instances of 800 different characters in four different fonts and three different font sizes. Of this set, 109 pages (83,452 characters, 512 unique) were fax versions and 108 pages (87,368 characters, 521 unique) were print versions. In terms of composition of training data, the print and fax versions each made up less than 10% of the data. As such, the overwhelming bulk of the training data consisted of synthetic images.

For testing, we used a set of 337 pages none of which were used for training. The test images contained a total of 188,854 character instances that spanned a set of 585 unique characters. Of the 337 pages, 26 were fax version (21,982 characters, 385 unique) images and 28 were scan versions (22,748 characters, 376 unique).

3 Experimental Results

3.1 Model Configuration

We modeled each basic glyph and ligature with a 14-state, left-to-right HMM with a maximum of 256 Gaussians per HMM. We used our standard set of features that include percentiles, horizontal and vertical derivatives of percentiles, angles, correlations, and energy. The computation of the features is described in detail in [1]. Linear discriminant analysis was used to reduce the dimensionality of the raw feature set from 81 to 15. HMM training (i.e., estimation of the parameters of the HMMs) was performed using the standard expectation-maximization procedure. For our language model we trained a tri-gram on characters using the text transcriptions that were used to train the character/glyph HMMs. We did not use a word lexicon during the recognition.

3.2 Recognition Performance

Table 1 shows the results of our initial experiments. As shown in the table, the CER was 1.0% on the synthetic image test set. The CER on print images is 1.40%, a small increase over the error rate on synthetic images. In the case of the fax images, the CER is much higher – 8.7%. There are two reasons for the higher error rate on fax data.

The first reason, of course, is that fax images are noisier and more degraded than print images. Further, standard fax transmission is at a resolution of 204 × 98 dpi. Thus, even though the resulting fax pages were scanned at a resolution of 300 dpi, the data itself exhibit characteristics associated with a much lower resolution. Such low-resolution data are known to present a serious challenge for most recognizers [3]. For comparison, the print images were printed at 600 dpi and scanned at 300 dpi.

The second reason for lower performance is that the fax images form a small fraction of the training data. Because the models are trained on data that consist mostly of synthetic images, there is a mismatch between the test data and the models. Based on our experience with other languages, we believe that by retraining the models on a more even mix of training data, and by including more fax data, we can bring the error rate on fax data down by a factor of 2, perhaps more.

Table 1 Hindi character error rates on different types of data

Test set type	Character error rate (%)
Synthetic (computer-generated images)	1.0
Print (printed on paper and scanned)	1.4
Fax (printed on paper, faxed, then scanned)	8.7

4 Conclusions

We were able to train Hindi models for our BBN Byblos OCR system in a relatively straightforward manner. On clean data (such as synthetic images and clean prints of the same), we observed a character error rate in the range of 1.0 – 1.4%. On fax data, we observed a CER of 8.7%. It is important to keep in mind that these numbers represent preliminary results on a data set of limited diversity. Nevertheless, it is also important to point out that these results are consistent with past experimental results for other scripts such as Arabic, English, and Chinese.

Looking ahead, we will be investigating various system optimizations in order to determine the best system configuration for Hindi OCR. We also intend to train and test the system on a corpus of "real" Hindi images consisting of scans from newspapers, magazines, faxes, etc. We also plan to apply adaptation methods developed for English [4] to improve the performance on degraded data.

References

1. P. Natarajan, Z. Lu, I. Bazzi, R. Schwartz, and J. Makhoul, "Multilingual machine printed OCR," International Journal of Pattern Recognition and Artificial Intelligence, 15:(1), 2001, pp. 43–63.
2. P. Natarajan, R. Schwartz, M. Decerbo, and T. Keller, "Porting the BBN BYBLOS OCR system to new languages," Symposium on Document Image Understanding Technologies, 2003, pp. 47–52.
3. S. V. Rice, J. Kanai, and T. A. Nartker, " An evaluation of OCR accuracy," Information Science Research Institute, 1993 Annual Research Report, pp. 9–20, University of Nevada, Las Vegas, 1993.
4. P. Natarajan, R. Schwartz, Z. Lu, I. Bazzi, and J. Makhoul, "Robust OCR of degraded documents," Proceedings of International Conference Document. Analysis and Recognition, Bangalore, India, 1999, pp. 357–361.
5. Z. Lu, R. Schwartz, P. Natarajan, I. Bazzi, 4nd J. Makhoul, "Advances in the BBN BYBLOS OCR system," Proc. of International Conference Document Analysis and Recognition, Bangalore, India, 1999, pp. 337–340.
6. O. E. Agazzi and S. Kuo, "Hidden Markov model based optical character recognition in the presence of deterministic transformations," Patt. Recognition, 1993, pp. 1813–1826.
7. H. Fujisawa, Y. Nakano, and K. Kurino, "Segmentation methods for character recognition: from segmentation to document structure analysis," Proceedings of the IEEE, 80, (7), 1992, pp. 1079–1092.

Generalization of Hindi OCR Using Adaptive Segmentation and Font Files

Mudit Agrawal, Huanfeng Ma, and David Doermann

Abstract In this chapter, we describe an adaptive Indic OCR system implemented as part of a rapidly retargetable language tool effort and extend work found in [20, 2]. The system includes script identification, character segmentation, training sample creation, and character recognition. For script identification, Hindi words are identified in bilingual or multilingual document images using features of the Devanagari script and support vector machine (SVM). Identified words are then segmented into individual characters, using a font-model-based intelligent character segmentation and recognition system. Using characteristics of structurally similar TrueType fonts, our system automatically builds a model to be used for the segmentation and recognition of the new script, independent of glyph composition. The key is a reliance on known font attributes. In our recognition system three feature extraction methods are used to demonstrate the importance of appropriate features for classification. The methods are tested on both Latin and non-Latin scripts. Results show that the character-level recognition accuracy exceeds 92% for non-Latin and 96% for Latin text on degraded documents. This work is a step toward the recognition of scripts of low-density languages which typically do not warrant the development of commercial OCR, yet often have complete TrueType font descriptions.

Keywords Adaptive segmentation · Hindi OCR · Font files

1 Introduction

Advances in digital document processing are driving the popularity of applications applied to office and library automation, bank and postal services, publishing houses and communication technology. An important task of automatic document processing is the reading of text. The procedure of automatically processing the text components of a complex document which contains text, graphics, and/or images

M. Agrawal (✉)
LAMP of UMIACS, University of Maryland, College Park, MD 20742, USA
e-mail: mudit@umd.edu

V. Govindaraju, S. Setlur (eds.), *Guide to OCR for Indic Scripts*, Advances in Pattern Recognition, DOI 10.1007/978-1-84800-330-9_10,

can be divided into three stages: (1) region extraction and text region classification using document layout analysis; (2) text line, and possibly word (glyphs separated by white space) and character segmentation; and (3) optical character recognition (OCR). Typically, the OCR character segmentation and classifier stage needs to be redesigned for each new script, while the other stages are easier to port and can be generalized over large classes of languages. OCR technology for some scripts like Roman and Chinese is fairly mature and commercial OCR systems are available with accuracy higher than 98%, including *OmniPage Pro* from Nuance or *FineReader* from ABBYY for Roman and Cyrillic scripts, and Nuance for Asian languages.

Despite ongoing research on non-Latin script recognition, most of the commercial OCR systems focus on Latin-based languages. OCR for Indian scripts, as well as many low-density languages, is still in the research and development stage. Efforts on non-Latin scripts are quite focused and continue to be tailored for specific scripts using their inherent features explicitly. The resulting systems are often costly and do little to advance the field.

1.1 Challenges of Segmentation

The literature often distinguishes between the recognition of isolated and continuous scripts. With isolated scripts, characters are written to be separable (although they may touch due to degradation) while connected scripts cannot be easily segmented. Scripts can also be broadly classified based on word composition into syllabic and non-syllabic. In non-syllabic scripts, characters are horizontally (or vertically) separable glyphs whereas in syllabic scripts, glyphs appear as syllables, which are in turn a complex combination of one or more characters. Sometimes, characters fuse together to form new shapes, called ligatures (Fig. 1). Indic, Cambodian (Khmer), and many south-east Asian scripts are examples of syllabic scripts.

The presence of language-specific constructs, in the domain of non-Latin scripts, such as shirorekha (Devanagari), modifiers (south-east Asian scripts), writing order, or irregular word spacing (Arabic and Chinese) requires different approaches to

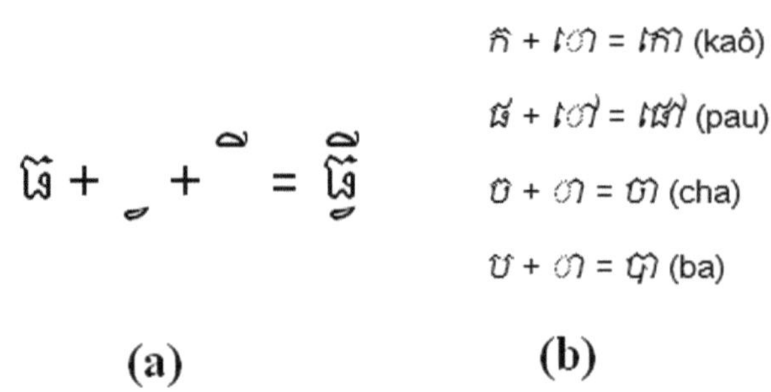

Fig. 1 (**a**) Syllable and (**b**) conjunct for Cambodian script

Fig. 2 (**a**) Burmese script; (**b**) Devanagari character composition; and (**c**) Arabic word rendering

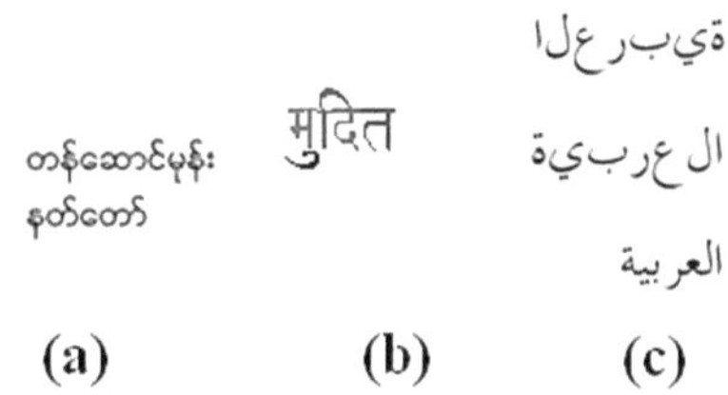

segmentation. Asian scripts, for example, share many common properties yet pose some unique challenges for segmentation. For example, in Burmese (Fig. 2a), a vowel can be used with diacritics to create other vowels. Figure 2b shows a word in Devanagari where characters are combined together to form a word. A character's appearance is affected by its ordering with respect to other characters, the font used to render the character, and the application or system environment. Figure 2c shows the word *al-arabiyyah*, in Arabic, at three stages of rendering. The first line shows the individual letters, the second line shows it with the bidirectional display mechanism, and the third line renders the letters using a glyph-shaping mechanism according to context. While conventional vertical or horizontal profiling methods fail to segment characters directly from words, character segmentation from syllables using only connected component analysis itself is a complex task which is highly correlated with the script characteristics.

Casey and Lecolinet define four methods of character segmentation [7] as follows:

1. The first is dissection based where the image is decomposed into classifiable units before feature extraction and classification. Due to its disconnectivity from the later modules, the feedback mechanism is expensive.
2. The second method tries to classify subsets of spatial features collected from a word image as a whole. Segmentation hypotheses are generated and choosing best hypothesis along the word gives best recognition result. The challenge of this approach is to come up with minimal number of possibly correct hypotheses.
3. The third involves over-segmenting the word image using heuristics. Though these techniques do fairly well in the handwriting domain, they have not yet been established in printed-character domain.
4. The fourth method recognizes an entire word as a unit and is a holistic strategy. A major drawback of this class of methods is that their use is usually restricted to a predefined lexicon.

1.2 Feature Extraction and Classification

Feature extraction [13, 31] and classification [11, 29] form the basis of most training and testing processes. Feature extraction approaches fall into two classes – spatial domain [12] and transform domain [14, 25] based. Spatial domain approaches derive features directly from the pixel representation of the pattern. With a transform domain technique, the pattern image is first transformed into another space using, for example, Fourier, cosine, slant, or wavelet transform and features are derived from the transformed images [14].

Classifiers like artificial neural network [5] or support vector machines (SVMs) [1] have been successful at recognizing various non-Latin scripts. These can work on either spatial- or transform-based features. Hidden Markov models (HMMs) [6] work on large number of training samples to estimate probability parameters. They have been quite successful in handwriting and speech recognition. Fuzzy rules [10, Mahalanobis and Hausdorff distance, and evolutionary algorithms [30] are other techniques used for recognition.

Most systems focus on feature extraction and classification to improve accuracy but they require training and the availability of class samples at the character or word levels. The objective of our work is to create a generic script recognizer which can be bootstrapped from font descriptors and can be trained using a minimal number of samples. Since our research is targeted toward low-density languages, the availability of large amounts of ground-truth data cannot be assumed [24]. For this reason, many techniques such as SVMs and HMMs which require large amounts of training data cannot be used. In addition, we feel that limited user feedback is a key to system's adaptiveness.

This chapter is organized as follows. Section 2 describes the complexity of various scripts and provides a high-level overview of our baseline recognition system. We overview the challenges and describe how a generic model can help simplify many of such challenges in Section 3, using font-file analysis, models, training and testing solutions. This is followed by experiments in Section 4 and by conclusions and directions for future work in Section 5.

2 Base Devanagari OCR System

The contributions of this work stem from observations about a base system we have described in [24, 20, designed for Devanagari script. In this section, we describe our base system which contains three different functional components: (1) hierarchical segmentation; (2) feature extraction; and (3) classification.

2.1 Background

Devanagari, an alphabetic script, is used by a number of Indian languages, including Sanskrit, Hindi, and Marathi. Many other Indian languages use close variants of this script. Although Sanskrit is an ancient language and is no longer spoken, written material still exists. Hindi is a direct descendant of Sanskrit through Prakrit and Apabhramsha, and has been influenced and enriched by Dravidian, Turkish, Farsi,

Arabic, Portuguese, and English. It is the world's third most commonly used language after Chinese and English, and there are approximately 500 million people all over the world that speak and write in Hindi. Thus, research on Devanagari script, mainly the Hindi language, attracts a lot of interest. In the rest of this document, Hindi, the language, and Devanagari, the script, are used interchangeably.

Unlike English and other Roman script languages, Hindi has few, if any, commercial OCR readers; and the ones that have products provide only custom enterprise solutions. Chaudhuri and Pal proposed a Devanagari OCR system that was ultimately purchased and is being marketed as a custom solution, but is not yet available as an off-the-shelf product. The basic components of the system, however, were described in the literature [8, 9]. After word and character segmentation, a feature-based tree classifier was used to recognize the basic characters. Error detection and correction based on a dictionary search brought the recognition accuracy of the OCR to 91.25% at the word level and 97.18% at the character level on clean images. In his Ph.D. thesis [3, Bansal designed a Devanagari text recognition system by integrating knowledge sources, features of characters such as horizontal zero crossings, moments, aspect ratios, pixel density in nine zones, number and position of vertex points, with structural descriptions of characters. These were used to classify characters and perform recognition. After correction, based on dictionary search, the average accuracy was about 87% at the character level for scanned document images.

It should be noted that both of the OCR systems mentioned above need vast amounts of training data with ground truth to achieve acceptable levels of performance. Collection and ground truthing of data is time consuming and labor intensive. Even so, before feeding a new font of a Hindi document to the OCR, the system must be retrained to obtain reasonable accuracy. In our application, we benefit from the need for only a small number of fonts for any given dictionary. This OCR does not need to be trained using a large number of training samples and is easily adapted to different types of documents.

2.2 System Design

Our Hindi OCR, designed to work on pure Devanagari, or bilingual and multilingual document images with one script Devanagari, is shown in Fig. 3. The system contains three different functional components: (1) document image preprocessing including denoising and deskewing; (2) segmentation and script identification at the word level; and (3) a classifier.

The system first scans pages of Hindi text at 300 or 400 dpi. Images are first preprocessed with denoising and deskewing [16, 15]. An implementation of DOCTRUM [28] is applied to the preprocessed images to segment them into zones, text lines, and words. Components of the page are segmented into entries based on the functional features of documents using the approach described in [21]. Figure 4 shows the segmented dictionary entries. Script identification [22, 20, 23] is applied

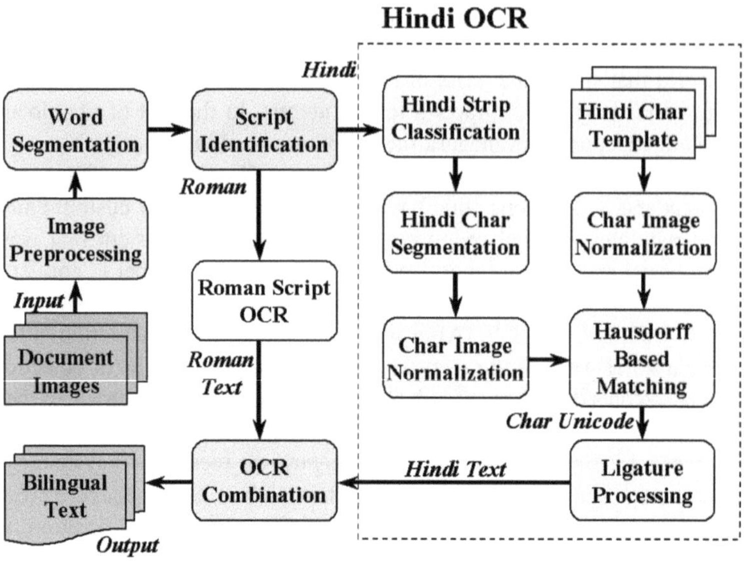

Fig. 3 System architecture

to the segmented word images to identify Devanagari script and Roman script words (including symbols neither Roman nor Devanagari). The identified Roman script word images are fed into a commercial English OCR, while the Hindi word images are first segmented into characters, and the character images are fed into a classifier to perform classification and recognition. After postprocessing, the output of the Hindi OCR is combined with the OCR output of Roman script to provide a complete result. The details of the approach and results are described in the following sections.

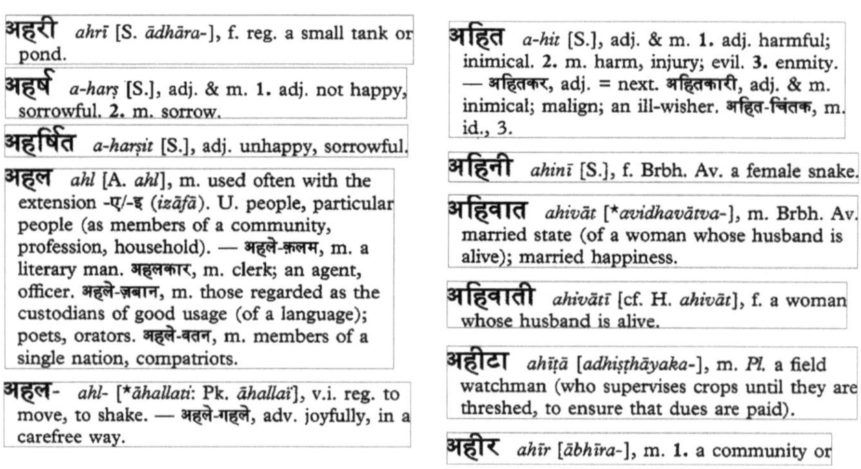

अहरी *ahrī* [S. *ādhāra-*], f. reg. a small tank or pond.

अहर्ष *a-harṣ* [S.], adj. & m. **1.** adj. not happy, sorrowful. **2.** m. sorrow.

अहर्षित *a-harṣit* [S.], adj. unhappy, sorrowful.

अहल *ahl* [A. *ahl*], m. used often with the extension -ए/-इ (*izāfā*). U. people, particular people (as members of a community, profession, household). — अहले-क़लम, m. a literary man. अहलकार, m. clerk; an agent, officer. अहले-ज़बान, m. those regarded as the custodians of good usage (of a language); poets, orators. अहले-वतन, m. members of a single nation, compatriots.

अहल- *ahl-* [**āhallati*: Pk. *āhallai*], v.i. reg. to move, to shake. — अहले-गहले, adv. joyfully, in a carefree way.

अहित *a-hit* [S.], adj. & m. **1.** adj. harmful; inimical. **2.** m. harm, injury; evil. **3.** enmity. — अहितकर, adj. = next. अहितकारी, adj. & m. inimical; malign; an ill-wisher. अहित-चिंतक, m. id., 3.

अहिनी *ahinī* [S.], f. Brbh. Av. a female snake.

अहिवात *ahivāt* [**avidhavātva-*], m. Brbh. Av. married state (of a woman whose husband is alive); married happiness.

अहिवाती *ahivātī* [cf. H. *ahivāt*], f. a woman whose husband is alive.

अहीटा *ahīṭā* [*adhiṣṭhāyaka-*], m. *Pl.* a field watchman (who supervises crops until they are threshed, to ensure that dues are paid).

अहीर *ahīr* [*ābhīra-*], m. **1.** a community or

Fig. 4 Segmented entries of the Hindi–English dictionary

2.3 *Character Segmentation*

2.3.1 Devanagari Script Overview

Devanagari has about 11 vowels (shown in the first row of Table 1) and about 33 consonants (shown in Table 2). Each vowel except अ corresponds to a modifier symbol as shown in the second row of Table 1. In Hindi, when consonants are combined with other consonants, the consonant with a vertical bar may appear as a *half-form*. Except for the characters क and फ , the half-forms of consonants are the left part of original consonants with the vertical bar and the part to the right of the bar removed. These half-consonants are shown in Table 3, where the order of characters corresponds to the character order in Table 2. Table 4 gives some examples of combinations of half-consonants with other consonants. The combination of half-consonants and other consonants are not always left–right structured. Sometimes the combination orientation is top-down, or even reorganized to become a new character. Some of these examples of special combinations are shown in Table 5. In addition to these special combinations, some special Hindi symbols are shown in Table 6. It should be noted that the list of special combinations is far from complete, so handling all these cases needs to be addressed. In [20] we address how to deal with these special cases with an operator's feedback.

2.3.2 Hindi Character Segmentation

The procedure to segment a Hindi word into characters (including core characters, and top and lower modifiers) is illustrated in Fig. 5 using the segmentation of the

Table 1 Vowels and corresponding modifiers

Vowels	अ	आ	इ	ई	उ	ऊ	ऋ	ए	ऐ	ओ	औ
Modifiers		ा	ि	ी	ु	ू	ृ	े	ै	ो	ौ

Table 2 Consonants

क	ख	ग	घ	ङ	च	छ	ज	झ	ञ	ट
ठ	ड	ढ	ण	त	थ	द	ध	न	प	फ
ब	भ	म	य	र	ल	व	श	ष	स	ह

Table 3 Half-forms of consonants with a vertical bar

क्‍	ख्‍	ग्‍	घ्‍		च्‍		ज्‍	झ्‍	ञ्‍	
			ण्‍	त्‍	थ्‍		ध्‍	न्‍	प्‍	फ्‍
ब्‍	भ्‍	म्‍	य्‍		ल्‍	व्‍	श्‍	ष्‍	स्‍	

Table 4 Examples of combination of half-consonants and consonants

क क क्क	क ल क्ल	घ न घ्न	च ञ च्ञ	ञ च ञ्च	त न त्न	प त प्त	प ल प्ल
ब व ब्व	भ न भ्न	म ल म्ल	ल ल ल्ल	श न श्न	श ब श्ब	श ल श्ल	स न स्न

Table 5 Examples of special combination of half-consonants and consonants

क ष क्ष	ज ञ ज्ञ	ट ट ट्ट	ट ठ ट्ठ	त र त्र	द द द्द
द ध द्ध	द व द्व	द व र द्व्र	श र श्र	द भ द्भ	द य द्य

Table 6 Special symbols

क़	ख़	ग़	ज़	फ़	ड़	ढ़	ँ		:	।	ऽ ँ	

Hindi word स्वीकृति as an example. The numbered arrows in Fig. 5 represent the steps of segmentation, and the characters with solid bounding boxes are the final segmentation results. The procedure to perform character segmentation has been described below. We denote the width of the Hindi word bounding box as W, the height as H, and the coordinates of the left-top corner are set to be (0, 0).

Step 1: Separate the top strip and the core-bottom strip. The separation of the top strip and the core-bottom strip is based on the location of the header line. For each word, we compute the horizontal projection (HP) and find the row (with Y-coordinate y) having the maximum value of HP. This is the candidate of the header line position. A header line candidate can be the real header line if $y \leq 0.4H$. If this condition is not satisfied, then set the HP value of this row to 0 and re-search the row with the maximum value until a real header line position is located. The maximum HP value is marked as HP_{max} and the position of the header line is marked as *hPosition*. Setting *hPosition* as the center, traverse the adjacent 10 HP values at each side of *hPosition*, and find the continuous rows whose HP values are

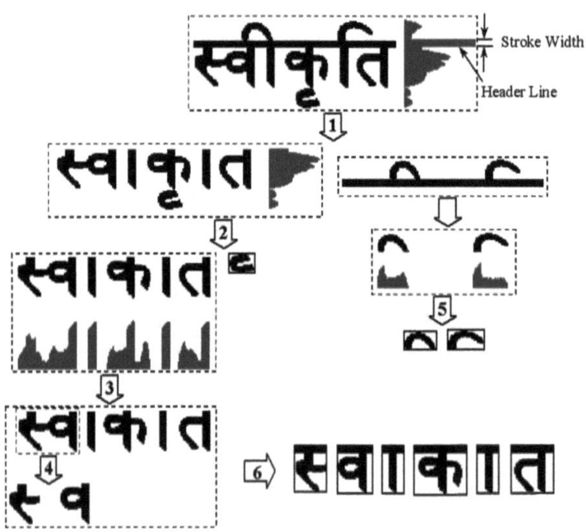

Fig. 5 The procedure of Hindi character segmentation

all greater than $0.8HP_{\max}$. The number of these continuous rows is the stroke width of this word which is marked as *StrokeWidth* and important for the postprocessing of segmentation. *hPosition* is updated as the first row's Y-coordinates of the header line. The header line separates the Hindi word into the top strip, including the header line, and the core-bottom strip. This procedure is shown in step 1 of Fig. 5.

Step 2: Identify the core strip and the bottom strip from the core-bottom strip. This procedure is briefly shown in step 2 of Fig. 5. Denoting the width and height of the core-bottom strip obtained in the last step as W_{cb} and H_{cb}, and using the Hindi word खुशनुमा which contains two lower modifiers, the detailed procedure is shown in Fig. 6, by dividing it into the following steps:

1. Compute the vertical projection VP_{cb} of the core-bottom strip (Fig. 6(a)).
2. The columns with no black pixels separate the Hindi word into several character candidates which may contain conjunct/shadow characters, or even incorrectly segmented characters (Fig. 6(b)).
3. Find the maximum height of these characters and denote it as $\mathrm{H}_{\max}$. The separated characters are divided into three groups. The first group contains all characters with height greater than $0.8\mathrm{H}_{\max}$, the second group contains characters whose height is between $0.8\mathrm{H}_{\max}$ and $0.64\mathrm{H}_{\max}$, and the remaining characters are put into the third group. The group with the maximum number of members is considered to contain normal characters without the lower modifiers, and the maximum height of members in this group is set as a threshold *hTh*. If $(H_{cb} - hTh) \geq H_{cb}/4$, the word contains at least one lower modifier (Fig. 6(b)).
4. For each separated character with a lower modifier, compute its horizontal projection HP_{cb}.
5. In the HP_{cb} obtained in the last step, setting *hTh* as the center, traverse the adjacent five values at each side of *hTh*. The row with the minimum HP_{cb} value is the boundary which segments the core-bottom strip character into the core character and the lower modifier (Fig. 6(c)).

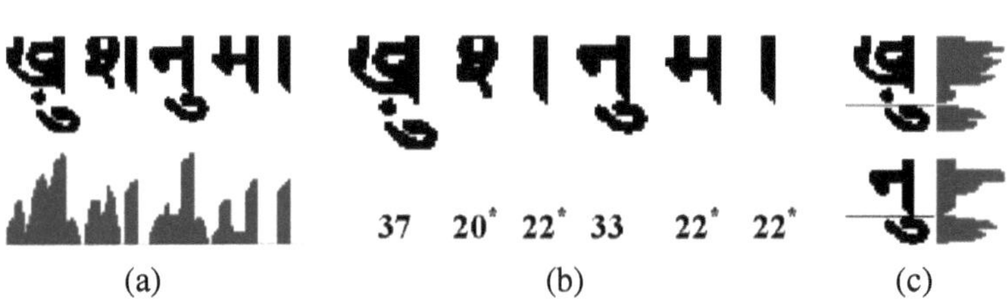

Fig. 6 Extraction of the lower modifiers from the core-bottom strip. (**a**) The core-bottom strip and its vertical projection; (**b**) separated characters based on the vertical projection, the number under each character is its height, and numbers with "*" are used to compute the threshold $hTh = 22$. Note that the second character is segmented into two characters incorrectly, while that does not affect the final result; (**c**) two characters with a lower modifier and their horizontal projections, where the two straight lines denote the separation positions

Step 3: Separate the core strip into characters. In this step, the core strip is separated into characters, and the conjunct/shadow characters, which need further segmentation, will be determined as well. We borrow the definition of shadow character from Bansal and Sinha [4]. A character is said to be under the shadow of another character if they do not physically touch each other but it is impossible to separate them merely by drawing a vertical line. In their paper, Bansal and Sinha proposed an approach to separate the core strip into characters and determine the conjunct/shadow characters based on the statistical information (such as average width, minimum and maximum width) of characters on the text line. The approach obviously cannot model our case because in the bilingual documents, Hindi words and English words are usually interlaced. It is impossible to obtain one Hindi text line which contains words with the same size. Therefore, we separate the Hindi word into characters and determine conjunct/shadow characters based on the statistical information obtained from the current Hindi word. Before extracting the information, it must be noted that the modifier ा in the Hindi word has a much smaller width than the regular characters after removing the header line, so this character cannot be applied in the computation of statistical information of character width. Fortunately, this character is easily located based on the obtained stroke width in the first step. The separation of the core strip and the determination of conjunct/shadow characters are shown in step 3 of Fig. 5, where one conjunct character is located. Taking the segmentation of another Hindi word इस्तेमाल as an example, the detailed procedure is shown in Fig. 7.

Step 4: Segmentation of the conjunct/shadow character. The segmentation of a conjunct character is complicated, and because of the different characteristics of conjunct and shadow characters, the segmentation operations of the conjunct character and the shadow character are different. They are described as follows:

Segmentation of the conjunct character. The basic idea to segment the conjunct character is to find the segmentation column from both the right and the left sides of the word image and then determine the final segmentation position by comparing these two segmentation columns. After examining all the consonants, we found the following four observations:

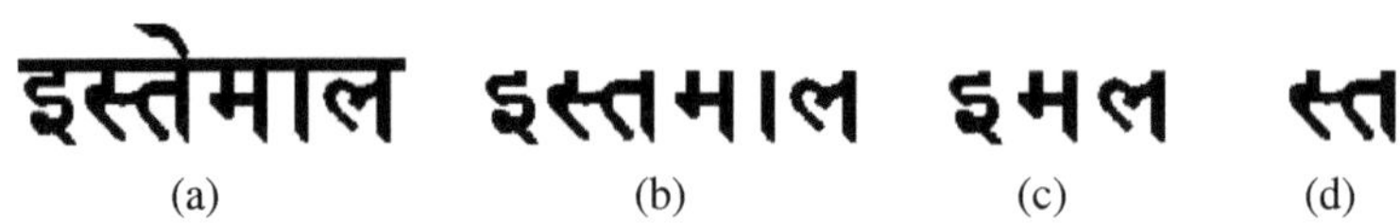

Fig. 7 Conjunct/shadow character determination. (**a**) Original word image (located header line provides *StrokeWidth* = 6); (**b**) five characters separated based on the vertical projection, with width 26, 51, 28, 7, 32, respectively; (**c**) three characters used to compute the average width, with width 26, 28, 32, respectively, where $W_{\min} = 26$ and $W_{\text{avg}} = 28.7$; and (**d**) detected conjunct character (with width 51)

1. In each conjunct character, the right part is a full consonant that is wider than the left part, and the left part is always a half-consonant.
2. For each consonant that can be combined with a half-consonant to create a conjunct character, after removing the header line, the vertical bar and the right part to the right of the vertical bar (if there is a vertical bar), the horizontal projection of the remaining part is always connected without any discontinuity.
3. Neither of the two parts of a conjunct character can be too short.
4. The pixel strength in the touching column of the two characters is usually less than that of other columns.

So the design of the segmentation algorithm which contains three steps is based on the above four observations. In the first step, segmentation column C1 is located by examining the right part of the conjunct character image (based on observations (1), (2), and (3)). Then in the second step, segmentation column C2 is located by examining the left part of the conjunct character image (based on observations (1), (3), and (4)). We use the same idea of computation of the *collapsed horizontal projection* (*CHP*) which was defined by Bansal and Sinha in their paper to detect the continuity of an inscribed image. Details of C1 and C2 measurements are shown in Figs. 8 and 9, respectively. In the last step, the final segmentation column C is determined by comparing C1 and C2 as follows:

Determine the segmentation column C by comparing C1 and C2: If a detected conjunct character is a real conjunct character, the found segmentation columns C1 and C2 should be very close. And considering the stop conditions of the searching

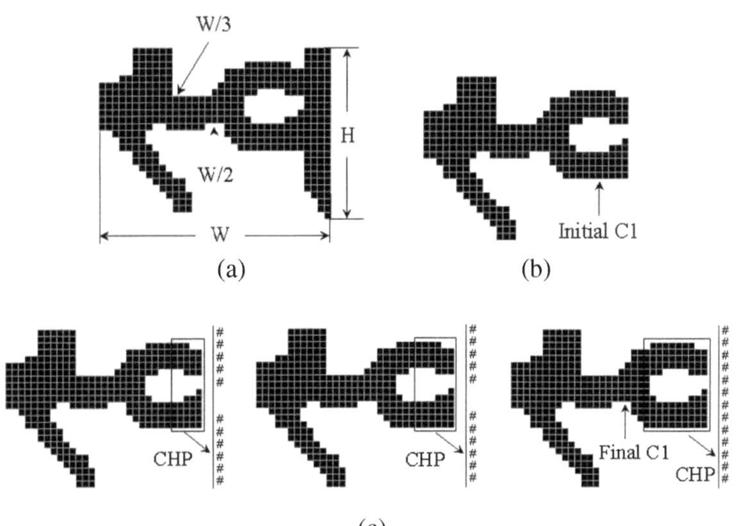

Fig. 8 Segmentation of the conjunct character (to find C1). (**a**) The conjunct character image; (**b**) the remaining character image with *vertical bar* removed; and (**c**) steps to search for C1

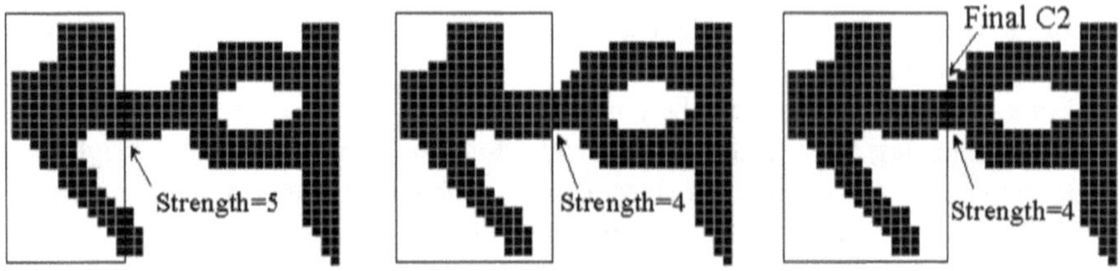

Fig. 9 Segmentation of a conjunct character (to find C2). The pixel strength of the column is defined as the number of *black pixels* in the column

iterations of C1 and C2, C1 cannot be less than C2 for a real conjunct character. So in this step, the decision of segmentation column C is made based on the following three situations that could be encountered:

(a) C1 is less than C2: Detected character is not a real conjunct character, so no further segmentation is needed.
(b) C1 is greater than C2 and C1, C2 are very close: If the difference between C1 and C2 is less than the stroke width, then the segmentation column C is set as the average of C1 and C2.
(c) C1 is one or more than one stroke width larger than C2: The segmentation column C is set as the column which is one stroke width left of C1, and only the right part will be extracted. The remaining left part will be considered as a new conjunct character image and further segmentation is needed.

Segmentation of the shadow character. The detection of a shadow character is straightforward. First we find the left most pixel of the character image. Then the connected component starting from this pixel is detected and the bounding box of this connected component is computed. If the right value of this bounding box is less than the right value of the original character image, then this character is considered a shadow character which needs further segmentation. The segmentation of a shadow character is clearly shown in Fig. 10. There are not many shadow cases in the Hindi words. Usually in the shadow character image, the right character is a character which can be represented as one single connected component. So the

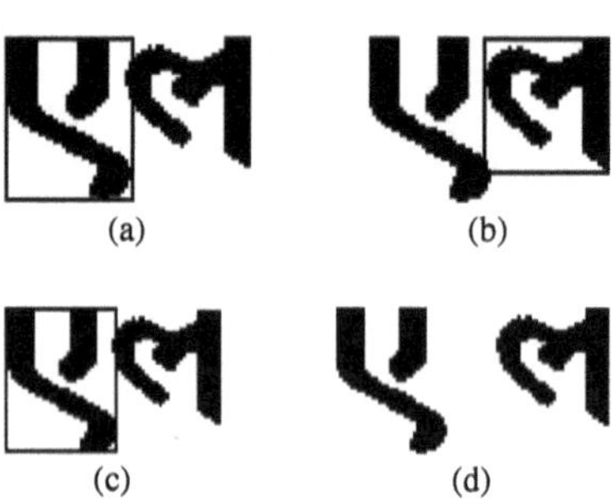

Fig. 10 Segmentation of the shadow character. (**a**) Determination of the shadow character; (**b**) bounding box of the connected component (the *right character*); (**c**) bounding box of the *left character*; and (**d**) segmented characters

segmentation of a shadow character starts from the right side of the image. First we find the right most black pixel of the image, then find the connected component starting from this pixel using eight-neighbor tracing. The connected component is considered the right character and separated from the original image. The left character is the remaining part with the detected connected component removed.

It should be noted that the above-mentioned segmentation can also be extended to the segmentation of the shadow top modifiers (the lower modifiers usually do not have shadow situations). Three examples of shadowed top modifiers are shown in Fig. 11.

Step 5: Extract the top modifiers. The extraction of the top modifiers from the top strip (shown in step 5 in Fig. 5) is simple and straightforward. The header line is removed from the top strip first, then the vertical projection of the remaining strip is computed. The boundary of a top modifier is located based on the column without any black pixels. There are some special cases that two top modifiers may touch each other, and they are separated as one single top modifier. Further segmentation of the top modifiers is handled as a special case [20].

Step 6: Put the header line back into the segmented characters. This step is straightforward, where the header line is put back to each segmented core character for the recognition in the next step.

In the above description of operations in all steps, there are some constants defined. Some of the constants depend on the natural characteristics of the Hindi character, such as factors 0.4, 0.8, 0.64, 1.2, 1/4, 1/3, and 1/2, which are usually fixed even for different fonts or different sizes of Hindi words. There are also some constants (such as 5 and 10 when traversing the projection profile) which depend on the sizes of Hindi words. We chose these constants based on the experimental results; they can be fixed as long as the font has the standard font size used in regular documents or they can be changed based on the new font size.

Fig. 11 Examples of shadow *top* modifiers

2.4 Feature Extraction

After character segmentation, each character is processed through a feature extraction routine where the most descriptive or differentiating features are extracted and used in training and testing. Three feature extraction routines have been developed and can be used interchangeably using configuration files:

1. *Template initialization:* Each character image is first resized to a 32×32 vector map. A probabilistic template is generated from all samples of each class from the training data [24]

2. *Zernike moments:* Moment descriptors have been studied for image recognition and computer vision since the 1960s. Teague [32] first introduced the use of Zernike moments to overcome the shortcomings of information redundancy present in the popular geometric moments. Zernike moments are a class of orthogonal moments which are rotation invariant and can be easily constructed to an arbitrary order. Khotanzad and Hong [18] proved that Zernike moments are effective for the optical character recognition (OCR).
3. *Directional features:* Templates are rigid, and can result in poor models for classification of noisy documents. Zernike moments, however, are a transform-based feature analysis method and more robust to shape variances, but do not utilize inherent "directional" property of complex scripts. The relative placement of neighboring pixels is more important than the overall placement of pixels forming the character. Directional features [17] record local pixel positions for each contour pixel and generate a feature vector using that information.
   For directional features, the character image is normalized, and the contour is extracted and mapped to a 64×64 mesh. The mesh is divided into 49 (7×7) sub-areas of 16×16 pixels where each sub-area overlaps 8 pixels of adjacent sub-area (Fig. 12). For each sub-area, a four-dimensional vector (x1, x2, x3, x4) is defined where x1, x2, x3, and x4 record the relative direction (vertical, horizontal, forward inclined, backward inclined) of neighboring pixels with respect to each foreground pixel in the sub-area. Hence, a $49 \times 4 = 196$ unit long feature vector is produced. Figure 12 shows the directional feature extraction process step by step.

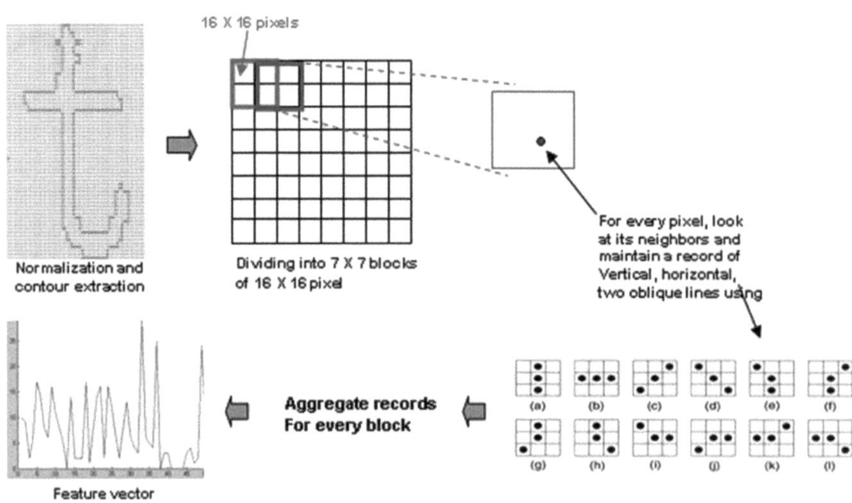

Fig. 12 Directional element feature extraction

2.5 Classification

2.5.1 Template Matching

Awarding probabilities when template pixel matches with the corresponding pixel in a candidate character image and penalizing otherwise forms the core objective of template matching. The template that has the best match is selected as the class. The candidate character image is binary, while the pixel values of the template map $g(x, y)$ are in a range $[0, N_{\text{inst}}]$. The similarity of a character image $f(x,y)$ and a template $g_b(x,y)$ is defined by a weighted similarity:

$$S_w(f,g) = 1.0 - \frac{1}{N^2} \sum_{x=1}^{N} \sum_{y=1}^{N} \omega(x,y) \, |f(x,y) - g_b(x,y)|$$

where the weight ω (x,y) is defined as

$$\omega(x,y) = \begin{cases} 1.0 & \text{if } g_b(x,y) \text{ is background} \\ \frac{g(x,y)}{N_{\text{inst}}} & \text{if } g_b(x,y) \text{ is background} \end{cases}$$

2.5.2 Generalized Hausdorff Image Comparison (GHIC)

Given two sets of points $A = \{a_1, \ldots, a_m\}$ and $B = \{b_1, \ldots, b_n$, the Hausdorff distance is defined as

$$H(A,B) = \max(h(A,B), h(B,A))$$

where $h(A,B) = \max_{a \in A} \min_{b \in B} ||a - b||$. The function $h(A,B)$ is called the "directed Hausdorff distance" from A to B (this function is not symmetric and thus is not a true distance). Therefore, when performing the recognition, rather than using $H(A,B)$, a generalization of the Hausdorff distance (which does not obey the metric properties on A and B, but does obey them on specific subsets of A and B) is used [20]. This generalized Hausdorff measure is given by taking the kth ranked distance rather than the maximum, or largest ranked one:

$$h_k(A,B) = k^{\text{th}}_{a \in A} \min_{b \in B} ||a - b||$$

where k^{th} denotes the kth ranked value (or equivalently the quantile of m values). For example, when $k = m$, then k^{th} is max. When $k = m/2$ then the median of the m individual point distances determines the overall distance. Therefore this measure generalizes the directed Hausdorff measure, by replacing the maximum with a quantile.

2.5.3 Nearest Neighbor Classifier and Weighted Euclidean Distance

Nearest neighbor classifier is used on Zernike moment features with a simple weighted Euclidean distance (WED). For each test sample, the classification is based on the distance between this sample and each class. The feature vector is in a d-dimensional space and the computed mean and standard deviation feature vectors for class i are $\mu^{(i)}$, $\alpha^{(i)}$, where $i = 1\ldots M$ and M is the number of classes. For each test sample $x \epsilon R^{d}$, the distance between this sample and each class is computed using the following formula:

$$d^{(i)}(x) = \sum_{k=1}^{d} \left| \frac{x_k - \mu_k^{(i)}}{\alpha_k^{(i)}} \right|$$

2.5.4 Hierarchical Classification

Kanji and south-east Asian scripts have a large number of symbols. Hence, one-stage discrimination does not generally suffice. In this approach, two-stage classification (coarse and fine) is used. The aim of coarse classification is to cluster similar-looking characters into groups and then perform fine classification to extract the right class [17].

1. *City Block Distance with Deviation (CBDD)*: Let $\nu = (\nu_1,\nu_2,\ldots,\nu_n)$ be an n-dimensional input vector and $\mu = (\mu_1, \mu_2, \ldots, \mu_n)$ be the standard vector of a category. The CBDD is defined as

$$d_{\mathrm{CBDD}}(\nu) = \sum_{j=1}^{n} \max\left\{0,|\nu_j - \mu_j| - \theta.s_j\right\}$$

   where s_j denotes the standard deviation of j_{th} element and θ is a constant.
2. *Asymmetric Mahalanobis Distance:* For each cluster, the correct class is obtained by finding the minimum asymmetric Mahalanobis distance from the templates in that cluster. The function is given by

$$d_{\mathrm{AMD}}(\nu) = \sum_{j=1}^{n} \frac{1}{\hat{\sigma}_j^2 + b}\left(\nu - \hat{\mu},\phi_j\right)^2$$

   where b is the bias, $\hat{\mu}$ is the quasi-mean vector of the samples of class m, ϕ_j is the eigenvector of covariance matrix of this category, and $\hat{\sigma}_j$ is the quasi-variance. In case of a tie, N-nearest neighbor is used, with $N = 3$.

2.6 Devanagari OCR Evaluation

The proposed system was applied to the 1083 pages of the Oxford Hindi–English dictionary [26] and to a collection of PDF-converted Hindi document images. The dictionary binding was burst and scanned at 400 dpi. The PDF-converted Hindi document images are obtained directly from the PDF file without the introduction of scanner noise, so they are considered ideal images.

To evaluate the accuracy of this OCR, we randomly chose seven pages and counted the number of Hindi words and characters recognized using generalized Hausdorff image comparison. The result evaluation is shown in Table 7.

The evaluation result in Table 7 shows that the recognition accuracy at the character level reaches 87.75%, while the accuracy at the word level reaches about 67%. The experiment was done on scanned images which obviously contain noise, and the result is the pure recognition result without any spell checking and word correction based on dictionary search

Table 7 Result evaluation of the Hindi–English dictionary, where "A1" is the character accuracy with respect to "Chars" and "A2" is the character accuracy with respect to "recognized." "A" is the word accuracy

Pages	Chars	Recognized	Correct	A1 (%)	A2 (%)	Words	Correct	A (%)
p0098	451	443	407	90.24	91.87	110	79	71.82
p0160	317	311	272	85.80	87.46	73	54	73.97
p0179	480	477	409	85.21	85.74	113	67	59.29
p0401	294	290	264	89.80	91.03	71	53	74.65
p0799	437	451	379	86.73	84.04	80	50	62.50
p0987	405	402	359	88.64	89.30	67	39	58.20
p1023	343	338	303	88.34	89.64	64	44	68.75
Total	2727	2712	2393	**87.75**	**88.24**	578	386	**66.78**

2.7 Additional Challenges

From our discussion, its clear that our base system has a character segmentation component that is specific to a given script. In addition, the approach must also be able to deal with different properties of characters, as follows:

1. *Classification of characters:* Based on the presence and position of the vertical bar and the number of connections of the character with the header line, the core Hindi characters can be divided into the following six groups shown in Table 8:
2. *Over-segmentation processing:* In the described character segmentation procedure, there may exist over-segmentation of characters, i.e., one single character could be segmented into two or more parts. The over-segmentation in the vertical direction only happens to long characters such as ए ह and other strongly

Table 8 Classes of core Hindi characters

Open header	अ थ ध भ
One end bar	च ज ञ त न व ज़
Multiple end bars	ख घ झ प म य ष स ख़
Middle bar	क्र क फ क़ फ़
No bar	इ उ ऊ ए ङ छ ट ठ ड ढ द र ह ड़ ढ़
Special case	ग ण श ग़

(a) (b)

Fig. 13 Examples of over-segmented characters added in the template. (**a**) Over-segmented characters and (**b**) original characters

combined forms of consonants such as द्द द्ध द्व द्र and ड्ड. Figure 13(a) shows some of the over-segmented characters we added to our templates, and characters in Fig. 13(b) are the original complete forms.

3. *Ligature processing:* Some Devanagari character combinations may result in a change in the order of the displayed glyphs. This re-ordering is not commonly seen in non-Indic scripts. One such character is Fig. 13(b), which is always displayed one consonant left of its real position. When exporting the codes of one Hindi word with such a character, the codes of characters must be reordered.

An analysis of results of the system described above shows that a large number of recognition errors are caused by incorrect character segmentation of complex syllabic scripts or by touching and broken characters (in degraded documents). Due to the large glyph set and possible conjunct set of such scripts, limited ground truth could not cover all the possibilities and hence many classes had no representation in the ground-truth data.

In [20], we listed solutions to the above problems, specific to Devanagari script. Nevertheless, a generic framework for any syllabic script was still a distant goal. The above problems imply that the benefits of good feature extraction modules (followed by classifiers or their combinations) cannot be realized until we have a robust generic solution for the character segmentation problem for any syllabic script. Having a header line is a characteristic property of Devanagari script that is not present in other Indic scripts like Gujarati, Dravidian scripts, or other south-east Asian scripts. In order to demonstrate our generic approach toward syllabic scripts, and to avoid the peculiarity of header line in Devanagari script, we compare our new approach on Khmer script. The Khmer script was one of the earliest writing systems used in Southeast Asia, first appearing in the 7th century CE. It is derived from the Pallava script, a variation of the Grantha script of south India, which in turn ultimately descended from the ancient Brahmi script of India. Like all Brahmi-derived scripts, Khmer has certain traits similar to those found in south Asian scripts. The direction of writing in Khmer is left to right, and downward when horizontal space runs out. Khmer is also a syllabic alphabet, and an ideal choice to evaluate our generic system.

3 Font-Based Intelligent Character Segmentation

3.1 Benefits and Font Models

Nearly every script we have considered has a representative TrueType font. One feature of a TrueType font file is layout. Given a character, the position of next character can be predicted using the properties of these fonts. This can be used to aid the segmentation of touching characters, the grouping of broken characters, and the processing of glyphs fused or overlapped. Another advantage of such an approach is that it does not involve script-dependent mechanisms for segmentation and aims at a generic character segmentation algorithm for any given script. This method branches off from second tier of character segmentation approaches (Section 1.1) by generating well-defined component extraction and segmentation hypotheses.

Font files have a wealth of information [19] and can be used to produce a generative model. Information in the font files includes a list of characters, glyphs of each character, font ascenders, and font descenders.

At a given font size, the file contains the following information for each character:

- Unicode value
- Height and width
- Horizontal advance (HA): the horizontal distance between the origins of present and next character in a word
- Vertical advance (VA): the vertical distance between the origins of present and next character in a word
- Bounding box (BB)
- Left bearing (LB): the horizontal distance between the left end of bounding box and its origin
- Right bearing (RB): the horizontal distance between the right end of bounding box and origin
- Combination rules of ligatures

Many parameters are redundant, as they can be derived from other parameters. For example

$$RB = HA - LB - width$$
$$\text{where } width = |BB\_right\_edge - BB\_left\_edge|$$

Font files for similar fonts can be analyzed for consistency in these model parameters. Figure 14 shows the location of characters for three fonts of Devanagari script

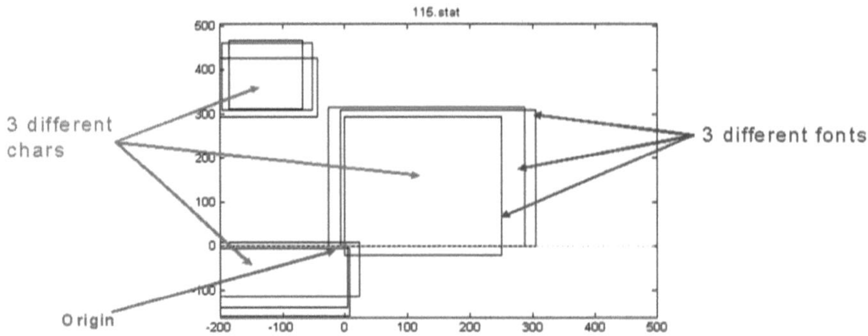

Fig. 14 Locations of three different characters of Devanagari script using three structurally similar Devanagari font files

(at the same font size). The fonts place each character at nearly same position (with respect to a given origin), hence demonstrating the consistency in these parameters. Similar analysis was done for non-syllabic scripts.

For a given font face and size, a word is rendered by placing the first character using its bounding box. Using the horizontal advance, vertical advance, and origin of present character, origin of next character is determined. Using this origin, the next character is placed in its bounding box and the process is repeated for the remaining characters in the word. Figure 15 shows the process.

Using a group of structurally similar fonts, glyphs can be extracted and used for training purposes. This eliminates the problem of unavailability of all characters in

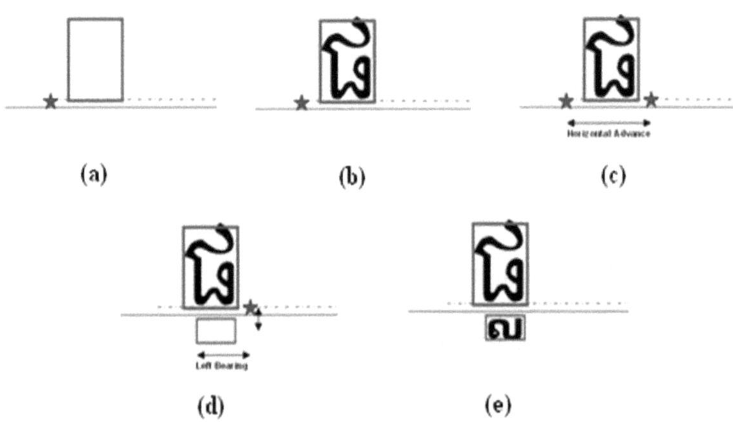

Fig. 15 The rendering of characters in a word in Khmer using font models. (**a**) Locating first character; (**b**) placing character into its bounding box; (**c**) determination of origin of next character; (**d**) determination of next character's bounding box; and (**e**) placing the second character

the large alphabet of syllabic scripts with limited ground truth. The glyphs extracted can substitute for missing or lesser available character classes from ground truth. The information is then used to segment characters from word images during training and testing using the process described above (Fig. 15).

3.2 Training Using Font Files

The following steps describe the process of training a system with limited ground-truth data.

Step 1: A group of similar fonts, resembling the text in documents to be processed, are provided along with electronic text.

Step 2: For each character, the average bounding box, horizontal and vertical advance values are computed from the font files.

Step 3: The character glyphs from font files are generated and passed through the feature extraction routines.

Step 4: Each document image along with its corresponding ground-truth file is passed through the segmentation module and a hierarchical structure (containing Page → Zone → Line → Word) is created with word alignments at its root.

Step 5: Each word in this structure is further segmented into characters using (a) aligned characters in the corresponding ground truth, (b) font parameters extracted in step 2, and (c) process explained in Fig. 15.

Step 6: For each character segmented in the document image, feature extraction is performed.

Step 7: Classes are modeled using the features of glyphs from training set and font files. Hence, limited ground-truth data with some unrepresented glyphs suffice, as those glyphs are processed from the font files.

3.3 Segmentation and Recognition

With the objective of grouping broken characters, segmenting conjuncts, and touching characters, the technique of font-model-based intelligent character segmentation and recognition was developed. As discussed earlier, it falls in the second category of character segmentation with an advantage of reducing the number of hypotheses by the knowledge of next character's position, given the present character. This is achieved using font parameters.

Algorithm: The document image is classified into zones, lines, and words. For each word, connected component analysis is performed. Assuming a maximum of N uncovered components can be combined together to form the ith character, there can be $C_1^N + C_2^N + ... + C_N^N$ possible nodes (η_i) for next character (typically $N = 3$). Given the present character, predictions (ρ_i) are made for next character's locations (using font-model). Those η_i which do not overlap (with threshold τ) with any ρ_i are discarded. η_i which overlap (with threshold τ) with any ρ_i are inserted into a set γ. η_i which enclose any ρ_i are inserted into a conjunct set δ. Nodes of set γ are ranked by their confidences returned from the recognizer. Nodes of the conjunct set δ are given for a conjunct test (described later). If they pass the test, the conjunct is broken into possible characters using Dijkstra's algorithm and individual character confidences are returned. Only the first character (along with its confidence) from every conjunct is kept in the set δ and later pieces are stacked back into the set of uncovered components. The highest confidence character is picked from set γ and δ combined. The process is repeated for the uncovered connected components in the next stage. In case of dead ends (when no possible character location coincides with the present connected component nodes), back-tracking is performed and the path is pruned (Fig. 16).

Conjunct test: Conjuncts form an integral part of any syllabic script. Many characters combine to form a single shape. Techniques so far have relied on a crude method of aspect ratio threshold (Section 2.3.2, Steps 3 and 4) to determine whether a character is a conjunct and needs to be broken down further. With font models, an intelligent conjunct detection procedure has been developed. A glyph is passed for conjunct analysis only if it encompasses the possibility of two or more characters of the given script under test. This position analysis can be done only through font models of a script, as illustrated in Fig. 17.

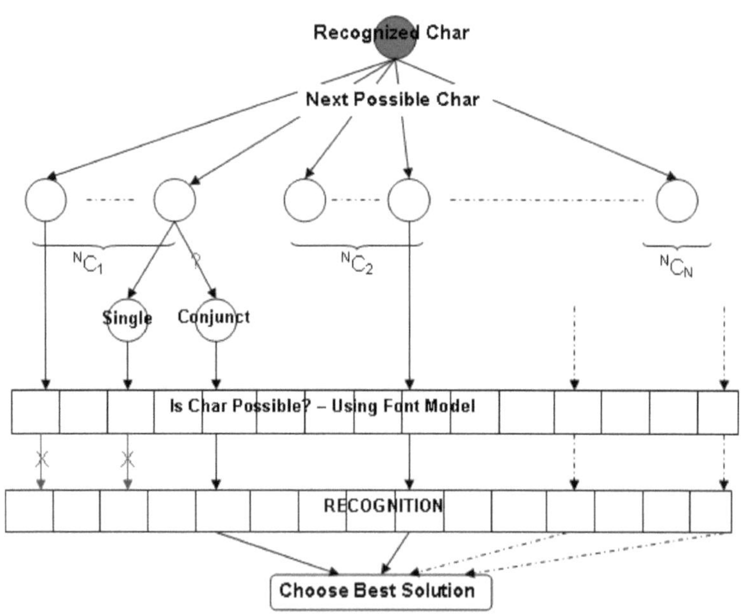

Fig. 16 Dynamic network created during best-path search of word recognition (using font models)

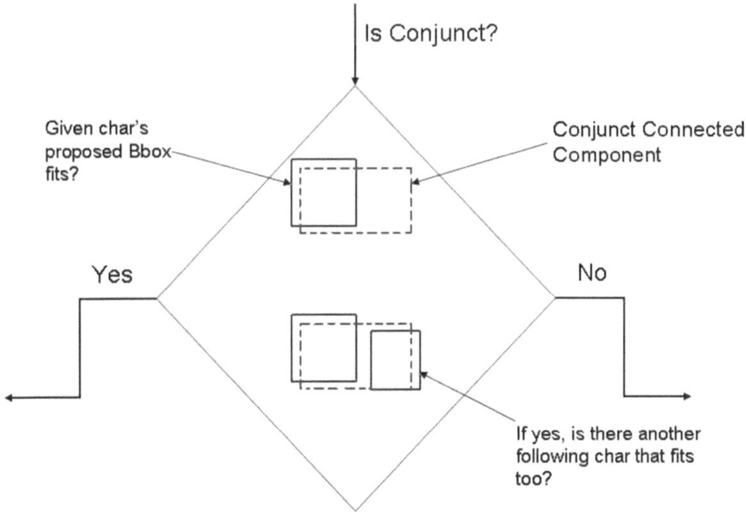

Fig. 17 Conjunct detection. Bigger (*dotted*) box shows a possible conjunct under detection. If two characters (*solid boxes*) fit in (using font model), it may be a conjunct

4 Experiments

4.1 Data Sets

Our experiments were performed on two classes of scripts – Latin (non-syllabic) and Khmer (syllabic). Two data sets for English and one for Khmer were used. First Latin data set has varying amounts of clarity across the pages which leads to a large number of broken and touching characters (Fig. 18). Apart from this, the documents contain noise introduced during printing and scanning process. The characters in words are also skewed and not aligned perfectly with word's bottom reference line. This imposes additional challenges for character segmentation and prediction of next character position using font models and verifies robustness of our approach. The closest font is *NSimSum*. The second Latin data set, on the other hand, is a much cleaner data set, with font resembling more closely to *Courier New*. A single English document had approximately 2000 characters and 330 words. The Khmer data set contains some documents from a Cambodian Gazetteer and documents scanned from other sources (15 pages total). These documents are dark and hence suffer badly from touching characters. This, combined with the presence of numerous conjuncts in Khmer script, becomes an ideal data set for evaluation of our techniques. The closest font to the documents is of *Limon S1*. A single Khmer document had approximately 1500 characters and 100 words. In each data set, three to five documents were chosen for training. The idea was to evaluate our approach with limited user feedback and a limited training set – which is generally the case for any new script under study. The figures reported are the average accuracy.

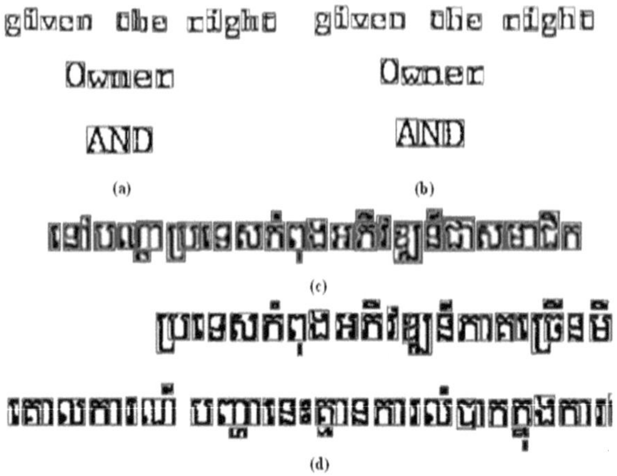

Fig. 18 Improvements of our technique over older dissection-based techniques. (**a**) and (**b**) show Latin script character segmentation using dissection font-model-based techniques, respectively; (**c**) and (**d**) show results for Khmer script using dissection and our font-model-based techniques, respectively

4.2 Protocols for Evaluation

The text returned by the OCR system is matched against the ground-truth data using a tool based on the UNLV Evaluation Toolkit [27]. The evaluation tool prints out an elaborate description of insertion, deletion, and substitution errors in form of one-to-one, one-to-two, two-to-one, two-to-two confusions. It also summarizes the most confused characters along with their confusions. Apart from character confusions, it also lists word confusion matrices in a similar fashion.

4.3 Character Segmentation

Ten percent of recognition errors in dissection-based character segmentation were due to bad character segmentation. The use of font models reduced those errors. Extraction of characters from fused ligatures is still a problem and is considered for our future work. Figure 18 shows the improvements in character segmentation for both broken and touching characters.

4.4 Feature Extraction

Table 9 compares template matching and directional element feature (DEF) extraction results, for both Latin and Khmer documents. A weighted similarity measure (Section 2) was used to classify templates and CBDD was used to classify the directional feature set.

Table 9 Compares character-level accuracy results for Latin and Khmer scripts using template and directional element features (DEF)

	English		Khmer	
Accuracy	Template matching (%)	DEF (%)	Template matching (%)	DEF (%)
Char	86	93	84	89

4.5 Recognition Results

Table 10 summarizes the improvements gained using our font-model-based character segmentation and recognition – for both English and Khmer data sets. Character accuracies and word accuracies have been reported. The accuracies reported are using directional feature extraction and the CBDD classifier. wo/FM is for with-out font model (following dissection-based segmentation) and w/FM is for with font model. Due to much higher word length in Khmer, the word accuracies are low compared to English.

Table 10 Compares dissection 2-based and font-model-based techniques

	English		Khmer	
Accuracy	wo/FM (%)	w/FM (%)	wo/FM (%)	w/FM (%)
Char	93	96	89	92
Word	83	89	38	37

5 Conclusion and Future Work

This chapter presents a novel technique to intelligently segment and recognize characters in complex syllabic scripts, using font models which are used to extend our base Hindi OCR system. The approach emphasizes the importance of a good feature extraction module (directional features over template or Zernike moments). These techniques not only enhance degraded text recognition results but also works with a limited number of training documents. An intelligent conjunct detection scheme was also described which is more intuitive than aspect ratio. These techniques do not differentiate syllabic or non-syllabic approaches for segmentation and hence carry out direct character segmentation from words even for syllabic scripts. The approach is targeted toward word based recognition and hence is ready for language models. This technique, however, is slower than dissection-based segmentation and recognition, as it requires the analysis of recognition results at every possible segmentation hypotheses. It is also susceptible to misrecognition if the font size of a character changes abruptly within a single word. This is because the model works on a self-learning approach by tuning its parameters using next recognized character.

Our OCR system was designed under the assumption that vast amount of training samples are unavailable, so it can be easily extended for the recognition of other languages or scripts under the following two conditions: (i) the language uses symbols of the same basic class and (ii) the words of this new language can be segmented into characters. Segmentation, however, is very different between Hindi and other non-Indic languages. Overall, our goal is to build a toolkit of components that can be reused for rapidly building OCR capabilities for new languages.

Complex ligature segmentation into its constituent characters using combination rules from font files will be our next goal. The next step for the recognition phase is to apply new, possibly multiclassifier techniques, and combine them with the current classifier to provide improved performance. The approach assumes we can train the system using a small number of samples, so the new classification techniques must also have this property.

References

1. Abd, M.A., Paschos, G.: Effective Arabic character recognition using Support Vector Machines. In: Innovations and Advanced Techniques in Computer and Information Sciences and Engineering, pp. 7–11. Springer-Verlag, London, UK (2007)
2. Agrawal, M., Doermann, D.: Re-targetable ocr with intelligent character segmentation. The Eighth IAPR International Workshop on Document Analysis Systems, 2008 (DAS '08) pp. 183–190 (2008)
3. Bansal, V.: Integrating knowledge sources in devanagari text recognition. Ph.D. thesis, Indian Institute of Technology, Kanpur, India (1999)
4. Bansal, V., Sinha, R.: Segmentation of touching and fused devanagari characters. Pattern Recognition **35**, 875–893 (2002)
5. Bhattacharya, U., Das, T., Datta, A., Parui, S., Chaudhuri, B.: A hybrid scheme for handprinted numeral recognition based on a self-organizing network and MLP classifiers. International Journal for Pattern Recognition and Artificial Intelligence **16**(7), 845–864 (2002)
6. Britto, A., Sabourin, R., Bortolozzi, F., Suen, C.: The recognition of handwritten numerals strings using a two-stage HMM based method. International Journal of Document Analysis and Recognition **5**, 102–117 (2003)
7. Casey, G., Lecolinet, E.: A survey of methods and strategies in character segmentation. IEEE on Pattern Analysis and Machine Intelligence **18**, 690–706 (1996)
8. Chaudhuri, B., Pal, U.: An ocr system to read two Indian language scripts: Bangla and devanagari (hindi). In: Proceedings of 4th International Conference on Document Analysis and Recognition, pp. 1011–1016. Germany (1997)
9. Chaudhuri, B., Pal, U.: Skew angle detection of digitized Indian script documents. IEEE Transactions on Pattern Analysis and Machine Intelligence **19**(2), 182–186 (1997)
10. Chi, Y., Yan, H.: Handwritten numeral recognition using self-organizing maps and fuzzy rules. Pattern Recognition **28**, 56–66 (1995)
11. Choisy, C., Belaid, A.: Cross-learning in analytic word recognition without segmentation. International Journal on Document Analysis and Recognition **4**, 281–289 (2002)
12. Dhanya, D., Ramakrishnan, A.G.: Optimal feature extraction for bilingual OCR. In: DAS '02: Proceedings of the 5th International Workshop on Document Analysis Systems V, pp. 25–36. Springer-Verlag, London, UK (2002)
13. Gorman, L.O., Kasturi, R.: Document image analysis: A bibliography. Machine Vision and Applications **5**(3), 231–243 (1992)
14. Granlund, G.H.: Fourier preprocessing for Hand Print Character Recognition. IEEE Transactions on Computers **C–21**(2), 195–201 (1972)
15. Hull, J.J.: Document image skew detection: Survey and annotated bibliography. In: J.J. Hull, S.L. Taylor (eds.) Document Analysis Systems II. Word Scientific (1998)

16. Ittner, D.J., Baird, H.S.: Language-free layout analysis. In: IAPR 2nd Int'l Conf. on Document Analysis and Recognition, pp. 336–340. Tsukuba Science City, Japan (1993)
17. Kato, N., Suzuki, M., Omachi, S., Aso, H., Nemoto, Y.: A handwritten character recognition system using directional element feature and asymmetric Mahalanobis distance. IEEE Transactions on Pattern Analysis and Machine Intelligence **21**(3), 258–262 (1999)
18. Khotanzad, A., Hong, Y.H.: Invariant image recognition by Zernike moments. IEEE Transactions on Pattern Analysis and Machine Intelligence **12**(5), 489–497 (1990)
19. Kopec, G., Chou, P.: Document image decoding using Markov source models. IEEE Transactions on Pattern Analysis and Machine Intelligence **16**(6), 602–617 (1994)
20. Ma, H., Doermann, D.: Adaptive Hindi OCR using generalized Hausdorff image comparison. ACM Transactions on Asian Language Information Processing **26**(2), 198–213 (2003)
21. Ma, H., Doermann, D.: Bootstrapping structured page segmentation. In: SPIE Conference Document Recognition and Retrieval, pp. 179–188. Santa Clara, CA (2003)
22. Ma, H., Doermann, D.: Gabor filter based multi-class classifier for scanned document images. In: 7th International Conference on Document Analysis and Recognition (ICDAR), pp. 968–972. Edinburgh, Scotland (2003)
23. Ma, H., Doermann, D.: Word level script identification for scanned document images. In: SPIE Conference Document Recognition and Retrieval. San Jose, CA (2004). To appear
24. Ma, H., Doermann, D.: Adaptive OCR with limited user feedback. International Conference on Document Analysis and Recognition, pp. 814–818 (2005)
25. Mahmoud, S.: Arabic character recognition using Fourier descriptors and character contour encoding. Pattern Recognition **27**, 815–824 (1994)
26. McGregor, R.: The OXFORD Hindi-English Dictionary. Oxford University Press, Oxford Delhi, (1993). ISBN 0-19-864339-X
27. Nartker, T.A., Rice, S.V., Lumos, S.E.: Software tools and test data for research and testing of page-reading OCR systems. Document Recognition and Retrieval XII **5676**, 37–47 (2005)
28. O'Gorman, L.: The document spectrum for page layout analysis. IEEE Transactions on Pattern Analysis and Machine Intelligence **15**(11), 1162–1173 (1993)
29. Plamondon, R., Srihari, S.: On-line and off-line handwritten recognition: A comprehensive survey. IEEE Transactions on Pattern Analysis and Machine Intelligence **22**, 62–84 (2000)
30. Stefano, D., Cioppa, A., Marcelli, A.: Handwritten numeral recognition by means of Evolutionary Algorithms. International Conference on Document Analysis and Recognition **00**, 804–807 (1999)
31. Suen, Y., Berthod, M., Mori, S.: Automatic recognition of hand-printed character-the state of art. Proceedings of IEEE **68**, 469–487 (1980)
32. Teague, M.: Image analysis via the general theory of moments. Journal of the Optical Society of America **70**(8), 920–930 (1979)

Online Handwriting Recognition for Indic Scripts

A. Bharath and Sriganesh Madhvanath

Abstract Online handwriting recognition refers to the problem of machine recognition of handwriting captured in the form of pen trajectories. The recognition technology holds significant promise for Indic scripts, given that the Indic languages are used by a sixth of the world's population, and the greater ease of use of handwriting-based text input for these scripts compared to keyboard-based methods. Even though the recognition of handwritten Devanagari, Bangla, and Tamil has received significant attention in recent times, one may say that research efforts directed at Indic script recognition in general are in their early stages. The structure of the scripts and the variety of shapes and writing styles pose challenges that are different from other scripts and hence require customized techniques for feature representation and recognition. In this chapter, we describe the challenges in recognizing online handwriting in Indic scripts and provide an overview of the state of the art for isolated character and word recognition. We then present in brief some of the promising applications, starting with handwriting-based text input systems (IMEs) that have been built for entering Indic scripts. In the last section, we provide a few pointers to resources such as tools and data sets that are currently available for online Indic script recognition research. endabstract

Keywords Online handwriting recognition · Indic scripts · Character recognition · Word recognition

1 Introduction

India plays host to 22 official languages and 10 scripts, in addition to a large number of others which do not have "official" status. The official languages invariably

A. Bharath (✉)
Hewlett-Packard Laboratories, Bangalore, India
e-mail: bharath.a@hp.com

V. Govindaraju, S. Setlur (eds.), *Guide to OCR for Indic Scripts*, Advances in Pattern Recognition, DOI 10.1007/978-1-84800-330-9_11, © Springer-Verlag London Limited 2009

have large numbers of speakers (e.g., approximately 500 million speakers of Hindi, 200 million of Bangla [1]). Many Indic languages have substantial global presence–Tamil, for instance, is also one of the official languages in countries such as Singapore, Malaysia, and Sri Lanka. The users of these languages and scripts constitute approximately a sixth of the world's population.

In India, information technology (IT) is still largely limited to the small fraction of the population that is English literate. One reason for this has been the complexity of text input in local Indic languages. Over the years a number of QWERTY overlays and specific keyboard layouts have been devised for different Indic languages, but they remain non-standard and difficult to learn and use. The large alphabet size typically requires multiple keystrokes for entering a character and mandates complex key-character mappings to be remembered, presenting a substantial barrier to use, especially for occasional users. The use of handwriting, on the other hand, is widely entrenched in the home, government, and business, and forms the basis for record keeping and communication.

In this setting, technology for the online recognition of handwriting (online HWR) in Indic languages and scripts can play a significant role in promoting IT in local languages. As compared to speech, the processing of handwriting input for text entry is less expensive computationally, and potentially more accurate, especially in the presence of ambient noise. Another useful aspect of machine recognition of online handwriting is that it can be easily customized to recognize an individual's own handwriting. Decades of research have made handwriting input a reality for several European and oriental languages represented, respectively, using the Latin and the Chinese, Japanese, Korean (CJK) scripts [2–5]. Such methods are now commonly built into mobile devices and tablet PCs and feature acceptably high recognition accuracies. However similar technology for the Indic languages and scripts is still in its infancy.

In this chapter we provide an overview of the state of the art in online HWR for Indic scripts. We first describe the structure of Indic scripts, and the challenges posed for online recognition. We then describe past and present research efforts directed at isolated character recognition and word recognition for Indic scripts. A glimpse of handwriting-based text input systems developed for Indic scripts is also presented along with some potential applications of online HWR. An overview of resources such as tools and data sets available for online HWR of Indic scripts may be found in the last section.

2 The Structure of Indic Scripts

The 10 official Indic scripts – Devanagari, Tamil, Gurmukhi, Telugu, Kannada, Gujarati, Oriya, Bangla, Malayalam, and Urdu – differ by varying degrees in their visual characteristics, but share some important similarities. With the exception of the Urdu script which is of Perso-Arabic origin, they have evolved from a single source, the phonographic Brahmi script, first documented extensively in the edicts of Emperor Ashoka of the third century BC. They are defined as "syllabic alphabets" or *abugidas* in that the unit of encoding is a syllable of speech, however, the corresponding orthographic units show distinctive internal structure and a constituent set of graphemes [6]. A word in these scripts is written as a sequence of these orthographic syllabic units. For simplicity, we will henceforth refer to these units as "characters," a term commonly used to refer to the building blocks of recognition systems (as in "isolated *character* recognition"). Some common rules for formation of orthographic syllables are discussed by Mudur et al. [7]. Some common classes of characters are described below with examples:

- V: An independent vowel */ii/* [1]
  Devanagari: ई Tamil: ஈ Telugu: ఈ
- C: An isolated consonant */ta/* with inherent neutral vowel */a/*
  Devanagari: त Tamil: த Telugu: త
- CH: An isolated consonant */t/* with the inherent vowel muted by a special diacritic called *halanth*. This form is used rarely; the linear form (CH)(C) of two consecutive consonant sounds is instead generally represented by a single consonant conjunct character (C'C), where C' denotes the half-form of the first consonant. A notable exception is Tamil, wherein the use of the CH form is the norm
  Devanagari: त् Tamil: த் Telugu: త్
- CV: A consonant */ta/* combined with vowel */ii/* to produce */tii/*. The vowel overrides the inherent */a/* and is indicated using a *matra* or diacritic symbol (also see Fig. 1)
  Devanagari: ती Tamil: தீ Telugu: తీ
- CVM: A CV character with a modifier M to indicate nasalization of the vowel V. Devanagari has four different kinds of nasalization, indicated using different kinds of diacritic marks, e.g., तीं */tii.n/*
- C'C: A conjunct that combines two consonant sounds – */k/* with */ta/* to produce */kta/*. In Devanagari, the leading consonant */k/* is indicated by a "half-form" to suggest that it is missing its inherent vowel. However in Telugu it is just the reverse– the leading consonant is in its full form but */ta/*, indicated by the horizontal diacritic at the bottom, is in its half-form. Tamil does not use half-forms. Instead, consonant conjuncts are "unraveled" into a linear sequence of (CH) characters followed by the base consonant C
  Devanagari: क्त Tamil: க்த Telugu: క్త
- CC: A distinct conjunct wherein the constituent consonants are not identifiable, e.g., consonant श् */sh/* combines with consonant र */ra/* to produce a distinct shape श्र */shra/* in Devanagari. Many C'C conjuncts have alternative representations as distinct conjuncts.

The above classes represent subsets of the set of all possible characters. In its most complex form a character is a *base consonant* C, optionally surrounded by modifiers for other consonants C', a vowel unit V, and modifier M. For example,

[1] ITRANS encoding: http://www.aczoom.com/itrans/tblall/tblall.html

ITRANS Encoding														
ka	kaa	ki	kii	ku	kuu	ke	kE	kai	ko	kO	kau	k.n	kaH	k
Devanagari														
क	का	कि	की	कु	कू	के	-	कै	को	-	कौ	कं	कः	क्
Telugu														
క	కా	కి	కీ	కు	కూ	కె	కే	కై	కొ	కో	కౌ	కం	కః	క్
Tamil														
க	கா	கி	கீ	கு	கூ	கெ	கே	கை	கொ	கோ	கௌ	-	-	க்

Fig. 1 Combinations of the consonant */ka/* with different vowels, and the vowel muting *halanth*

क्तीं */ktii.n/* in Devanagari has the structure C'CVM. This example also shows an alternative representation of */kta/* as a distinct conjunct. The first two classes of characters C and V are sometimes collectively called "simple characters" and have been the focus of early efforts at recognizing Indic scripts. Most Indic scripts have an order of 600 CV characters and as many as 20,000 C'CV ones in theory, although a much smaller subset of C'CV characters are used in practice. While Devanagari has 35 consonants, 11 vowels, and 4 vowel modifiers, Telugu consists of 18 vowels and 36 consonants. The number of characters in both the scripts run into thousands (1500 for Devanagari and around 5000 for Telugu). Tamil has 12 vowels, 18 consonants, 6 Grantha letters (that can combine with vowels for writing Sanskrit words) and a special symbol, with the number of characters summing up to 325 [8], though a smaller number is in common usage. The much smaller number is largely due to consonant conjunct characters such as C'C being written as linear sequences of separate characters CH and C, as previously mentioned.

3 Challenges for Online HWR

The structure of characters in Indic scripts was introduced in the previous section. In this section we describe some of the challenges for online HWR of characters and words in Indic scripts, and highlight key differences from Latin and CJK scripts. Some of these stem from the structure of these scripts, others from established writing practice.

3.1 Large Alphabet Size

As mentioned earlier, most Indic scripts use a large (>1000) number of characters, as opposed to less than 100 in English. The internal graphemic structure makes a divide-and-conquer approach to recognition feasible in theory. However many consonant conjuncts are represented by visually distinct conjuncts bearing no resemblance to the constituent consonant shapes (Fig. 2). Similarly, many consonant and vowel combinations give rise to new symbols (e.g., "து" */thu/* in Tamil) which cannot be segmented into the base consonant and matra. These may need to be dealt

Fig. 2 Combination of consonants resulting in a distinct conjunct character in Devanagari

with as opaque symbols and exceptions in a divide-and-conquer recognition strategy. Other challenges for this strategy (discussed in detail later) include cursive styles and stroke- and symbol-order variations across different writers.

3.2 Two-Dimensional Structure

As is evident from Fig. 1, *matras* or vowel diacritics can occur to the left, right, bottom, top, or even as multiple components surrounding the base consonant. Some possible vowel matras for a consonant symbol in Devanagari are shown in Fig. 3(a). In Fig. 3(b), a two-part matra with components occurring on the left as well as on the right of a base consonant in Tamil is shown. Similarly, half-consonant forms in consonant conjuncts can occur in different positions around the base consonant. In the case of Telugu, they are aligned vertically below the consonant as shown in Fig. 3(c). Position is also important to distinguish certain matras and consonant forms that have very similar shapes and differ only in their position relative to the base consonant, e.g., half-consonant */n/* and matras */e/* and */uu/* shown in Fig. 4. Thus Indic scripts exhibit a two-dimensional structure much like the CJK scripts. Modeling Indic characters for recognition in terms of the constituent strokes or graphemes requires modeling of their spatial relationships in addition to their shapes. Further, the two-dimensional structure results in added variability in symbol and stroke order across writers, unlike the linear left-to-right ordering of the Latin script.

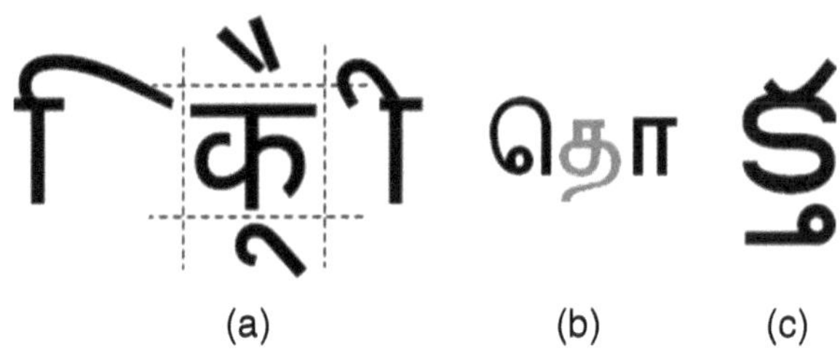

Fig. 3 Two-dimensional structure: (**a**) some possible matras for a consonant in Devanagari, (**b**) two-part matra surrounding the consonant in Tamil, and (**c**) consonant conjunct in Telugu

3.3 Inter-class Similarity

In certain Indic scripts, there is intrinsically high inter-class similarity between some pairs of symbols. Figure 5(a) shows two characters from Malayalam that look very similar except for the small loop present in the first. Figure 5(b) shows two Tamil characters with a subtle difference in the shapes of their matras. This calls for

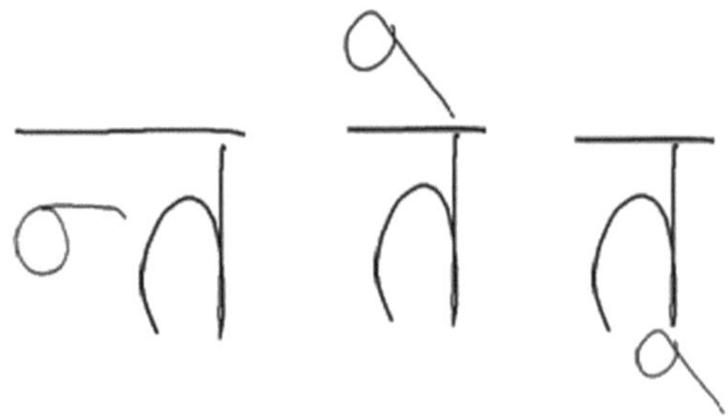

Fig. 4 Similar-looking half-consonant and matras varying only in their position relative to the base consonant */ta/*

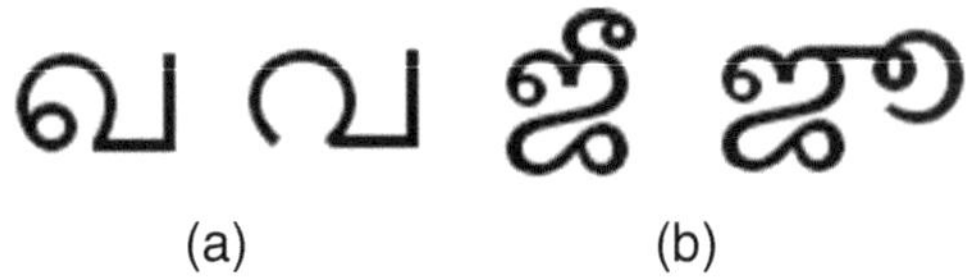

Fig. 5 Similar-looking characters in (**a**) Malayalam and (**b**) Tamil

reliable, highly distinctive features to describe the shapes of characters and graphemes.

3.4 Issues with Writing Styles

Indic scripts with the exception of Urdu are written as a left-to-right sequence of characters (syllabic units). As already discussed, the characters themselves have two-dimensional arrangements of graphemes corresponding to consonants, vowels, and vowel modifiers. Since characters can vary widely in width, height, and complexity, there is no boxed style. This is a key difference from CJK scripts, wherein characters are complex but of approximately the same size and may be written in boxes.

In general, character transitions are marked by pen lifts. Writing an entire word cursively is possible in some Indic scripts (e.g., Bangla), but rare. One might say that the "run-on" style is the most common for Indic scripts. However cursiveness is common within characters, and found generally wherever a pen-up requires additional effort.

While writing a character, users are generally concerned with reconstructing its visual appearance rather than its phonological structure. Various factors such as the relative positions of different strokes, the effort required to move from one stroke to the next given the overall flow of writing, and writing styles taught in school – all have an influence on the stroke order that is eventually used. The consequences for online HWR are many:

Symbol-order variations – The sequence of writing of consonant and vowel units in a character need not correspond to the phonological order of their occurrence in the corresponding syllable. For instance, " ि" matra in Devanagari and " െ" in Tamil are often written before writing the base consonant, since they occur to its left. In contrast, the Unicode representation of CV characters in Indic scripts is based on their phonological structure and encodes the consonant before the vowel. While modeling characters and the lexicon, the recognition system should take this discrepancy into account.

Stroke-order variations spanning multiple symbols – Strokes from different graphemes may be interleaved while writing a character. For example, a two-stroke matra may be written partially and completed only after the base consonant is written. This is loosely related to the phenomenon of delayed strokes in English, wherein some strokes are entered only after the completion of the entire word. However for Indic scripts it happens at the level of individual characters, and the variations are widespread and not limited to a small number of strokes such as t-crossings and i-dots in English. Further, because of the 2-D arrangement, it is often not possible to use heuristics to reorder out-of-order strokes as is common practice for dealing with delayed strokes in English.

Stroke-order, -number, and -direction variations within symbols – The ordering of strokes is likely to vary even within a symbol. For example, Fig. 6 shows different styles of writing the consonant */pha/* in Devanagari, where each style (shown along the columns) differs in the number of strokes and/or their ordering.

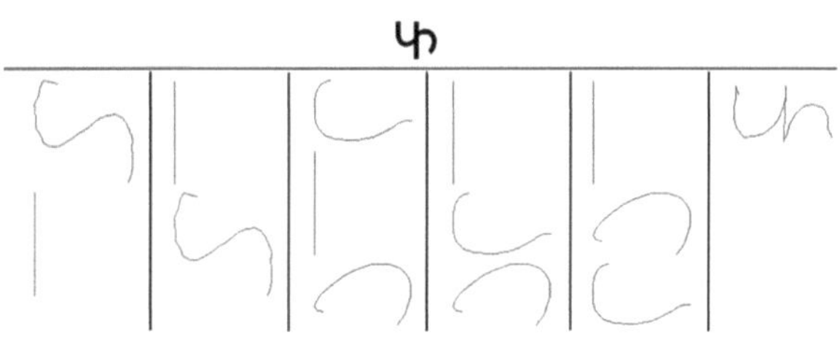

Fig. 6 Writing styles identified for a Devanagari character

In general, stroke-order, -number, and -direction variations are quite high in Indic characters and constitute one of the central challenges in online recognition of Indic scripts. These variations may be discovered automatically from the data samples by applying unsupervised learning techniques such as clustering [9].

3.5 Language-Specific and Regional Differences in Usage

Marked differences in the use of symbols may be observed in the use of a script like Devanagari across languages such as Hindi, Sanskrit, Marathi, and Nepali. For instance, the *halanth* (vowel muting diacritic) and the CH form are used frequently in Sanskrit, but rarely in Hindi. The shapes of symbols show regional variations, influenced by other languages and scripts in use in the region and its surrounding areas. Due to the fact that languages such as Tamil and Bangla span multiple countries, one may also expect country-specific differences in the use of the corresponding scripts. In all these cases, the language models, which are often used in the handwriting recognition system to improve accuracy, need to be substantially unique.

The challenges for online recognition of Indic scripts are sufficiently different from those of Latin. Chief among them are the large number of classes, the stroke-order/number variation, and the two-dimensional nature of the script. There are several others. For example, small vowel modifiers may get interpreted as noise in the input, and the *shirorekha* or headline which is often written after completing the word requires special treatment (Fig. 7). Indic script recognition also differs from that of CJK scripts in a few significant ways. In the case of CJK scripts, the shape of each stroke in a character is generally a straight line and hence stroke direction-based features are often sufficient. But in the case of Indic scripts, the basic strokes are often nonlinear or curved, and hence features that provide more information than just the directional properties are required. Moreover, in CJK scripts, a word is generally written discretely and hence segmenting it into characters is much easier when compared to Indic scripts where the most common style of writing is run-on. Table 1 summarizes the salient characteristics of Indic, Latin, and CJK scripts from the perspective of online HWR.

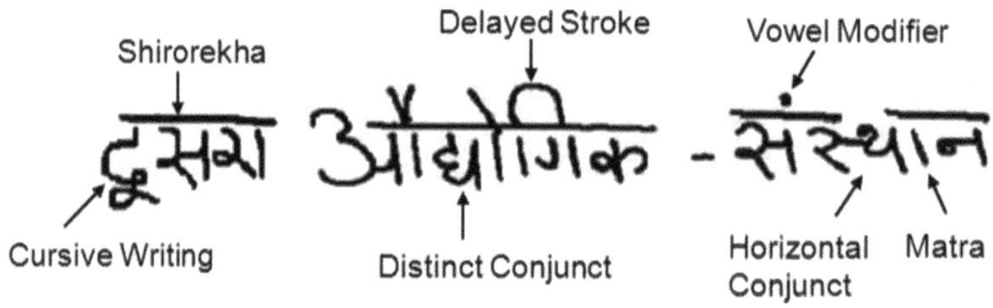

Fig. 7 Some challenges for online HWR of Devanagari script

Table 1 Comparison of Indic, Latin, and CJK scripts [6]

Property	Indic	Latin	CJK
Writing system	Syllabic alphabet	Alphabetic	Chinese and Kanji: pictographic–ideographic, Kana: syllabary, Hangul: syllabic alphabet
Number of units	>1500	<100	Chinese and Kanji: few thousands, Kana: 48, Hangul: few thousands
Common style of writing a word	Run-on	Cursive	Discrete
Structure of writing	2-D	1-D	2-D
Stroke shape complexity	High	High	Low
Stroke-order/number variation	High	Low	High

4 Recognition of Isolated Characters

We have seen that syllabic units or characters of varying complexities form the basic building blocks of Indic scripts and are difficult to recognize for a number of reasons. A number of early efforts in the literature have focused on recognition of simple characters such as independent vowels and isolated consonants. The primary challenges in recognizing complex characters as previously outlined come from their number, shape complexity, and symbol and stroke-order variations.

4.1 Strategies

There are several strategies possible for recognition of isolated (complex) characters:

1. Characters may be viewed as compositions of strokes
2. Characters may be viewed as compositions of C, C', V, and M graphemes
3. Characters may be viewed as indivisible units

In the stroke-centric strategy, a set of unique stroke shapes that constitute all characters are found and characters expressed as combinations of these strokes. The number of unique strokes in most Indic scripts is believed to be less than 300. A key problem with this strategy is that these strokes are not known in advance for a given script and are a function of writing styles. The approaches developed at IIT-M [10–13] adopt this strategy. The determination of unique strokes is performed manually by analysis of training data and are estimated as 123 and 98 for Devanagari and Tamil, respectively [13]. However these approaches are rule based, script specific, and may require significant manual intervention in the training phase.

The second strategy leverages the internal graphemic structure of the character. Recognition of a character is a result of recognizing the (much smaller set of) constituent graphemes. Potential segmentation points are typically at stroke transitions and alignment using dynamic programming may be used for segmentation. Hidden Markov models (HMM) may also be used to solve this problem implicitly. For Telugu script recognition [14], basic graphemes including core characters and ligatures, summing up to 141 when their positions are ignored, are manually identified and then HMMs are used to model each one of them. A major advantage of this strategy is the reduced effort involved in data collection as only samples of the identified graphemes are required. In its simplest form, this strategy does not address stroke-order variations across symbols in the character, symbol-order variations, co-articulation effects, and the cases where opaque symbols are created by CC and CV combinations. It is highly effective when constraints may be imposed on the writer to aid recognition.

The last strategy of treating complex characters directly as pattern classes has to deal with their large numbers. It also requires large quantities of data for training.

Consequently this strategy has been explored primarily for simple characters such as isolated vowels and consonants in different Indic scripts. It has also been used for Tamil characters, which as mentioned earlier are limited in number due to the linearization of consonant conjuncts [15, 16, 12, 17]. An obvious advantage of this strategy is that standard character recognition techniques in the literature may be used without much knowledge of the structure of the script, as is evident from the results of the Tamil character recognition competition organized in conjunction with IWFHR-10 [18]. Joshi et al. [19] assume that Devanagari can be "linearized" like Tamil by constraining writers to unravel consonant clusters into sequences of vowel-muted consonant characters. The linearization assumption reduces the number of characters to 441 – still a large number – when vowel modifiers are not considered. An accuracy of around 90% is reported for writer-dependent recognition using the subspace-based method.

4.2 Preprocessing

Preprocessing techniques for Indic scripts are similar to those used for other scripts. Dehooking, smoothing, resampling, size normalization, etc., are commonly performed. In the work by Swethalakshmi [13], different types of size normalization for Devanagari strokes are investigated. Genetic programming has also been explored as a way of designing an optimal scaling function that reduces classification error [20].

Nonlinear normalization that has been found to be effective for CJK scripts does not appear useful for Indic scripts [13]. In the case of Devanagari, the *shirorekha* is often detected and removed prior to recognition. During word recognition the shirorekha also serves as a valuable cue for detecting reference lines.

4.3 Features

Features used for Latin scripts have been found to be useful for Indic scripts as well. Low-level features such as the normalized x- and y-coordinates have been widely used. Additional features such as normalized first and second derivatives and curvature have shown promising results for Tamil and Telugu [21, 22]. Structural features such as cusps, bumps, loops, and semi-loops have also been explored for Tamil [12, 23] and Devanagari [13] character recognition. In some early work on Tamil character recognition [24], angle features, Fourier coefficients, and wavelet features are compared using a neural network classifier. Angle features are shown to be susceptible to noise leading to high intra-class variability. On the other hand, Fourier coefficients do not capture subtle differences between two characters as the change in the values of x and y over a small interval of time gets nullified over the entire frequency domain. Wavelet features are shown to be the most effective for Tamil as they retain both the intra-class similarity and inter-class differences. In general, directional coding approaches popular for CJK scripts are not effective for Indic scripts since the strokes do not have simple shapes.

In the work of Toselli et al. [21], a combination of time-domain and frequency-domain features is shown to improve recognition accuracy on Tamil characters. For Telugu character recognition, Rao and Ajitha [25] propose the use of x- and y-extrema, direction of pen motion (clockwise/anticlockwise), and relative displacement from the previous point of the same extrema category (x or y).

Offline features that model the input as a raster image rather than a trajectory may also be used to improve recognition accuracy when compared to using online features alone [26]. Being invariant to stroke-order, -number, and -direction variations, offline features are very promising in the context of Indic script recognition.

4.4 Classification

A number of different classification techniques have been applied to the problem of Indic script character recognition. While some approaches [13] are aimed at recognizing all the characters in the script, others [26, 14] only address specific subsets. These classification approaches may broadly be categorized as follows:

- Template matching
- Rule-based approaches
- Neural networks
- Hidden Markov models
- Subspace-based approach

Template matching – In this approach, the features extracted from the test character are compared with those of stored prototypes or templates. The test character is assigned the label of the template that is most similar to it. The templates could either be samples selected from the training set or a categorical representation [27]. In the context of Indic script recognition, efforts based on template matching are aplenty and a majority of them have reported encouraging results. For example, a two-stage classification scheme [17] using nearest neighbor classifiers is described for *writer-dependent* Tamil character recognition. The first stage filters the templates based on the Euclidean distance from the test sample and the second stage computes the more expensive dynamic time warping (DTW) distance (Fig. 8) from the short-listed templates. The label of the nearest template is assigned to the test sample.

The same scheme has also been applied for *writer-independent* Telugu and Tamil character recognition using a different set of features [22]. For the problem of Telugu character recognition, Rao and Ajitha [25] perform a coarse matching with the templates using the number of X–Y extrema points in the test sample and a fine matching using dynamic programming.

In another effort on Tamil character recognition [28], templates are identified from the training set using agglomerative hierarchical clustering and learning vector

Fig. 8 Dynamic time warping (DTW) for matching two samples of a Tamil character (see also Plate 4 on page 317 in the Color Plate Section)

quantization (LVQ) with DTW as the distance measure. A DTW-based nearest neighbor classifier is then employed for matching the test sample.

Rule-based approaches – These approaches do not have an explicit training phase; instead they exploit human knowledge about the problem. The task of classification now becomes a deterministic verification procedure. Although the approach has the advantage of requiring minimal training data, it suffers from being labor intensive and highly script specific. Another disadvantage is that the approach typically does not provide alternate recognition choices. In a recent effort on Devanagari character recognition [13], strokes are first classified using support vector machines (SVM) and predefined rules are then used for grouping the stroke labels into characters.

In the work of Ranade [27] for the Devanagari script, a set of stroke templates is derived from analysis of common writing styles of different Devanagari characters, and each character is represented by a set of combinations of these stroke templates.

In another effort [12], Tamil strokes are represented as strings of shape features. In order to recognize an unknown stroke, its equivalent feature string is computed. The test stroke is then identified by searching the database using a flexible string-matching algorithm. Once all the strokes in the input are known, the character is determined using a finite state automaton.

Prior knowledge about popular writing styles has also been exploited to design a first-stage classifier for Tamil characters [23]. The authors observe that the start of any Tamil character is either a line, semi-loop, or a loop. Accordingly, the candidate choices are pruned during recognition.

Neural networks – In the work of Kunte and Samuel [29], feed-forward neural networks with a single hidden layer are used for the recognition of handwritten Kannada characters. The authors use approximation coefficients derived from wavelet decomposition on the preprocessed (x, y) as features for representing characters. The input character is initially classified into its consonant group (defined as a consonant and any of its vowel combinations), and separate neural networks are used for further classification within the consonant group.

The neural network-based approach is also adopted by Sundaresan and Keerthi [24] for the recognition of online Tamil characters. Their work compares the performance of time delay neural network (TDNN) and a single hidden layer network for the classification task. Due to the presence of similar-looking characters and high dimensionality of the input, TDNN exhibits poor performance when compared to the single hidden layer network. The work also studies the relevance of different features such as (x, y) coordinates, sequence of directions, curvature, sequence of cosine angles, and wavelet features.

Another example is the use of multi-layer perceptrons (MLP) trained on eight-direction code histogram features for the problem of Bangla character recognition [30].

Hidden Markov models – While HMMs have been used widely for English character recognition, they have seen limited application for Indic scripts. Connell et al. [26] use a combination of two HMM classifiers trained with online features, and three nearest neighbor classifiers each trained on different sets of offline features, for Devanagari character recognition. The combination of online and offline classifiers is shown to improve the accuracy from 69.2% (online, HMM alone) to 86.5%.

HMMs have also been used for Telugu [14] and Tamil [21] character recognition. Each character is modeled as a left-to-right HMM and a combination of time-domain and frequency-domain features is shown to result in accuracies higher than using either of them alone.

Subspace-based approach – In this approach, principal component analysis (PCA) is applied separately to feature vectors extracted from the training samples of each class. The subspace formed by the first few eigenvectors is considered to represent the model for that class. During recognition, the test sample is projected onto each subspace and the class corresponding to the one that is closest is declared as the recognition result (Fig. 9). Joshi et al. [19] apply the subspace method to writer-dependent Devanagari character recognition. The shirorekha and vowel modifiers are preclassified using heuristics before recognizing the core character using the subspace method. The approach has also been employed for Tamil character recog-

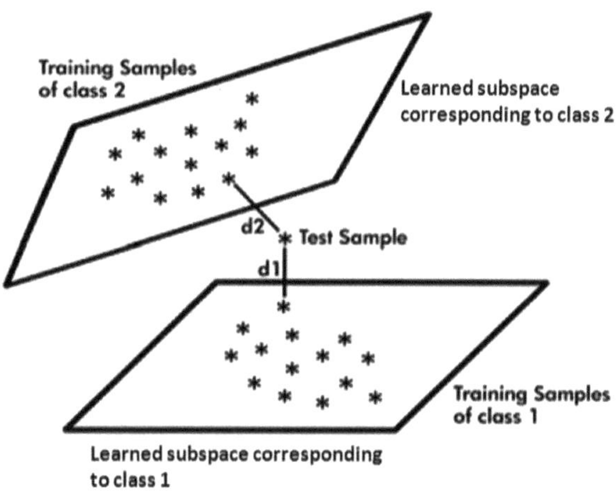

Fig. 9 Subspace-based approach for character recognition [31]

nition [15]. In these efforts, the feature vectors used for eigenanalysis are composed of the normalized (x, y) coordinates extracted following equi-spaced resampling of the character trajectory. Consequently different feature dimensions may not have stable interpretations (e.g., as salient points along the trajectory), and the method as used is outperformed by DTW-based template matching [16].

Recognition accuracies of some of the systems described above are shown in Table 2. The accuracies in the case of Devanagari are not comparable as the data sets used and the classes defined differ widely.

Table 2 Reported accuracies for isolated character recognition

System	Number of classes	Features	Classification	Accuracy (%)
		Devanagari		
Swethalakshmi [13]	123 strokes	*X–Y* coordinates, Fourier descriptors and structural features	SVM and rule-based stroke regrouping	89.88
Connell et al. [26]	40 simple characters	Online and off-line	Combination of HMM and nearest neighbor classifiers	86.5
		Tamil		
Vision objects [18]	156 characters	Online and off-line	Neural networks	93.53
Bulacu M. [18]	156 characters	*X–Y* coordinates	Nearest neighbor classifier using dynamic time warping (DTW) distance	91.20
Toselli et al. [18, 21]	156 characters	Time domain and frequency domain	HMM	90.72
		Telugu		
Prashanth et al. [22]	141 core characters and ligatures	*X-Y* coordinates, normalized first and second derivatives and curvature	Nearest neighbor classifier using Euclidean and DTW distance	89.77
Babu et al. [14]	141 core characters and ligatures	Time domain and frequency domain	HMM	91.6
		Bangla		
Bhattacharya et al. [30]	50 simple characters	Eight-direction code histogram	MLP	83.61

5 Word Recognition

Word recognition for Indic scripts is a nascent area of research, and published literature on the topic is limited. The general strategies for word recognition for Indic scripts may be classified broadly along the lines of those available for Latin scripts [32–35] into analytic approaches based on explicit segmentation, those based on implicit segmentation, and holistic approaches.

5.1 Preprocessing

When part of larger systems [36], line and word segmentation are needed in order to isolate words. There has not been much work in the area of layout analysis or page segmentation specially directed at Indic scripts. In general since writing is structured into lines and lines into words, strategies used for English may be adapted for Indic scripts. In the case of Devanagari, the shirorekha may be used to simplify segmentation of lines into words.

Given an isolated word sample, common preprocessing steps performed at the word level include the determination of reference lines, baseline skew correction, and character slant correction. For a script such as Devanagari, reference lines generally delineate the upper matra zone, the middle zone, and the lower matra zone (Fig. 10). Shirorekhas where present may be used for determination of reference lines and are also frequently removed before further processing.

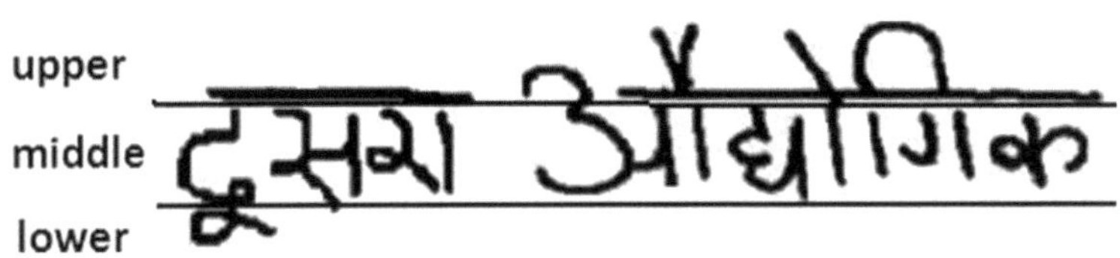

Fig. 10 Reference lines identified during Devanagari word preprocessing

5.2 Analytic Approaches Based on Explicit Segmentation

Explicit segmentation strategies are based on explicitly segmenting the handwritten word into simpler units, recognizing those units and thereby deriving the graphemes or character identities, typically by imposing some constraints on the writer. Explicit segmentation is often error prone because of Sayre's paradox [32]: "To recognize a letter, one must know where it starts and where it ends; to isolate a letter, one must recognize it first." Some efforts that adopt this approach [19, 37] presuppose that Indic scripts may be written as a sequence of space separated or boxed characters. As already observed, this is not natural given that syllabic units can vary greatly in size and complexity. Further, there may be multiple ways of decomposing syllabic units

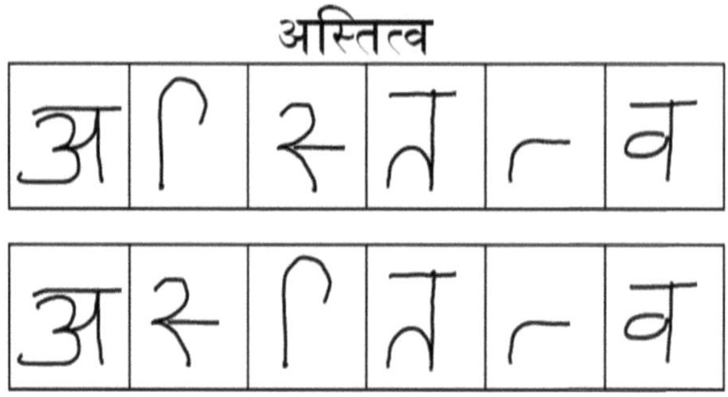

Fig. 11 Alternate ways of writing the Devanagari word */astitva/* in boxed form

into simpler symbols, and different possible symbol orders adopted while writing in boxed form (Fig. 11). However preliminary studies suggest that "standard" ways of decomposing complex characters and ordering symbols can be successfully learned as part of a training phase [37].

The stroke-based approach adopted by Swethalakshmi [13] does not require boxed input, but performs explicit segmentation based on proximity analysis for grouping strokes into characters. Proximity analysis is conventionally carried out based on the spatial information between consecutive strokes in a character. For scripts such as Devanagari where the most proximal strokes need not be consecutively written (e.g., */ko/*, " को"), a two-stage proximity analysis is proposed. In the first stage, consecutive strokes are grouped together based on the spacing between their bounding rectangles. In a second stage, character-like units whose bounding box overlap with each other are grouped together. Any residual oversegmentation or undersegmentation of characters is resolved in a postprocessing step when the stroke labels are used to classify the characters. Given the interpretation of individual syllabic units, the best word-level interpretation is determined using a lexicon or other language model.

5.3 Analytic Approaches Based on Implicit Segmentation

Approaches based on implicit segmentation address the segmentation problem implicitly by adopting a strategy of "over-segmentation." The word input is segmented into a number of small segments with the only criterion that none of the segments should contain parts of more than one symbol. In other words, the intention is that the actual segmentation points are always covered as a subset of the segmentation boundaries obtained by over-segmenting the word. Analytic approaches based on implicit segmentation typically use models of an underlying set of symbols to analyze the word sample to recognize the word. Segmentation is a byproduct of recognition, and for this reason, this approach is also known as "recognition-based segmentation." The two most popular techniques employed for implicit

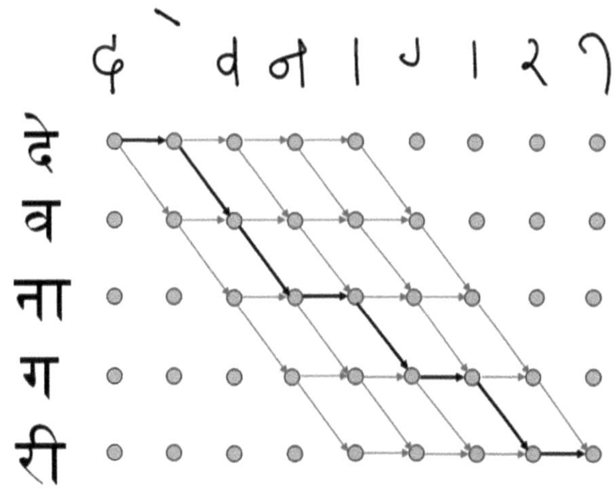

Fig. 12 Implicit segmentation at stroke boundaries based on dynamic programming. The *arrows* illustrate all the possible paths for matching the Devanagari word/*devanaagarii*/. The *black arrows* show the minimum cost path

segmentation are dynamic programming (DP) (Fig. 12) and hidden markov models (HMM). Segmentation is performed implicitly by aligning the input with a dictionary word model composed from the symbol models.

An example of this class of approaches applied to Tamil word recognition is that of the authors [38] which uses a set of 83 C, V, and "opaque" CV characters in Tamil as the underlying symbol set. Characters are not modeled explicitly; the lexicon is represented as a network of HMMs corresponding to these symbols. The system uses normalized y-value, normalized first and second derivatives, writing angle, and pen-up/down information as features. Stroke-order variation within a symbol is captured implicitly by the symbol model; however, symbol-order variation is not captured; instead a standard symbol order is assumed. This assumption is broadly true for Tamil which is more linear than two dimensional, but may not hold for other scripts such as Devanagari. This approach also assumes that one symbol is completed before another is initiated; in practice, strokes of different symbols may be temporally intermingled in creating the character (e.g., the delayed stroke in Fig. 7). Under the constraints mentioned, recognition accuracy of 98% is obtained for lexicons of size 1000, decreasing to 92% on lexicons of size 20,000.

5.4 Holistic Approaches

Techniques that follow the segmentation free or holistic approach circumvent the problem of segmentation completely. Feature vectors are extracted at the word level and the most similar lexicon word is considered as the recognition result. The training of holistic recognition algorithms is inseparable from the lexicon because adding a new word to the lexicon typically requires retraining the recognizer with samples of that word. As the lexicon size increases, similarities between words increase and hence the recognition accuracy deteriorates. However, the approach has its own advantages. As it uses the global word shape, it is less sensitive to local shape variations that are common in unconstrained writing. To the best of our knowledge, there is no Indic script recognition system that adopts this approach. However there has been some research on synthesis of words in Indic languages [39]. A collection of handwritten documents may be searched by aligning handwriting synthesized from search keywords, with handwritten words in the documents, using a DTW-like algorithm.

5.5 *Language Models*

Lexicons and other language models are an important aspect of achieving acceptable accuracy for online HWR. Barring a few reported methods that use lexicons, the use of language models has not been explored substantially for online HWR of Indic scripts. In general these may be derived from available text corpora for Indic languages [40, 41], or from increasingly available web content especially in the form of online versions of newspapers and magazines. In addition, a number of such resources are being created by research communities working on natural language processing, machine translation, optical character recognition, off-line handwriting recognition, and automatic speech recognition for Indic languages.

Unicode [42] is the most popular standard for representing strings in Indic languages, although ISCII [43] is still available. One of the issues with Unicode is that it imposes the phonological symbol ordering, for example, a CV is expressed as a C followed by a V. This can be an issue when the V is actually written before the C.

A second issue especially with languages such as Sanskrit is that of compounds words, which makes it difficult to enumerate all possible words. Also in the case of lexicon-driven and stroke-based approaches, where each grapheme has different stroke-order representations, the number of possible definitions of a lexicon word in terms of stroke labels tends to increase exponentially. This could be an important problem to address in implementing such an approach.

6 Applications

The principal application of online HWR is to support input of text into devices of various form factors, by providing an alternative to hard and soft keyboards. Online HWR may also be used (in conjunction with ink parsing and layout analysis techniques) for subsequent interpretation of handwritten notes captured as digital ink – either to support transcription or indexing and keyword search. Online HWR may also be used to complement or supplement speech input as a part of multimodal interfaces and systems [44, 45].

While the recognition of unconstrained handwriting is clearly the end objective of research, a number of practical Indic text input solutions (also called input method editors or IMEs) can be obtained by imposing constraints on the writer. Further, since text input is interactive, partial recognition may be performed periodically during the course of writing a word or character rather than at the end.

One such constraint is symbol order imposing the phonological order of the occurrence of consonant and vowels in the syllable: for example, constraining the writer to complete the consonant (C) before the vowel diacritic (V) while writing a CV character (even when the vowel diacritic appears to the left of the consonant and is typically written before). This allows a two-step IME in which the consonant is first written and recognized (and manually corrected by selecting from an n-best list), and the vowel diacritic written and recognized in a second step. A second constraint could be to ask the user to unravel consonant clusters or conjuncts into sequences of CH characters using the vowel-muting diacritic, rather than by using the half-forms or consonant conjuncts. When used together, these constraints allow recognition of complex characters such as C'C'CV using only isolated symbol recognizers for C and V. Such strategies are used by IMEs such as the gesture keyboard [31], guided handwriting [46], compact IME [47] and IndicDasher [48]. The gesture keyboard uses a combination of coarse pen position in a grid of base consonants, and recognition of the written matra, to interpret the user's CV input (Fig. 13). Guided handwriting uses a set of basic stroke and substroke shapes together with rules to predict a consonant even as it is being written. In contrast to these approaches which only recognize isolated consonants or matras, FreePad [49] is an IME based on word recognition which assumes phonological symbol order and pen lifts between symbols, but does not require any explicit indication of symbol transition. Despite supporting "eyes-free" input using a stylus or finger, recognition accuracy is reported to be on par with conventional handwriting input, at least for Tamil.

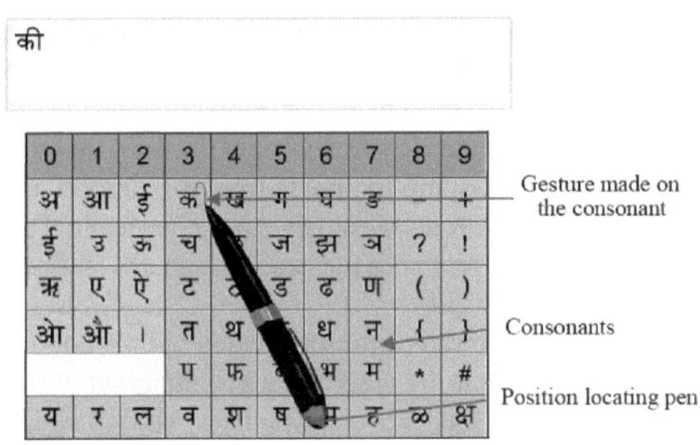

Fig. 13 Gesture keyboard for entering Devanagari characters [31]

Another specialized application of online handwriting recognition is pen-based form filling. These forms may be electronic in nature or printed on paper for use with a device capable of capturing electronic ink. In either case, they are filled by hand, and the handwriting captured as digital ink and recognized. As mentioned earlier, boxed styles are not natural for Indic scripts since characters may be of different sizes, but users may be trained to adopt a standard decomposition and ordering [37]. In the general case and to support walk-up use, form-filling applications would need to support recognition of words and phrases with all of the attendant variations and issues. Electronic forms may alternatively be filled using an appropriate IME.

The PATRAM system [36] is an interactive handwritten notes capture application for Indic languages. It allows a handwritten document to be created, edited, and exported into standard formats such as InkML. The system also integrates layout analysis and character recognition algorithms to interpret the document and a spell checker to correct misrecognized words.

7 Resources

One of the major stumbling blocks for language technology research in the Indian context has been the lack of significant publicly available linguistic resources, and this is especially true for HWR. It is imperative that tools and data formats be standardized and validated data sets be created and made available to change the status quo. It should be mentioned that such data sets would also benefit research in handwritten document analysis, writer identification, script identification, handwritten document indexing and retrieval, and so forth.

Data collection is a challenge for Indic scripts due to the large number of characters. It is generally easy to collect symbols of the basic C and V characters, since they are a small number. However data collection should ideally cover all possible characters in order to capture different coarticulation effects and stroke- and symbol-order variations.

Different strategies have been used to address this challenge in practice. For CV characters, one common strategy is to collect samples of isolated matras under the assumption that the shape does not change as a function of the consonant being modified. As seen earlier, there are clearly several exceptions that this strategy does not address. Even where this assumption holds true, it is important to capture the relative position of the matra with respect to the base consonant. Therefore another possible strategy is to pre-print or render the base consonants and instruct writers to mark only the matras over them [14].

Data collection to support word recognition is often optimized to suit the specific recognition approach, for example, by identifying a minimal set of words that covers all the basic graphemes used. A set cover algorithm may be employed to discover the optimal set of words from a text corpus [50]. The word data thus collected still need to be annotated at the grapheme level in order to provide training samples for the grapheme models. In order to avoid the labor-intensive task of labeling the collected word samples at the character level, dynamic programming has been explored to propagate the word truth to the constituent characters [51]. Propagation of manual character or grapheme-level annotation between samples of the same word written by the same writer has also been explored [52]. Some of the practical challenges encountered in creating a handwriting corpus for an Indic script are described by Agrawal et al. [53].

7.1 Data Set Standards

Standards are important for the creation of handwriting data sets, in order to ensure that resources created can be used by others. UNIPEN 1.0 [54] is still the de facto standard for encoding of handwriting data because of its simplicity and widespread use. However it suffers from some shortcomings [55] and hence new standards such as hwDataset [52] and UNIPEN XML (UPX) [55] have been proposed. UPX in particular is being seen as an XML-based successor to the (ASCII-based) UNIPEN standard. UPX provides a hierarchical and structured solution for the representation of online handwriting data and uses W3C digital ink markup language (InkML) [56] as the underlying representation of digital ink. However the use of UPX has been hampered by the lack of implementations and tools; this is expected to change with InkML itself expected to become a standard with available implementations.

A second aspect of standardization is the development of conventions for the annotation hierarchy and labels to be used for annotating handwriting in Indic scripts. It is clear that a standard should minimally allow markup of words, syllabic units, the core graphemes, and perhaps strokes. While there is agreement at the word and syllabic unit level because of their linguistic significance, no standards are as yet available for the core graphemes or for strokes. There is no consistent definition of these units, and also a clear dependence on the recognition strategy, since, for example, certain CV characters or CC conjuncts may be treated as opaque graphemes for the purposes of recognition. Hence a requirement of the standard may be the ability to support customizations of a standard annotation hierarchy, especially below a certain level.

Since Unicode for Indic scripts [57] is an encoding of the sound of the word, it may at best be used for labeling at the level of words and syllabic units. Unicode labels are clearly insufficient to encode lower level visual structures that a recognition strategy may adopt. For example, Unicode does not have any labels for half-consonant forms, since these do not occur in isolation in the phonological sense.

7.2 Tools

The UNIPEN Project [54] created tools for visualization and annotation of English handwriting data in the UNIPEN 1.0 format, as well as a library of preprocessing functions. While the original project is no longer active, the tools are still available [58] and usable for Indic scripts.

The Lipi Toolkit Project [59, 60] provides open-source tools and recognizers for online HWR of Indic scripts. The focus at the present time is recognition of isolated characters. The tools and recognizers are in fact generic and may be used for arbitrary character/symbol sets. The project provides handwriting data collection tools for different devices such as TabletPCs and ACECAD DigiMemo [61], an inexpensive paper-based electronic clipboard device which allows handwriting capture simultaneously in the form of digital ink and paper. The toolkit uses the UNIPEN format for storage of ink data. The "Core Toolkit" provides common preprocessing operations and feature extractors, and a k-NN classifier based on DTW distance. The project also provides an interactive recognizer development (IDE) tool which allows creation of a simple recognizer using a few training samples, as well as "pre-built" recognizers for different scripts. An annotation tool for Indic (and other) scripts that supports UNIPEN, W3C InkML, and hwDataset/UPX [52] is likely to be released as part of the Lipi Toolkit Project once InkML and UPX are standardized.

7.3 Data Sets

Publicly available data sets of handwriting at the time of writing are limited to those used for the IWFHR-10 Tamil character recognition competition [62] and some data sets of simple characters such as core consonants [63]. A partial list of available resources for Indic (and other) languages is hosted at the Lipi Toolkit project web site [64].

The Technology Development for Indian Languages (TDIL) program of the Ministry of Information Technology of the Government of India has recently funded a consortium of universities to create resources as well as technology for online HWR of Indic scripts [65]. The consortium is collecting word data for several Indian languages and scripts. It is hoped that many of the tools and data sets created in the process will become publicly available for research purposes.

8 Summary

Online handwriting recognition for Indic scripts is still in its infancy. Given the large number of scripts and millions of users, two-dimensional layout, and stroke- and symbol-order variations, there are a number of aspects that make the problem different from Latin and CJK scripts, and worthy of serious investigation. The benefits of developing such a technology are also very significant, given the large user population both within and outside the Indian subcontinent, and the lack of standardized or convenient keyboard-based text input solutions.

Much research is needed on recognition of complex characters and whole words in the different Indic scripts. Given the issues of stroke-order, stroke-direction, and stroke-number variations in Indic scripts, off-line features and approaches stand a good chance of improving recognition accuracy when used in combination with online features and approaches. For continuous handwriting input to become a reality, research on language models is imperative as well. There is also a clear need that approaches to recognition be as data-driven as possible, given the challenges of covering a large number of languages and scripts. There is an urgent need for standardized data sets using well-defined sets of characters and graphemes to be created and made available for all Indic scripts, in order to allow meaningful comparison of different published approaches. Resources such as tools and data sets for a few scripts are gradually becoming available in the public domain, and should provide a significant fillip to research. The next 5–10 years are likely to produce interesting new approaches and new levels of performance, hopefully leading to widespread adoption of online HWR technology, especially for mobile devices.

Acknowledgments We gratefully acknowledge the contributions and influence over the years, of various present and former colleagues at HP Labs India – notably Deepu Vijayasenan, M. Dinesh, Ajay Bhaskarabhatla, Mudit Agrawal, Kalika Bali, and K.S.R. Anjaneyulu, collaborators Prof. A.G. Ramakrishnan at the Indian Institute of Science (IISc), Prof. Srinivasa Chakravarthy at Indian Institute of Technology-Madras (IIT-M), and Prof. C.V. Jawahar at International Institute of Information Technology-Hyderabad (IIIT-H), their students, and various interns who have worked with us at sometime or the other.

References

1. List of Languages by Number of Native Speakers, http://en.wikipedia.org/wiki/List_of_languages_by_number_of_native_speakers
2. Tappert, C., Suen, C., Wakahara, T.: State of the Art in On-Line Handwriting Recognition.IEEE Transactions on Pattern Analysis and Machine Intelligence (PAMI) **12**(8) (1990) 787–808
3. Plamondon, R., Srihari, S.N.: Online and Off-Line Handwriting Recognition: A Comprehensive Survey. IEEE Transactions on Pattern Analysis and Machine Intelligence (PAMI) **22**(1) (2000) 63–84
4. Liu, C.L., Jaeger, S., Nakagawa, M.: Online Recognition of Chinese Characters: The State-of-the-Art. IEEE Transactions on Pattern Analysis and Machine Intelligence (PAMI) **26**(2) (2004) 1489–1500
5. Jaeger, S., Liu, Nakagawa, M.:The State of the Art in Japanese On-Line Handwriting Recognition Compared to Techniques in Western Handwriting Recognition. International Journal on Document Analysis and Recognition (IJDAR) **6**(2) (2003) 75–88
6. Coulmas, F.: The Blackwell Encyclopedia of Writing Systems. Blackwell, Oxford (1996)
7. Mudur, S.P., Nayak, N., Shanbhag, S., Joshi, R.K.: An Architecture for the Shaping of Indic Texts. Computers & Graphics **23**(1) (1999) 7–24
8. Tamil Script, http://en.wikipedia.org/wiki/Tamil_script
9. Bharath, A., Deepu, V., Madhvanath, S.: An Approach to Identify Unique Styles in Online Handwriting Recognition. In: 8th International Conference on Document Analysis and Recognition (ICDAR 2005), Seoul, Korea (August–September 2005)
10. Swethalakshmi, H., Jayaraman, A., Chakravarthy, V.S., Sekhar, C.C.: Online Handwritten Character Recognition of Devanagari and Telugu Characters using Support Vector Machines. In: 10th International Workshop on Frontiers in Handwriting Recognition (IWFHR 2006), La Baule, France (October 2006)
11. Jayaraman, A., Sekhar, C.C., Chakravarthy, V.S.: Modular Approach to Recognition of Strokes in Telugu Script. In: 9th International Conference on Document Analysis and Recognition (ICDAR 2007), Curitiba, Brazil (September 2007)

12. Aparna, K.H., Subramanian, V., Kasirajan, M., Prakash, G.V., Chakravarthy, V.S., Madhvanath, S.: Online Handwriting Recognition for Tamil. In: 9th International Workshop on Frontiers in Handwriting Recognition (IWFHR 2004), Tokyo, Japan (October 2004)
13. Swethalakshmi, H.: Online Handwritten Character Recognition for Devanagari and Tamil Scripts Using Support Vector Machines. Master's thesis, Indian Institute of Technology, Madras, India (October 2007)
14. Babu, V.J., Prasanth, L., Sharma, R.R., Rao, G.V.P., Bharath, A.: HMM-Based Online Handwriting Recognition System for Telugu Symbols. In: 9th International Conference on Document Analysis and Recognition (ICDAR 2007), Curitiba, Brazil (September 2007)
15. Deepu, V., Madhvanath, S., Ramakrishnan, A.G.: Principal Component Analysis for Online Handwritten Character Recognition. In: 17th International Conference on Pattern Recognition (ICPR 2004), Cambridge, UK (August 2004)
16. Joshi, N., Sita, G., Ramakrishnan, A.G., Madhvanath, S.: Tamil Handwriting Recognition Using Subspace and DTW Based Classifiers. In: 11th International Conference on Neural Information Processing (ICONIP 2004), Calcutta, India (November 2004)
17. Joshi, N., Sita, G., Ramakrishnan, A.G., Madhvanath, S.: Comparison of Elastic Matching Algorithms for Online Tamil Handwritten Character Recognition. In: 9th International Workshop on Frontiers in Handwriting Recognition (IWFHR 2004), Tokyo, Japan (October 2004)
18. Madhvanath, S., Lucas, S.M.: IWFHR 2006 Online Tamil Handwritten Character Recognition Competition. In: 10th International Workshop on Frontiers in Handwriting Recognition (IWFHR 2006), La Baule, France (October 2006)
19. Joshi, N., Sita, G., Ramakrishnan, A.G., Deepu, V., Madhvanath, S.: Machine Recognition of Online Handwritten Devanagari Characters. In: 8th International Conference on Document Analysis and Recognition (ICDAR 2005), Seoul, Korea (August–September 2005)
20. Deepu, V., Madhvanath, S.: Genetically Evolved Transformations for Rescaling Online Handwritten Characters. In: IEEE India Annual Conference (INDICON 2004), Kharagpur, India (December 2004)
21. Toselli, A.H., Pastor, M., Vidal, E.: On-Line Handwriting Recognition System for Tamil Handwritten Characters. In:Pattern Recognition and Image Analysis. Springer Berlin/Heidelberg (July 2007) 370–377
22. Prasanth, L., Babu, V.J., Sharma, R.R., Rao, G.V.P., Dinesh, M.: Elastic Matching of Online Handwritten Tamil and Telugu Scripts Using Local Features. In: 9th International Conference on Document Analysis and Recognition (ICDAR 2007), Curitiba, Brazil (September 2007)
23. Sundaram, S., Ramakrishnan, A.G.: A Novel Hierarchical Classification Scheme for Online Tamil Character Recognition. In: 9th International Conference on Document Analysis and Recognition (ICDAR 2007), Curitiba, Brazil (September 2007)
24. Sundaresan, C.S., Keerthi, S.S.: A Study of Representations for Pen Based Handwriting Recognition of Tamil Characters. In: 5th International Conference on Document Analysis and Recognition (ICDAR 1999), Bangalore, India (September 1999)
25. Rao, P.V.S., Ajitha, T.M.: Telugu Script Recognition – A Feature Based Approach. In: 3rd International Conference on Document Analysis and Recognition (ICDAR 1995), Montreal, Canada (August 1995)
26. Connell, S.D., Sinha, R.M.K., Jain, A.K.: Recognition of Unconstrained On-Line Devanagari Characters. In: 15th International Conference on Pattern Recognition (ICPR 2000), Barcelona, Spain (September 2000)
27. Ranade, A., Ranade, M.: Devanagari Pen-Written Character Recognition. In: 9th International Conference on Advanced Computing and Communications (ADCOM 2001), Bhubaneshwar, India (December 2001)
28. Niels, R., Vuurpijl, L.: Dynamic Time Warping Applied to Tamil Character Recognition. In: 8th International Conference on Document Analysis and Recognition (ICDAR 2005), Seoul, Korea (August–September 2005)
29. Kunte, R.S.R., Samuel, R.D.S.: On-Line Character Recognition System for HandWritten Characters/Script with Bilingual Facility Employing Neural Classifiers and Wavelet Features.

In: International Conference on Knowledge Based Computer Systems (KBCS 2000), Mumbai, India (December 2000)
30. Bhattacharya, U., Gupta, B.K., Parui, S.K.: Direction Code Based Features for Recognition of Online Handwritten Characters of Bangla. In: 9th International Conference on Document Analysis and Recognition (ICDAR 2007), Curitiba, Brazil (September 2007)
31. Balaji, R., Deepu, V., Madhvanath, S., Prabhakaran, J.: Handwritten Gesture Recognition for Gesture Keyboard. In: 10th International Workshop on Frontiers in Handwriting Recognition (IWFHR 2006), La Baule, France (October 2006)
32. Vinciarelli, A.: A Survey on Off-Line Cursive Word Recognition. Pattern Recognition **35**(7) (2002) 1433–1446
33. Lecolinet, E., Baret, O.: Cursive Word Recognition: Methods and Strategies. In: Fundamentals in Handwriting Recognition. Springer-Verlag, New York (1994) 235–263
34. Steinherz, T., Rivlin, E., Intrator, N.: Offline Cursive Script Word Recognition – A Survey. International Journal on Document Analysis and Recognition (IJDAR) **2**(2–3) (1999) 90–110
35. Madhvanath, S., Govindaraju, V.: The Role of Holistic Paradigms in Handwritten Word Recognition. IEEE Transactions on Pattern Analysis and Machine Intelligence (PAMI) **23**(2) (2001) 149–164
36. Madduri, K., Aparna, K.H., Chakravarthy, V.S.: PATRAM – A Handwritten Word Processor for Indian Languages. In: 9th International Workshop on Frontiers in Handwriting Recognition (IWFHR 2004), Tokyo, Japan (October 2004)
37. Krishna, A., Prabhu, G., Bali, K., Madhvanath, S.: Indic Scripts Based Online Form Filling – A Usability Exploration. In: 11th International Conference on Human–Computer Interaction (HCII 2005), Las Vegas, USA (July 2005)
38. Bharath, A., Madhvanath, S.: Hidden Markov Models for Online Handwritten Tamil Word Recognition. In: 9th International Conference on Document Analysis and Recognition (ICDAR 2007), Curitiba, Brazil (September 2007)
39. Balasubramanian, A.: Document Annotation and Retrieval Systems. Master's Thesis, International Institute of Information Technology, Hyderabad, India (2006)
40. Indian Languages Corpora, http://www.ciilcorpora.net/
41. Baker, P., Hardie, A., McEnery, T., Cunningham, H., Gaizauskas, R.: EMILLE, A 67-Million Word Corpus of Indic Languages: Data Collection, Mark-up and Harmonisation. In: 3rd International Conference on Language Resources and Evaluation (LREC 2002), Canary Islands, Spain (May 2002)
42. The Unicode Consortium: The Unicode Standard Version 5.0. Addison Professional, MA (2006)
43. Indian Script Code for Information Interchange (ISCII), Ministry of Information Technology, Government of India, http://tdil.mit.gov.in/standards.htm (April 2003)
44. Manohar, P.: The Multimodal Interaction for the Computer: An Application-Independent Approach. Master's Thesis, Indian Institute of Technology, Madras, India (2006)
45. Barthelmess, P., Kaiser, E., McGee, D.: Toward Content-Aware Multimodal Tagging of Personal Photo Collections. In: 9th International Conference on Multimodal Interfaces (ICMI 2007), Nagoya, Japan (November 2007)
46. Prasad, A., Prashant, A., Borgaonkar, S.: Guided Handwriting: Predictive Writing Input Method Environment. Internal Technical Report, HP Labs India (December 2005)
47. Manish Kumar: Compact Stylus-Based Input Method for Indic Scripts. Diploma Thesis, National Institute of Design, Ahmedabad, India (2007)
48. Srinivas, N.K., Varghese, N., Raman, R.K.V.S.: IndicDasher: A Stroke and Gesture Based Input Mechanism for Indic Scripts. In: Workshop on Intelligent User Interfaces for Developing Regions (IUI4DR 2008), Canary Islands, Spain (January 2008)
49. Bharath, A., Madhvanath, S.: Recognition of Eyes-Free Handwriting Input for Pen and Touch Interfaces. In: 11th International Conference on Frontiers in Handwriting Recognition (ICFHR 2008), Montreal, Canada (August 2008)

50. Bhaskarabhatla, A.S., Madhvanath, S.: Experiences in Collection of Handwriting Data for Online Handwriting Recognition in Indic Scripts. In: 4th International Conference on Language Resources and Evaluation (LREC 2004), Lisbon, Portugal (May 2004)
51. Kumar, A., Balasubramanian, A., Namboodiri, A., Jawahar, C.V.: Model-Based Annotation of Online Handwritten Datasets. In: 10th International Workshop on Frontiers in Handwriting Recognition (IWFHR 2006), La Baule, France (October 2006)
52. Bhaskarabhatla, A.S., Madhvanath, S., Kumar, M.N.S.S.K.P., Balasubramanian, A., Jawahar, C.V.: Representation and Annotation of Online Handwritten Data. In: 9th International Workshop on Frontiers in Handwriting Recognition (IWFHR 2004), Tokyo, Japan (October 2004)
53. Agrawal, M., Bhaskarabhatla, A.S., Madhvanath, S.: Data Collection for HandWriting Corpus Creation in Indic Scripts. In: International Conference on Speech and Language Technology and Oriental COCOSDA (ICSLT-COCOSDA 2004), New Delhi, India (November 2004)
54. Guyon, I., Schomaker, L., Plamondon, R., Liberman, M., Janet, S.: UNIPEN Project of Online Data Exchange and Recognizer Benchmarks. In: International Conference on Pattern Recognition (ICPR 1994), Jerusalem, Israel (October 1994)
55. Agrawal, M., Bali, K., Madhvanath, S., Vuurpijl, L.: UPX – A New XML Representation for Annotated Datasets of Online Handwriting Data. In: 8th International Conference on Document Analysis and Recognition (ICDAR 2005), Seoul, Korea (October 2005)
56. W3C Working Group: Ink Markup Language, http://www.w3.org/2002/mmi/ink (2003)
57. Richard Ishida: Unicode Technical Note #10: An Introduction to Indic Scripts, http://unicode.org/notes/tn10/ (August 2003)
58. International Unipen Foundation: The Unipen Project, http://www.unipen.org (1994)
59. Madhvanath, S., Deepu, V., Kadiresan, T.M.: Lipitk: A Generic Toolkit for Online Handwriting Recognition. In:10th International Workshop on Frontiers in Handwriting Recognition (IWFHR 2006), La Baule, France (October 2006)
60. The Lipi Toolkit, http://lipitk.sourceforge.net
61. ACECAD DigiMemo, http://www.acecad.com.tw/products.html
62. HP Labs Isolated Handwritten Tamil Character Dataset hpl-tamil-iso-char, http://www.hpl.hp.com/india/research/penhw/resources/tamil-iso-char.html
63. Handwritten Character Databases of Indic Scripts, http://www.isical.ac.in/ujjwal/download/database.html
64. Online HWR Resources, http://lipitk.sourceforge.net/resources.htm
65. Online Handwriting Recognition System for Indian Languages (OHWR), http://ragashri.ee.iisc.ernet.in/ohwr/

Part II
Retrieval of Indic Documents

Enhancing Access to Primary Cultural Heritage Materials of India

Peter M. Scharf and Malcolm Hyman

Abstract This chapter is about enhancing access to primary cultural heritage materials of India housed in academic libraries by integrating them with machine-readable texts, lexical resources, and linguistic software in a digital library. Integrating primary cultural materials with a digital library can enable broad use of Indic collections for research and education. For the purposes of illustrating this procedure, we outline here the development of a prototype using the collections of Sanskrit manuscripts in the libraries at Brown University and the University of Pennsylvania and integrating them with The Sanskrit Library. The result is extendable to collections of Indic materials throughout the world and can serve as a model for digitization projects of cultural materials in other major culture-bearing languages such as Greek, Latin, Arabic, Persian, and Chinese.

Keywords Heritage materials · Digital libraries · Sanskrit documents

1 Introduction

Access to primary cultural heritage materials in non-European languages is severely hampered by distance to collections, isolation of artifacts from complementary research materials, deficiency or lack of metadata, and disarray within collections and within individual items of a collection. Arranging, cataloguing, scanning, and web-hosting of digital images of artifacts obviously address these problems. Yet an additional impediment confronts users of web-based primary literary sources in non-European languages: information-processing technology that has developed primarily in the environment of the Roman alphabet is incompatible with non-European languages. Internet users expect to find what they are looking for on the web in seconds. One expects to be able to search a PDF file. One expects to be able to run optical character recognition (OCR) software on a document image

P.M. Scharf (✉)
Department of Classics, Brown University, Providence, RI, USA
e-mail: scharf@brown.edu

V. Govindaraju, S. Setlur (eds.), *Guide to OCR for Indic Scripts*, Advances in Pattern Recognition, DOI 10.1007/978-1-84800-330-9_12,

file to extract machine-readable text. One expects to find material so extracted in a Google search. The seamless fulfillment of these expectations depends upon information-processing technology that has developed primarily in the environment of the Roman alphabet. However, generalized information extraction and search techniques cannot adequately handle literary materials for which there is a lack of adequate optical character recognition software, inconsistent encoding, obscure word boundaries, complex morphology, and free syntax. Functionality that is taken for granted for European languages has not yet been developed for languages such as Sanskrit. Fortunately, however, linguistic and OCR software currently being developed overcomes this impediment for Sanskrit and other Indic languages and makes possible for the first time the development of formats and interoperability protocols necessary to provide web access to the primary cultural heritage materials of India.

The potential impact of allowing wide-audience access to the large number of Sanskrit manuscripts is enormous. These texts constitute an enormous body of knowledge in diverse domains that are grossly underrepresented in the world academic community. Sanskrit has had a continuous production of literature in all fields of human endeavor over the course of four millennia. Preceded by a strong oral tradition of knowledge transmission, records of written Sanskrit remain in the form of inscriptions dating back to the first century BCE. Extant manuscripts in Sanskrit number over 30 million, 100 times those in Greek and Latin combined, constituting the largest cultural heritage that any civilization has produced prior to the invention of the printing press. While the Sanskrit language is of preeminent importance to the intellectual and cultural heritage of India, it has also been a major factor in the development of the world's religions, languages, literature, arts, sciences, and history. The prototype outlined below establishes a framework to allow projects to dramatically increase the accessibility of scanned Indic books and manuscripts which are currently accessible only to highly trained specialists. This access will be profoundly valuable to students, scholars, and the wider public concerned with such fields as historical and general linguistics, philosophy and religious studies, pharmacology and medicine, history of science and mathematics, and general history and literature of south Asia. Moreover the protocols, formats, and software described for Sanskrit in this prototype establish exemplary standards for accessing books and manuscripts in other non-European languages as well and indeed for cultural heritage literature in general (Fig. 1).

Of the 30 million extant Sanskrit manuscripts, more than 6500 are housed in 25 libraries and museums in the United States and Canada. Principal collections in the United States include Fitz-Edward Hall's collection of philosophical and literary manuscripts at Harvard, William Dwight Whitney's Vedic manuscripts at Yale, Charles Lanman's heterogeneous collection at Harvard, Albrecht Weber's Vedic manuscripts at the Library of Congress, David Eugene Smith's astronomical manuscripts at Columbia, and W. Norman Brown's diverse collection at the University of Pennsylvania. For our model, we select a set of 162 manuscripts of two centrally important Sanskrit texts for which the Sanskrit Library has the corresponding machine-readable texts, namely the *Mahābhārata*and *Bhāgavata Purāṇa*.

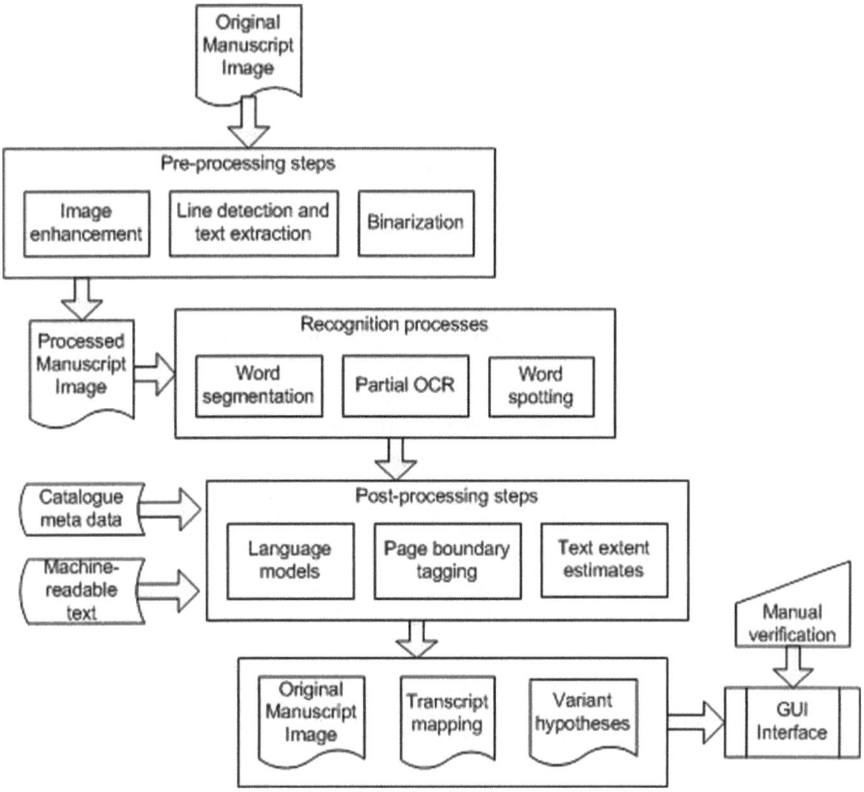

Fig. 1 Process for enhancing access to heritage materials

The Sanskrit Library[1] is a digital library at Brown University, founded in 2002, dedicated to facilitating education and research in Sanskrit by providing access to digitized primary texts in Sanskrit and computerized research and study tools to analyze and maximize the utility of digitized Sanskrit text. Housed on the server of the Center for Language Studies at Brown University,[2] the Sanskrit Library is achieving its aim through Brown University's collaboration with the University of Buffalo, the Thesaurus Indogermanischer Text- und Sprachmaterialien at Johann Wolfgang Goethe Universität, Frankfurt am Main (TITUS), and the Cologne Digital Sanskrit Lexicon project at Universität zu Köln (CDSL). The collaborative NSF-funded project "International Digital Sanskrit Library Integration" is currently integrating the linguistic tools being developed at Brown, lexical sources from CDSL, and the TITUS machine-readable text base in an integrated educational and research environment for Sanskrit analogous to what the Perseus Digital Library provides for classical Greek and Latin literature.

[1] http://sanskritlibrary.org/

[2] http://www.language.brown.edu

The Sanskrit Library utilizes the expertise of Brown's Scholarly Technology Group (STG) to support scholarly work in the digital medium by exploring critical new technologies that transform scholarly work and help to maintain its longevity. These technologies include data and metadata standards, XML publication tools, text encoding methods, database design, and accessibility standards. The library also cooperates closely with the Archimedes Project at Harvard University and the Max Planck Institute for the History of Science in Berlin, which is developing standardized tools to serve as a unified front end to diverse sources of linguistic and lexical data in any language. These tools serve as middleware between editing and browsing applications on the one hand and linguistic and reference services on the other. The Donatus system provides a unified interface to morphological analysis software and databases. The Pollux system provides a unified means of access to dictionaries or to any other reference work that is organized by alphabetized headwords, in any natural language. These tools enrich the digital Sanskrit Library, shorten the development cycle for our digital library applications, and provide interoperability with other digital library resources.

In this chapter, we describe techniques that can provide access to documents of Indic heritage materials and their metadata to enable generalized search and information extraction. We also outline techniques and infrastructure to utilize OCR and linguistic software to integrate Sanskrit manuscripts with machine-readable text, lexical resources, and linguistic software.

We are developing protocols, formats, and software to integrate digital images of manuscript pages with the corresponding machine-readable text and thereby provide direct and focused access to specifically sought passages on individual manuscript pages. Since OCR technology for Indic scripts is still not mature, it is necessary to provide linguistic and contextual constraints to successfully correlate text with its image. These constraints reduce the possible alternatives to a set small enough and differentiated enough to allow correct image identification.

Generally, as critical editions are digitized, they are segregated from the critical apparatus that accompanies the original printed edition, thereby isolating them from the manuscripts that constituted the text. In contrast, text-image alignment techniques outlined below allow identification of significant spans of variant readings in manuscripts and permit them to be examined in context. Integration of the machine-readable text of the critical edition with linguistic software can provide the facility for systematic interrogation of manuscripts. Significantly, this facility can be provided even for manuscripts not utilized to constitute the critical edition. Indexing variants in these manuscripts will bring them to the notice of the scholarly community for the first time and provide scholars with access to hitherto unnoticed passages.

2 Linguistic Tools

Software we are developing at Brown generates dynamic links from inflected forms in Sanskrit texts to the relevant dictionary entries in lexica supplied by the CDSL and revised under the Sanskrit Library project. Linguistic tools being developed under the Sanskrit Library project preserve all stages in the derivation of a form, and it will be possible to present the digital library user with a considerable amount of grammatical information relevant for education and research. Since the tools are based on XML, it is possible to devise innovative application interfaces involving hyperlinks. For instance, we are able to provide links to the Pāninian sūtras that describe all the rules that apply in the derivation of a particular form. This constitutes a novel and extremely powerful application of technology that will be useful to the communities of Sanskrit scholars and students.

While some users want to view texts in Devanāgarī script, others prefer the traditional transliteration or another Romanization. Software has been developed to allow for dynamic switching of text display in accordance with a user's preferences. The system accommodates a variety of fonts and encodings that may be available on an end-user's system. A prototype of this software is currently employed for the display of Whitney's *Roots* and inflectional software in the digital Sanskrit Library.

The inflection software created allows users to enter a stem using the Sanskrit Library Phonetic encoding (SLP) and to view the results in Roman or Devanagari Unicode as well as in other standard encodings. SLP associates each Sanskrit sound with a single character as shown in Fig. 2. The display of the nominal paradigm of *aśva* in Roman Unicode and Devanagari Unicode appears in Figs. 3 and 4. By running the inflection software on nominal stems extracted from Monier Williams, a full-form lexicon associating each inflected form with its inflectional identifier and stem was created. For the stem *aśva*, the full-form lexicon contains entries shown in Fig. 5. The full-form lexicon has allowed the building of a prototype morphological analyzer that already recognizes over 6 million inflected forms of nominals. Although the prototype is limited in scope, the number of forms recognized already exceeds by more than 4 orders of magnitude the capacity of a competing system. The analyzer displays all possible analyses of the inflected nominal form entered in the analyzer input field. This analysis consists of the inflectional identifier and stem. Results for the form *aśvena*, masculine instrumental singular of *aśva* "horse" are shown in Fig. 6.

The stem *aśva*, shown in Fig. 6 in Devanāgarī script, is a live link to the digital version of Monier-Williams' *A Sanskrit—English Dictionary*. We are working with our collaborators Malten and Funderburk to revise and extend tagging of CDSL's edition of Monier-Williams' (1899) *A Sanskrit—English Dictionary* (MW), the most complete English language dictionary of Sanskrit. Prior to our work, CDSL generated the display of the entry for *aśva* "horse" shown in Fig. 7. Since the present CDSL search form does not distinguish between uppercase and lowercase and utilizes the Harvard-Kyoto encoding which does, the results show the stem ā*śva* as well as two entries for *aśva*. Our improved and extended mark-up allows software to differentiate different types of information in the entry by associating it with different text types, such as color and italic, in the HTML used to create the display. The current display, shown in Fig. 8, displays lexical tags in italics, Sanskrit forms in blue, class names or proper nouns in aqua, and citations and etymology in green,

अ a **a**	आ ā **A**	इ i **i**	ई ī **I**	उ u **u**	ऊ ū **U**
ऋ ṛ **f**	ॠ ṝ **F**	ऌ ḷ **x**	ॡ ḹ **X**	*	
ए e **e**	ऐ ai **E**	ओ o **o**	औ au **O**		

क् k **k**	ख् kh **K**	ग् g **g**	घ् gh **G**	ङ् ṅ **N**
च् c **c**	छ् ch **C**	ज् j **j**	झ् jh **J**	ञ् ñ **Y**
ट् ṭ **w**	ठ् ṭh **W**	ड् ḍ **q**	ढ् ḍh **Q**	ण् ṇ **R**
त् t **t**	थ् th **T**	द् d **d**	ध् dh **D**	न् n **n**
प् p **p**	फ् ph **P**	ब् b **b**	भ् bh **B**	म् m **m**

य् y **y**	र् r **r**	ल् l **l**	व् v **v**
श् ś **S**	ष् ṣ **z**	स् s **s**	ह् h **h**

* anusvāra = **M**; visarga = **H**

Fig. 2 Sanskrit Library Phonetic encoding

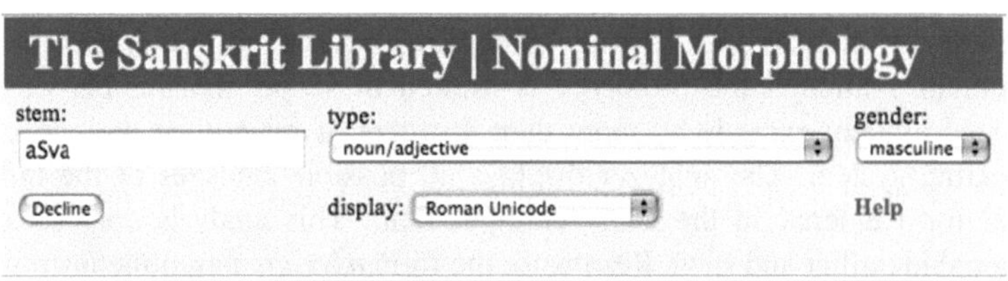

	s	d	p
1	aśvaḥ	aśvau	aśvāḥ
v	aśva	aśvau	aśvāḥ
2	aśvam	aśvau	aśvān
3	aśvena	aśvābhyām	aśvaiḥ
4	aśvāya	aśvābhyām	aśvebhyaḥ
5	aśvāt	aśvābhyām	aśvebhyaḥ
6	aśvasya	aśvayoḥ	aśvānām
7	aśve	aśvayoḥ	aśveṣu

Fig. 3 Nominal inflection displayed in Roman Unicode

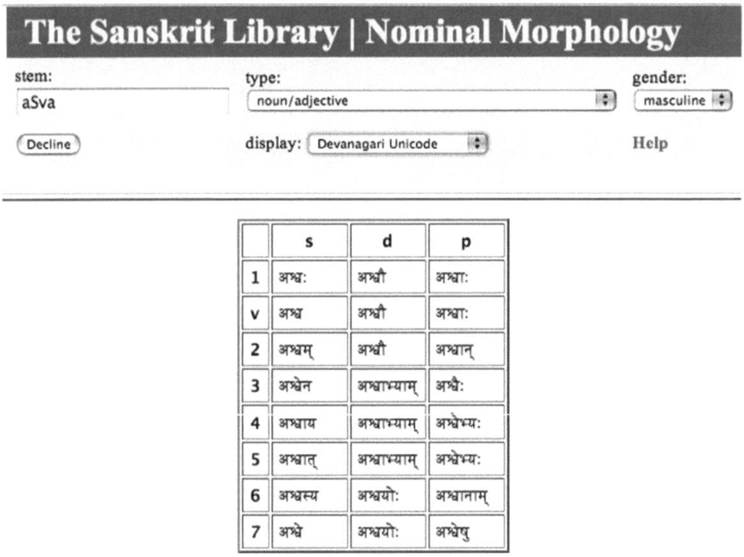

	s	d	p
1	अश्वः	अश्वौ	अश्वाः
v	अश्व	अश्वौ	अश्वाः
2	अश्वम्	अश्वौ	अश्वान्
3	अश्वेन	अश्वाभ्याम्	अश्वैः
4	अश्वाय	अश्वाभ्याम्	अश्वेभ्यः
5	अश्वात्	अश्वाभ्याम्	अश्वेभ्यः
6	अश्वस्य	अश्वयोः	अश्वानाम्
7	अश्वे	अश्वयोः	अश्वेषु

Fig. 4 Nominal inflection displayed in Devanagari Unicode

aSvaH	m1s	aSvam	m2s	aSvAya	m4s	aSvasya	m6s
aSvO	m1d	aSvO	m2d	aSvAByAm	m4d	aSvayoH	m6d
aSvAH	m1p	aSvAn	m2p	aSveByaH	m4p	aSvAnAm	m6p
aSva	mvs	aSvena	m3s	aSvAt	m5s	aSve	m7s
aSvO	mvd	aSvAByAm	m3d	aSvAByAm	m5d	aSvayoH	m7d
aSvAH	mvp	aSvEH	m3p	aSveByaH	m5p	aSvezu	m7p

Fig. 5 Full-form lexicon entries for *aśva*

making it easier to read. The display can be altered just by changing parameters in the software display without further altering the markup of the data.

The revised Sanskrit lexicon display in Fig. 8 contains a number beneath the head word (114 in the phrase [*p*=114, 3]) that is a link to the digital image file of the page in MW. Clicking it brings up the image file of the entire page. The entry of *aśva* in the digital image is shown in Fig. 9. While options to display compounds could be added, compound words formed by combining a subsequent element with a head word are not currently displayed in the digital lexica unless the compound word is entered in the entry form. The first two of several subsequent compound elements are shown in the digital image of the entry for *aśva* in Fig. 9.

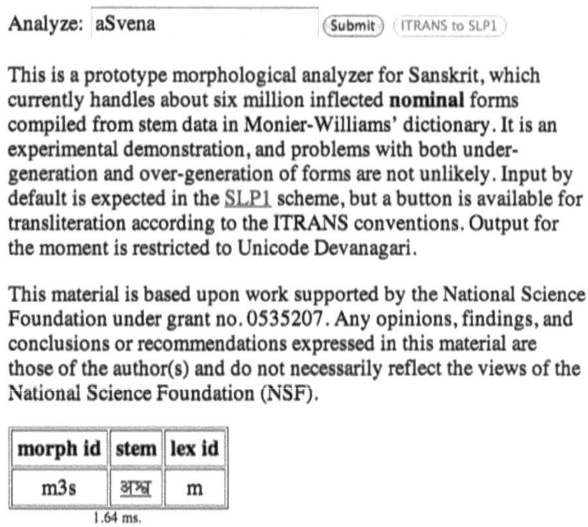

Fig. 6 Morphological analyzer results for *aśvena*

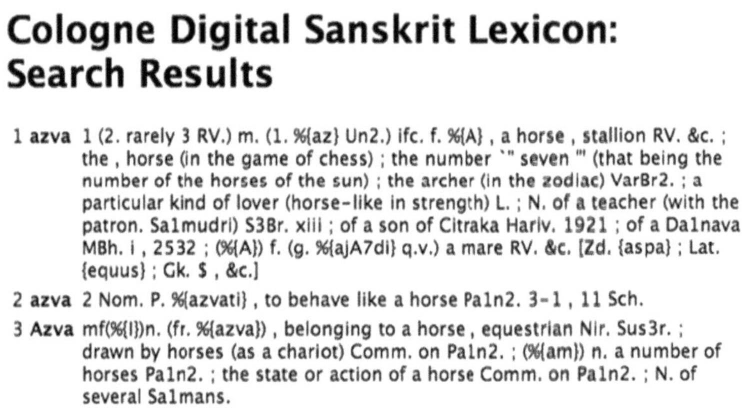

Fig. 7 CDSL digital Sanskrit lexicon display

This demonstration of our work linking image files of the MW with the digital lexicon and inflection software demonstrates in principle our ability to associate machine-readable Sanskrit text with digital images of manuscripts. In our prototype, we integrate manuscripts of the *Mahābhārata* and *Bhāgavata Purāna* with machine-readable editions of the texts they represent and with linguistic tools and lexical resources in the Sanskrit Library. The Sanskrit Library's lemmatized searching currently under development allows one to find passages and morphological and prosodic variants of words in these texts. Search results refer to the locations of sought passages in the editions. Users can display the manuscript pages with the sought items highlighted (Fig. 10). Conversely, the prototype allows users

Fig. 8 Sanskrit Library revised digital Sanskrit lexicon display

aśva

(H1Y) áśva 1 [p= 114,3] [L=19869]	(2. rarely 3 RV.) m. (√1. aś Un2.) (ifc.) f. ā , a horse , stallion RV. &c ; the , horse (in the game of chess) ; the number " seven " (that being the number of the horses of the sun) ; the archer (in the zodiac) VarBr2. ; a particular kind of lover (horse-like in strength) L. ; N. of a teacher (with the patron. sāmudri) S3Br. xiii ; of a son of citraka Hariv. 1921 ; of a dānava MBh. i , 2532 ; (ā) f. (g. ajā*di (qv)) a mare RV. &c [Zd. aspa ; Lat. equus ; Gk. $, &c]
(H2) aśva 2 [p= 115,3] [L=20089]	(Nom.) P. aśvati , to behave like a horse Pa1n2. 3-1 , 11 Sch.

अश्व 1. *áśva* (2. rarely 3, RV.), *as*, m. (√1. *aś*, Uṇ.), ifc. f. *ā*, a horse, stallion, RV. &c.; the horse (in the game of chess); the number 'seven' (that being the number of the horses of the sun); the archer (in the Zodiac), VarBṛ.; a particular kind of lover (horse-like in strength), L.; N. of a teacher (with the patron. Sāmudri), ŚBr. xiii; of a son of Citraka, Hariv. 1921; of a Dānava, MBh. i, 2532; (*ā*), f. (gaṇa *ajâdi*, q.v.) a mare, RV. &c. [Zd. *aspa*; Lat. *equus*; Gk. ἵππος, &c.] **-kandikā**, f. = *-gandhā*, q. v., L. **-karṇa**, m. the ear of a horse, KātyŚr.; (mfn.) 'resembling the ear of a horse,' said

Fig 9 The entry *aśva* as in the digital image

viewing a manuscript page to locate a passage of interest in the corresponding machine-readable text and to submit the passage to parsing software currently under development that will perform sandhi analysis, morphological analysis, and lead to digital lexica.

3 Image-Processing Tools

To achieve the integration of manuscripts with the Sanskrit Library texts, software, and lexica requires aligning the manuscripts with the machine readable texts. The prototype software facilitates the correlation of manuscripts with the corresponding machine-readable text and supports their display. Since OCR technology by

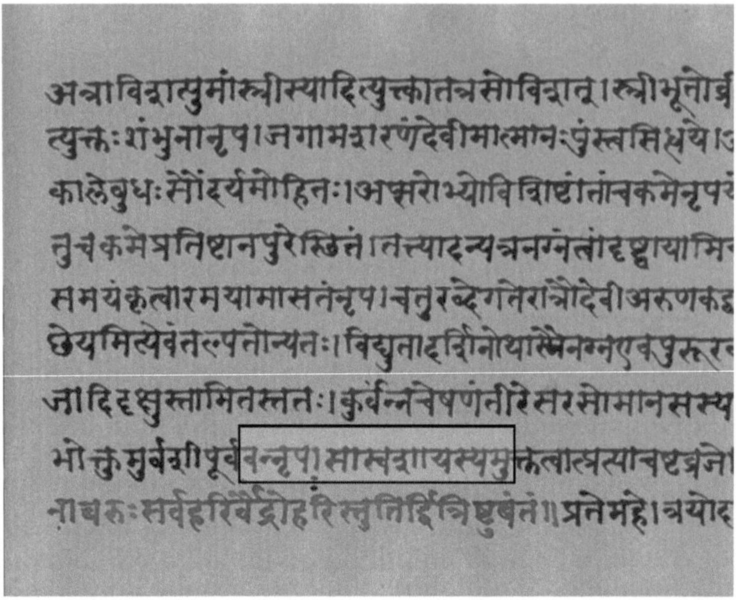

Fig 10 A highlighted passage in a manuscript of Sadgurusishya's Vedarthadipika: Wai 321, folio 131, recto, line 8

itself is not capable of generating accurate Sanskrit text from an image of an Indic manuscript, or even of a printed book, known characteristics of the manuscript, of the text, and the fact that the manuscript mostly corresponds to the text can supply additional constraints for use with existing OCR software.

Although transcribing an unknown text is a difficult OCR task, it is in general significantly easier to correlate a partial OCR transcription with machine-readable text. In the prototype the availability of machine-readable texts and metadata render the problem of identifying and highlighting relevant sections of the manuscripts and estimating the text extent very tractable. Given accurate segmentation of lines, demarcated linguistic strings, and characters, partial OCR of the text will provide sufficient information to reliably identify and highlight the portion of an image that corresponds to a span of text. A group at the University of Massachusetts has demonstrated the tractability of providing probabilistic holistic word search over a real-world manuscript corpus, with an actual web-accessible retrieval system that provides access to a thousand handwritten pages of George Washington's personal papers.

The known extent of text between confirmed termini can assist in segmenting sub-domains and in locating passages in scanned images. Manuscript cataloging includes specifying the number of folios, incipits, excipits, colophons, and the range of lines per page. Matching the incipits, excipits, and colophons with the machine-readable text specifies shared termini. The number of folios in the manuscript and the number of lines per page can then be used to estimate the apportionment of the text, whose extent is known from the machine-readable text, between the shared termini.

Partial OCR can automatically insert page boundary tags in the machine-readable text for subsequent review. Known page boundaries significantly enhance the accuracy of text-image alignment. Utilizing correlation and extent stochastics, it is possible to flag segments of text that do not correlate with the machine-readable text. Scholars can then manually confirm whether these represent insertions, deletions, or variants.

The use of techniques such as transcript mapping and partial OCR allows for automatic display of a passage of interest without need for full OCR or machine-readable transcription of each manuscript. Depending on the quality of the manuscript and the sophistication of the underlying technologies, it is possible to display the relevant page image and highlight a region of interest with granularity that corresponds to the confidence of the machine recognition. Thus much of the functionality normally available only with full transcriptions can be supplied for the digital images.

Digital Image Enhancement of Indic Historical Manuscripts

Zhixin Shi, Srirangaraj Setlur and Venu Govindaraju

Abstract Historical documents in Indic scripts can be found on a wide range of media such as paper, palm leaves, and parchment. Palm leaves are believed to be one of the earliest forms of writing media and their use as writing material has been recorded in various parts of the world including India. Ancient palm leaf manuscripts relating to religion, science, medicine, astronomy are still available for reference today due to many ongoing efforts for preservation of ancient documents by libraries and universities around the world. These manuscripts typically last a few centuries but with time the leaves degrade and the writing becomes illegible. Image processing techniques can help enhance the images of these manuscripts so as to enable readability of the written text. In this chapter, we propose methods for enhancing digital images of palm leaf and other historical manuscripts. We approximate the background of a gray-scale image using piece-wise linear and nonlinear models. Normalization algorithms are used on the color channels of the palm leaf image to obtain an enhanced gray-scale image. Experimental results show significant improvement in readability. An adaptive local connectivity map is used to try to segment lines of text from the enhanced images with the objective of facilitating techniques such as keyword spotting or partial OCR and thereby making it possible to index these documents for retrieval from a digital library.

Keywords Image enhancement · Image processing · Document pre-processing · Historical documents · Palm leaf manuscripts · Indic scripts · OCR · Text line extraction

1 Introduction

Digital libraries can be repositories of not just scanned images of books but also images of manuscripts written on media such as palm leaves and parchment

Z. Shi (✉)
Department of Computer Science and Engineering, University at Buffalo, Buffalo, NY, USA
e-mail: zshi@buffalo.edu

V. Govindaraju, S. Setlur (eds.), *Guide to OCR for Indic Scripts*, Advances in Pattern Recognition, DOI 10.1007/978-1-84800-330-9_13, © Springer-Verlag London Limited 2009

and even images of stone inscriptions. Palm leaves have been a popular writing medium for over two millennia in south and Southeast Asia. They have been used for recording literary and scientific texts and documents dating from about the second century AD have been preserved in museums.The manuscripts were produced primarily from two types of palms: palmyra and talipot. A metallic stylus was used to etch letters into the dried leaf. Contrast and legibility of the script were sometimes enhanced by applying lampblack or turmeric mixed with aromatic oils.

Most existing manuscripts are nearing the end of their natural lifetime or are facing destruction from elements. See page of ink and smearing along cracks, damage to the leaf due to the holes used for binding the manuscript leaves (Fig. 1), and dirt and other discoloration add to the problem. The leaves are prone to desiccation, which causes loss of flexibility making them brittle. Often, this dryness is treated by reapplying oil, which has a darkening effect. These processes result in uneven coloration across the image and a darkening of the background leading to poor contrast rendering the text illegible.

Another problem is introduced during the digitization of leaf manuscripts. Since these fragile manuscripts cannot be flattened without damaging them, digitization is carried out primarily with the aid of digital cameras and due to the warped surface of the manuscripts, the light intensities across the image are uneven. This has spurred preservation projects to protect these valuable historical documents.

Most document image enhancement algorithms have been designed primarily for binarization of modern documents. An overview of the traditional thresholding algorithms for text segmentation are given in [1] which compares Otsu's thresholding technique [2], entropy techniques proposed by Kapur et al. [3], and the minimal

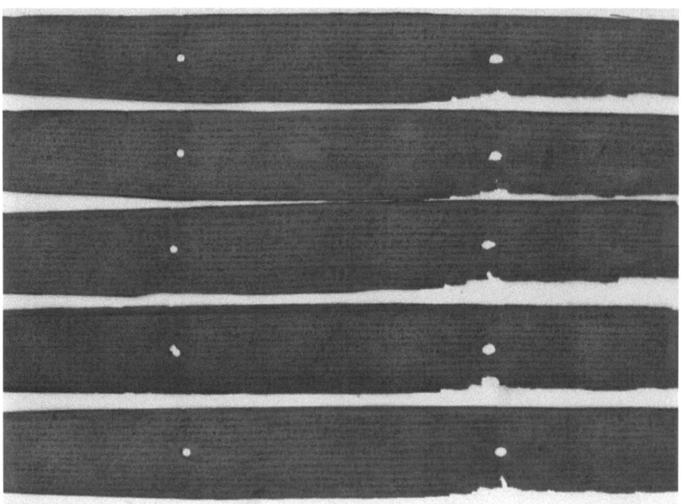

Fig. 1 Sample palm leaf manuscripts (see also Plate 5 on page 317 in the Color Plate Section)

error technique by Kittler and Illingworth [4]. Another entropy-based method specifically designed for historical document segmentation [5] deals with the noise inherent in the paper especially in documents written on both sides. Tan et al. presented methods to separate text from background noise and bleed-through text (from the backside of the paper) using direct image matching [6] and directional wavelets [7]. These techniques are designed mainly as preparation stages for subsequent OCR processing. Other methods are designed for improving human readability whilemaintaining the original “look and feel” of the documents [8]. These previous methods fail on palm leaf manuscripts due to low contrast and varying color intensity of the background.

In this chapter we present methods for enhancing digital images of palm leaf manuscripts and other historical documents. First, we describe a method that approximates the background of a gray-scale image using (i) piece-wise linear and (ii) nonlinear models. The approximations are designed to overcome the unevenness of the document background given that the palm leaves are not flat when photographed with digital cameras.

We also describe a method for extracting enhanced gray-scale images directly from color images of palm leaf manuscripts.

We have tested these techniques on a set of palm leaf and historical document images from publicly available sources. Experimental results show significant improvement in readability.

2 Image Enhancement

A background normalization algorithm for gray-scale images is presented based on two mathematical models [9]. In the piece-wise linear model, we first partition an image into small rectangular regions. In each region, we search for the best fitting linear plane. In the nonlinear model, the approximation is performed along each scan line. We first filter the pixels to leave behind only those that belong to the background. A moving window is then used to compute a nonlinear curve approximating the background.

For enhancing color images of palm leaf manuscripts, we apply the background normalization algorithms to the color component images separately and then combine the components to obtain an enhanced color image.

We also describe an alternate method using a predominant color projection for conversion of color images to contrast-enhanced gray-scale images.

2.1 Background Normalization

The problem of uneven background color intensity across an image is often seen in historical document images. Figure 2 depicts the scan line view of a typical degraded historical document, which shows how the intensities of the document image background and the foreground text vary across the image.

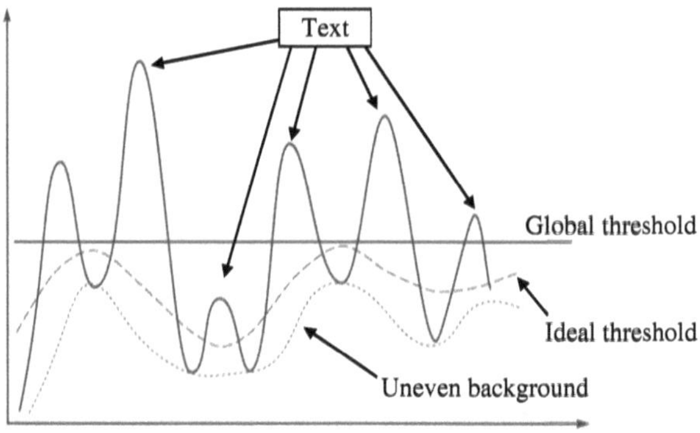

Fig. 2 Scan line view of a typical historical document illustrating the problem of uneven intensities

Our approach to background normalization is to approximate the background of a document image and adjust pixel intensities with respect to the approximated background.

2.1.1 Background Normalization Using a Piece-Wise Linear Model

Traditional document binarization algorithms separate document text from its background using either a global thresholding approach or a local adaptive thresholding approach. Global thresholding methods find a single cutoff level at which pixels in a gray-scale image can be separated into two groups, one for foreground text and the other for the background. For complex document images, it is difficult to find such a global threshold. Therefore, some thresholding techniques use adaptive approaches that find multiple threshold levels for local regions of an image. The assumption made is that there exist relatively flat backgrounds, at least in those small local regions. This assumption does not hold well for historical document images. Let us treat an image as a three-dimensional object whose positional coordinates are in the x–y plane and the pixel gray values are in the z plane. Consider the extreme case when a document image does not include any textual content. Then the image merely represents the paper surface.The traditional thresholding applied to this image should find a plane H parallel to the x–y plane above the paper surface. The plane H should also be very close to the paper surface if it is sufficiently flat. In the case of historical documents with uneven backgrounds, while it is not easy to find such a plane H strictly above the background surface, with a carefully chosen threshold we can find a plane K with almost all of the foreground pixels above the plane. Figure 3 shows the selected background, in which the non-background pixels are replaced with white pixels.

We now address the problem of detecting background pixels that have been misclassified as foreground pixels. We use linear functions to approximate the background in small local regions. The image is first partitioned into m by n smaller

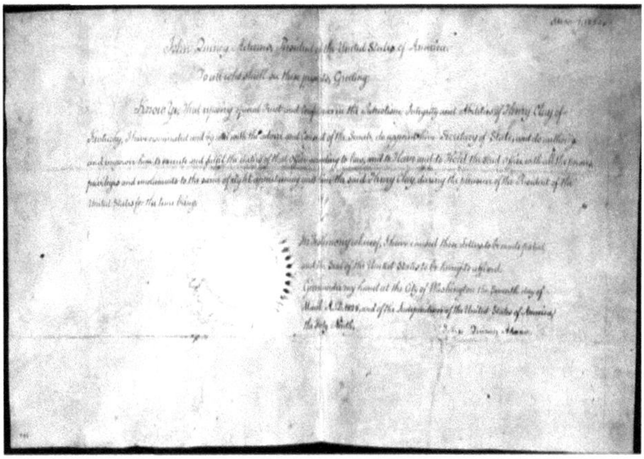

a

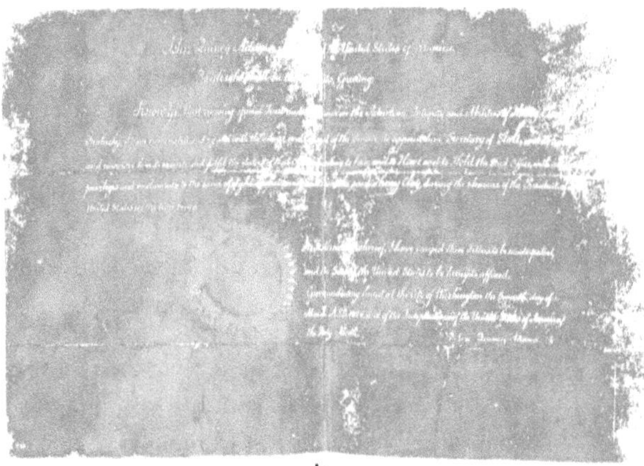

b

Fig. 3 Background pixel selection: (**a**) Original historical document of Henry Clay's appointment as secretary of state, March 7, 1825. (**b**) The selected background after a rough thresholding to keep most of the background pixels for background approximation

regions each approximating a flat surface. In each region, we find a linear function in the form

$$Ax + By - z + D = 0 \tag{1}$$

The selected background pixels are represented as points in the form $< x_i, y_i, z_i >$ where $< x_i, y_i >$ is the position of a pixel and z_i is the pixel value. We minimize the sum of distances

$$\min \sum_i (Ax_i + By_i - z_i + D)^2 \tag{2}$$

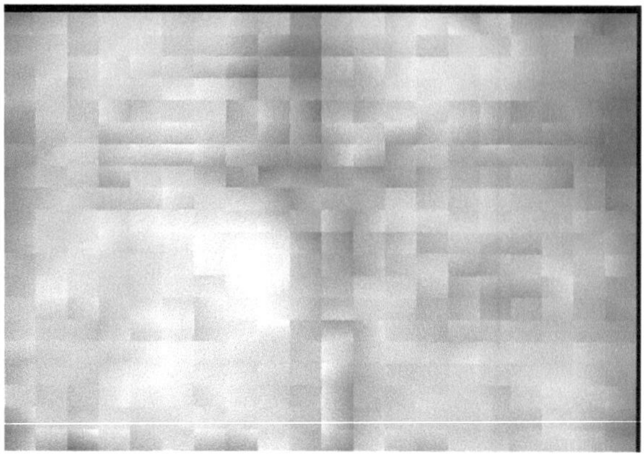

Fig. 4 Piece-wise linear approximation of the background for the image in Fig. 3

where the sum is taken for all the available points in the selected background image. The minimization gives the "best-fit" linear plane (1) because the distance from any point $< x_i, y_i, z_i >$ to the plane in (1) is a constant proportional to $|Ax_i + By_i - z_i + D|$. The solution for A, B, and D is obtained by solving a system of linear equations that are derived from the first derivatives of function (2) with respect to the coefficients. Thus in each local block we find a plane that is the best approximation of the background in the block. The pixel value of the plane is given by

$$z = Ax + By + D \tag{3}$$

for each pixel located at $< x, y >$. The background approximation is shown in Fig. 4. It exhibits a tile-like pattern due to the partition of the image in Fig. 3 into square blocks.

2.1.2 Background Normalization Using a Nonlinear Model

We have also approximated the uneven background by a nonlinear curve that best fits the background color values. For efficiency, we compute a nonlinear approximation for the image background color along each scan line, as shown in Fig. 5.

Consider the histogram of foreground pixel color intensity. The histogram exhibits taller peaks with higher variations at text locations. The non-text locations in the histogram appear as a lower and less variant distribution. The number of background pixels in the document image is significantly larger than the number of foreground pixels for text. Based on these observations, we first compute the mean level of the histogram. We use the mean level as a reference to set a background level at each pixel position along the scan line. In a left-to-right sweep along the scan line, if the pixel level at a current position is less than the mean, then we take that pixel value as the level for the next computation of our approximation. If the current level is higher than the mean, we retain the previous low value as the background level at the current location for the following computation of our approximation.

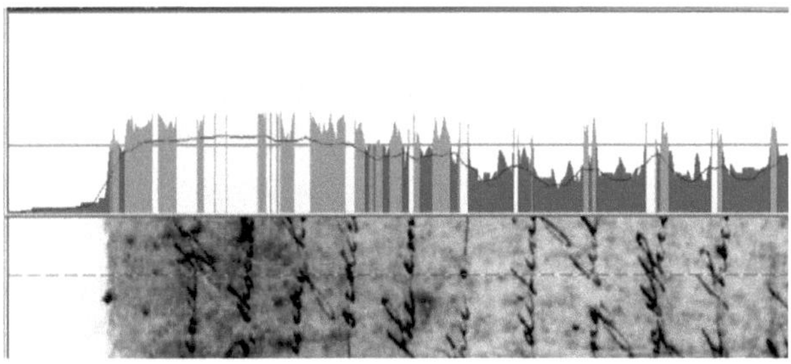

Fig. 5 Scan line histogram and background approximation. The histogram of *black pixel* intensity along a selected scan line is shown above the *gray-scale* document. The *horizontal line* is the calculated average level. The *curve* is the approximation of the background

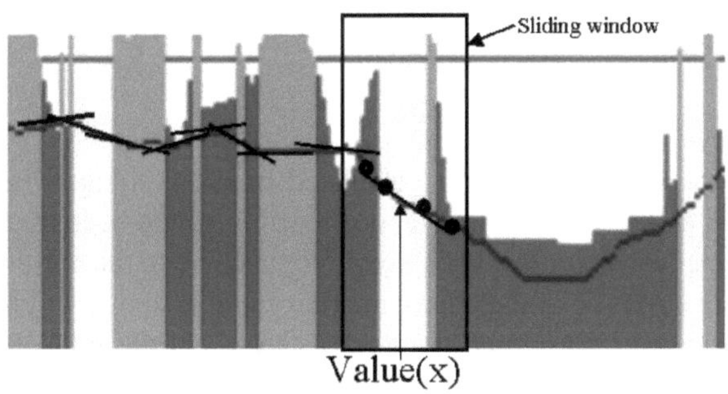

Fig. 6 Background approximation along a scan line: Step 1: Filter foreground pixels. Step 2: For each scan line derive new intensity values. Use a sliding window positioned at the point x. Use sliding window for local line fitting to derive Value (x) from the existing background pixel values. The approximated *curve* is an envelope of the line segments

Thus far, we have set an approximate background level for each pixel position on the scan line. This rough background is not very accurate for two reasons. First, at the foreground pixel location, the foreground level is set using a previously remembered background level which may be used multiple times for a consecutive run of foreground pixels. Second, due to the low image quality even the real background pixels may be locally very distant from the desired globally dominant document background level. We therefore propose to use this roughly selected and estimated background (SEB) to obtain a better approximation of the normalized background level.

Using the SEB pixel levels on a scan line, the approximation of the normalized document background level can be achieved in two ways. One approach is to use a *sliding window* paradigm. At each pixel position, the approximated background level is computed from an average of the SEB values in the local neighborhood of the pixel position.

A better approximation is computed using a best fitting straight line in each of the above neighborhoods. At each position, we use all the SEB values in its neigh-

Fig. 7 Nonlinear approximation of the background for the image in Fig. 3

borhood to find a best fitting line using the least-squares method. Then the approximation value for a pixel position is calculated from the straight line value corresponding to the position. If the final approximation of the background is a curve, the line segments going through each point on the curve at the corresponding pixel position form an envelope of the approximation curve as shown in Fig. 6.

The approximated background image consists of all the scan line approximations. Figure 7 shows an example of an approximated background for the image in Fig. 3 using the nonlinear model. It can be seen that this image is smoother than the approximation using the linear model in Fig. 4.

2.2 Image Normalization

The pixels in the gray-scale image are normalized using the linear or nonlinear approximations described above. There are two ways to adjust the pixels. The first approach is by translation. For any pixel at location $< x, y >$ with pixel value z_{orig}, the normalized pixel value is computed by a linear translation:

$$z_{\text{new}} = z_{\text{orig}} - z_{\text{back}} + c \tag{4}$$

where $z_{\text{back}} = Ax + By + D$ for the linear approximation method,$z_{\text{back}} = \text{Value}(x, y)$ for the nonlinear approximation, and Value(x, y) is a value taken from the nonlinear approximation at $< x, y >$. c is a constant close to the white color value of 255.

The second approach is by stretching. For any pixel $< x, y >$ the enhanced pixel value is given by

$$z_{\text{new}} = \frac{z_{\text{original}}}{z_{\text{back}}} C \tag{5}$$

To ensure that the value does not exceed 255, C is set to 255 (usually) to make the background color white.

The resultant normalized images are shown in Figs. 8 (linear) and 9 (nonlinear).

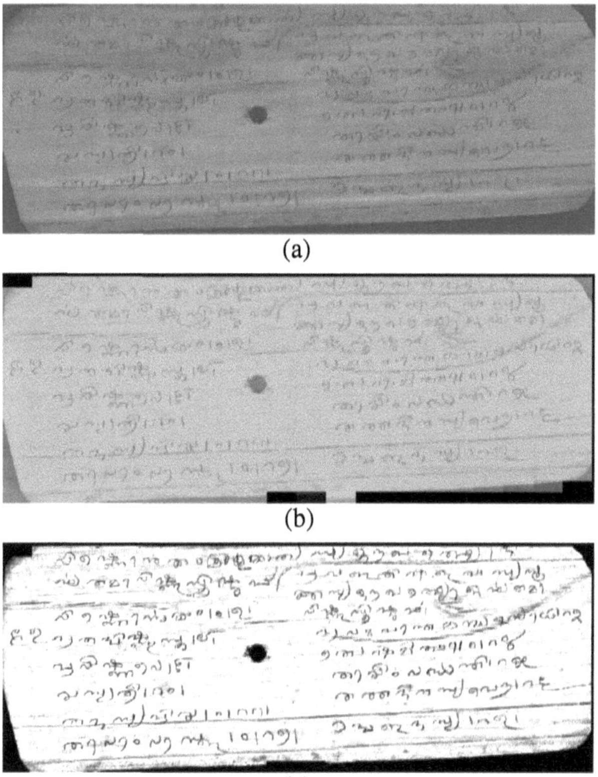

(a)

(b)

(c)

Fig. 8 Background normalization using the linear model: (**a**) original palm leaf image, (**b**) by translation and (**c**) by stretching

2.3 Background Normalization for Color Images

We have applied the background normalization algorithms to the component channel images of a color document image to generate an enhanced color image.

We consider a color image in the RGB system. We take each channel image as a gray-scale image and apply the background normalization algorithm for enhancement. We take the enhanced channel images as the new channels in the same color system. This results in an enhanced color image represented by the enhanced channel images (See example in Fig. 10).

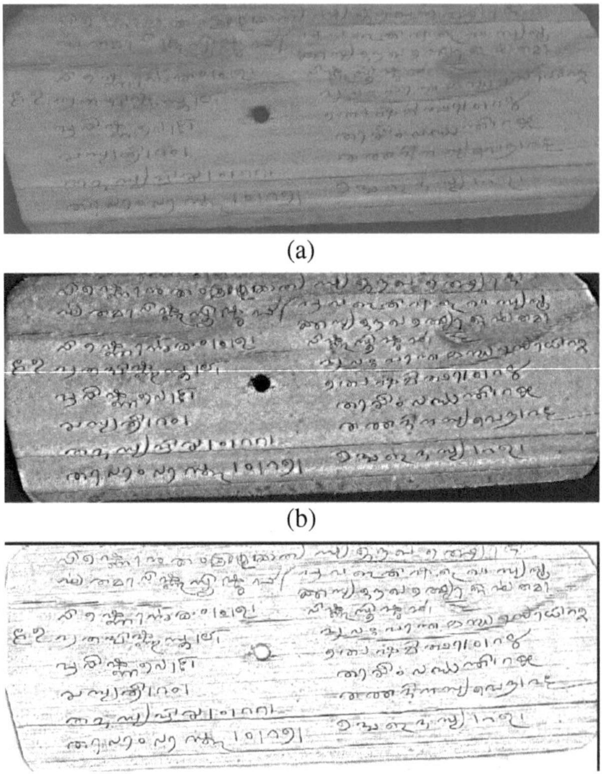

(a)

(b)

(c)

Fig. 9 Background normalization using the nonlinear model: (**a**) original palm leave image, (**b**) by translation and (**c**) by stretching

2.4 Color Document Image Enhancement

Since most OCR techniques require a binary image of characters or words for recognition, conversion of a color document image to a gray-scale image with high contrast can be a critical pre-processing step to facilitate good binarization.

We identify a base color for the background. In the case of palm leaf images, the background colors vary due to differences in age or material. Hence, the background color has to be dynamically determined for each leaf manuscript. The simplest way of approximating the background color is by calculating a color histogram. Our assumption is that the most dominant colors from a leaf are from the background. We first locate a range for the most frequently occurring colors on a leaf, then take the mean of the colors in the range as the background base color.

After calculating the base background color (r_0, g_0, b_0), we apply the following transform:

$$L = R \cdot r_0 + G \cdot g_0 + B \cdot b_0 \tag{6}$$

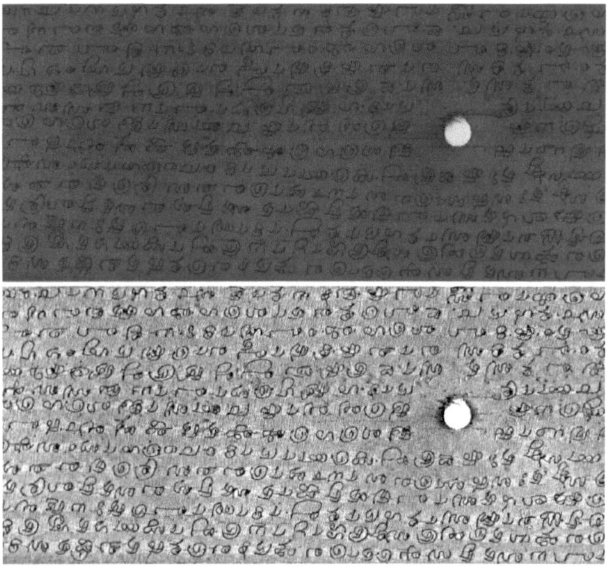

Fig. 10 Component channel background normalization for color palm leaf image enhancement (see also Plate 6 on page 318 in the Color Plate Section)

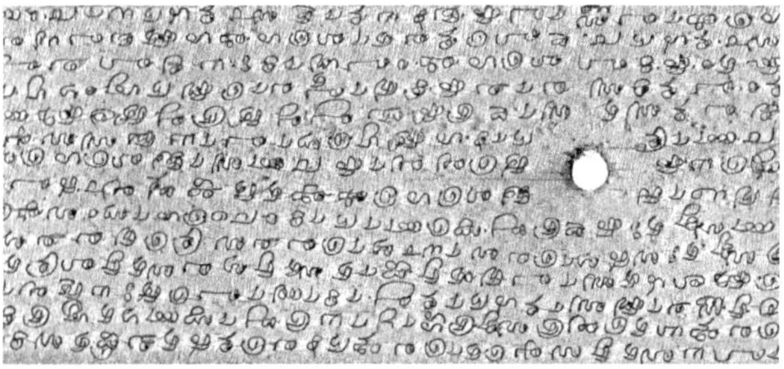

Fig. 11 Result of the color projection transform (*color-* to *gray-scale* conversion) applied to the palm leaf image in Fig. 10

Equation (6) can be interpreted as a projection of a pixel's color vector on the direction of the estimated predominant background color vector. This is similar to using a lens of the estimated background color. A result of the application of this technique is shown in Fig. 11.

3 Experiments

The techniques described were tested on over 50 historical palm leaf manuscript images downloaded from several online repositories. Most of the images had uneven background colors and low contrast. Visual inspection of the enhanced images showed a marked improvement in image quality for human reading. Due to the lack of published binarization techniques for color historical documents and the lack of readily available recognition systems in general for historical handwritten documents, the tests on the historical palm leaf manuscript images were based on human visual inspection only.

A binarized image produced from our example palm leaf manuscript is shown in Fig. 12.

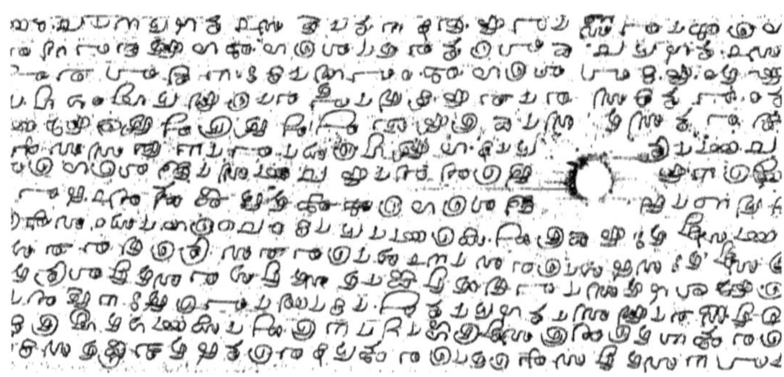

Fig. 12 Binary image obtained using a simple thresholding for the image in Fig. 11

The background normalization methods described were also tested on historical handwritten manuscript images from Library of Congress. One hundred randomly selected old handwritten manuscript document images were used for the experiments. The images were enhanced using both the linear and the nonlinear background normalization methods. The enhanced images were binarized using a simple global threshold.Visual inspection of the enhanced gray-scale images showed a general improvement in readability over the original images. The binary images generated using our methods also produced more readable images when compared with the binary images produced by other methods such as Otsu's global thresholding method [2], Giuliano, Paitra, and Stringer's local adaptive method [13], and Niblack's local adaptive method [14].

A quantitative evaluation of our methods is presented by comparing the performance of the methods described in this chapter on 10 randomly chosen images from the Abraham Lincoln Papers at the Library of Congress with three other binarization methods. Each of the 10 images was binarized using our enhancement methods followed by a fixed global thresholding. They were also binarized using three-other thresholding methods: Otsu's global thresholding method [2], Giuliano's local adaptive method [13], and Niblack's local adaptive method [14]. The number of words in each original document was manually counted. The number of readable words in the binarized image produced by each of the methods is shown in Table 1. The table shows the methods presented in this paper produced better quality binarized images than the other three methods.

Table 1 Comparison of number of readable words in the binarized images of Lincoln's papers generated using different methods

	Earlier methods				Our methods	
Document number	Words	Otsu's	Giuliano	Niblack	Piece-wise linear	Nonlinear
1	120	63	12	3	88	121
2	154	93	114	85	115	121
3	78	9	0	0	42	75
4	110	49	24	7	80	84
5	94	63	19	1	90	91
6	157	51	81	43	121	124
7	70	60	47	45	63	67
8	17	7	4	1	13	12
9	70	42	46	31	51	56
10	182	87	30	3	138	173

4 Extract Text Lines from Images

Humans are able to locate text lines in document images relying on recognition of the geometrical layout features of the lines without the need for recognizing characters and understanding the document. Usually the text line patterns in an image can be easily detected by reducing the scale of the image. Reducing scale of a document image is equivalent to looking at the image from a farther distance. On a reduced scale the line patterns appear distinct and the touching between lines loses prominence. The touching or connections between text lines are sparse since they are usually made by oversized characters or characters with long ascenders or descenders running through the neighboring lines. Another observation of handwritten documents is that although the text lines may be fluctuating across an entire text block, there still exists a general orientation of a line.

Based on these observations, we use an adaptive local connectivity feature to change the scale of a document image. For each pixel we define its connectivity measure by cumulatively collecting its neighboring pixels' intensities along the horizontal direction.This connectivity measure can be intuitively understood as the measure of how likely it is for a pixel to belong to a line. With the connectivity measure, the pixels in between lines are less likely to influence the location of text lines even if some of these pixels are part of the text that is between the lines.

In [10], a method using fuzzy run length was proposed, in which a relaxed version of run length computed for background pixels in a binary image, is considered. The method emphasizes using background features in grouping and separating text lines and can efficiently extract text lines even in complex documents including a mix of graphics, handwritten and printed text.

The method proposed in this chapter is inspired by several well-known methods. The traditional projection profile method computes a global histogram over an entire text block. The computation is done on a binary image. Our connectivity measure is computed adaptively for each pixel in its neighborhood. The computation can be done on a gray-scale image. Another method that we use is run length smearing. Run length smearing [11] is usually used for tolerating noise and run-away strokes.The desired run length such as foreground runs are created by skipping small runs in background color. The expected result from this process is that the most of the foreground text characters are grouped together. The text lines and text blocks are extracted by using a connected component analysis approach. The method again works well for printed documents with mostly text. It will fail on documents with touching lines or connection between text lines and text blocks. Our method is also inspired by scale-space techniques [12] in which non-uniform Gaussian filers are used in convolutions on the image of a text line to create a smoothed/smeared image for extracting handwritten words. The filters are functions of two variables that act as scale parameters. By carefully choosing the parameters, the convolved image shows the separated words each as a distinct connected component.

4.1 ALCM Method

Our method for text line location and extraction consists of the following steps. (1) We convert a gray-scale document image into an adaptive local connectivity map (ALCM), which is also a gray-scale image. (2) We then apply a thresholding algorithm on the ALCM to reveal the text line patterns in terms of connected components. (3) Using a straightforward grouping algorithm we can easily group the connected components into location masks for each text line. (4) Finally, the text lines from a binarized version of the document image (using any standard thresholding algorithm) can be extracted by mapping the location masks back onto the binary image to collect the text line components. For those components touching multiple lines, a splitting algorithm is applied.

4.1.1 ALCM Transform

Let $f\colon R^2 \rightarrow R$ represent any given signal. Its discrete version with the domain limited to $\{0,1,...,n-1\} \times \{0,1,...,m-1\}$ and values in $\{0,...,255\}$ is our gray-scale document image. Then the adaptive local connectivity map is defined as a transform

$$\text{ALCM}\colon f \rightarrow A$$

by a one-direction convolution:

$$A(x,y) = \int_R f(x,y) G_c(t-x,y) dt \tag{7}$$

where

$$G_c(x,y) = \begin{cases} 1 \text{ if } |x| < c \\ 0 \text{ otherwise} \end{cases} \tag{8}$$

The implementation of the transform is as follows. For convenience,we first reverse the input gray-scale image so that 255 represents the strongest level of intensity for foreground text. Most handwritten historical images are scanned with resolution ranging from 200 to 300 dpi. We first down-sample the image to 1/4 of its original size (1/2 in each direction). Then we scan the image along each of its scan lines twice, from left to right and right to left, using a sliding window of size $2c$, to compute the cumulative intensity at a pixel by adding up all the intensity values in a neighborhood of size $2c$. Finally, we re-scale the resulting image to a gray-scale image with values ranging from 0 to 255; see Fig. 13.

In the above algorithm c is a value for determining the size of the sliding window prior to scanning the image for calculating ALCM transform. It can be set as a fixed value for an application running similar set of images or determined at runtime dynamically. A good initial value of c for the sliding window would be 120 which is approximately equal to three times the average height of text. The average height of text in a document image could be roughly estimated using a projection profile on a portion of a text block or other connected component-based methods, after a rough binarization. Our experiments found that our method can tolerate a wide range in the value of c.

Fig. 13 ALCM pattern shown for the palm leaf example from Fig. 10

4.1.2 Locations of Possible Text Lines

Each pixel value in an ALCM image represents the cumulative foreground pixel density for the original document image. As with a projection profile, a higher value in the ACLM means that the pixel is in a dense text region. We therefore binarize ALCM to two values for separation of highly likely text areas from the background. Generally, binarization for document images is not an easy task especially when the document images are from handwritten historical manuscripts. Binarization for document images is used to not only separate the text in an image from its background but also keep the integrity of the writing for later recognition. Unlike document image binarization, binarization for our ALCM is much easier due to two reasons. First, as a gray-scale image, ALCM shows clear bi-modal pixel distribution most of the time, which allows for a global thresholding. Second, binarization of the ALCM is to detect general patterns of text lines. Each pattern represents loosely a central location of a textline or part of a line. The binarization of the ALCM works equally well with different binarization algorithms. Figure 14 shows a binarization result using Otsu's algorithm [2].

The binarized ALCM image in Fig. 14 consists of connected components which represent either the entire line or part of a line. Instead of using the connected components to form the complete line pattern we do some filtering and reconstruction as follows:

1. Filter out the small pieces. Based on experiments, some small pieces whose width is significantly smaller than most other components are filtered out.

Fig. 14 Binarization of ALCM shows the patterns of text line (see also Plate 7 on page 318 in the Color Plate Section)

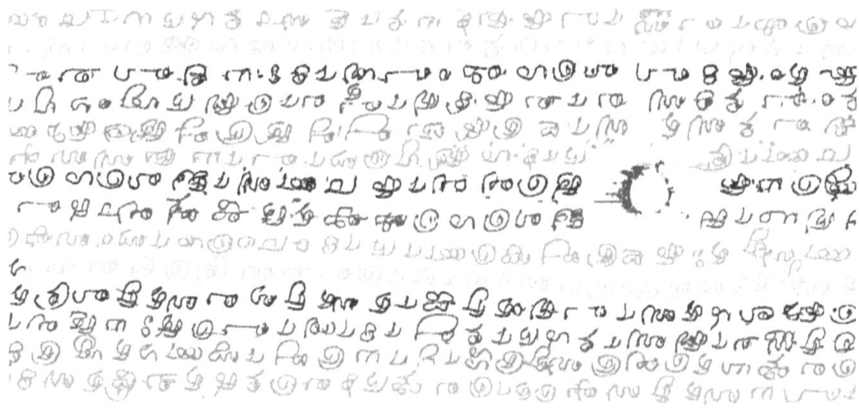

Fig. 15 Text line extraction result of image in Fig. 13 (see also Plate 8 on page 319 in the Color Plate Section)

2. For each connected component, we calculate its upper, lower profiles and also the center points. Filling in each pair of upper and lower profile points, we reconstruct the connected components and extract the text line (Fig. 15).

In the ideal case, each connected component represents a complete text line. But sometimes a text line pattern is made up of two to three components and requires grouping. A straightforward approach would be using horizontal alignment and rules based on whether a grouping of two neighboring components is too wide for a line or not.

4.1.3 Extraction of Text

The text line patterns that we have extracted are location masks of text lines. The extraction of text from a gray-scale image using these locations brings up two issues. The first is how we represent the text and how to get the text information. The second issue is dealing with touching characters crossing different lines.

Most document recognition systems require binary images of text lines, words, and characters. However binarization of handwritten historical document images is still a challenging problem. Our proposed method for text line location in this chapter explores local adaptive binarization. After we find the locations of the text lines, an adaptive binarization algorithm is designed to focus on only the line locations. It allows us to not only concentrate on a much smaller document region but also avoid much of the non-text noise.

After binarization, extraction of the text lines is done by a connected component collection and grouping. We first generate the connected component representation. For each text line pattern, we collect all the connected components touching the pattern; these components together make up the text line. If there are some connected components that do not touch any line pattern, we find the closest line pattern to group them with. Figure 14 shows the line patterns that are superimposed on a binary image and text lines are identified in different colors after collecting and grouping of the connected components.

Some connected components may belong to more than one line pattern. These components represent the touching characters crossing lines (see the red color components in Fig. 14). Since these crossing pieces are easily detected, splitting them according to their relation to the nearby lines is trivial.

5 Conclusion

In this chapter we present image enhancement techniques for historical manuscript images such as palm leaf documents. Experimental observations show that the methods described can be successfully used to improve readability of these poor contrast images and produce high-quality binarized images. The methods described are effective not only on palm leaf manuscripts but also on other aged and degraded historical paper documents. A technique to separate lines of text from the enhanced image using an adaptive local connectivity map has also been described. These steps could potentially facilitate keyword spotting or partial OCR of these manuscripts for indexing and retrieval in a digital library. At the very least, these methods would provide a way for digital libraries to publish enhanced digital images of historical manuscripts in Indic and other scripts to facilitate literary scholars and researchers in the study of such documents.

References

1. Leedham, G., Varma, S., Patankar, A., Govindaraju, V.: Separating text and background in degraded document images–a comparison of global thresholding techniques for multi-stage thresholding. In: Proceedings Eighth International Workshop on Frontiers of Handwriting Recognition (September 2002)
2. Otsu, N.: A threshold selection method from gray level histogram. IEEE Transactions in Systems, Man, and Cybernetics **9** (1979) 62–66
3. Kapur, J.N., Sahoo, P.K., Wong, A.K.C.: A new method for gray-level picture thresholding using the entropy of the histogram. Computer Vision, Graphics, and Image Processing **29** (1985) 273–285
4. Kittler, J. Illingworth, J.: Minimum error thresholding. Pattern Recognition **19**(1) (1986) 41–47
5. Mello, C.A.B., Lins, R.D.: Image segmentation of historical documents. In: Visual 2000, Mexico City, Mexico (September 2000)
6. Wang, Q., Tan, C.: Matching of double-sided document images to remove interference. In: IEEE Conference on Computer Vision and Pattern Recognition, Hawaii, USA (2001)
7. Wang, Q., Xia, T., Li, L., Tan, C.: Document image enhancement using directional wavelet. In: Proceedings of the 2003 IEEE Conference on Computer Vision and Pattern Recognition, Madison, WI (June 2003)
8. Mello, C.A.B., Lins, R.D.: Generation of images of historical documents by composition. In: ACM Symposium on Document Engineering, McLean, VA (2002)
9. Shi, Z., Govindaraju, V.: Historical document image enhancement using background light intensity normalization. 17th International Conference on Pattern Recognition, Cambridge, UK (23–26 August 2004)

10. Shi, Z., Govindaraju, V.: Line separation for complex document images using fuzzy runlength. In: DIAL '04: Proceedings of the First International Workshop on Document Image Analysis for Libraries (DIAL'04), IEEE Computer Society, Los Alamitos, CA (2004) 306
11. Srihari, S., Govindaraju, V.: Analysis of textual images using the Hough transform. Machine Vision and Applications **2** (1989) 141–153
12. Manmatha, R., Srimal, N.: Scale space technique for word segmentation in handwritten documents. In: SCALE-SPACE '99: Proceedings of the Second International Conference on Scale-Space Theories in Computer Vision, Springer-Verlag, London (1999) 22–33
13. Giuliano, E., Paitra, O., Stringer, L.: Electronic character reading system. U.S. Patent No. 4,047,15 (September 1977)
14. Niblack, W.: An Introduction to Digital Image Processing. Prentice Hall, English Cliffs, NJ (1986)

GFG-Based Compression and Retrieval of Document Images in Indian Scripts

Gaurav Harit, Santanu Chaudhury and Ritu Garg

Abstract Indexing and retrieval of Indian language documents is an important problem. We present an interactive access scheme for Indian language document collection using techniques for word-image-based search. The compression and retrieval paradigm we propose is applicable even for those Indian scripts for which reliable OCR technology is not available. Our technique for word spotting is based on exploiting the geometrical features of the word image. The word image features are represented in the form of a graph called geometric feature graph (GFG). The GFG is encoded as a string which serves as a compressed representation of the word image skeleton. We have also augmented the GFG-based word image spotting with latent semantic analysis for more effective retrieval. The query is specified as a set of word images and the documents that best match with the query representation in the latent semantic space are retrieved. The retrieval paradigm is further enhanced to the conceptual level with the use of document image content-domain knowledge specified in the form of an ontology.

Keywords Geometric feature graph (GFG) · Word spotting · Latent semantic analysis · Indic scripts

1 Introduction

Word spotting [1] is widely used for indexing and retrieval of word (printed or handwritten) images in documents. Many of the recent works [2, 3] have devised features and matching measures for word spotting and analysis. However none of these schemes allow synthesis of the word images from feature-based representations. Moreover, to index a large document image collection we need a compressed representation of the textual components to facilitate faster indexing. In this chapter we present techniques for indexing and retrieval of documents using a compressed

G. Harit (✉)
IIT Delhi, New Delhi 110016, India
e-mail: gharit@ee.iitd.ac.in

V. Govindaraju, S. Setlur (eds.), *Guide to OCR for Indic Scripts*, Advances in Pattern Recognition, DOI 10.1007/978-1-84800-330-9_14, © Springer-Verlag London Limited 2009

representation of the textual component of document images. Variations in font and size of the word do not vary the structural shape of the word. The skeleton of a word image best characterizes the word structure using a minimal set of pixels obtained by applying a thinning operation to the word image. This helps to get rid of the redundant information that does not contribute to the word structure but rather to the word font or thickness. The word image skeleton is converted into a symbolic string representation known as the GFG string. The significance of this conversion is that it makes it amenable to apply traditional text indexing techniques based on string similarity measures.

Word spotting does not ensure semantic relevance of the retrieved documents to the user's query. Users may use very different terms to specify concepts and all of them may refer to the same semantic object. Latent semantic analysis (LSA) has been successfully applied for analysis and retrieval of text documents [4–6]. Unlike electronic text documents, an indexing technique for document images has to deal with additional preprocessing issues like word segmentation, character segmentation, and character recognition, in order to extract the *word* (in unicode/ASCII form) which can then be processed for LSA. However, for many scripts, especially Indian languages, character segmentation is a difficult problem and reliable OCR techniques do not exist. We show through experiments that our symbolic descriptor-based representation for word images can be used with LSA and provides improvements in retrieval precision as is the case with electronic text documents.

Concept-based access of document images can be made a reality if the retrieval techniques (using annotations, word images, layout, etc.) can be employed in a unified framework driven by an ontological model of the concepts associated with the document images. An ontology is a formal, explicit specification of a shared conceptualization. It includes a vocabulary of the terms and their meaning. It indicates how concepts are inter-related. It imposes a structure on the domain and constrains the possible interpretation of terms. Specification of the concepts with reference to a collection of documents which exist in the form of images pose a difficult problem because the textual blocks are not OCRed. In the last part of this chapter we describe the use of content-domain ontologies to represent concepts in the document image. Such ontologies are enhancements to the traditional ontologies describing the textual domain knowledge because they need to take into account the relations between concepts and the observable features in the media domain.

The organization of this chapter is as follows. In Section 2 we discuss the GFG representation for word images. Specifically we describe the GFG extraction scheme, conversion of a GFG to a string representation, reconstruction of word image structure using the GFG, and the compression achieved by using the GFG string representation. In Section 3 we describe the scheme to index word images represented using GFG string. Use of LSA to improve the retrieval performance is described in Section 4. Finally in Section 5 we present the ontology-based paradigm for conceptual access to document images. We conclude this chapter in Section 6.

2 Geometric Feature Graph (GFG) of a Word Image

In order to compress textual component of document images we have exploited a structural model of word images in the form of its skeleton. To extract simpler shape segments from the word skeleton, a set of key points on the word skeleton needs to be identified so that they would form end points of the possible segments. A graph is the most informative way to represent the set of segments and their end points. We call such a graph formally as a geometric feature graph or simply a GFG of the word skeleton. A GFG is a representation of a word image structure (in the form of geometric features) expressed as a graph where the nodes represent certain key points identified on the word image and the links represent shape primitives that best characterize the structural segments connecting pairs of neighboring nodes. Representing the word image using a GFG makes it possible to achieve compression because the number of shape primitives required to approximate different possible segments in a word image is very less compared to the total number of pixels in the word image. The repertoire of shape primitives is limited, implying that the size of the dictionary is small and thus the length of the indices required to refer to a shape primitive is small at both the encoder and the decoder. Shape primitives can be parametrized, for example, on length, curvature so that better approximation is possible with a small set of shape primitives.

We have used two basic types of parametrized shape primitives: A line segment and a curve segment. A line segment drawn from a given end point is characterized by its length and its orientation. We model a curve segment as a semicircle. Thus a curve drawn from a given point is characterized by the orientation and the length of its diameter. The shape primitives are shown in Fig. 1. A line segment is referred to as the shape primitive "L" and specified with notation "L-*len-orient*," where the attributes – length and orientation – are also included as parameters, and thus uniquely identify a line segment to be drawn from a given point. A curve segment is referred to as the shape primitive "C" and specified with notation "C-*side-*

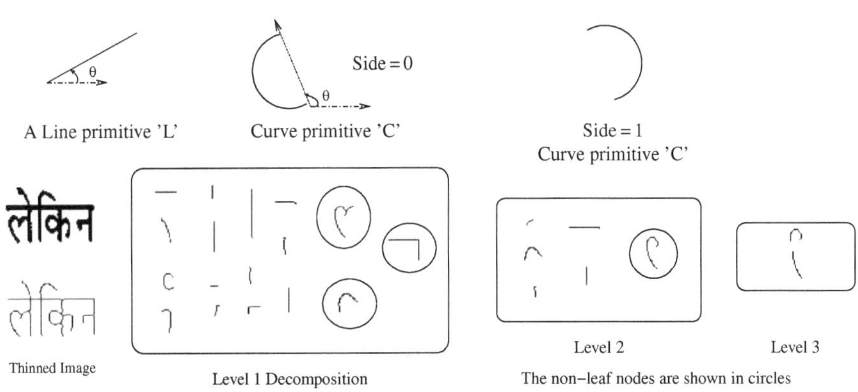

Fig. 1 Shape primitives; word decomposition organized in the form of a tree

len-orient," where the attributes are the side of the diameter which the curve takes (0 for left and 1 for right), and the length and the orientation of the curve diameter, respectively.

2.1 GFG Extraction

In this section we first list the main steps of the GFG extraction algorithm, followed by explanations. The GFG is then converted to a string-based representation. Subsequently we discuss the method for reconstruction of the word image from the GFG string:

1. Binarize the word image
2. Preprocess the word image with a closing operation
3. Obtain the word image skeleton using a thinning operation
4. Mark the junction points and end points of the GFG skeleton
5. Identify the skeleton segments as bounded by the junction points and end points
6. *Do* for all *Segments*:

   (a) Arrange the skeleton points sequentially such that the points on a segment follow the parametrized notation:

   $$C(t) = [x(t), y(t)]$$

   (b) The local tangent information is computed at each pixel. We make a tangent angle plot [7] θ vs t, where t is the curve parameter (sequence number of the pixel). For regions on the curve that belong to a straight line, θ is almost constant. For curved sections θ varies as shown in Fig. 2.
   (c) Identify the straight lines on the tangent angle plot. This is done using the regression algorithm for line fitting.
   (d) The curved regions on the tangent angle plot are approximated using a semi-circle. If the approximation error is large, the curved segment is subdivided using line fitting and regression. Subdivision is stopped when the approximation error is within acceptable bounds or when the number of pixels in the segment to be approximated falls below a threshold. In the latter case the segment is approximated using a straight line segment.

7. Choose one of the end points of the skeleton and do a depth first traversal to generate the GFG string.

A gray-level image is binarized using a suitable threshold obtained as the prominent valley point of the gray-scale histogram. A closing operation is then applied to this binarized image to fill in possible gaps arising from binarization. For Step 3 we obtain the skeleton of the word image using a thinning algorithm [8]. Step 4 involves marking the junction points and end points on the skeleton. A point is marked as a

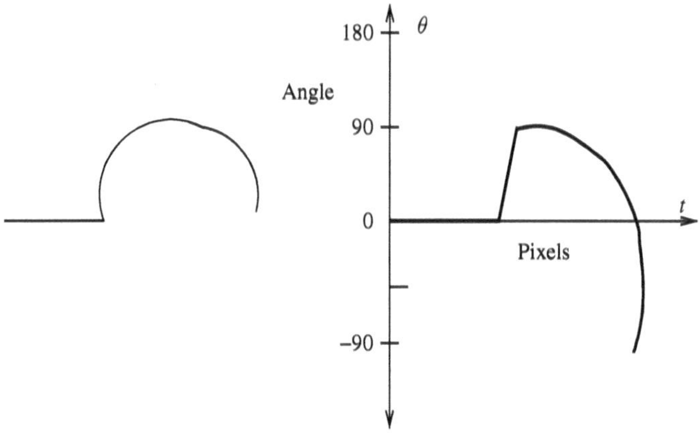

Fig. 2 Tangent angle plot

junction point (where branching occurs) if it has 3 or more non-contiguous neighboring pixels. We further check that each of these neighboring pixels gives rise to branches of reasonable length to eliminate false junction. An end point has exactly one contiguous set of neighboring pixels. In Step 6, the word skeleton is decomposed recursively into smaller segments till a segment can be approximated by one of the primitives either line or curve. Step 7 forms the GFG using the junction/end points as the nodes and the segments as the branches connecting the nodes. The process of fitting segments of constant curvature makes the representation robust against noisy output of the skeletonization process.

2.2 Converting the GFG to a String Representation

We need a way to encode the GFG in the form of a string such that the reconstruction of the original GFG, and thus the word skeleton, is possible given just the encoded GFG string. Step 8 of the GFG extraction algorithm does this task by following a depth first traversal (DFT) of the graph. We select a node, typically the left most node in the skeleton, and do the DFT of the GFG. The parameters of a segment are calculated according to the direction in which it is traversed. The labels of the branches are concatenated in the sequence in which the branches are visited. The concatenated string is called as the GFG string for the given word skeleton. During DFT, as we reach a dead end of a branch, we need to backtrack to a previous node so that any unvisited branches emanating from it may now be visited. DFT is implemented using a stack and backtracking amounts to popping nodes out of the stack. When a node is popped out from the stack, we insert a special symbol "$" to the GFG string (Fig. 3).

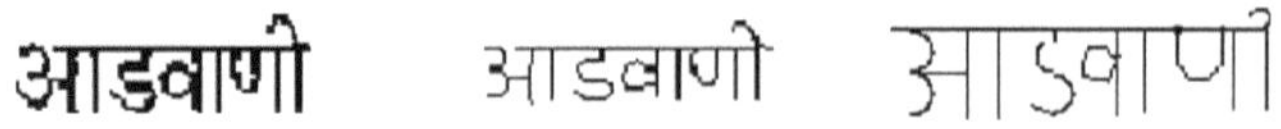

(A) (B) (C)

C–1–16−−90.0 C–1–17−−90 $ L–20–0.0 L–17−−90.0 $ L–17–90.0 L–27–180.0 $ L–11–0.0 L–34−−90.0 $ L–
C–0–13−−90.0 C–1–14−−90.0 L–9–160.0 $ $ $ $ L–22–0.0 L–12−−90.0 L–7–130.0 L–6–180.0 L–5–250.0 L–
L–11–70.0 $ $ $ $ $ $ L–20−−90.0 $ $ L–10–0.0 L–31−−90.0 $ L–13–0.0 C–0–20–0 L–20–0.0 L–20–0.0 C–0–

(D)

Fig. 3 Reconstruction of word skeleton using GFG string: (A) original word image; (B) thinned image; (C) reconstructed word skeleton; and (D) GFG string representation

2.3 Reconstruction of Word Images Using GFG

The GFG is decoded from the GFG string by traversing the string in depth first order. A stack is used to store the end points (nodes) of the branches. The node at the top of the stack gives the position of the point from which a new branch is to be drawn. The other end point of drawn branch is pushed into the stack. The backtracking symbol "$" is used to pop out nodes from the stack. Once all the branches have been drawn, we have the reconstruction of the word image. The reconstruction can be done at various sizes by multiplying the values of the primitive length with a chosen scale factor. The shape primitives are drawn using a rasterization algorithm with antialiasing. We have achieved a fairly reasonable reconstruction of word images with 1 byte representation for branch labels. The results of word image reconstruction from GFG string are shown in Fig. 4. The results show satisfactory reconstruction for word images from three languages (Hindi, Bengali, and Telugu). Despite minor artifacts because of misrecognition of certain noisy branches, almost all the reconstructed word images were quite legible. Though the GFG string depends on the choice of the start node, the reconstruction of the word skeleton from the GFG string is not dependent on the choice of the start node. The GFG representation of a word image skeleton is not unique. Depending on the segment from which the DFT is done, we can have different GFG strings which all correspond to the same word image. We start GFG traversal from the top-left end point to avoid different strings referring to the same word image. Further, this method of GFG representation is for

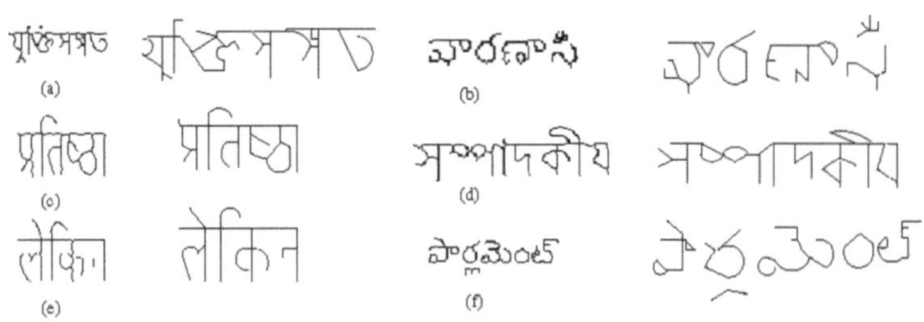

Fig. 4 Reconstruction using GFG string

a skeleton which has all segments as connected. To encode the disconnected segments, a "D" primitive is used which is actually the specification of a line (a dummy line segment which is *not drawn*) signifying the displacement of the start point of the disconnected segment from the start point of the previous segment of the same word image.

2.4 GFG Compression

We represent each GFG branch label with 1 byte. The first bit indicates the type of shape primitive (whether "L" or "C"). The second bit is used to indicate the *side* parameter value for the case of "C" primitive. The next 3 bits store the quantized *length* and the last 3 bits store the quantized orientation. With a 3 bits representation the length gets quantized to eight levels and the orientation is approximated with one of the eight quantized directions. A word image often comprises disconnected alphabets giving rise to more than one connected components. Since the complete word image needs to be represented as a single GFG, a dummy branch (straight line) is introduced between the nearest nodes of two connected components of the word skeleton. The dummy branch serves as a link so that the position of the disconnected segment can be localized. While rendering the word image corresponding to the GFG string the dummy branch is not shown. For the "L" primitives the second bit is set to 0 to indicate a dummy segment. The number of bytes used to store the complete GFG string is equal to the number of branches in the GFG and the number of times the backtracking symbol "$" (represented in 1 byte with all zero bits) is inserted in the string. We have achieved high compression rates with the GFG string representation of word images. For the word images (Fig. 4(a–f)) of three different languages (Hindi, Bengali, and Telugu) the byte size of the obtained GFG string is shown in Table 1. This shows that our GFG string representation offers compression of around 60–85% over the JBIG-compressed thinned word images. For more accurate representation of branches, we can use 2 bytes for the label, which offers a finer quantization of length and orientation.

Table 1 Table shows the percentage compression achieved by GFG representation compared to JBIG

Word image in Fig. No.	JBIG compression (bytes)	GFG compression (bytes)	Reduction in bytes required (%)
4(a)	158	54	66
4(b)	163	51	69
4(c)	199	36	82
4(d)	196	43	78
4(e)	192	27	86
4(f)	137	56	59

3 GFG-Based Indexing

Each word image of a document page gets represented as a string of symbolic descriptors in the form of a GFG string. The problem of indexing word images in a collection of documents is basically reduced to that of string-based indexing. To accommodate the possibility of matching with root words and also to withstand image processing errors we need an indexing scheme with the facility for approximate match. The indexing problem is formulated as follows: given a *text* of length n and pattern of length m retrieve all the text segments (or "occurrences") whose *edit distance* to the pattern is at most k. The *edit distance* between two strings is defined as the minimum number of character insertions, deletions and replacements needed to make them equal.

We have used suffix tree for indexing. The pattern is partitioned into sub-patterns which are searched for. All the occurrences of the sub-patterns are later verified for a complete match. The goal is to balance between the cost to search in the suffix tree (which grows with the size of the sub-patterns) and the cost to verify the potential occurrences (which grows when shorter patterns are searched). The suffix tree is constructed using the Ukkonen's linear-time algorithm [9]. A query image is first processed to get the symbolic descriptor string corresponding to the image. For searching the pattern in the suffix tree, we sub-divide the pattern. The size of the sub-patterns considered is a function of length of the pattern ($>0.4*$ length of query pattern). All the strings having the sub patterns are selected for verification. Verification is done by calculating the edit distance between the full pattern and each of the retrieved string. All the strings having edit distance within a given threshold are considered for indexing on to the documents. The threshold is taken as a function of the length of the query pattern. Use of a suitable threshold allows the retrieval of "stem" words. The recall–precision curves (labeled as without LSA) for a Hindi and Bengali document collection are shown in Fig. 6.

4 Latent Semantic Indexing Using GFG

In the previous section we discussed techniques for indexing word images. However the performance of any indexing and retrieval scheme using word matching would still have limited precision because simply retrieving documents which have words that match to the query does not ensure that they would be relevant in the semantic sense. Users may use very different set of terms to specify concepts and all the ways may refer to the same semantic object. This is the *synonymy* problem which tends to decrease the recall performance. Another problem which mostly affects the precision performance is the *polysemy* problem, which refers to the fact that most words have more than one distinct meaning. Thus a word may assume different meanings in different contexts. In this section we describe an application of latent semantic analysis (LSA) for indexing and retrieval of document images with text. The query is specified as a set of word images and the documents which best match

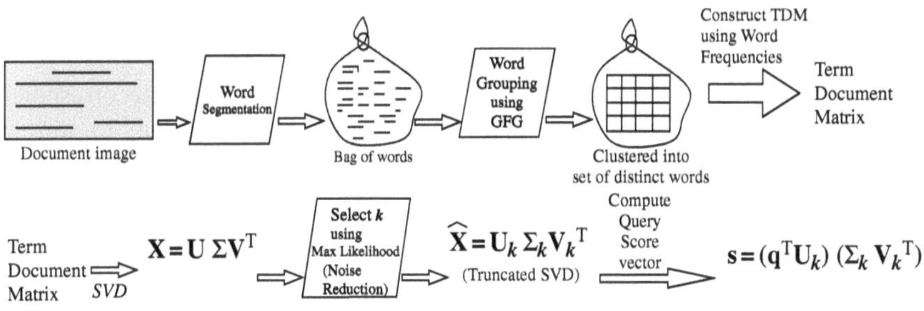

Fig. 5 Overview of methodology

with the query representation in the latent semantic space are retrieved. We show through extensive experiments that the use of LSA for document images provides improvements in retrieval precision as is the case with electronic text documents.

Latent semantic analysis [4, 10] is an approach for automatic indexing and information retrieval that attempts to overcome these problems by mapping documents as well as terms to a representation in the so-called *latent semantic space*. Latent semantic space is a lower rank approximation of the term document matrix using SVD [11]. Squeezing the term/documents down to a k-dimensional space (k being far smaller than the original rank of TDM), SVD brings together the terms with similar co-occurrences. Thus improving the retrieval quality. The rationale is that documents that share frequently co-occurring terms will have a similar representation in the latent space, even if they have no terms in common. LSA thus performs some sort of noise reduction and provides the benefit to detect synonyms as well as words that refer to the same topic. Probabilistic latent semantic analysis (PLSA) [12] is an enhancement of LSA with solid statistical framework since it is based on the likelihood principle and defines a proper generative model of the data. It can deal with polysemous words and can explicitly distinguish between different meanings and different types of word usage.

Below we provide a listing of the steps in our application of LSA/PLSA for indexing and retrieval of documents using the latent semantic space. Figure 5 shows the flow of the complete methodology.

For every document (Steps 1–4)

1. Identify the text region in the document image using the wavelet-based text/non-text region classification tool developed in [13].
2. Extract the text lines using horizontal projection profiles of intensity, and segment every text line into constituent word images using vertical projection profiles.
3. The complete set of word images (with many repeated words) is then grouped into sets of distinct words using GFG-based pairwise word matching. Two words are labeled to be same if the match cost is small (below a threshold).
4. The statistics of word occurrence count in each document is used to update the term document matrix (TDM) X.

5. The TDM is transformed into the latent semantic space using SVD as $X \backsimeq U_k \Sigma_k V_k^T$.
6. We then select the optimal number of semantic dimensions, K, which correspond to the larger singular values in Σ. This is done by exhaustively trying for different values of K and selecting the one for which the likelihood is maximum as follows:

$$\mathcal{L} = \sum_{d \in \mathcal{D}} \sum_{w \in \mathcal{W}} n(d,w) \log P(d,w), \tag{1}$$

   where $P(d,w)$ denotes the joint probability of the word w occurring in the document d, and $n(d,w)$ denotes the term frequency, i.e., the number of times w occurred in d.
7. A query is specified as a set of word images selected from the document(s). A query word image would correspond to a term, which is identified (of all the terms used for TDM and represented using GFG) as the one for which the computed GFG match cost is minimum. The set of query word images is represented as a query vector $\mathbf{q}$ with the matching terms having entry 1, and all other entries as 0.
8. The similarity score of the query with all the documents in the latent semantic space is computed using the following equation:

$$\mathbf{s} = (\mathbf{q}^T U_k)(\Sigma_k V_k^T). \tag{2}$$

   The documents are ranked according to their scores and retrieved in the ranked order.

The formulation for PLSA makes use of the latent semantic classes $\mathcal{Z}$ and the EM-based model fitting to derive the TDM as explained in [12,14].

4.1 Results of Using LSA and PLSA

We have developed the retrieval scheme for two different collections – one having 390 documents of Hindi script with a total of 2556 distinct words and the other having 225 documents of Bengali script with a total of 2108 distinct words. The latent semantic space was constructed separately for the two collections. For our experiments with LSA, the optimal number of dimensions K for the latent semantic space was selected as 110 and 98 for the Hindi and Bengali collections, respectively. The selection was done by constructing the likelihood curve for different values of K, and selecting the point at the onset of a plateau (on which the variance of the likelihood score was $<1\%$) on the likelihood curve. The recall vs precision curves

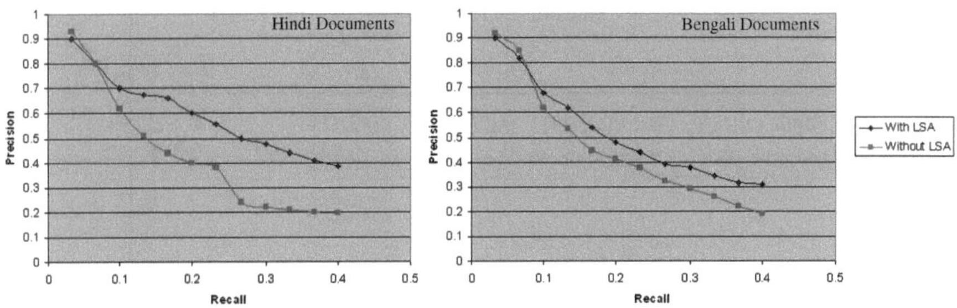

Fig. 6 Retrieval statistics using LSA for Hindi and Bengali collections

for the Hindi and Bengali collections are shown in Fig. 6. The results for Hindi collection have been plotted for over 1200 queries by five users. The precision of the retrieved results was judged by each of the five users. Every point on the curve is the average of the precision scores by five users for all the 1200 queries. The performance evaluation of Bengali collection was done by four users with about 600 queries. For comparison we also show the precision vs recall curves for naive word-match-based retrieval, i.e., without using LSA. We see that the document retrieval using LSA results in an improvement of about 10–30% for the case of Hindi and about 10–24% for the case of Bengali collection.

We also measured the mean average precision (MAP) value of our retrieval system for 1200 queries for Hindi collection and 600 queries for Bengali collection. MAP provides a measure of retrieval quality across recall levels. To compute the MAP measure we identified the set of relevant documents for each query q as $R^q = d_1^q, d_2^q, \ldots, d_{r_q}^q$. Denoting the set of retrieved (in response to query q) ranked documents up to $d_k^q \in R^q$ as T_k^q, i.e., T_k^q includes all retrieved documents (relevant or non-relevant) which were ranked higher than or equal to d_k^q, we have

$$\text{MAP} = \underset{\forall q}{\text{Mean}} \frac{1}{r_q} \sum_{k=1}^{r_q} \text{Precision}(T_k^q).$$

The MAP values for the retrieval system using LSA and PLSA are tabulated in Tables 2 and 3. We have obtained higher MAP values for the test collection when the retrieval system uses LSA and PLSA (K=115).

For the retrieval scheme using PLSA, we have evaluated the retrieval performance for four different values of $K = \{60, 90, 115, 180\}$, i.e., the number of semantic classes $z_k \in \mathcal{Z}$. We have found that as the number of semantic classes is increased, the retrieval performance improves, however, as seen in Fig. 7(a, b), the

Table 2 MAP values of the retrieval system using LSA and without using LSA

	With LSA	Without LSA
Hindi	0.365	0.181
Bengali	0.283	0.150

Table 3 MAP values of the retrieval system using PLSA

	K=60	K=90	K=115	K=180
Hindi	0.175	0.237	0.411	0.403
Bengali	0.118	0.315	0.421	0.396

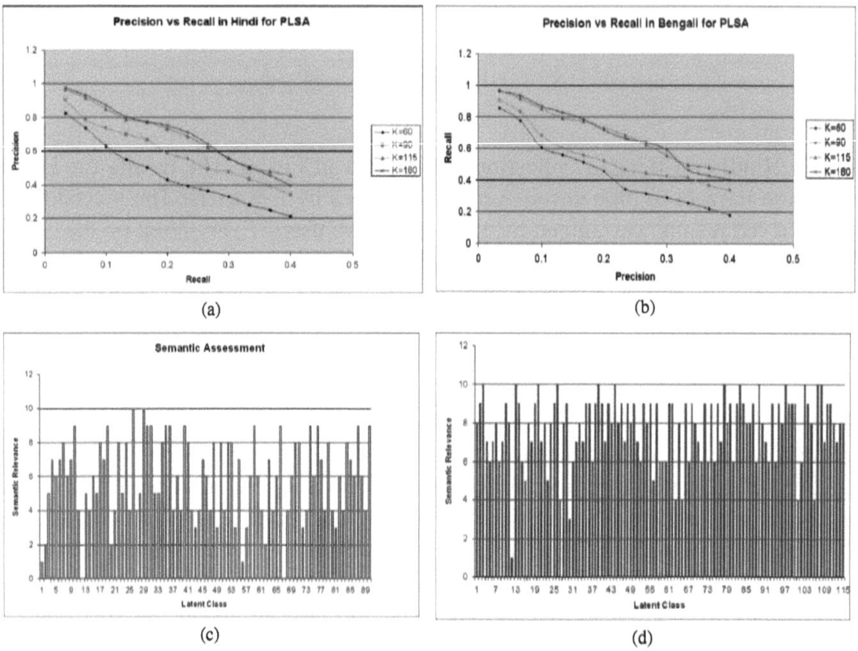

Fig. 7 Retrieval statistics using PLSA for Hindi and Bengali collections: (a) retrieval statistics using PLSA for Hindi documents; (b) retrieval statistics using PLSA for Bengali documents; (c) subject assessment for $K = 90$ for PLSA latent classes; and (d) subject assessment for $K = 115$ for PLSA latent classes

improvement is only marginal when K is increased from 115 to 180. We observed that with $K = 90$, the retrieval results are comparable to what we have obtained for LSA. For $K = 115$, there is a noticeable improvement in the retrieval performance by PLSA compared to LSA for both Hindi and Bengali collections.

Further, we have done a subjective analysis of the semantic coherence of the semantic classes z_k in the probabilistic model for PLSA. This was done by computing the cosine distance of each word image from every axis in the latent semantic space. For every axis, the best adhering word images were identified as the ones which had the smallest cosine distance. The closest 10 word images for each axis were taken as characterizing the semantic *topic* and were assessed by five users for semantic coherence. Figure 7(c, d) shows the average of the coherence score for each semantic class by all five users for two PLSA models for two cases – with

$K = 90$ for Bengali and with $K = 115$ for Hindi documents. The average semantic relevance assessed is 6.3 and 8.1, respectively, for the two cases.

Our experimental results on two document image collections have established that even for the domain of document images, LSA and PLSA extend the benefits of improved precision results as in the case of conventional electronic text documents.

5 Ontology-Based Access with GFG

In this section we discuss how GFG-based representation of word images can be used in a paradigm of conceptual access to document image collections. Many conceptual entities manifest in document images in the form of observable patterns, for example, the words or the pictures in the document. For non-OCR'able documents, the words exist as word images and not electronic text. The observable patterns in document media can be described using feature descriptors or an example. A concept can be embedded in a set of word images or in a picture, or as a graphical pattern. Moreover, the word images can be different for different scripts. A document image ontology should have a mechanism for associating the media (observable) pattern descriptors to concepts. The media pattern can be described in the form of feature descriptors or examples. It should also have the provision to specify the uncertainty inherent in the associations of media properties with concepts. Uncertainties arise in associating a concept to a media pattern because of different possible ways in which the concept can manifest into a media pattern and also due to the presence of noise or distortions in the media.

For encoding document image ontologies we use MOWL [15, 16] which is an extension of OWL. MOWL uses a probabilistic reasoning framework for inferencing to deal with uncertainties in the multimedia domain. Uncertainty is encoded by specifying a *causal strength* of association between concepts or between a concept and a media property specification. The causal strength is expressed as a pair of probability values $P(M \mid C)$ and $P(M \mid \neg C)$, where C is a concept and M represents an associated concept or an associated media pattern.

5.1 Concept-Driven Document Image Retrieval

Conceptual querying of documents is done by forming an observation model (OM) [17] for the concept which is to be queried. The MOWL ontology is used to construct the observation model which is a graphical structure depicting the concepts (nodes) linked up to their observable media properties as well as to their related concepts. An example of an OM for a query "carnatic music in 1980s" is shown in Fig. 8. Since the ontology specifies probabilistic relations between concepts and media features, the OM can be used as a belief network with the concept being queried as the root node. The evidence nodes for the concept correspond to keywords in annotations, word image features as GFG string, metadata related to the

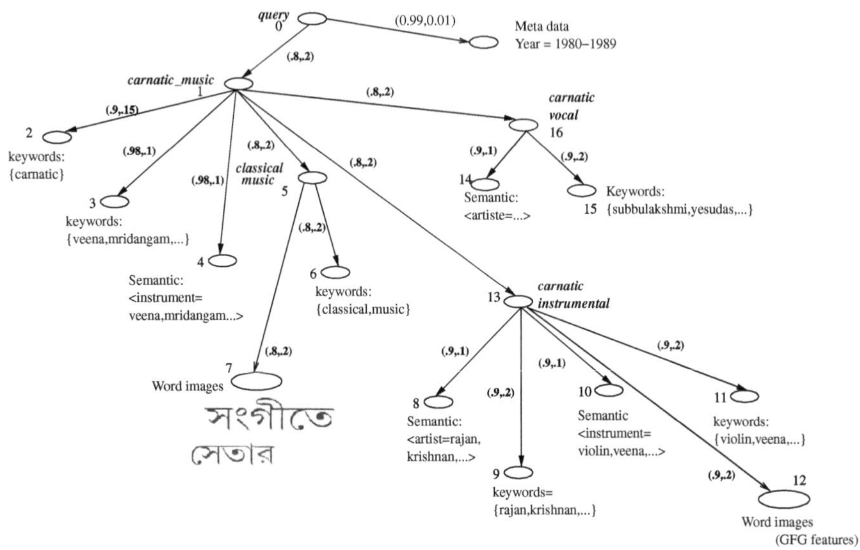

Fig. 8 Observation model for query "carnatic music in 1980s"

document, and features/examples associated with the pictures relevant to the concept. Instantiation of evidences invokes a feature detection process corresponding to leaf nodes (evidence nodes) of the observation model. Belief propagation takes place and the a posteriori probability is computed for every concept node. The probability value indicates the relevance of a document with respect to the queried concept. Documents are ordered according to this relevance score for presentation to the user.

5.2 Results

We show an example illustrating the retrieval of documents providing information on vocal *carnatic music* during the period 1980s. The query is interpreted as *carnatic music* and is related to the broader class of *classical music* and the narrower classes: *carnatic vocal* and *carnatic instrumental*. The generated OM consists of a set of keywords and parametric specifications for some general descriptors, the musical instruments normally associated with carnatic music, and some celebrities in the field. As shown in the OM (Fig. 8), the media patterns to be searched are keywords (in annotations) and word images related to the concept nodes and the metainformation associated with the documents. A retrieved document has a relevance score same as the a posteriori probability evaluated at the query node as a result of belief propagation due to evidence instantiation. All the retrieved documents (shown in Fig. 9) belonged to the specified period of time. Among them, three referred to carnatic music. However, the retrieved documents

Fig. 9 Results of document retrieval for query "carnatic music in 1980s"

had others related to the broader class of classical music. They scored good relevance to node 5 in the OM, and hence contributed to the queried concept and were retrieved.

6 Conclusion

We have described the geometric feature graph-based representation of the structural features of the word image. The scheme offers a compressed representation of the word images while offering reconstruction and indexing. We have presented an application of LSA and probabilistic LSA for the purpose of retrieving image documents with text. Our experimental results on two document image collections have established that even for the domain of document images, LSA and PLSA extend the benefits of improved precision results as in the case of conventional electronic text documents. We have proposed the use of document image ontologies to construct an observation model which is a belief network depicting association of concepts with observable features of document media. We have demonstrated retrieval of documents using word image spotting, embedded picture similarity, and annotation keywords as evidences to establish relevance of concepts.

References

1. R. Manmath, C. Han, and E. Riseman, "Word spotting: A new approach to indexing hand writing," in *Proceedings of IEEE CVPR*, pp. 631–637, 1996.
2. A. K. Jain and A. M. Namboodiri, "Indexing and retrieval of on-line handwritten documents," in *Proceedings of IEEE ICDAR*, pp. 655–659, 2003.
3. T. M. Rath and R. Manmatha, "Word image matching using dynamic time warping ," in *Proceedings of IEEE CVPR*, vol. 2, pp. 521–527, 2003.
4. Deerwester, S. Dumais, Furnas, Lanouauer, and Harshman, "Indexing by latent semantic analysis," *Journal American Society for Information Retrieval*, 41 (6), pp. 391–407, 1990.
5. G. W. Furnas, S. Deerwester, S. T. Dumais, T. K. Landauer, R. A. Harshman, L. A. Streeter, and K. E. Lochbaum, "Information retrieval using a singular value decomposition model of latent semantic structure," in *Proceedings of ACM SIGIR Conference on Research and Development in Information Retrieval*, (Grenoble, France), pp. 465–480, 1988.
6. S. T. Dumais, "Latent semantic indexing (LSI)," in *Proceedings of the Text Retrieval Conference (TREC-3)*, 1995.
7. S. Chaudhury, A. Roy, and L. Dey, "An MIMD algorithm for constant curvature feature extraction using curvature based data partitioning," *Pattern Recognition Letters*, 20 (6), pp. 573–583, 1999.
8. R. C. Gonzalez and R. E. Woods, *Digital Image Processing*. Prentice Hall, Upper Saddle River, NJ, 3rd ed., 2008.
9. E. Ukkonen, "Finding approximate patterns in string," *Journal of Algorithms*, 6 (1), pp. 132–137, 1985.
10. S. Banerjee, G. Harit, and S. Chaudhury, "Word image based latent semantic indexing for conceptual querying in document image databases," in *Proceedings of IEEE ICDAR*, vol. 2, pp. 1208–1212, 2007.
11. P. R. Christopher, D. Manning, and H. Schtze, *Introduction to Information Retrieval*. Cambridge University Press, Cambridge, 1st ed., 2008.
12. T. Hofmann, "Probabilistic latent semantic indexing," in *Proceedings of SIGIR*, 1999.
13. S. Kumar, N. Khanna, S. Chaudhury, and S. D. Joshi, "Locating text in images using matched wavelets," in *Proceedings of IEEE ICDAR*, vol. 2, pp. 595–599, 2005.
14. L. Saul and F. Pereira, "Aggregate and mixed order Markov models for statistical language processing," in *Proceedings of the 2nd International Conference on Empirical Methods Natural Language Processing*, pp. 81–89, 1997.
15. H. Ghosh, S. Chaudhury, K. Kashyap, and B. Maiti, *Ontologies A Handbook of Principles, Concepts and Applications in Information Systems*, ch. Ontology Specification and Integration for Multimedia Applications. Springer-Verlag New York, Inc., Secaucus, NJ, USA 2006.
16. G. Harit, S. Chaudhury, and J. Paranjpe, "Ontology guided access to document images," in *Proceedings of IEEE ICDAR*, vol. 1, pp. 292–296, 2005.
17. H. Ghosh and S. Chaudhury, "Distributed and reactive query planning in R-MAGIC: An agent based multimedia retrieval system," *IEEE Transactions on Knowledge and Data Engineering*, vol. 16, pp. 1082–1095, September 2004.

Word Spotting for Indic Documents to Facilitate Retrieval

Anurag Bhardwaj, Srirangaraj Setlur, and Venu Govindaraju

Abstract With advances in the field of digitization of printed documents and several mass digitization projects underway, information retrieval and document search have emerged as key research areas. However, most of the current work in these areas is limited to English and a few oriental languages. The lack of efficient solutions for Indic scripts has hampered information extraction from a large body of documents of cultural and historical importance. This chapter presents two relevant topics in this area. First, we describe the use of a script-specific keyword spotting for Devanagari documents that makes use of domain knowledge of the script. Second, we address the needs of a digital library to provide access to a collection of documents from multiple scripts. This requires intelligent solutions which scale across different scripts. We present a script-independent keyword spotting approach for this purpose. Experimental results illustrate the efficacy of our methods.

Keywords Document analysis · Keyword spotting · Optical character recognition · Document retrieval · Indic scripts

1 Introduction

For decades, optical character recognition (OCR) has been considered as the primary enabling technology for automatic interpretation of handwritten or machine-print document images. Given the relatively easy access to large numbers of document images in English and certain oriental scripts, OCR solutions have primarily focused on these scripts. However, the information boom of the last decade has led to a remarkable growth in the digital collection of documents in non-European and non-oriental scripts such as Indic scripts. Unfortunately, the

A. Bhardwaj (✉)
Department of Computer Science and Engineering, Center for Unified Biometrics and Sensors, University at Buffalo, Amherst, NY 14228, USA
e-mail: ab94@cubs.buffalo.edu

V. Govindaraju, S. Setlur (eds.), *Guide to OCR for Indic Scripts*, Advances in Pattern Recognition, DOI 10.1007/978-1-84800-330-9_15,

progress in recognition technologies for Indic scripts such as Devanagari (used for Sanskrit, Hindi, and other languages) has not been at par with the growth in the digital document collections. This can be attributed to a number of challenges in the form of poor-quality documents, complex nature of the scripts, and relatively fewer years of research on Indic OCR.

Fortunately, recent advances in information retrieval have led to the emergence of keyword spotting as a viable method and an alternative to full OCR. Keyword spotting essentially finds all occurrences of a typed input word in a set of handwritten/printed documents. Using this method, it is possible to obtain information from documents without relying on robust recognition strategies. Figure 1 illustrates the concept where the boxed word image represents the spotted keyword.

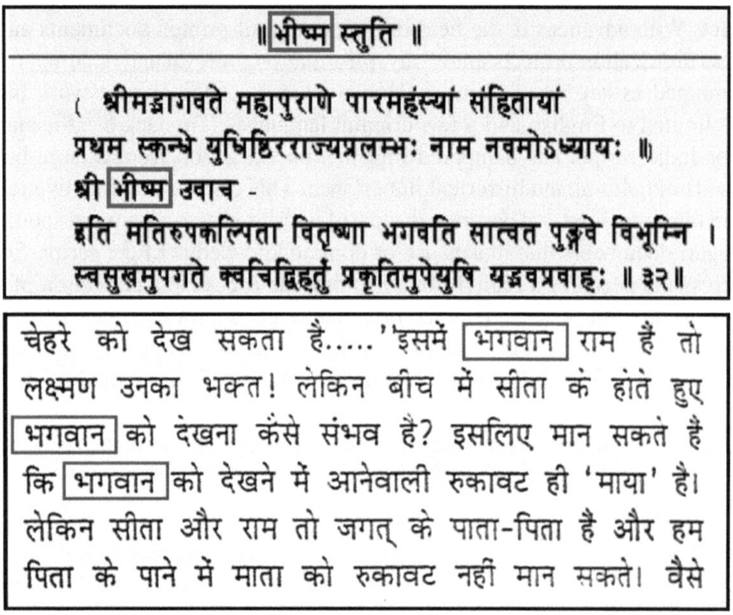

॥ भीष्म स्तुति ॥

(श्रीमद्भागवते महापुराणे पारमहंस्यां संहितायां
प्रथम स्कन्धे युधिष्ठिरराज्यप्रलम्भः नाम नवमोऽध्यायः ॥)
श्री भीष्म उवाच -
इति मतिरुपकल्पिता वितृष्णा भगवति सात्वत पुङ्गवे विभूम्नि ।
स्वसुखमुपगते क्वचिद्विहर्तुं प्रकृतिमुपेयुषि यद्भवप्रवाहः ॥ ३२॥

चेहरे को देख सकता है.....''इसमें भगवान राम है तो
लक्ष्मण उनका भक्त! लेकिन बीच में सीता के होते हुए
भगवान को देखना कैसे संभव है? इसलिए मान सकते हैं
कि भगवान को देखने में आनेवाली रुकावट ही 'माया' है।
लेकिन सीता और राम तो जगत् के पाता-पिता है और हम
पिता के पाने में माता को रुकावट नहीं मान सकते। वैसे

Fig. 1 Sample Sanskrit and Hindi document images with keyword boxed

We present two different approaches to Devanagari keyword spotting. In the first approach, we describe a block adjacency graph (BAG)-based scheme for word recognition. It includes a BAG-based document cleanup technique that uses a graph to maintain the overall ligature structure while removing noise that does not conform to a ligature shape. We use multiple hypotheses generated in the recognition phase to determine the similarity between a query word and a document word image. This ensures that even if the top choice result of an OCR is not correct, based on the similarity with the query, multiple word hypotheses returned by the OCR are considered. The second approach extends the idea of keyword spotting to multilingual documents. We use a moment-based word matching technique which maintains a script-invariant representation of all word images. Word matching is performed using the cosine similarity. We also employ a relevance feedback technique to refine the word spotting results. The rest of the chapter is organized as follows: Section 2 describes background work in this area. Section 3 explains the proposed methodologies. Section 4 discusses the scope of the proposed methods. Conclusions are drawn in Section 5.

2 Related Work

Existing keyword spotting approaches can be broadly classified into two categories (Fig. 2): (i) OCR-based approaches and (ii) Image feature-based approaches. The OCR-based techniques are suitable only for applications where the documents are of good quality and involve relatively small lexicons. Thus, instead of indexing the OCR'ed text of images for keyword retrieval, approaches based on indexing intermediate OCR likelihood or matching distance have been proposed for retrieving English documents [1–3]. However, such OCR systems are still not available for Devanagari. This is because of several challenges in Devanagari word recognition including (i) a large number of ligatures resulting from all possible permutations of graphemes, (ii) ligature shapes made of complex primitives that cannot be easily segmented using conventional approaches, (iii) multiple font styles, and (iv) poor-quality documents. To the best of our knowledge, our method is the first that uses a recognition-based approach for keyword spotting in Devanagari documents.

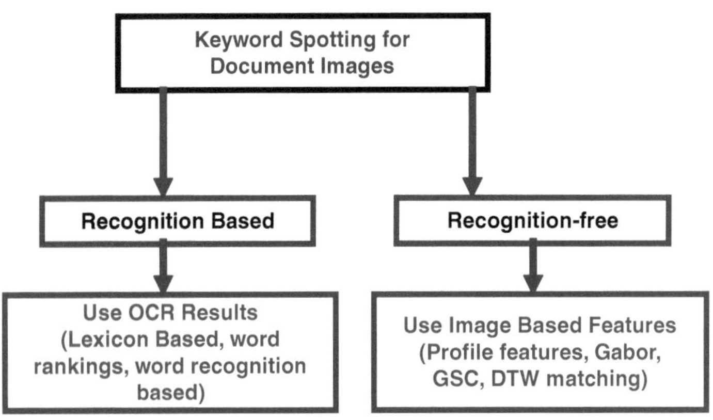

Fig. 2 Classification of existing keyword spotting techniques

In recognition-free keyword spotting approaches (Fig. 2), after preprocessing of document images and word segmentation, feature vectors are extracted from word images and stored in a database. When a user provides a query word, the similarity between the query and the word image in the database is computed, and word images are returned in decreasing order of similarity [4–6]. The comparison functions accommodate inexact matches by using dynamic time warping (DTW) or string edit distance measures. Some methods use probabilistic similarity metrics or clustering to compute the similarity between the query word image and the document word image [6, 7]. Global shape features have been found to be not as discriminative as using an OCR specific to the script and are prone to failure in the case of scripts like Devanagari that have a large and complex set of ligatures. The extracted global word shape features are not very reliable in poor-quality Devanagari documents.

Manmatha et al. [8] study various types of features for indexing handwritten English documents including profile-based features, gradient features, and Gabor-based features [7]. Dynamic time warping (DTW) is used for finding similarity between the query word image and other word images. Though these features work fairly well with English documents, they have proved to be inadequate for Devanagari given the complexity of class labels calling for more specific modeling of word images. Moreover, the presence of the top horizontal line (head line) or "Shirorekha" renders most of the profile-based features ineffective. Also, DTW-based approaches are slow. The keyword spotting method for Devanagari proposed by Harish et al. [9] uses a gradient, structural, and concavity (GSC) feature set to measure the image characteristics at local, intermediate, and large scales. The method specifies a sliding window approach. Local image features are computed from every window. However, in the presence of noisy word images, feature extraction is fragile. Template-based approaches such as these perform image matching in the feature space and hence require an image-based model of the query word (template). Therefore the method does not scale with a large number of query words.

3 Proposed Methodologies

This section describes two different approaches to Devanagari keyword spotting. The first is based on a common framework for both recognition and retrieval of Devanagari documents. A font-independent OCR generates results at the (sub)grapheme level (atomic graphs) for a given word image. These results are used by a document retrieval system which defines a "string edit"-based cost metric to align OCR results with an input query word. The second approach uses a script-independent representation of word images to match the input query word with every indexed word image and retrieves the corresponding documents. The latter approach is recognition free but needs a query template consisting of word images of each query word to be searched. The following sections describe these methodologies in detail.

3.1 Recognition-Based Keyword Spotting

Our system (Fig. 3) consists of three phases: (a) preprocessing phase, (b) recognition phase, and (c) matching phase. In the preprocessing phase, the horizontal profiles of the document image are used to segment the document into line images. The vertical

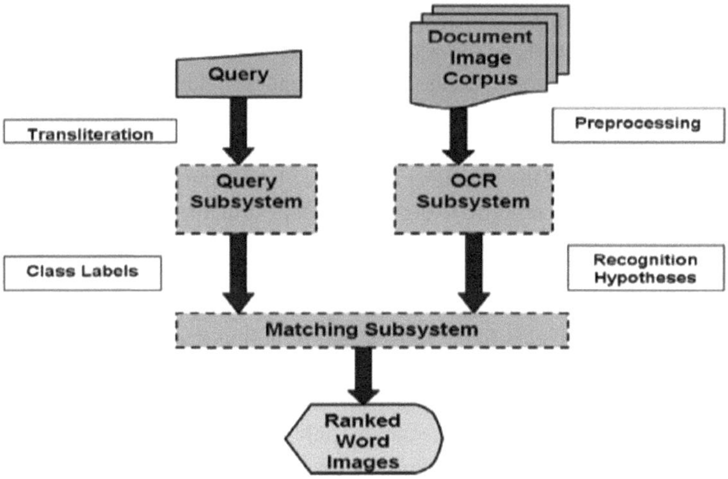

Fig. 3 System architecture for OCR-based keyword spotting [10]

profile of each line image is used to extract individual word images. Since the document images are often of poor print quality, the extracted word images are noisy. Therefore, the word images are cleaned by performing a block adjacency graph (BAG)-based smoothing procedure before initiating the recognition phase [10].

A block adjacency graph (BAG) can be created by classifying runs as *merging*, *splitting*, or *continuing* runs. BAGs can be constructed using both horizontal runs and vertical runs. Horizontal runs are classified based on the number of runs present above and below a given run. Runs that have one or no runs above them are labeled *splitting* runs, and runs that have one or no run below are labeled *merging* runs. The remaining runs are classified as *continuing*. Adjacent runs that are classified as *continuing* are merged into a single block. A *splitting* run is added to the block above it, and a *merging* run is added to the block below it. A graph can be constructed by connecting the centroid of the neighboring blocks. Information pertaining to the image structure can be inferred from the edges in the graph. An example of BAG construction is shown in Fig. 4.

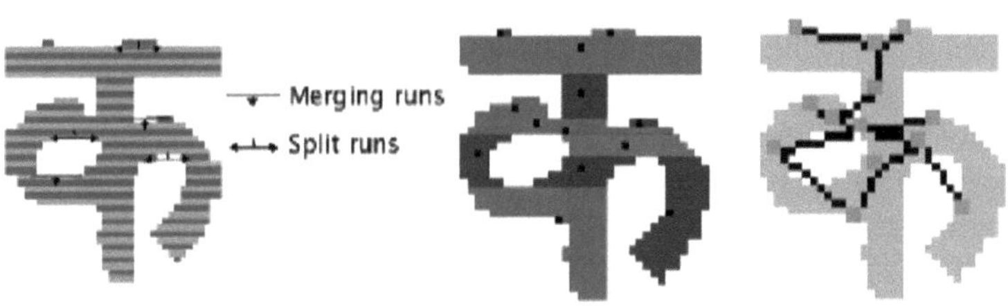

Fig. 4 BAG construction using horizontal runs for a sample grapheme [10] (see also Plate 9 on page 319 in the Color Plate Section)

The poor quality of many Devanagari documents poses a significant challenge to word spotting. Noisy pixels on the contour boundaries and holes in the interior make feature extraction inaccurate. Image enhancement techniques like morphological operations or filters often cannot discriminate between the noise and natural ligature structures like junctions or holes. We perform BAG-based contour smoothing [10] which takes into account the junctions and holes that are inherent in ligature shapes. In this method, a pixel is modified not only by using structuring elements but also by considering its connectivity to other parts of the ligature. Each pixel of an image can be mapped to a block in the BAG structure. If the corresponding BAG has multiple edges, it indicates that the block is connected to many other blocks of the graph. This implies that the pixel is likely to be a part of a joint that connects two or more parts of the image. In our implementation, we compute the average stroke width of the horizontal runs and the average block size. Blocks that have an area smaller than the average block size and are connected by only one edge are flagged as noise and removed. Since merging and splitting runs are grouped into larger adjacent blocks, thin sections at the trailing ends of a ligature are retained. Figure 5 shows an example of how noisy pixels are removed using this method.

Fig. 5 Illustration of BAG-based noise removal – *Left*: (1, 2) sample with noise, (3) thin joint, (4) thin ligature boundary; *Right*: result of BAG-based noise removal [10] (see also Plate 10 on page 319 in the Color Plate Section)

In the recognition phase, the cleaned documents are input to a font-independent Devanagari OCR [10]. The OCR generates multiple segmentation hypotheses by selecting different combinations of blocks from the BAG. A naive approach is to exhaustively segment sub-graphs from the BAG. Such a scheme is computationally inefficient, since the number of possible hypotheses grows exponentially. The hypotheses search space is pruned by using the following constraints: (i) the primitives in the class space are assumed to be joined from left to right or top to bottom and (ii) all of the primitives are assumed to consist of a single connected component. The equivalent conditions for sub-graph selection are as follows (i) a node cannot be selected if it is to the right (bottom for descender ligatures) of a node that has not been selected and (ii) sub-graphs representing primitives in our class space cannot have disconnected nodes.

A neural network-based classifier is used to output recognition scores corresponding to every segmentation hypothesis. Figure 6 (left) shows the Devanagari primitives classified by our OCR. Figure 6 (right) shows a sample segmentation hypotheses lattice generated by the sub-graph selection scheme.

We make use of the multiple recognition hypotheses provided by the OCR for each word in the document image. A similarity metric is designed to obtain the best match between the hypotheses and class labels corresponding to the query word.

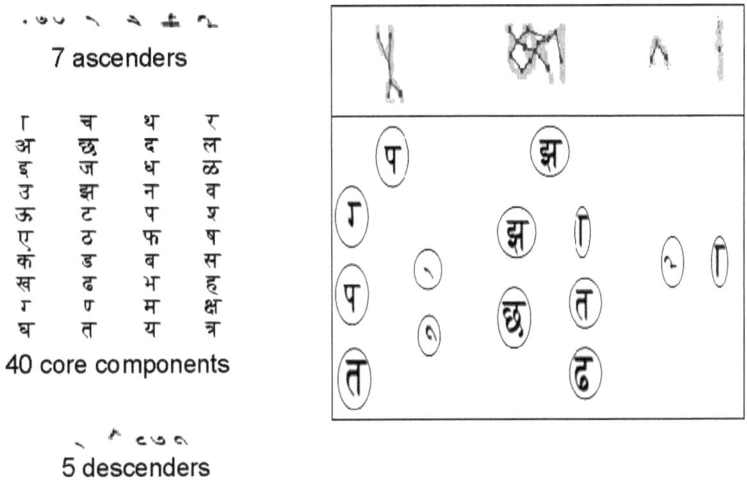

Fig. 6 *Left*: Devanagari OCR class space. *Right*: segmentation hypotheses lattice generation using sub-graph selection

Therefore, the task of keyword spotting involves finding the best match between the input query word and the hypotheses. All the occurrences of the query word in the document are found by ranking the candidate words using a cost-based model. This is based on "string edit" distance and represents the cost of aligning a combination of recognition hypotheses for a given word image with the query word. Since the hypotheses are associated with classifier scores for class labels for the Devanagari graphemes at each position, our model incorporates both (i) classifier score and (ii) class label position within a hypotheses combination. A class label c here represents the Unicode value of a single Devanagari grapheme present in the query text. The model takes a sequence of the desired class labels (ordering of individual Devanagari graphemes in the query word) generated by transliteration of the queried text. For each class label in this sequence, the model finds the best position of occurrence of the class label among all the hypotheses corresponding to a single word image of the document (Fig. 7). It marks this position as the "BestPos" found and computes the difference "MinDiff" between the desired position and the actual position of the class label. It also stores the classifier score "CScore" which is the OCR output for this position of the class label. Thus the model computes the alignment cost. All the words are ranked in order of increasing cost and constitute the keyword spotting output. The overall cost model is as shown below:

$$\mathrm{MinDiff}(c) = \mathrm{BestPos}(c) - \mathrm{ReqdPos}(c)$$

$$\alpha(c) = \frac{1}{1 + \mathrm{MinDiff}(c)}$$

$$\mathrm{Cost}(w \mid q) = \sum_{c} 1 - (\alpha(c)^{*}\mathrm{CScore}(c))$$

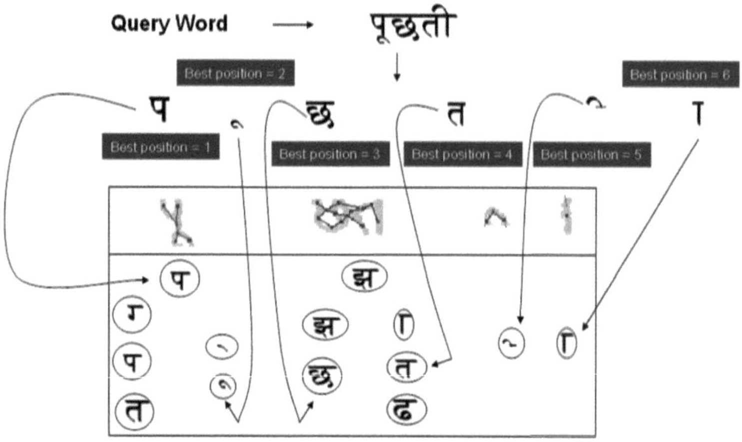

Fig. 7 Hypothesis search for best position of class labels

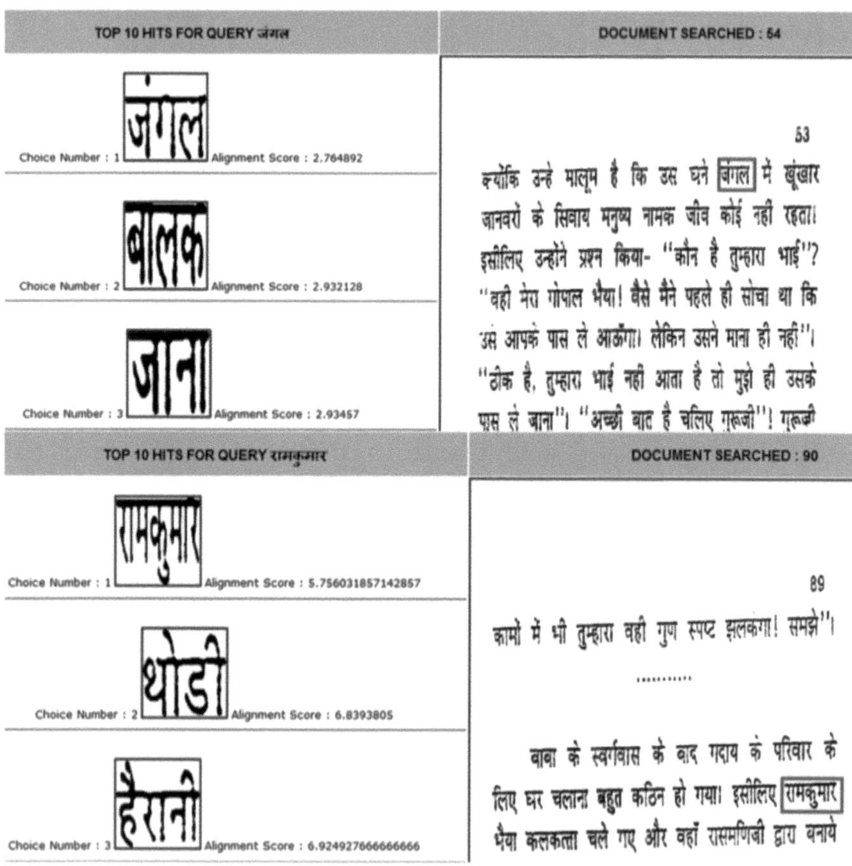

Fig. 8 Devanagari keyword spotting results for two queries (OCR-based approach)

3.1.1 Performance

The recognition-based strategy is lexicon free because the segmentation hypotheses are generated at the ligature-primitive level. We do not assume any query-specific template and therefore our method is extensible to multiple queries. To evaluate this method, we implement some of the previously reported template-based word spotting methods (Table 1, Fig. 9). Three feature extraction schemes are studied:

- *Gabor Features:* Arrays of Gabor filters are designed corresponding to different scales and orientations. We experimented with two scales and eight orientations [0, 45 90, 135, 180, −45, −90, −135], making a total of 16 Gabor filters. To extract features from every image, we convolve the input image with every Gabor

Table 1 Comparative performance of different keyword spotting methods

Query	OCR	GSC	Gradient	Gabor
Baba	0.62	0.8	0.41	0.41
Bandar	1.0	0.092	1.0	1.0
Bhakt	0.75	0.52	0.41	0.41
Jungal	0.65	0.74	0.1	0.1
Machali	0.79	0.93	0.89	0.89
Mata	0.63	0.35	0.38	1.0
Naksha	1.0	0.77	1.0	0.41
Raat	0.70	0.72	0.41	0.38
Ramkumar	1.0	0.89	0.22	0.24
Vachan	0.86	0.67	0.24	0.22
Mean for 10	**0.80**	**0.65**	**0.50**	**0.50**
Mean for 20	**0.67**	**0.60**	**0.29**	**0.29**

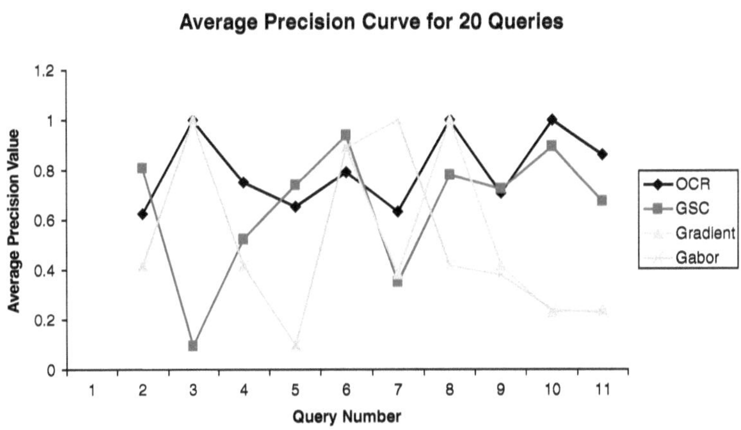

Fig. 9 Average precision curve for different keyword spotting methods (see also Plate 11 on page 320 in the Color Plate Section)

filter and generate an output image. A block-based feature extraction mechanism is performed by dividing the output image into five vertical zones. For every vertical zone, we find the centroid of the image block and compute a weighted Gaussian-based positive and negative component of the filter output. This yields two features per image block per filter, resulting in a total of 5*2 = 10 features per filter. By applying all the filters in a similar fashion, we obtain a feature set of 160 features per image.

– *Gradient Features:* Images are divided into a 3×3 grid and the gradient magnitude and direction is computed in each block using a Sobel operator. A gradient map is computed by applying an empirical threshold on the gradient magnitudes. The gradient directions in each cell are quantized into eight bins: horizontal, vertical, and the two diagonals in each direction. Concatenation of the gradient vectors for the nine cells forms a 72-element feature vector.
– *Gradient, Structural, and Concavity Features:* As reported in [9], GSC has 512 features that represent three types of image attributes: (a) 192 gradient features, which represent the local edge and curvature information of the image, (b) 192 structural features, representing short strokes of different angles, and (c) 128 concavity features which reflect holes and concavities that are oriented in different directions.

Two templates are designed to test the performance of template-based matching. The first template "A" is designed using fonts that are different from fonts seen in the document image collection. The second template "B" is constructed by selecting word images from the document collection itself. Experimental results show that in both cases, the recognition-based approach outperforms the template-based methods. Moreover, we observe a large variation in the performance of the template-based methods. Template B shows better performance compared to template A, since the query word images in template A have the same font as the document image collection. Figure 8 shows results for two sample queries obtained using the OCR-based approach described above. However, this is a script-specific solution which does not generalize over scripts other than Devanagari. An error analysis of this method suggests that most of the errors are due to the misclassification of ligatures by the OCR as a result of confusion between classes that are similar in appearance. For instance, in the case of keywords such as टोलि (Toli) and सोने (Sone),  is often incorrectly recognized as . Such confusion is also observed between र and स. One possible solution to this problem is to use a confusion matrix for post-processing the OCR results and to integrate this with the retrieval mechanism.

3.2 Recognition-Free Keyword Spotting

The recognition-based approach to keyword spotting is very promising but has the disadvantage of being specific to a single script type. Digital libraries contain many documents that involve multiple scripts. Our goal is to enable access to these documents without having to use a script-specific solution for every script in the document collection. A script-invariant representation of document images is needed to achieve this goal. Figure 10 illustrates such a process where the input query gets translated into multiple languages and a script-independent keyword spotting solution searches the entire collection for multiple translations and returns the relevant documents from each script.

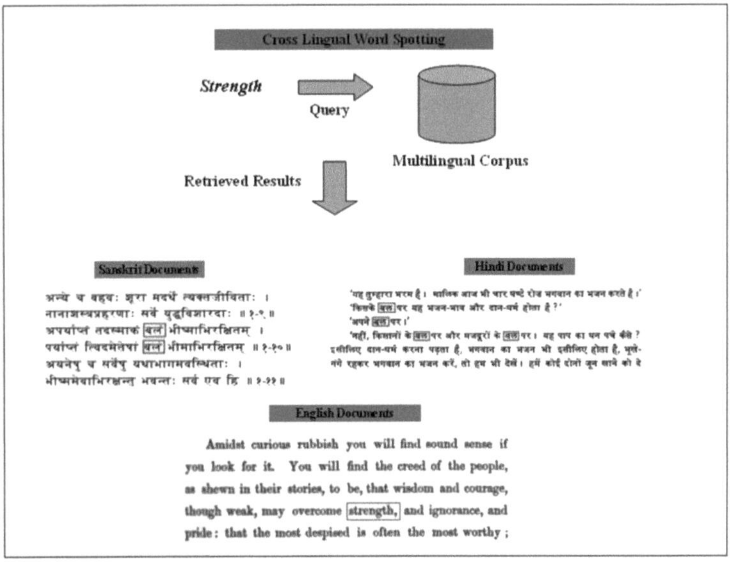

Fig. 10. Script-independent keyword spotting solution

We present a script-independent solution using image-based features which are invariant to script type, image scale, and translation. Previously proposed structural features such as GSC are not suitable as they are dependent on scale. Filter-based features such as Gabor features have similar issues. Moreover, filter-based feature extraction schemes are computationally expensive. We propose the use of moment-based image features that have been previously used to achieve an invariant representation of a two-dimensional image pattern [11]. Geometric moments also have the desirable property of being invariant under image translation, scale, and stretching and shear in either X or Y direction. Mathematically, such affine transformations are of the form of $X^* = aX + b$ and $Y^* = cY + d$ [12].

Geometrical moments (GM) of order $(p + q)$ for a continuous image function $f(x,y)$ are defined as follows:

$$M_{pq} = \int_{-\infty}^{\infty} \int_{-\infty}^{\infty} x^p y^q f(x,y)\, dx\, dy$$

The function $f(x,y)$ has only two possible values of 0 and 1, thus

$$M_{pq} = \sum_X \sum_Y x^p y^q f(x,y)$$

The center of gravity of image has co-ordinates

$$\bar{x} = \frac{M_{10}}{M_{00}}, \bar{y} = \frac{M_{01}}{M_{00}}$$

If we refer to the center of gravity as origin, we get

$$\bar{M}_{pq} = \sum_X \sum_Y (x - \bar{x})^p (y - \bar{y})^q f(x,y)$$

These moments are also referred to as central moments and can be expressed as combinations of moments of lower order. The variances of the moments are defined as

$$\sigma_x = \sqrt{\frac{\bar{M}_{20}}{M_{00}}}, \sigma_y = \sqrt{\frac{\bar{M}_{02}}{M_{00}}}$$

They are used to normalize the co-ordinates by setting

$$x^* = \frac{(x - \bar{x})}{\sigma_x}, y^* = \frac{(y - \bar{y})}{\sigma_y}$$

Using the normalized values of coordinates as obtained in equation above, the moment equation is as follows:

$$m_{pq} = \frac{\sum_X \sum_Y (x^*)^p (y^*)^q f(x,y)}{M_{00}}$$

This moment equation is invariant under image translations and scale transformations. Using this equation, we extract moment features up to the seventh order. A feature vector consisting of 30 moment values corresponding to each word image is stored in the primary index. The index construction is followed by query template construction. A set of query words is chosen and a template is created which maps each query word to a query feature vector. A similar feature extraction scheme is employed to generate query feature vector from the query word image.

A standard vector space model is used to represent the query word and all the candidate words. The index is maintained in the form of a word-feature matrix, where each word image "*w*" occupies one row of the matrix and all columns in a single row correspond to the moment values computed for the given word image. When the user enters any query word, a lookup operation is performed in the stored template to obtain the corresponding normalized word image for the input text. Feature extraction is performed on the word image to construct the query feature vector

"q". A cosine similarity score is computed for this query feature vector and all the rows of the word-feature matrix.

The cosine similarity is calculated as follows:

$$\mathrm{SIM}(q,w) = \frac{\vec{q}\,.\,\vec{w}}{|\vec{q}| * |\vec{w}|}$$

Figure 11 describes the overall procedure for similarity matching. Since the word images present in the document corpus can be of poor print quality and noisy, the moment features computed may not be effective in assigning a high rank to all relevant word images. Also, the presence of higher order moments may be unstable. To overcome this limitation, we also implement a relevance feedback mechanism based on Rocchio's formula. This mechanism re-formulates the query feature vector by adjusting the values of the individual moment orders present in the query vector. The relevance feedback mechanism assumes a user input after the presentation of the initial results. A user enters a 1 for a relevant result or a 0 for an irrelevant result. The new query vector is computed as follows:

$$q_{\text{new}} = \gamma \cdot q_{\text{old}} + \frac{\alpha}{|R|} \cdot \sum_{i=1}^{i=R} d_i - \frac{\beta}{|NR|} \cdot \sum_{j=1}^{j=NR} d_j$$

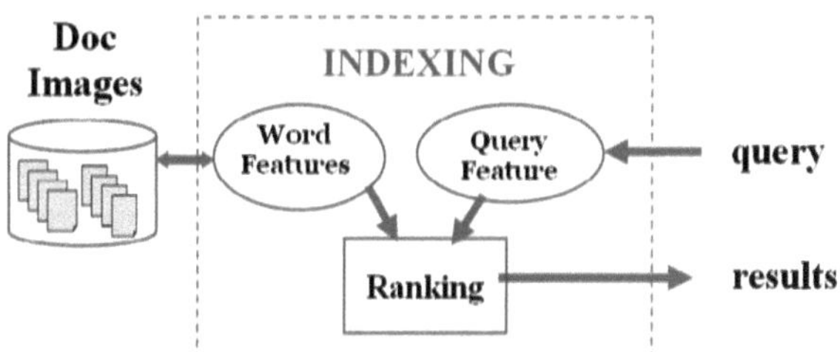

Fig. 11 Similarity matching using cosine similarity

In the above equation, α, β, and γ represent term re-weighting constants and R and NR represent relevant and non-relevant word images, respectively. Figure 12 describes the relevance feedback mechanism.

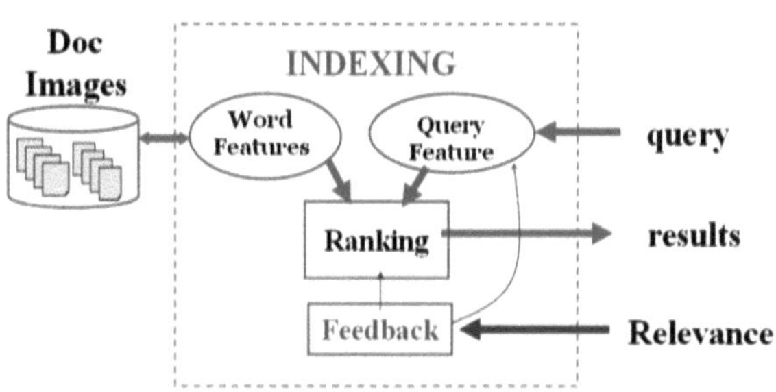

Fig. 12 Relevance feedback using Rocchio's formula

3.2.1 Performance

A script-independent solution is desirable when dealing with multi-script document collections. The solution described in Section 3.2 is recognition free but requires a query template for every query into the corpus and is not scalable to multiple queries. Moreover, this method suffers from the same drawback of font dependence as mentioned above. Table 2 shows the average precision rate for three different scripts using the proposed method. As shown in the table, the proposed method performs better with Sanskrit and Hindi document images compared to English. Figure 13 shows the result for a single query on a Sanskrit document using the script-independent approach.

Table 2 Average precision rate for different scripts

Script	Before relevance feedback	After relevance feedback
English	0.66	0.69
Hindi	0.71	0.74
Sanskrit	0.87	0.92

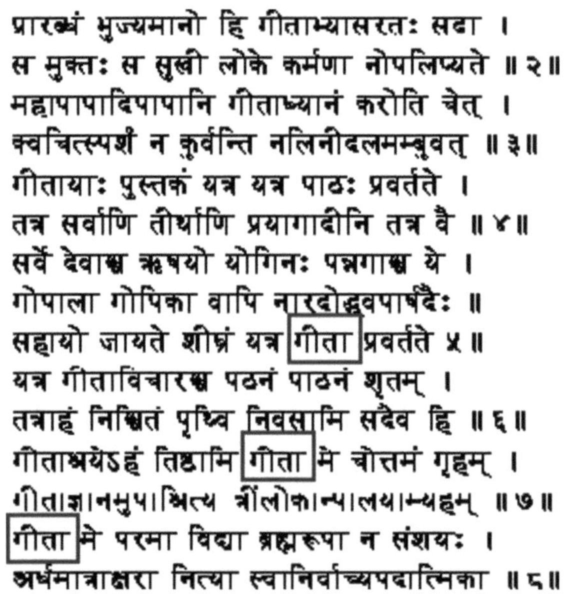
प्रारब्धं भुज्यमानो हि गीताभ्यासरतः सदा ।
स मुक्तः स सुखी लोके कर्मणा नोपलिप्यते ॥२॥
महापापादिपापानि गीताध्यानं करोति चेत् ।
क्वचित्स्पर्शं न कुर्वन्ति नलिनीदलमम्बुवत् ॥३॥
गीतायाः पुस्तकं यत्र यत्र पाठः प्रवर्तते ।
तत्र सर्वाणि तीर्थानि प्रयागादीनि तत्र वै ॥४॥
सर्वे देवाश्च ऋषयो योगिनः पन्नगाश्च ये ।
गोपाला गोपिका वापि नारदोद्धवपार्षदैः ॥
सहायो जायते शीघ्रं यत्र गीता प्रवर्तते ५ ॥
यत्र गीताविचारश्च पठनं पाठनं श्रुतम् ।
तत्राहं निश्चितं पृथ्वि निवसामि सदैव हि ॥६॥
गीताश्रयेऽहं तिष्ठामि गीता मे चोत्तमं गृहम् ।
गीताज्ञानमुपाश्रित्य त्रींलोकान्पालयाम्यहम् ॥७॥
गीता मे परमा विद्या ब्रह्मरूपा न संशयः ।
अर्धमात्राक्षरा नित्या स्वानिर्वाच्यपदात्मिका ॥८॥

Fig. 13 Sanskrit keyword spotting results for a query (script-independent approach)

4 Conclusion

We have described two different approaches for keyword spotting in printed Sanskrit documents. The first approach which is script specific uses Devanagari OCR based on block adjacency graph (BAG) representation of word images. The recognition phase selectively segments ligatures by extracting sub-graphs from the initial BAG representation of the input word image. Multiple segmentation hypotheses are retained in the form of grapheme class labels and scores returned by the OCR. Finally, a string edit distance-based cost model is used to retrieve the relevant documents by computing the alignment cost between the query word and multiple segmentation hypotheses for candidate words in the document corpus. The second approach, which is script independent, uses an image moment-based keyword spotting method to handle multi-script document collections.

Acknowledgment This material is based upon work supported by the National Science Foundation under grant no. IIS-0112059, IIS-0535038, and IIS-0849511.

References

1. N. R. Howe, T. M. Rath and R. Manmatha. Boosted decision trees for word recognition in handwritten document retrievals. In *Proceedings of the SIGIR*, pp. 377–383, 2005.
2. D. R. Lee, W. Y. Kim and I. S. Oh. Hangul document image retrieval system using rank-based recognition. In *Proceedings of the International Conference on Document Analysis and Recognition*, vol. 2, pp. 615–619, 2005.
3. T. M. Rath, R. Manmatha and V. Layrenko. A search engine for historical manuscripts. In *Proceedings of the 27th Annual International ACM SIGIR Conference on Research and Development in Information Retrieval*, 2004.
4. M. Burl and P. Perona. Using hierarchical shape models to spot keywords in cursive handwriting. In *IEEECS Conference on Computer Vision and Pattern Recognition*, pp. 535–540, 1998.
5. J. L. Decurtins and E. C. Chen. Keyword spotting via word shape recognition. In *Proceedings of SPIE Document Recognition II*, L. M. Vincent, H. S. Baird; Eds., vol. 2422, pp. 270–277, 1995.
6. T. M. Rath and R. Manmatha. Word image matching using dynamic time warping. In *Proceedings of the Conference on Computer Vision and Pattern Recognition*, vol. 2, pp. 521–527, 2003.
7. H. Cao and V. Govindaraju. Template-free word spotting in low-quality manuscripts. In *Proceedings of the 6th International Conference on Advances in Pattern Recognition*, pp. 135–139, 2007.
8. T. Rath and R. Manmatha. Features for word spotting in historical manuscripts. In *Proceedings of the 7th International Conference on Document Analysis and Recognition*, pages 218–222, 2003.
9. S. N. Srihari, H. Srinivasan, C. Huang and S. Shetty. Spotting words in Latin, Devanagari and Arabic scripts. *Vivek: Indian Journal of Artificial Intelligence*, Vol. 16, no. 3, pp. 2–9, 2006.
10. A. Bhardwaj, S. Kompalli, S. Setlur and V. Govindaraju. An OCR based approach to word spotting in Devanagari documents. In *Proceedings of the 15th SPIE – Document Recognition and Retrieval*, vol. 6815, 2008.
11. C.-H. Teh and R. T. Chin On image analysis by the methods of moments. *IEEE Trans actions on Pattern Analysis and Machine Intelligence*, 10(4), 496–513, 1988.
12. Franz L. Alt. Digital pattern recognition by moments. *The Journal of the ACM*, 9(2), 240–258, 1962.

Indian Language Information Retrieval

Prasenjit Majumder and Mandar Mitra

Abstract With the proliferation of the Internet in south Asia over the last decade, the availability of digital documents in Indian languages has increased considerably. The need for effective information access methods for these languages is being increasingly felt. Although Indian language information retrieval (ILIR) research is in a relatively nascent stage (especially with regard to large-scale quantitative evaluation), several research efforts in this area have been reported in the recent past. This chapter reviews the current state of the art in mono-lingual and cross-lingual information access in Indian languages and outlines a recent project that aims to create a comprehensive, end-to-end IR system for Indian languages, along with a standardized evaluation framework (in the spirit of TREC, CLEF, or NTCIR) that will provide a sound empirical basis for further work.

Keywords Indian languages · Information retrieval (IR) · Mono lingual IR · Cross lingual IR

1 Introduction

The word "information" was first used in popular English literature sometime before 1258. Dictionaries have a wide range of definitions of this term:

> [**Webster**] A collection of facts from which conclusions may be drawn; Knowledge acquired through study or experience or instruction.
> [**Wikipedia**] Information is a term with many meanings depending on context, but is as a rule closely related to such concepts as meaning, knowledge, instruction, communication, representation, and mental stimulus.

P. Majumder (✉)
CVPR Unit, Indian Statistical Institute, Kolkata, West Bengal, India
e-mail:prasenjit_t,mandar@isical.ac.in

Parts of this chapter appeared earlier in [1].

V. Govindaraju, S. Setlur (eds.), *Guide to OCR for Indic Scripts*, Advances in Pattern Recognition, DOI 10.1007/978-1-84800-330-9_16, © Springer-Verlag London Limited 2009

Information storage and retrieval is an age-old practice. Over the last half century, information retrieval (IR) has emerged as a well-focused, inter-disciplinary research area involving computer scientists, librarians, and statisticians.

The field of information retrieval (IR) is concerned with the retrieval of information that is relevant to a user's information need. Information retrieval is often regarded as being synonymous with document retrieval and text retrieval, though many IR systems also retrieve pictures, audio, multimedia, or other types of non-textual information. Text document retrieval subsumes two related activities: indexing and searching. Indexing refers to the way *documents* (i.e., information items) are represented by the information retrieval system; searching refers to the process whereby a *query* (i.e., a statement of a user's information need) is used to produce a set of (possibly ranked) documents that are relevant to the query.

The textual information contained in documents and articles is written in natural language. The unstructured nature of this information makes IR more challenging compared to data retrieval, which uses deductive and Boolean logic to find data items that precisely match a query. Unlike data retrieval, IR has to deal with imprecise, unstructured, and abstract forms of information.

Over the years, various methods for indexing and retrieval have been proposed. Some major approaches are the vector space model, the probabilistic model, and knowledge-based approaches. The first two approach the problem without attempting to analyze the semantics of the documents. The knowledge-based approach retrieves relevant documents based on a semantic analysis of queries and documents: the conceptual models of queries and documents are compared directly based on their abstract meanings. Finding information where the query is given in the same language as the documents is called mono lingual information retrieval and finding information where the query and the document language are different is called cross-lingual information retrieval.

Besides retrieval, several other information-processing tasks have been investigated by researchers in the IR community. Text filtering, question answering, and online new event detection and tracking are some of the tasks besides retrieval which have been studied recently. The text filtering task addresses a situation where the user's information need is stable (and some relevant documents are known), but there is a stream of new documents. For each document, the system must make a binary decision as to whether the document meets the user's information need. Documents that are considered relevant are passed on (or "routed") to the user; all other documents are rejected. No ranking of documents is required. Question answering (QA) is designed to take the state of the art a step closer to *information* retrieval rather than document retrieval. Instead of returning a ranked list of documents, QA systems attempt to return precise answers to natural language questions. New event detection is a challenging task where a system has to identify news stories that discuss an event that has not already been reported in earlier stories. Event tracking consists of starting from a few sample stories and finding all subsequent stories that discuss the same event. Thus the scope of textual information retrieval encompasses several interesting and challenging problems, each of which has practical significance.

1.1 Background

Digital information processing in Indian languages can be traced back to the 1970s, when the ISCII (Indian Standard Code for Information Interchange) character encoding scheme[1] was proposed for storing Indic data. Over the next three decades, machine translation and the development of related natural language processing tools were a major research focus.

The last decade has witnessed the increasing proliferation of the Internet in India. With more and more people accessing the World Wide Web in the country, the amount of Indian language content available in electronic form has reached (indeed, crossed) critical mass. A large number of newspapers have online editions. There are also several magazines and information portals serving content in various Indian languages. In addition to online material, the Indian parliament publishes proceedings of every session in Hindi. The government is also encouraging the introduction of local languages in official activities. Naturally, there is a growing need for techniques for effectively managing all the available information.

While several successful techniques developed in the context of English language IR are likely to be directly applicable to indian language information retrieval (ILIR), some important issues need to be investigated within the specific context of Indian languages for better performance. For some tasks, existing techniques need to be refined to suit Indian languages. For certain other tasks, existing techniques may not be suitable, and new methodologies may have to be designed. Thus, information retrieval research for Indian languages is a relatively new area that has come into focus in the last 5 years due to the rapidly increasing availability of electronic content in Indian languages.

The aim of this chapter is twofold: to provide an overview of work done so far in the area of ILIR and to present a standardized evaluation framework for ILIR, which is expected to provide a firm, empirical basis for further research in this area.

2 Overview of Indian Language IR

In this section, we first enumerate the various sources of digital information in Indian languages; next, we review some of the prominent research efforts in the area of ILIR.

2.1 Information Sources

With the proliferation of personal computers in the Indian subcontinent over the last decade, creating documents in Indian languages has become easier than ever before.

---

[1] http://tdil.mit.gov.in/standards.htm#iscii

Table 1 Indian Internet statistics

1.1 billion	Population (2007 est.)
5 million	Internet users (2000)
60 million	Internet users (2007)
1100%	Use growth (2000–2007)
5.3%	Penetration (% population)
13.0%	(%) users in Asia

In many cases, desktop publishing has replaced the traditional press. Electronic publications can be broadly divided into two categories, *off-line* and *online*.

Off-line documents: CD-ROMs with Indian language content, covering subjects like music and the arts, mythology, traditional medicine are becoming increasingly popular. In addition, the Government of India has set up four mega-centers for creating digital libraries of primarily literary material. This huge collection of digitized documents is gradually being uploaded to the Web. One of the possible frameworks for organizing this collection is provided by the Greenstone digital library package,[2] available in a wide range of language interfaces including Bengali, Hindi, Marathi, Tamil, and Urdu. Shivaram and Rajashekar [2] have described their experience of creating Hindi and Kannada text collections using Greenstone, which was found to be effective for indexing, searching, and displaying the collections. Another Indian language digital library, Vidyanidhi [3], was created by localizing DSpace,[3] and contains about a thousand doctoral theses in Hindi and Kannada. The central and state governments of India are also promoting the use of the local language for official work. For example, the proceedings of the Indian Parliament are available as multilingual documents. Thus, there is a growing archive of official documents written in Indian languages.

Online documents: Table 1 shows some statistics collected recently about the Internet in India.[4] Among the 25 official languages in India, about 10 languages have regular online publications in the form of news, weekly and monthly magazines, individual homepages, and blogs. For example, there are 41 regular Internet publications in Hindi, the major language in India, 20 in Bengali, 16 in Marathi, 67 in Tamil, and 14 in Gujarati. Besides these, all government and major academic institutions have Hindi versions of their web sites. A more comprehensive picture of the Indian web is given in [4, 5].

2.2 Research Efforts

Among the major research efforts focused on ILIR, the most prominent one was the DARPA-sponsored surprise language exercise (SLE) under the TIDES (Translin-

[2] http://www.greenstone.org
[3] http://www.dspace.org
[4] http://www.internetworldstats.com/stats3.htm

gual Information Detection, Extraction, and Summarization) program,[5] where many interesting experiments were carried out for the first time on ILs. Besides TIDES, some noteworthy efforts in IL information processing have been reported in various national and international conferences.

2.2.1 Text Retrieval

In 2003, DARPA organized a surprise language exercise, where the participants started with no language resources, and tried to construct workable IR/IE systems within a short time frame (10–29 days). TIDES was intended to show the portability of existing information-processing tools to new languages. Besides Cubano, Hindi was announced as a surprise language on June 1, 2003; participants were to complete their tasks by June 30. Participants worked on various tasks like cross-lingual IR, named-entity identification (NEI), part-of-speech tagging, and other language-processing components. A slightly modified version of Unicode (UTF-8), designed by the surprise language group's encoding and normalization sub-committee, was the official exchange format for all Hindi text.

For retrieval evaluation, 15 English topics, Hindi translations of these topics, and a collection of 41,697 Hindi news articles from several different sources were distributed. Topics consisted of a title, description, narrative, and search terms. About 16 institutions prepared this evaluation data collaboratively, in an effort that involved frequent conference calls, hundreds of e-mails in a common mailing list, and resources sharing. Text encoding issues and obtaining parallel news corpora turned out to be the biggest challenges, and the final version of standardized text was eventually made available only a few days before the final evaluation.

Among the participants, He et al. [6] ported MIRACLE (Maryland Interactive Retrieval Advanced Cross-Language Engine) to Hindi. MIRACLE is a document retrieval system that was previously used to search French, German, and Spanish documents using English queries. The main features of MIRACLE are

- user-assisted query translation,
- rapid feedback-based progressive refinement,
- weighted structured query methods,
- configurable translation.

For user-assisted query translation, MIRACLE provides the following four types of cues to help searchers who know only English to decide which of the available translations to use:

- pronunciation,
- synonyms,

[5] http://www.darpa.mil/ipto/programs/tides/

– examples of usage, and
– translation probabilities.

As in many other cross-language retrieval systems, the query translation module is a crucial component of MIRACLE. In their work, the authors addressed the following three key questions:

– What terms should be translated (root forms, words, or phrases)?
– How should multiple candidate translations for a term be ranked?
– How should those translations be used to rank the documents?

A probabilistic Hindi–English dictionary was constructed using several sources, including bilingual term lists obtained from IIIT Hyderabad,[6] a list of Hindi translations of country names and Indian city names, and a lexicon prepared by IBM for this task. Out-of-vocabulary terms were transliterated by breaking the words into English phonemes using the Festival text-to-speech system, and each phoneme was then replaced by its nearest Hindi character(s). Translation polysemy was disambiguated using Pirkola's structured query translation method [7]. The impact of multi-word or phrase-based query translation on retrieval effectiveness was also studied.

He et al. also tried indexing based on overlapping character n-grams instead of words. This approach is typically useful when stemming tools are not available for a language, or when the text is erroneous, as in OCR-ed text [8].

The unavailability of a relevance-judged text collection in Hindi precluded the use of mean average precision (MAP) for evaluating and tuning the system components during the developmental stage; mean reciprocal rank (MRR)-based evaluation was used instead. For tuning, the authors constructed a Hindi collection of approximately 3000 BBC Hindi news articles from 2001, along with 29 topics.

For the final evaluation using the NIST-LDC test collections, two automatic CLIR runs were submitted using the same queries for both runs, combining all terms in the title, description, and narrative fields of the topic description. Both runs used the probabilistic lexicon, a Hindi stemmer from UC Berkeley, and a Hindi stop-word list from the University of Massachusetts. The MAP scores for the two cross-lingual and one mono-lingual Hindi runs were 0.28, 0.32, and 0.34 respectively. The differences between these scores were not found to be statistically significant.

Larkey et al. [9] adapted an English–Arabic CLIR system for Hindi. A Hindi stop-word list of 275 words was produced by manual selection from the 1000 most frequent words in the BBC corpus, and the *Naidunia* news collection (www.naidunia.com) obtained from LDC. A stemmer that removed 27 common Hindi suffixes was constructed and compared with a stemmer contributed by BBN

[6]http://www.iiit.net/ltrc/Dictionaries/Shabdanjali/Shabdanjali.tgz

[10], which removed 65 inflectional suffixes. Interestingly, both the stemmers hurt retrieval performance in terms of mean average precision on the test queries (this group used the same training data as that used by He et al.). For the official evaluation runs, therefore, no stemming was used.

Structured query translation from English to Hindi was done to search the Hindi corpus. Three dictionaries prepared by the UMass group, IBM, and ISI, were used in this step. To handle out-of-vocabulary words, a generative statistical transliteration model was used, which produced a string of Hindi characters from a string of English characters by replacing English characters or n-grams with Hindi characters/n-grams. This model was trained from English/Hindi proper noun pairs using GIZA++ [11]. Query expansion using pseudo-relevance feedback was tried on both English and Hindi queries (before and after translation, respectively).

Two search engines, INQUERY [12] and a language-modeling (LM)-based system [13], were used for retrieval, and the two sets of results obtained were fused to create the final ranked list.

In the mono-lingual task, the UMass runs achieved MAP scores of 0.4661 and 0.4738 (with and without expansion of the Hindi queries, respectively). For the cross-lingual task, the MAP figures were 0.4067 (0.4298) when only English queries (respectively, both English and Hindi queries) were expanded. No statistical significance tests were reported by this group.

Xu and Weischedel [14] applied previously used techniques for retrieving Chinese and Arabic documents in response to English queries. A probabilistic retrieval method [13] was used. Translation probabilities were estimated from a number of sources and were combined linearly. The sources include the LDC lexicon, the statistical lexicon from IBM, two sentence-aligned parallel corpora from UC Berkeley and LDC, and a pseudo-parallel corpus from USC/ISI's machine translation system. One mono-lingual and four cross-lingual runs were submitted. For the cross-lingual run, query expansion was tried on English and Hindi queries. Surprisingly, all cross-lingual runs outperformed the mono-lingual run in terms of precision at 5, 10, 15, and 20 document cutoffs.

Leuski et al. [15] built a Java-based, Hindi–English CLIR system called Lighthouse. The Hindi stop-word list of 543 words used by this system was provided by UC Berkeley. No Hindi stemmer was used. The English–Hindi probabilistic dictionary provided by UMD was used for query translation. During translation, matching long phrases in the query were preferred over matching individual words. If an English term had multiple Hindi translations, all translation variants were used. No quantitative results for this system on the TIDES test data were reported in this chapter.

The specific task of sense tagging in a cross-lingual setting was also studied at the SENSEVAL-3 [16] workshop. Given an ambiguous English word in context, participants were required to select the correct Hindi translation for that word from a list of possible candidates. Five teams participated in this workshop, and the best performance was achieved by Lee et al. [17], who used a supervised learning approach based on support vector machines.

2.2.2 Information Extraction

Much attention has been devoted to machine translation (MT) research in India over the last three decades. Related NLP tasks like part-of-speech tagging, named-entity identification have also been studied. However, it is difficult to compare techniques or measure progress because of the lack of standardized benchmark data (e.g., the collections used at the message understanding conferences).

The Hindi NEI task at TIDES involved finding all occurrences of three types of entities: PERSON, LOCATION, and ORGANIZATION. For evaluation, NIST provided a set of 25 previously unseen documents, consisting of 50,000 words. The entity counts in these documents for the above categories were 152, 232, and 92, respectively.

May et al. [18] from BBN built an NEI engine and a name co-reference algorithm for Hindi. Their system uses a hidden Markov model to label the data into different named-entity classes. More details of their system can be found in [19].

Annotated training data are crucial for this NEI system. For Hindi, LDC made available a 600,000 word corpus of online news drawn from several different sources. The sources were BBC Hindi news (58%), the EMILLE corpus (34%), India News Daily (1%), Naidunia (2%), Rediff (1%), United News of India (3%), and Voice of America (2%).

One major obstacle that had to be tackled before the data could be annotated was the different (and sometimes proprietary) character encoding schemes used by the various sources. Annotation was done jointly by LDC, BBN, and NYU. A maximum *F*-measure score of 80 was obtained on the Hindi evaluation set. For the name co-reference identification task, a set of heuristic rules were used.

Li et al. [20] applied conditional random fields (CRF) with feature induction for Hindi NEI. Atomic features used in this approach include the entire word text, character n-grams ($n = 2, 3, 4$), word prefixes and suffixes of lengths 2, 3, and 4, their positional values, and 24 Hindi gazetteer lists provided by the surprise language resource web site. The training set consisted of 4540 \textsc{person}, 7342 \textsc{location}, and 3181 \textsc{organization} entities collected from 601 BBC and 27 EMI documents. A first-order CRF was trained using the whole training set and the maximum F^1 score obtained was 71.50.

Huang et al. [21] presented an automatic approach to extract Hindi–English translingual named-entity equivalences from sentence-aligned bilingual parallel corpora. The basic assumption behind this task was that person and location names are often phonetically translated. The authors first proposed an automatic approach to iteratively learn the transliteration model between romanized Hindi and English letters. The Nymble [19] NEI system was then used to detect the named entities in an English corpus. For each entity, the romanized Hindi strings for which the transliteration cost is minimal were identified. The parallel corpus used in this experiment was the *India Today* news corpus, with 10,096 sentence pairs. This approach extracted 1000 Hindi–English NE pairs with a precision of 91.8%. Similar experiments with Chinese and English yielded an *F*-score of 81%.

We have also tried a similar approach for English and Bengali, using a noisy comparable corpus (since a sentence-aligned parallel corpus was not readily available), obtaining an MRR score of 0.615 over a test set consisting of 153 pairs of English and Bengali names. More details about this study have been reported in [22].

Besides TIDES, the most significant work for identifying names from Indian language text was by Cucerzan et al. [23], who used a language-independent bootstrapping algorithm. The precision, recall, and *F*-measure scores obtained by this approach were 83, 28, and 42%, respectively, for Hindi.

2.2.3 Question Answering

Sekine et al. [24] developed a cross-lingual question answering (CLQA) system for Hindi and English. Questions are posed in English, and the system finds candidate answers from Hindi newspapers. The system also translates the answers back to English. Using a tagger created by May et al. [18] for the TIDES SLE, person, location, and organization names were first identified in the corpus. A numeric expression tagger was developed by this group using simple pattern matching rules to identify amounts involving money, time, length, volume, etc. An initial question examiner module examines English questions and determines the expected answer types (3 name types or 15 numeric expression types). An English–Hindi bilingual dictionary-based CLIR system was then used to retrieve Hindi news articles. The top 20 articles retrieved were analyzed to find candidate answers. Finally, the Hindi answers were translated back into English. For this final stage, two options were provided in the user interface: (a) the MT system created by ISI [15] and (b) a bilingual dictionary with transition probabilities. Fifty-six questions were used for evaluation and an MRR of 0.25 was achieved (considering the top five answers).

2.2.4 Topic Detection and Tracking

Topic detection and tracking (TDT)[7] is among the more recent problems being investigated by the IR community. TDT research started with a pilot study in 1996 and continued with open evaluations from 1998 to 2000 [25]. Five major sub-tasks are studied:

- story segmentation – detecting changes between topically cohesive sections,
- topic tracking – keeping track of stories similar to a set of example stories,
- topic detection – building clusters of stories that discuss the same topic,
- new event detection – detecting if a story is the first story of a new, unknown topic,
- link detection – detecting whether or not two stories are topically linked.

Allan et al. [26] attempted three TDT tasks, namely cross-language topic tracking (TT), topic detection (TD), and new event detection (NED) for TIDES 2003 by

[7] http://www.itl.nist.gov/iaui/894.01/tests/tdt/

modifying their existing TDT system. For the TT task, the system was trained with a few ($N_t = 4$) news stories sharing a common topic, and the system was then used to identify stories of the same topic from a stream of news stories. For the TD task, an unsupervised approach was adopted.

The TDT evaluation corpus consisted of 77 Mbytes of text, comprising 41,697 Hindi documents. It was assumed that the news stream was not sorted chronologically. Fifteen topics and four Hindi stories on each topic were identified by LDC for training. Allan et al. tried both mono-lingual and cross-lingual topic tracking, as well as topic detection and new event detection. The performance of the mono- and cross-lingual TT system was found to be comparable to that achieved in earlier work with English and Arabic. However, the miss rates for the topic detection and new event detection tasks were unexpectedly high (59.5 and 54.6, respectively).

2.2.5 Indian Language Subtrack at CLEF 2007

More recently, cross-lingual IR has been studied by a few groups within the CLEF framework. Since appropriate Indian language corpora were not available, experiments used an English document collection (articles from the *Los Angeles Times* published in 2002), with 50 search topics in Indian languages. The topics were originally created in English and later translated into other languages. Table 2 lists the groups that participated in the Indian language subtrack at CLEF 2007.

All groups used at least the most elementary language-specific resources required for IR, viz., a stop-word list and a stemmer or morphological analyzer. Also, all groups used transliteration as a fallback for converting query words that were not translatable using a bilingual dictionary.

Mandal et al. [27] (IIT Kharagpur) used a manually constructed list of about 1500 named entities (including country/city names, abbreviations, diseases) along with their translations, but otherwise had no access to a Bengali–English bilingual lexicon or parallel corpora. Consequently, the results for queries involving named entities were better than those for other queries.

Jagarlamudi and Kumaran [28] used a word alignment table that was learnt using a statistical machine translation (SMT) system trained on aligned parallel sentences. For a given Hindi word, only selected English translations (either all words having translation probabilities above a threshold or the *n* most probable translations) were

Table 2 Participants in the Indian language sub-track at CLEF 2007

Group	Languages
IIIT Hyderabad (IIITH)	Hindi, Telugu
IIT Bombay (IITB)	Hindi, Marathi
IIT Kharagpur (IITK)	Hindi, Bengali
Jadavpur U (JU)	Hindi, Bengali
MSR India (MSR)	Hindi

included in the final English query. The retrieval engine used the language modeling approach. The MAP reported by this group on Hindi → English CLIR was 0.2156.

Pingali and Varma [29] created new "quick and dirty" bilingual dictionaries, the Telugu–English and Hindi–English language pairs. A set of Telugu and Hindi words were selected (based on their *tf* × *idf* values in a large corpus collected from a mono-lingual web search engine). These words were translated by native speakers, who were asked to provide equivalent words that would be topically related to the source language word, rather than being literal translations. The final Hindi–English dictionary had 5175 entries, while the Telugu–English dictionary had 26,182 entries. Not surprisingly, performance was better on the Telugu task than on the Hindi one.

The best results on the Hindi–English task (as well as the English mono-lingual task) were reported by Chinnakotla et al. [30]. This group used a Hindi–English bilingual dictionary containing around 115,571 entries,[8] and a Marathi–English dictionary with around 6110 entries. This is the only group that used a proper translation disambiguation module, based on a page-rank style iterative disambiguation algorithm proposed by Monz and Dorr [31] that returned the most probable English translation of the entire query to the mono-lingual IR engine. The system achieved a MAP score of 0.2952.

Overall, the results obtained by the various groups indicate that the richness of the language resources used has a direct bearing on retrieval effectiveness for the CLIR task. Selectively using translation candidates (as opposed to using all translations) also seems to improve performance.

3 The CLIA Project

While the preceding section gives an overview of a fair number of research efforts that have been made in the area of ILIR, thus far, no complete, end-to-end ILIR system has emerged that is both capable of handling the major information-processing tasks and is available freely for research use. There is also a general lack of readily available language resources – like standard relevance-judged corpora, stemmers, named-entity identifiers, multilingual dictionaries, part-of-speech taggers – that are useful for ILIR system development and evaluation.

These problems are expected to be addressed by a large project on cross-lingual information access systems for Indian languages, that is being funded by the Government of India, and is being executed by a consortium of several academic and industrial institutions. The major aims of this project are

1. to build a cross-lingual information access portal, where a user will be able to present a query in one of six[9] Indian languages, and get back information from various sources in his/her own language

[8] Available online at http://www.cfilt.iitb.ac.in/~hdict/webinterface_user/dict_search_user.php

[9] Bengali, Hindi, Marathi, Punjabi, Tamil, Telugu

2. to create a standardized evaluation framework that can be used to quantitatively measure and compare the effectiveness of various IR tools and techniques

3.1 The Forum for Information Retrieval Evaluation (FIRE)

The importance of reusable, large-scale standard test collections in information access research has been widely recognized. In particular, the success of TREC, CLEF, and NTCIR has clearly established the importance of an evaluation workshop that facilitates research by providing the data and a common forum for comparing models and techniques. Inspired by these initiatives, the Forum for Information Retrieval Evaluation (FIRE)[10] has been formed as a part of the CLIA project with the following aims:

- to encourage research in Indian language information access technologies by providing reusable large-scale test collections for ILIR experiments
- to provide a common evaluation infrastructure for comparing the performance of different IR system
- to investigate evaluation methods for information access techniques and methods for constructing a reusable large-scale data set for ILIR experiments.

Specifically, the goal of FIRE is to create sizeable benchmark corpora in the six selected languages. Some of the language corpora have already been constructed. These consist predominantly of news articles published during September 2004 to September 2007 in various online news sources. Besides news articles, the corpus also includes some documents from the health and tourism domains. A set of 95 search topics have also been created based on manual inspection of the corpus. As at CLEF (see Section 2.2), the topics were originally formulated in English and then translated to all the six languages. A typical topic has a title, a description, and a narrative section. Some of these topics are expected to be discarded as either too easy or too difficult on the basis of preliminary experiments. Of the remainder, 50 topics will be used for the final evaluation and 30 topics will be used as training data. More details about this evaluation framework can be found in [32].

4 Conclusion

The increasing availability of digital information in Indian languages has led to the growth of research activity in the area of ILIR. In this chapter, we have provided an overview of various research efforts in this area. We have also outlined the goals of the CLIA project as well as FIRE, a framework for ILIR evaluation that follows the tradition established by TREC, CLEF, and NTCIR. The basic language tools

[10] www.isical.ac.in/~fire

and resources, along with benchmark data, that will be created as a result of these initiatives should provide a strong impetus to further research in this area.

References

1. Majumder, P., Mitra, M., Datta, K.: Multilingual information access: an Indian language perspective. In Gey, F., Peters, C., eds.: Proceedings of ACM SIGIR Workshop on MLIR (2006)
2. Rajashekar, T.: Building Indian language digital library collections: Some experiences with Greenstone software. In: Digital Libraries: International Collaboration and Cross-Fertilization: 7th International Conference on Asian Digital Libraries, ICADL 2004, Springer Berlin/Heidelberg (2004)
3. Urs, S.R., Raghavan, K.S.: Vidyanidhi: Indian digital library of electronic theses. Commun. ACM **44**(5) (2001) 88–89
4. Mitra, M., Chaudhuri, B.B.: An OCR-based architecture for indexing Indian language web documents. In: Proceedings 2nd Symposium on Indian Morphology, Phonology and Language Engineering (SIMPLE 05) (2005)
5. Pingali, P., Jagarlamudi, J., Varma, V.: Webkhoj: Indian language IR from multiple character encodings. In: Proceedings of WWW2006 Workshop (May 2006)
6. He, D., Oard, D.W., Wang, J., Luo, J., Demner-Fushman, D., Darwish, K., Resnik, P., Khudanpur, S., Nossal, M., Subotin, M., Leuski, A.: Making miracles: Interactive translingual search for Cebuano and Hindi. ACM Transactions on Asian Language Information Processing (TALIP) **2**(3) (2003) 219–244
7. Pirkola, A.: The effects of query structure and dictionary setups in dictionary-based cross-language information retrieval. In: SIGIR '98: Proceedings of the 21st Annual International ACM SIGIR Conference on Research and Development in Information Retrieval, New York, NY, ACM Press (1998) 55–63
8. Mitra, M., Chaudhuri, B.: Information retrieval from documents: A survey. Information Retrieval **2**(2/3) (2000) 141–163
9. Larkey, L.S., Connell, M.E., Abduljaleel, N.: Hindi CLIR in thirty days. ACM Transactions on Asian Language Information Processing (TALIP) **2**(2) (2003) 130–142
10. Ramanathan, A., Rao, D.: A lightweight stemmer for Hindi. In: EACL Workshop on Computational Linguistics for South Asian Languages (2003)
11. Och, F.J., Ney, H.: A systematic comparison of various statistical alignment models. Computational Linguistics **29**(1) (2003) 19–51
12. Callan, J.P., Croft, W.B., Broglio, J.: TREC and Tipster experiments with Inquery. Information Processing and Management **31**(3) (1995) 327–343
13. Weischedel, R., Nguyen, C.: Evaluating a probabilistic model for cross-lingual information retrieval. In: SIGIR '01: Proceedings of the 24th Annual International ACM SIGIR Conference on Research and Development in Information Retrieval, New York, NY, ACM Press (2001) 105–110
14. Xu, J., Weischedel, R.: Cross-lingual retrieval for Hindi. ACM Transactions on Asian Language Information Processing (TALIP) **2**(2) (2003) 164–168
15. Leuski, A., Lin, C.Y., Zhou, L., Germann, U., Och, F.J., Hovy, E.: Cross-lingual (c∗st∗rd): English access to Hindi information. ACM Transactions on Asian Language Information Processing (TALIP) **2**(3) (2003) 245–269
16. Chklovski, T., Mihalcea, R., Pedersen, T., Purandare, A.: The Senseval-3 multilingual EnglishHindi lexical sample task. In Mihalcea, R., Edmonds, P., eds.: Senseval-3: Third International Workshop on the Evaluation of Systems for the Semantic Analysis of Text, Association for Computational Linguistics (July 2004) 5–8
17. Lee, Y.K., Ng, H.T., Chia, T.K.: Supervised word sense disambiguation with support vector machines and multiple knowledge sources. In Mihalcea, R., Edmonds, P., eds.: Senseval-3:

Third International Workshop on the Evaluation of Systems for the Semantic Analysis of Text (July 2004) 137–140
18. May, J., Brunstein, A., Natarajan, P., Weischedel, R.: Surprise! what's in a Cebuano or Hindi name? ACM Transactions on Asian Language Information Processing (TALIP) **2**(3) (2003) 169–180
19. Bikel, D.M., Miller, S., Schwartz, R.L., Weischedel, R.M.: Nymble: a high-performance learning name-finder. In: ANLP Washington, DC, ACL (1997) 194–201
20. Li, W., McCallum, A.: Rapid development of Hindi named entity recognition using conditional random fields and feature induction. ACM Transactions on Asian Language Information Processing (TALIP) **2**(3) (2003) 290–294
21. Huang, F., Vogel, S., Waibel, A.: Extracting named entity translingual equivalence with limited resources. ACM Transactions on Asian Language Information Processing (TALIP) **2**(2) (2003) 124–129
22. Majumder, P., Mitra, M., Sarkar, N., Mitra, P., Datta, K.: Bengali name identification using a noisy comparable corpus. In: International Conference on Emerging Applications of IT (2006) 41–44
23. Cucerzan, S., Yarowsky, D.: Language independent named entity recognition combining morphological and contextual evidence. In: Proceedings of Joint SIGDAT Conference on Empirical Methods in NLP and Very Large Corpora (1999) 90–99
24. Sekine, S., Grishman, R.: Hindi-English cross-lingual question-answering system. ACM Transactions on Asian Language Information Processing (TALIP) **2**(3) (2003) 181–192
25. Allan, J.: Introduction to topic detection and tracking. Norwell, MA, Kluwer Academic Publishers (2002)
26. Allan, J., Lavrenko, V., Connell, M.E.: A month to topic detection and tracking in Hindi. ACM Transactions on Asian Language Information Processing (TALIP) **2**(2) (2003) 85–100
27. Mandal, D., Gupta, M., Dandapat, S., Banerjee, P., Sarkar, S.: Bengali and Hindi to English CLIR evaluation. In: Advances in Multilingual and Multimodal Information Retrieval (8th Workshop of the Cross-Language Evaluation Forum, CLEF 2007). Number 5152 in LNCS, Budapest, Hungary Springer Verlag (2008) 95–102
28. Jagarlamudi, J., Kumaran, A.: Cross-Lingual Information Retrieval System for Indian Languages. In: Advances in Multilingual and Multimodal Information Retrieval (8th Workshop of the Cross-Language Evaluation Forum, CLEF 2007). Number 5152 in LNCS, Budapset, Hungary Springer Verlag (2008) 80–87
29. Pingali, P., Tune, K., Varma, V.: Improving Recall for Hindi, Telugu, Oromo to English CLIR. In: Advances in Multilingual and Multimodal Information Retrieval (8th Workshop of the Cross-Language Evaluation Forum, CLEF 2007). Number 5152 in LNCS, Budapset, Hungary Springer Verlag (2008) 103–110
30. Chinnakotla, M., Ranadive, S., Damani, O., Bhattacharyya, P.: Hindi to English and Marathi to English cross language information retrieval evaluation. In: Advances in Multilingual and Multimodal Information Retrieval (8th Workshop of the Cross-Language Evaluation Forum, CLEF 2007). Number 5152 in LNCS, Budapest, Hungary Springer Verlag (2008) 111–118
31. Monz, C., Dorr, B.J.: Iterative translation disambiguation for cross-language information retrieval. In: Proceedings of 28th ACM SIGIR (2005) 520527
32. Majumder, P., Mitra, M., Pal, D., Bandyopadhyay, A., Maiti, S., Mitra, S., Sen, A., Pal, S.: Text collections for FIRE. In: Proceedings of ACM SIGIR (2008) 699–700

Colour Plates

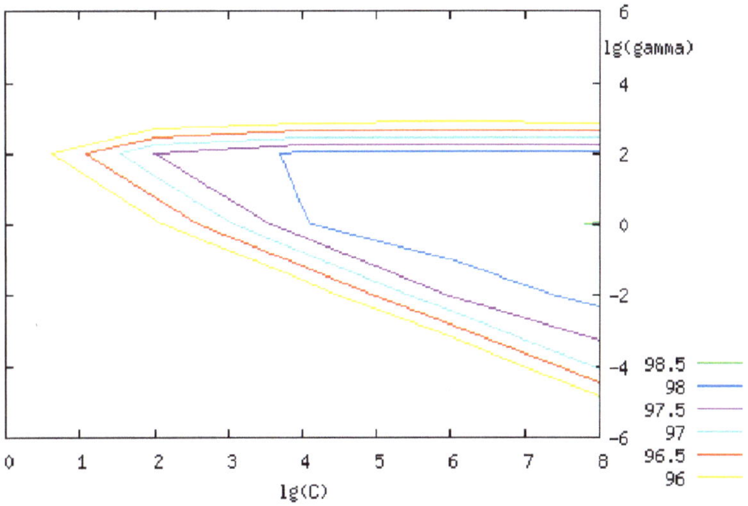

Plate 1 Cross-validation results obtained using a multi-class SVM (RBF kernel) for objects of kind 4, with 25 2D-spline features. The log scales of the axes are in base 2 (See also Fig. 10 on page 113)

V. Govindaraju, S. Setlur (eds.), *Guide to OCR for Indic Scripts*, Advances in Pattern Recognition, DOI 10.1007/978-1-84800-330-9_BM2, © Springer-Verlag London Limited 2009

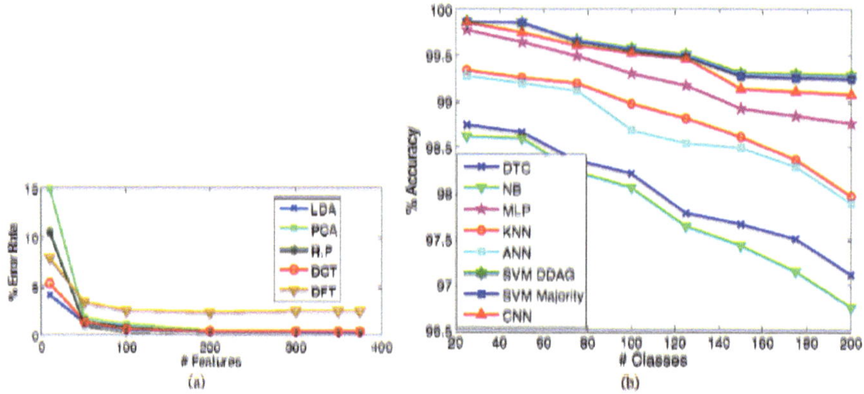

Plate 2 Classifier performance with varying number of **(a)** features and **(b)** classes (See also Fig. 9 on page 143)

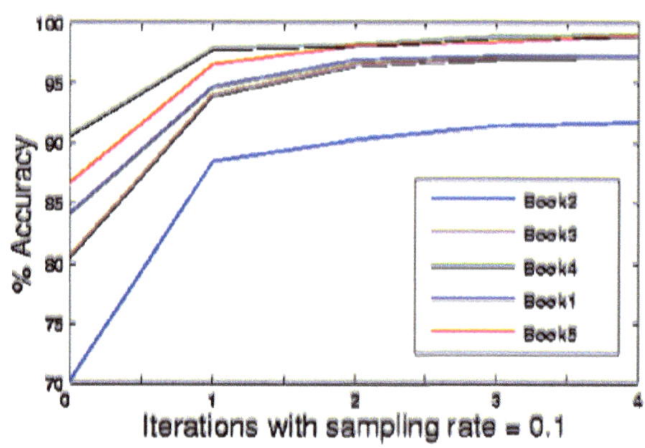

Plate 3 Improvement in the performance of recognition of a book over iterations (See also Fig. 10 on page 144)

Plate 4 Dynamic time warping (DTW) for matching two samples of a Tamil character (See also Fig. 8 on page 220)

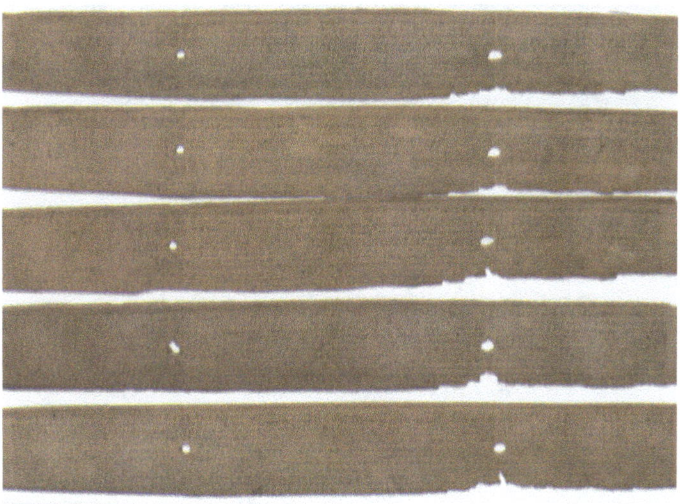

Plate 5 Sample palm leaf manuscripts (See also Fig. 1 on page 250)

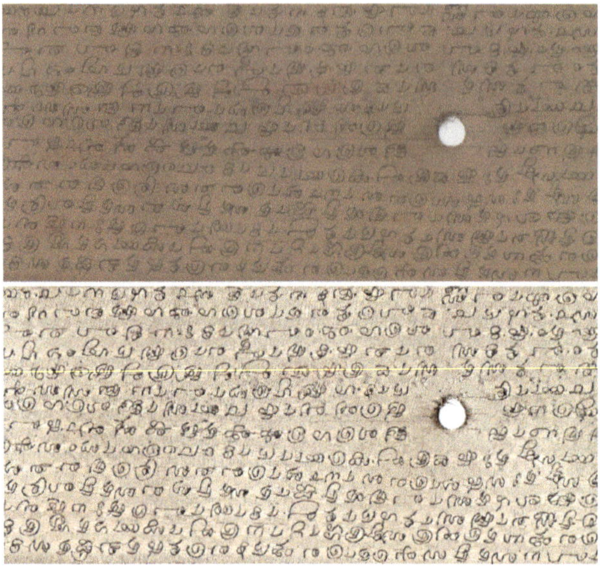

Plate 6 Component channel background normalization for color palm leaf image enhancement (See also Fig. 10 on page 259)

Plate 7 Binarization of ALCM shows the patterns of text line (See also Fig. 14 on page 264)

Plate 8 Text line extraction result of image in Fig. 13 (See also Fig. 15 on page 265)

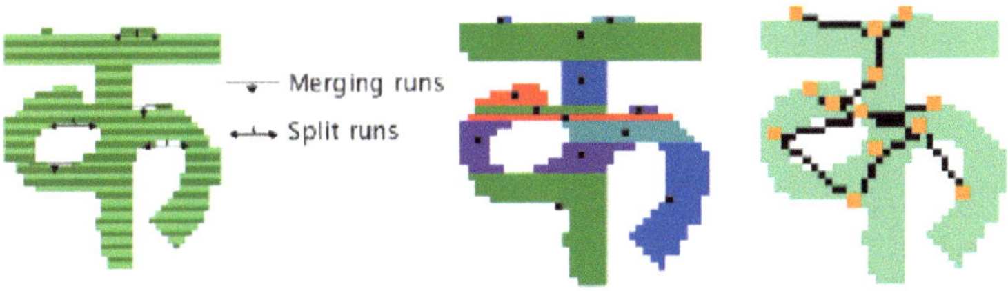

Plate 9 BAG construction using horizontal runs for a sample grapheme [10] (See also Fig. 4 on page 289)

Plate 10 Illustration of BAG-based noise removal – *Left*: (1, 2) sample with noise, (3) thin joint, (4) thin ligature boundary; *Right*: result of BAG-based noise removal [10] (See also Fig. 5 on page 290)

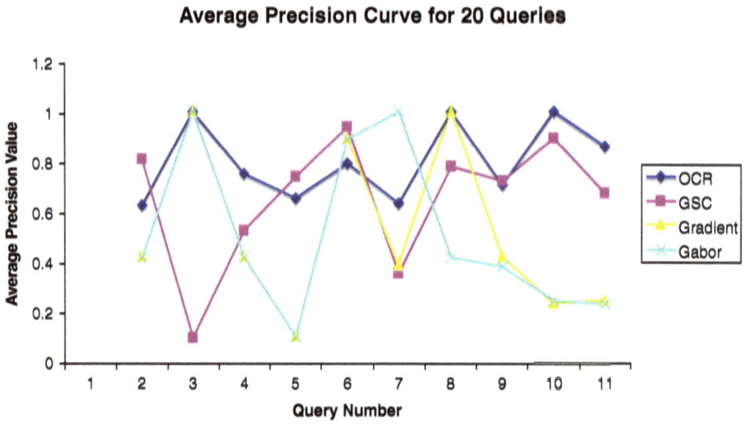

Plate 11 Average precision curve for different keyword spotting methods (See also Fig. 9 on page 293)

Index

N

O

P

Q

R

S

MIX
Papier aus verantwortungsvollen Quellen
Paper from responsible sources
FSC® C105338

If you have any concerns about our products,
you can contact us on
ProductSafety@springernature.com

In case Publisher is established outside the EU,
the EU authorized representative is:
Springer Nature Customer Service Center GmbH
Europaplatz 3, 69115 Heidelberg, Germany

Printed by Libri Plureos GmbH
in Hamburg, Germany